Hyperspectral Remote Sensing for Sustainable Agriculture

Edited by

Sartajvir Singh
Centre of Excellence, Socio-Environmental Sustainability for River Sand-Mining (SEnSRS)
Indian Institute of Technology
Ropar, Punjab, India

Neelam Dahiya
Department of Computer Applications
Chitkara University Institute of Engineering and Technology
Chitkara University, Punjab, India

Maged Mohammed
Department of Agricultural and Biosystems Engineering
Faculty of Agriculture, Menoufia University
Shebin El Koum, Egypt

Abdullah Alzharihi
Department of Electrical and Computer Engineering
Oakland University
Rochester Hills, MI, USA

&

Vishal Dutt
Department of Computer Science and Engineering
Chandigarh University
Punjab, India

Hyperspectral Remote Sensing for Sustainable Agriculture

Editors: Sartajvir Singh, Neelam Dahiya, Maged Mohammed, Abdullah Alzharihi & Vishal Dutt

ISBN (Online): 979-8-89881-396-3

ISBN (Print): 979-8-89881-397-0

ISBN (Paperback): 979-8-89881-398-7

Published by Bentham Science Publishers Pte. Ltd. Singapore, in collaboration with Eureka Conferences, USA.

First published in 2026.

Bentham Science Publishers Pte. Ltd.
No. 9 Raffles Place
Office No. 26-01
Singapore 048619
Singapore
Email: subscriptions@benthamscience.net

CONTENTS

PREFACE i

LIST OF CONTRIBUTORS iii

CHAPTER 1 ADVANCING SMART IRRIGATION PRACTICES IN SMALL-SCALE AGRICULTURE BY COMBINING HYPERSPECTRAL REMOTE SENSING WITH IOT SOLUTIONS 1

Suryavanshi Bhagyeshkumar Vijaybhai, Mohammad Sohail Pervez, Ramesh Chandra Nayak, Kirti Khandelwal, Shresthashree Swain and *Akshata Musale*

- **INTRODUCTION** 2
- **EXPERIMENTAL SETUP AND PROCEDURE** 8
- **RESULT AND DISCUSSION** 11
  - IoT Programming 12
  - Execution of the Program 15
- **LIMITATIONS AND FUTURE WORK** 17
- **CONCLUSION** 18
- **REFERENCES** 19

CHAPTER 2 LAND COVER CLASSIFICATION USING HYPERION EO-1 DATA: A CASE STUDY IN UTTAR PRADESH, INDIA 23

Neelam Dahiya, Nitin Arora, Sartajvir Singh and *Gurwinder Singh*

- **INTRODUCTION** 23
- **STUDY SITE AND DATASET** 25
- **METHODOLOGY** 26
  - Pre-Processing 27
  - Classification 28
  - Accuracy Assessment 29
    - *Class Categories* 30
- **RESULTS AND DISCUSSION** 31
- **CONCLUSION** 32
- **REFERENCES** 33

CHAPTER 3 EMERGING TRENDS AND CHALLENGES IN REMOTE SENSING FOR IRRIGATION OF HORTICULTURAL CROPS 36

Rupinder Singh, Amanpreet Singh and *Jaswinder Singh*

- **INTRODUCTION** 36
- **LITERATURE REVIEW** 37
  - Satellite-Based Remote Sensing 37
  - UAV-Based Remote Sensing 37
  - Ground-Based Sensors 38
  - Hyperspectral Imaging in Irrigation Management 38
  - How AI and Machine Learning are Changing the Game 38
  - Challenges and Opportunities 39
    - *Challenges* 39
    - *Opportunities* 39
- **HOW REMOTE SENSING IS USED FOR SMARTER IRRIGATION** 40
  - How Data Gets Collected 40
    - *Satellites* 40
    - *Drones (UAVs)* 41
    - *Ground Sensors* 41
  - How the Data Gets Processed and Analyzed 41

Image Correction ... 41
Calculating Plant Health ... 42
Combining Data (Data Fusion) ... 42
Turning Data into Action: Automated Irrigation ... 42
How Do We Know Remote Sensing Data is Reliable? (Validation Techniques) ... 43
WHAT ARE THE KEY TAKEAWAYS FROM USING REMOTE SENSING IN IRRIGATION? ... 44
Monitoring Crop Water Status ... 44
Measuring Evapotranspiration (ET) ... 45
Creating Precision Irrigation Zones ... 45
DISCUSSION ... 45
Why Remote Sensing Matters ... 45
What is Still Hard? ... 46
How AI and Machine Learning Help ... 46
What Needs More Work? ... 46
Future Directions ... 46
Practical Tips for Farmers and Advisors ... 46
CONCLUSION ... 47
REFERENCES ... 47

CHAPTER 4 ROLE OF REMOTE SENSING AND GEOGRAPHIC INFORMATION SYSTEM (GIS) IN INTEGRATED PEST MANAGEMENT (IPM) ... 50
Kalirajan Murugasridevi, Venunathan Dhivya, Lincy Kirubhadharshini B., VR Mageshen and *S. Sowjanya*
INTRODUCTION ... 51
WORKING PRINCIPLE OF REMOTE SENSING ... 53
Elements of Remote Sensing ... 54
Energy Source ... 54
Interaction with the Target ... 54
Sensors ... 54
Platforms ... 55
Transmission, Reception, and Processing ... 55
Interpretation and Analysis ... 55
Implementation ... 55
Implementation of Remote Sensing in IPM ... 55
Pest Monitoring Through Remote Sensing ... 56
Attributes of Remote Sensing for Pest Monitoring ... 57
VIS - NIR Spectral Attributes ... 58
Prediction of Pest Outbreak by Employing Remote Sensing ... 60
Pest Mapping Using Remote Sensing ... 61
WORKING PRINCIPLE OF GEOGRAPHIC INFORMATION SYSTEM (GIS) ... 62
APPLICATIONS OF GIS IN IPM ... 63
Monitoring of Pest ... 63
Prediction of Pest Outbreaks with Environmental Change ... 65
Mapping of Pest Incidence ... 66
APPLICATION OF HYPERSPECTRAL REMOTE SENSING IN IPM ... 66
Early Pest Detection and Stress Monitoring ... 67
Species-Specific Pest Identification ... 67
Precision Pesticide Application and Residue Management ... 67
Tracking Pest Dynamics & Climate Change Impacts ... 67
Post-Harvest Pest Detection ... 67

Hyperspectral Sensorsfor Pest Detection 67
APPLICATION OF MULTISPECTRAL AND UAV-BASED (UNMANNED AERIAL VEHICLE) IMAGERY IN IPM 68
Early Pest Detection and Monitoring 69
Precision Pesticide Application 69
Tracking Pest Movement and Population Dynamics 69
Assessing Pesticide Efficacy 69
Climate Change & Insect Behavior Analysis 69
Large-Scale Pest Outbreak Monitoring 69
Multispectral Sensors for Pest Detection 70
CONCLUSION 71
REFERENCES 72

CHAPTER 5 A SMART IOT-BASED FRAMEWORK FOR PREDICTIVE CROP HEALTH MONITORING AND PRECISION FARMING 79
Hashmat Fida, Jaspreet Kaur, Binod Kumar Mishra and *Vinod Kumar*
INTRODUCTION 79
Precision Agriculture and its Importance 80
The Role of IoT in Precision Agriculture 81
Comprehensive Soil and Crop Health Monitoring 82
Preemptive Management of Physiological Disorders 83
Optimized Resource Management and Sustainability 84
AI in Remote Sensing Applications 85
LITERATURE SURVEY 85
AIMS OF THE RESEARCH 87
RESEARCH SUMMARY 88
PROPOSED METHODOLOGY 89
Hyperspectral Imaging and AI-Based Analysis 95
AI-Driven Analysis of Remote Sensing Datasets 96
AI Models and Their Role in Remote Sensing Data Processing 96
I. Specific Remote Sensing Datasets Employed for Crop Health Monitoring 97
THE FUTURE OF SMART AGRICULTURE 97
Limitations 98
LESSONS FROM PILOT DEPLOYMENTS 98
CASE STUDY 99
CONCLUSION 99
REFERENCES 99

CHAPTER 6 PRECISION AGRICULTURE PRACTICES FOR CROP YIELD MANAGEMENT WITH AI MODELS 101
Rishikesh Ratan, Arshdeep Singh, Krishna Rawat, Danish Monga, Adarsh Tripathi Sakshi Sinha, Jyotsana Patel and *Amish Goyal*
INTRODUCTION 101
TECHNOLOGIES ENABLING PRECISION AGRICULTURE 103
ARTIFICIAL INTELLIGENCE (AI) ALGORITHMS USED IN AGRICULTURE 105
AI in Agriculture 105
Types of AI Models Used in Crop Yield Prediction 107
Machine Learning (ML) in Agriculture 107
Deep Learning(DL) in Agriculture 108
Artificial Intelligence for Hyperspectral Remote Sensing in Precision Agriculture 109
AI Methods for Hyperspectral Image Data Analysis in Agriculture 109
Comparative Analysis of AI Models 111

Integration of AI Models with Precision Agriculture 112
AI-DRIVEN CROP YIELD MANAGEMENT TECHNIQUES 115
AI-Based Soil Analysis and Fertiliser Optimisation 115
Computer Vision-Based Crop Health Monitoring 115
Weather Forecasting and Irrigation Scheduling 116
Transformative Impact and Future Outlook 117
REAL-WORLD USE CASES AND APPLICATIONS IN AGRICULTURE 118
Success Stories of AI in Crop Yield Management 118
Precision Agriculture Practices for Various Crops 119
Wheat and Maize 119
Paddy Cultivation 119
Horticultural Crops 119
AI Implementation Challenges in Agriculture 120
ECONOMIC AND ENVIRONMENTAL IMPACT 121
Cost-Benefit Analysis of Precision Agriculture 121
AI Technologies for Sustainable Farming 122
Environmental Footprint Reduction through Precision Agriculture 123
FUTURE TRENDS IN PRECISION AGRICULTURE 123
AI Innovations for Smart Farming 123
Future of AI in Global Agricultural Systems 124
CONCLUSION 124
REFERENCES 125

CHAPTER 7 LAND COVER CLASSIFICATION IN BHATINDA AND COMPARATIVE ANALYSIS OF MACHINE LEARNING ALGORITHMS USING GOOGLE EARTH ENGINE 136
Vishal Dutt, Sartajvir Singh and *Ganesh Kumar Sethi*
INTRODUCTION 136
Importance of Land Cover Classification in Bhatinda, Punjab 137
Google Earth Engine (GEE) as a Tool 138
Research Objectives 138
STUDY AREA 138
METHODOLOGY 139
Data Preparation in Google Earth Engine 139
Machine Learning Algorithms 140
Classification Process 141
Comparative Analysis 143
RESULT AND DISCUSSION 144
Classification Results 144
Comparative Analysis 146
LIMITATIONS AND FUTURE DIRECTIONS 147
CONCLUSION 147
REFERENCES 148

CHAPTER 8 SIGNIFICANCE OF REMOTE SENSING IN OPTIMIZING FERTILIZER USE FOR NUTRIENT MAPPING 150
Akinchan Maity, Sangeetha Annam and *Jay Arindam Maity*
INTRODUCTION 150
Role of Hyperspectral Remote Sensing in Agriculture 152
Role of Hyperspectral Remote Sensing in Precision Agriculture 153
Use of Hyperspectral Remote Sensing for Fertilizer Optimization 154
LITERATURE REVIEW 154
Applications of Hyperspectral Remote Sensing in Agriculture 154

Application of Hyperspectral Remote Sensing in Fertilizer Optimization ... 156
SOIL HEALTH MONITORING THROUGH HYPERSPECTRAL REMOTE SENSING ... 157
INTEGRATION WITH DECISION SUPPORT SYSTEMS ... 159
Architecture of Hyperspectral Remote Monitoring for Fertilizer Optimization and Nutrient Mapping ... 160
Discussion on Fertilizer Optimization using Hyperspectral Remote Sensing ... 161
Cost Effectiveness ... 162
Environmental Benefits ... 162
CHALLENGES AND LIMITATIONS ... 163
FUTURE PROSPECTS OF HYPERSPECTRAL REMOTE SENSING IN FERTILIZER MANAGEMENT ... 164
CONCLUSION ... 164
REFERENCES ... 164

CHAPTER 9 STUDY ON HARNESSING REMOTE SENSING FOR ADVANCED WILDLIFE MONITORING AND CONSERVATION ... 169
Anamika Larhgotra and *Navpreet Kaur Walia*
INTRODUCTION ... 170
METHODOLOGIES ... 171
LITERATURE REVIEW ... 172
ADVANCES WITH AI/ML TECHNIQUES ... 175
Data Acquisition Using IoT Sensors ... 175
Habitat Mapping Using AI/ML ... 175
Species Identification by means of ML Models ... 175
Poaching and Threat Detection Using IoT ... 175
MERITS AND DEMERITS ... 178
Merits ... 178
Wildlife Monitoring ... 178
Sustainable Agriculture ... 178
Demerits ... 178
Wildlife Monitoring ... 178
Sustainable Agriculture ... 178
COMPARISON AND CONNECTION TO SUSTAINABLE AGRICULTURE ... 179
Common Usage Scenarios and Intersections ... 180
APPLICATIONS ... 182
Case Study 1: Integrated Remote Sensing in Wildlife Conservation and Sustainable Agriculture ... 182
Case Study 2: AI-facilitated Cameras for Early Bushfire Detection in Australia ... 183
Case Study 3: AI in US Agroecosystems Regenerative Agriculture ... 183
Case Study 4: AI-Cattle Monitoring in Queensland, Australia ... 183
DEVICES AND TOOLS ... 184
RESEARCH ANALYSIS ... 187
Wildlife Monitoring ... 188
Sustainable Agriculture ... 189
Integrated Research Scope ... 189
CONCLUSION ... 190
REFERENCES ... 192

CHAPTER 10 ADVANCEMENT IN REMOTE SENSING AND GIS FOR SUSTAINABLE GROUNDWATER MONITORING ... 194
Neha Bhati, Narayan Vyas and *Ashutosh Pagrotra*
INTRODUCTION ... 194

Overview of Groundwater Importance and Global Water Crisis 194
Need for Remote Sensing and GIS in Groundwater Monitoring 195
Objectives of the Chapter 196
UNDERSTANDING GROUND WATER SYSTEMS 196
Basics of Ground Water Hydrology 196
Key Challenges in Groundwater Management 197
The Crucial Role of Sustainable Groundwater Monitoring 198
EVOLUTION OF REMOTE SENSING FOR GROUNDWATER MONITORING 198
Traditional Groundwater Monitoring Techniques 198
Introduction to Remote Sensing: Key Technologies and Advancements 199
Satellite-Based Groundwater Monitoring: GRACE, Landsat, and Other Key Platforms 199
REMOTE SENSING TECHNOLOGY ADVANCEMENTS 201
Remote Sensing Techniques for Groundwater Monitoring (Optical, Radar, and Microwave) 201
Integration of AI and Machine Learning (ML) in Remote Sensing for Groundwater Analysis 201
ROLE OF GIS IN GROUNDWATER MAPPING 202
INTEGRATION OF IMAGERY AND GIS FOR GROUNDWATER DETECTION 203
Remote Sensing And GIS Technologies Synergy 203
Remote Sensing and GIS-Integrated Groundwater Model Development 203
Predictive Modelling and Forecasting for Groundwater Sustainability 203
REMOTE SENSING AND GIS APPLICATIONS IN SUSTAINABLE GROUNDWATER MANAGEMENT 204
CONCLUSION 204
REFERENCES 205

CHAPTER 11 PRECISION AGRICULTURE, IRRIGATION MANAGEMENT, AND MONITORING USING HYPERSPECTRAL REMOTE SENSING AND AI 210
Jaswinder Singh, Rupinder Singh and *Amanpreet Singh*
INTRODUCTION 210
LITERATURE REVIEW 211
METHODOLOGY 212
IMPLEMENTATIONS 213
DATA COLLECTION AND ANALYSIS 215
EXPECTED RESULTS 215
HYPOTHESIS 216
COMPARISONS 216
REMOTE SENSING APPLICATIONS IN AI-BASED IRRIGATION 219
HOW AI MODELS PROCESS SATELLITE AND UAV DATA FOR IRRIGATION MANAGEMENT 220
AUTOMATION IN SMART IRRIGATION SYSTEMS 221
CONCLUSION 221
REFERENCES 222

CHAPTER 12 EVALUATION OF SOIL FERTILITY USING DEEP LEARNING AND MACHINE LEARNING ALGORITHMS 224
VR Mageshen, C. Krithika, V. Dhayalan, K. Murugasridevi and *G. Manimaran*
INTRODUCTION 225
DEEP LEARNING ALGORITHMS 226
Artificial Neural Network 226
Key Features 227
Challenges 227
Convolutional Neural Network 227
Key layers of CNN 228

Challenges ... 229
Recurrent Neural Network ... 229
Strengths of RNN ... 230
Challengesof RNN ... 230
Deep Belief Network ... 230
Key Features of Deep Belief Networks ... 231
Challenges ... 231
MACHINE LEARNING ALGORITHMS ... 231
Random Forest Regression ... 231
Key Features of Random Forest Aggression ... 233
Challenges in Random Forest Aggression ... 234
Linear Regression ... 234
Key Features in Linear Regression ... 235
Challenges in Linear Regression ... 235
Naive Bayes Algorithm ... 235
Strength of Naive Bayes Algorithm ... 237
Challenges of the Naive BayesAlgorithm ... 237
Multinomial Logistic Regression (MLR) ... 237
Strength of Multinomial Logistic Regression ... 238
Challenges of Multinomial Logistic Regression ... 238
HYPERSPECTRA REMOTE SENSING IN SOIL FERTILITY MAPPING ... 238
CONCLUSION ... 239
REFERENCES ... 239

CHAPTER 13 ADVANCED REMOTE SENSING TECHNIQUES FOR MONITORING AGRICULTURAL CHANGES ... 242
Jay Arindam Maity, Sangeetha Annam and *Akinchan Maity*
INTRODUCTION ... 242
Remote Sensing Evolution ... 243
Methods and Techniques of Remote Sensing ... 243
Satellite-Based Remote Sensing ... 243
Aerial Remote Sensing ... 244
Use of Hyperspectral Remote Sensing in Agriculture ... 244
METHODOLOGIES USED IN HYPERSPECTRAL RS ... 245
AGRICULTURAL FACTORS TO MONITOR WITH HYPERSPECTRAL RS ... 247
Soil Health ... 247
Nutrient Level ... 248
Soil Type and Soil Texture ... 248
Moisture Index ... 248
pH Level ... 249
Soil Organic Matter ... 249
Presence of Contaminants ... 249
Plant Growth and Health ... 249
Growth Rate and Structure ... 250
Leaf Colour and Condition ... 250
Flowering and Fruit Production ... 250
Pest and Disease Signs ... 251
Weather and Environmental Indices ... 251
Effects of Temperature ... 252
Effects of Humidity ... 252
Effects of Light ... 252

Effects of Wind ... 252
TECHNIQUES FOR PROCESSING AND MONITORING THE DATA THROUGH HYPERSPECTRAL REMOTE SENSING ... 253
Workflow and Integration with Decision Support Systems ... 254
Current Limitations ... 254
FUTURE SCOPE ... 255
CONCLUSION ... 256
REFERENCES ... 256

CHAPTER 14 REMOTE SENSING FOR PRECISION AGRICULTURE: OPTIMIZING FERTILIZER USE THROUGH NUTRIENT MAPPING ... 261
Jaspreet Singh, Rupinder Singh, Amanpreet Singh and *Jaswinder Singh*
INTRODUCTION ... 261
Benefits of Remote Sensing in Nutrient Management ... 263
REMOTE SENSING TECHNIQUES FOR NUTRIENT MAPPING ... 263
Multispectral and Hyperspectral Imaging ... 264
Thermal Imaging ... 265
LiDAR (Light Detection and Ranging) ... 266
Satellite-Based Remote Sensing ... 266
UAV (Drone) Remote Sensing ... 266
Spectral Vegetation Indices for Nutrient Mapping ... 266
Ground-Based Remote Sensing ... 267
ROLE OF REMOTE SENSING IN FERTILIZER OPTIMIZATION ... 267
Site-Specific Nutrient Management (SSNM) ... 267
Variable Rate Technology (VRT) Integration ... 268
Reduction of Environmental Impact ... 269
Real-Time Decision Support Systems ... 269
Practical Implementation Tips ... 269
CHALLENGES AND LIMITATIONS ... 271
Technological Challenges ... 271
Data Processing and Interpretation Complexity ... 271
Accuracy Limitations in Nutrient Detection ... 272
Financial and Infrastructure Challenges ... 272
High Initial Investment and Maintenance Costs ... 272
Limited Accessibility for Small-Scale Farmers ... 272
Environmental and Operational Constraints ... 272
Influence of Weather and Atmospheric Conditions ... 272
Data Integration Challenges with Traditional Farming Practices ... 272
FUTURE PROSPECTS AND TECHNOLOGICAL ADVANCEMENTS IN REMOTE SENSING FOR FERTILIZER OPTIMIZATION ... 273
Emerging Trends in Remote Sensing for Agriculture ... 273
Integration of Artificial Intelligence (AI) and Machine Learning (ML) ... 273
Adoption of Internet of Things (IoT) and Smart Sensors ... 273
Advances in Hyperspectral and Thermal Imaging ... 273
Technological Advancements Driving Future Adoption ... 273
Integration of Blockchain for Data Security and Transparency ... 273
Autonomous Drones and Robotics in Fertilizer Application ... 274
Development of Cost-Effective Satellite Imagery Solutions ... 274
Government Policies and Global Initiatives Supporting Remote Sensing Adoption ... 274
Challenges in Implementing Future Technologies ... 274
CONCLUSION ... 275

REFERENCES ... 276

CHAPTER 15 SMART IRRIGATION SYSTEMS: A REVIEW OF CURRENT TRENDS AND FUTURE PROSPECTS ... 278

Nishu Bali and *Deepika Chaudhary*

INTRODUCTION ... 278

ROLE OF TECHNOLOGY FOR SMART IRRIGATION ... 279

Sensors ... 279

Soil Moisture Sensor ... 280

Rainfall Sensors ... 280

Temperature Sensors ... 281

Solar Radiation Sensor ... 282

Weather Stations ... 282

Flowmeters ... 283

Leaf Wetness Sensors ... 284

UV Radiation Sensor ... 284

Automation and Control Systems ... 285

Machine Learning and Artificial Intelligence ... 286

Automated Valves and Pumps ... 286

METHODOLOGY ... 286

EMERGING TECHNOLOGIES IN SMART IRRIGATION ... 288

CONCLUSION ... 294

FUTURE SCOPE ... 295

REFERENCES ... 296

SUBJECT INDEX ... 299

PREFACE

Over the past decades, the challenges facing global agriculture—climate change, soil degradation, water scarcity, and feeding an ever-growing population—have made it very clear that traditional agriculture alone will not be sufficient. The demand for sustainable, efficient, and data-driven farming practices has never been more pressing. Hyperspectral remote sensing has assumed its position as a significant part of innovation among the many technological innovations shaping the future of agriculture. With its ability to capture and quantify intricate spectral information across hundreds of adjacent bands, hyperspectral imaging enables researchers and practitioners to detect subtle differences in vegetation, soil health, water stress, and more—long before they are apparent to the human eye. Coupled with recent advances in artificial intelligence and geospatial analysis, the possible applications for this technology in agriculture are nothing less than revolutionary.

This book, "Hyperspectral Remote Sensing for Sustainable Agriculture", brings together a broad range of research works encompassing not only the theoretical foundations of hyperspectral sensing but also its actual applications along the agricultural value chain—from crop monitoring and disease detection to nutrient management and irrigation planning.

What makes this book especially valuable is the balance it achieves between depth and accessibility. It speaks to students and early researchers without oversimplifying the complexity of the subject, and, simultaneously, it offers veteran scientists and practitioners a thoughtfully chosen overview of the contemporary trends, challenges, and future prospects. The fact that artificial intelligence is included in most of the chapters shows the forward-looking nature of this work and how interdisciplinary approaches hold the key to achieving true agricultural sustainability. I commend the vision and academic effort of the editors and contributors in compiling this important work. This book contains resources, references, and, most importantly, calls for responsible innovation. I am confident that "Hyperspectral Remote Sensing for Sustainable Agriculture" will serve as a useful guide for academic researchers, practitioners in the field, and policymakers as well, and will continue to inspire innovations in this important field.

Sartajvir Singh
Centre of Excellence
Socio-Environmental Sustainability for River Sand-Mining (SEnSRS)
Indian Institute of Technology
Ropar, Punjab, India

Neelam Dahiya
Department of Computer Applications
Chitkara University Institute of Engineering and Technology
Chitkara University, Punjab, India

Maged Mohammed
Department of Agricultural and Biosystems Engineering
Faculty of Agriculture, Menoufia University
Shebin El Koum, Egypt

Abdullah Alzharihi
Department of Electrical and Computer Engineering
Oakland University
Rochester hills, MI, USA

&

Vishal Dutt
Department of Computer Science and Engineering
Chandigarh University
Punjab, India

List of Contributors

Adarsh Tripathi	Department of Agricultural and Food Engineering, Indian Institute of Technology Kharagpur, Kharagpur, West Bengal, India
Akinchan Maity	Chitkara University Institute of Engineering and Technology, Chitkara University, Punjab, India
Akshata Musale	Department of Civil Engineering, Jain College of Engineering and Technology, Hubballi, Karnataka, India
Amanpreet Singh	Chitkara University Institute of Engineering and Technology, Chitkara University, Punjab, India
Amish Goyal	Department of Agricultural and Food Engineering, Indian Institute of Technology Kharagpur, Kharagpur, West Bengal, India
Anamika Larhgotra	Department of CSE, Chandigarh University, Mohali, India
Arshdeep Singh	Department of Agricultural and Food Engineering, Indian Institute of Technology Kharagpur, Kharagpur, West Bengal, India
Ashutosh Pagrotra	Department of Biomechatronics, National Taiwan University, Taipei, Taiwan
Binod Kumar Mishra	Department of Computer Science and Engineering, Chandigarh University, Mohali, Punjab, India
C. Krithika	Department of Soil Science and Agricultural Chemistry, College of Agriculture and Technology, Theni-625562, Tamil Nadu, India
Danish Monga	Department of Agricultural and Food Engineering, Indian Institute of Technology Kharagpur, Kharagpur, West Bengal, India
Deepika Chaudhary	Chitkara University Institute of Engineering & Technology, Chitkara University, Punjab, India
G. Manimaran	Department of Soil Science and Agricultural Chemistry, Tamil Nadu Agricultural University, Coimbatore-641 003, India
Ganesh Kumar Sethi	Department of Computer Science, MM Modi College, Patiala, Punjab, India
Gurwinder Singh	Department of Computer Application, Chandigarh Group of Colleges, Jhanjeri, India
Hashmat Fida	School of Computer Science and Engineering, Presidency University, Bangaluru, India
Jaspreet Kaur	Department of Computer Science and Engineering, Chandigarh University, Mohali, Punjab, India
Jaspreet Singh	Department of Computer Science & Engineering, Chandigarh University, Mohali-140413, Punjab, India
Jaswinder Singh	Chitkara University Institute of Engineering and Technology, Chitkara University, Punjab, India
Jay Arindam Maity	Chitkara University Institute of Engineering and Technology, Chitkara University, Punjab, India

Jyotsana Patel	Department of Agricultural and Food Engineering, Indian Institute of Technology Kharagpur, Kharagpur, West Bengal, India
K. Murugasridevi	Amrita School of Agricultural Sciences, Amrita Vishwa Vidyapeetham, Coimbatore-642109, India
Kalirajan Murugasridevi	Amrita School of Agricultural Sciences, Amrita Vishwa Vidyapeetham, Coimbatore -642 109, India
Kirti Khandelwal	Department of Mechanical Engineering, Anjuman College of Engineering and Technology, Nagpur-440001, India
Krishna Rawat	School of Water Resources, Indian Institute of Technology Kharagpur, Kharagpur, West Bengal, India
Lincy Kirubhadharshini B.	VIT School of Agricultural Innovations and Advanced Learning (VAIAL), Vellore Institute of Technology (VIT), Vellore - 632 014, India
Mohammad Sohail Pervez	Department of Mechanical Engineering, Anjuman College of Engineering and Technology, Nagpur-440001, India
Narayan Vyas	Department of Computer Science and Engineering, Vivekananda Global University, Jaipur, India
Navpreet Kaur Walia	Department of CSE, Chandigarh University, Mohali, India
Neelam Dahiya	Department of Computer Applications, Chitkara University Institute of Engineering and Technology, Chitkara University, Punjab, India
Neha Bhati	Department of Research and Development, Flexxited, Bangalore, India
Nishu Bali	Chitkara University Institute of Engineering & Technology, Chitkara University, Punjab, India
Nitin Arora	University Institute of Engineering, Chandigarh University, Mohali, Punjab, India
Ramesh Chandra Nayak	Department of Mechanical Engineering, Synergy Institute of Technology, Bhubaneswar, Odisha, India iHubAnubhuti-IIITD Foundation, Okhla Industrial Estate, New Delhi, India
Rishikesh Ratan	Department of Agricultural and Food Engineering, Indian Institute of Technology Kharagpur, Kharagpur, West Bengal, India
Rupinder Singh	Chitkara University Institute of Engineering and Technology, Chitkara University, Punjab, India
S. Sowjanya	VIT School of Agricultural Innovations and Advanced Learning (VAIAL), Vellore Institute of Technology (VIT), Vellore - 632 014, India School of Biosciences and Technology, Vellore Institute of Technology (VIT), Vellore - 632014, India
Sakshi Sinha	Department of Dairy Sciences and Food Technology, Banaras Hindu University, Varanasi, 221005, Uttar Pradesh, India
Sangeetha Annam	Chitkara University Institute of Engineering and Technology, Chitkara University, Punjab, India
Sartajvir Singh	Centre of Excellence, Socio-Environmental Sustainability for River Sand-Mining (SEnSRS), Indian Institute of Technology, Ropar, Punjab, India

Shresthashree Swain	School of Oceanographic Studies, Jadavpur University, Kolkata - 700032, West Bengal, India
Suryavanshi Bhagyeshkumar Vijaybhai	Department of Mechanical Engineering, Birla Vishwakarma Mahavidhyalya (BVM) Engineering College, Anand, Gujarat, India
V. Dhayalan	Department of Agricultural Engineering, Hindusthan College of Engineering and Technology, Coimbatore-641050, India
Venunathan Dhivya	Department of Agricultural Entomology, Tamil Nadu Agricultural University, Coimbatore - 641 003, India
Vinod Kumar	Department of Computer Science and Engineering, Chandigarh University, Mohali, Punjab, India
Vishal Dutt	Department of Computer Science, Punjabi University, Patiala, Punjab, India Department of Computer Science and Engineering, Chandigarh University, Mohali, Punjab, India
VR Mageshen	Amrita School of Agricultural Sciences, Amrita Vishwa Vidyapeetham, Coimbatore-642109, India

CHAPTER 1

Advancing Smart Irrigation Practices in Small-Scale Agriculture by Combining Hyperspectral Remote Sensing with IoT Solutions

Suryavanshi Bhagyeshkumar Vijaybhai[1], Mohammad Sohail Pervez[2], Ramesh Chandra Nayak[3,4,*], Kirti Khandelwal[2], Shresthashree Swain[5] and **Akshata Musale[6]**

[1] *Department of Mechanical Engineering, Birla Vishwakarma Mahavidhyalya (BVM) Engineering College, Anand, Gujarat, India*

[2] *Department of Mechanical Engineering, Anjuman College of Engineering and Technology, Nagpur-440001, India*

[3] *Department of Mechanical Engineering, Synergy Institute of Technology, Bhubaneswar, Odisha, India*

[4] *iHubAnubhuti-IIITD Foundation, Okhla Industrial Estate, New Delhi, India*

[5] *School of Oceanographic Studies, Jadavpur University, Kolkata - 700032, West Bengal, India*

[6] *Department of Civil Engineering, Jain College of Engineering and Technology, Hubballi, Karnataka, India*

Abstract: Technology in agriculture has advanced significantly over the past few decades. However, small and medium-sized agricultural enterprises often face challenges in accessing and adopting these technological innovations. In India, the majority of farmers are marginal or smallholders cultivating up to 2 hectares of land. Because the productivity of these agricultural systems is typically lower than that of large-scale operations, it is essential to manage resource requirements precisely to maximize benefits. Irrigation remains one of the most critical needs in all types of agriculture. Appropriate and cost-effective irrigation methods can enable farmers to improve yields while conserving resources. This study presents an integrated approach combining hyperspectral remote sensing with an IoT-based manual irrigation system tailored for small-scale agriculture. Hyperspectral imagery is leveraged to assess spatial variability in crop health, soil moisture distribution, and stress indicators across fields, providing actionable insights to optimize water application. The designed system consists of an epicyclic gear train arrangement powered by solar energy and interfaced with IoT technology. An advanced circuit incorporating an ESP8266 microcontroller is implemented to monitor key environmental parameters, such as soil moisture content, relative humidity, and air dry bulb temperature. The integration of hyperspectral data

* **Corresponding author Ramesh Chandra Nayak:** Department of Mechanical Engineering, Synergy Institute of Technology, Bhubaneswar, Odisha, India; iHubAnubhuti-IIITD Foundation, Okhla Industrial Estate, New Delhi, India; E-mail: rameshnayak23@gmail.com

Sartajvir Singh, Neelam Dahiya, Maged Mohammed, Abdullah Alzharihi & Vishal Dutt (Eds.)

with real-time sensor measurements enables more informed irrigation scheduling and targeted water delivery. The system offers programmable control to maintain ideal soil moisture content at 80% saturation, supporting sustainable water management and improved productivity for small and marginal farmers. This combined strategy demonstrates the potential of merging hyperspectral remote sensing and IoT solutions to advance precision irrigation practices in smallholder agriculture.

Keywords: Epicyclic gear train, External source, Farmer, Hand pump, IoT, Irrigation, Technology.

INTRODUCTION

Water scarcity and the rising demand for food production worldwide pose challenges for agriculture. Traditional irrigation methods lead to inefficient use of water and wastage. The need for sustainable farming practices and the presence of unfavourable climatic conditions are driving the adoption of advanced irrigation systems. Markom *et al.* demonstrated the digital technological farming process using IoT and artificial intelligence [1]. They concluded that farmers are satisfied with technology-based irrigation and other methods for agriculture. Technological growth is therefore a suitable pathway for farmers towards sustainability, as also indicated in their work.

Naim, A investigated how cutting-edge computing tools and artificial intelligence can be used to address urgent environmental issues [2]. The study demonstrated that processing large amounts of information on biodiversity, resource management, and climate change using High-Performance Computing (HPC) can result in more precise modelling and forecasts. The author reviewed several case examples where AI systems enhance resource efficiency, improve environmental monitoring, and promote sustainable practices across various industries. The study also emphasizes the necessity of multidisciplinary cooperation and policy guidelines for the successful incorporation of these developments into sustainability initiatives.

Peng *et al.* examined the application of artificial intelligence to optimize multi-energy systems for rural areas [3]. Their goal was to encourage a sustainable energy economy and a green transition in rural energy planning. The authors proposed a model integrating AI with multi-energy optimization, leading to efficient and environmentally friendly energy systems. This research contributed to a more sustainable and green rural energy landscape.

Uddin *et al.* examined the basic ideas that define autonomous systems, describing how AI-powered analytics and IoT connectivity could simplify resource management and operating procedures [4]. They provide examples in fields including smart cities, smart agriculture, and factory automation, showing how these technologies can support instantaneous decisions and adaptive reactions to environmental change. The report highlights several implementation challenges, including scalability, compatibility, and data security, and makes recommendations for future research directions to address these issues.

S. Neethirajan demonstrated the possible application of AI with big data to achieve net-zero carbon dairy production [5]. By improving feed efficiency, waste management, and animal health tracking, among other aspects of dairy production, these developments can increase productivity and ultimately reduce greenhouse gas emissions.

Alazzai *et al.* studied the application of AI and IoT in agriculture to optimize crop management [6]. The research demonstrated the potential of these technologies to maximize resources, boost production, and enhance agricultural efficiency, highlighting their role in promoting sustainable and productive farming practices.

Hussein *et al.* discussed the use of AI and IoT in agriculture, emphasizing their ability to maximize resource utilization, enhance crop production, and encourage more efficient and sustainable agricultural practices [7].

Matar *et al.* investigated advancements in intelligent modular agricultural systems, demonstrating how technologies such as data analysis, automated processes, and the Internet of Things can improve farm operations [8]. The authors advocate a modular strategy because it allows farmers to scale and adapt to different conditions. Key advantages include improved crop yields, reduced environmental impact, and efficient resource management. The paper also addresses challenges, including the need for farmer training and the cost of initial investment, ultimately presenting intelligent modular farming as a viable approach for sustainable agriculture to meet global food demands.

The conference proceedings focused on advances in data-driven computing and intelligent systems, with major areas of focus including new approaches such as extreme gradient boosting for ship classification and deep learning techniques for seizure detection and skin disease diagnosis.

Other significant studies focus on open innovation in the Greek food sector, the fusion of multiple sensors for detecting mental stress, and real-time object detection in aerial images. Also discussed are problems of energy efficiency in telecommunications and anti-forensic image processing. The range of research demonstrates the increasing influence of data-driven strategies in different domains, showcasing the potential to maximize sustainability, efficiency, and innovation. Akavova *et al.* delve into the importance of machine learning and AI for the progress of sustainable development [9]. They discuss how resources can be better managed, environmental monitoring enhanced, and more informed decisions made across various industries. The authors present practical applications of AI that can significantly minimize environmental impacts, including waste management, energy efficiency, and intelligent agriculture. To fully capitalize on AI's sustainability potential, the article also stresses the need for cooperative research and supportive policy environments. Ultimately, it suggests leveraging AI-powered solutions to support the achievement of the United Nations Sustainable Development Goals.

Implementation of AI in combating climate change was reviewed by Chen *et al.* [10]. They explore AI-driven methods for enhancing data analysis, predictive modelling, and climate monitoring, all of which support environmental management. The authors investigate how machine learning and deep learning might optimize resource utilization and enhance energy efficiency across several industries, particularly in agriculture, transportation, and urban planning. To increase AI's efficacy in tackling climate-related concerns, they provide case examples demonstrating the impact of these algorithms and emphasize the significance of multidisciplinary cooperation and policy support.

To maximise indoor agriculture, Hadj Abdelkader *et al.* proposed an energy-efficient IoT-based lighting control system [11]. Its main aim was to strike a balance between energy savings and plant-enhancing requirements. The device continuously monitors ambient conditions and adjusts illumination based on sensor data and IoT technology. The research indicates that this method can significantly reduce energy consumption while maintaining agricultural productivity. In his discussion of the profound effects of IoT and artificial intelligence on the bioeconomy, J. Lourenço investigated investigated the application of IoT and AI and concluded that they can enhance efficiency, sustainability, innovation, and economic and environmental performance, though further development is needed [12]. Priyanka *et al.* proposed an energy-efficient IoT network for agriculture [13]. To improve data transfer, they used the most efficient routing and region-based segmentation. Their aim was to promote a sustainable agricultural ecosystem by optimizing the energy consumption of IoT networking. Husaini and Sohail examined how robotics and biotechnology could enhance organic farming for sustainable and healthy food production [14]. They challenged the simple GM *vs.* organic crop debate, suggesting a combined approach. Their research, published in the Journal of Biotechnology, proposed integrating these technologies for a comprehensive and environmentally conscious food system. The study by Kumar Tyagi *et al.* [15] explores how AI might transform sustainable business practices and improve organisational independence. The article discusses the advantages of employing various AI technologies to simplify decision-making, reduce waste, and enhance resource management. According to the authors, AI enables businesses to achieve sustainability through efficient operations and adapt to evolving environmental standards. The case studies in the paper demonstrate successful applications of AI that have substantially reduced operating costs and environmental impact. The universal message encourages corporate planning that applies AI to support both business returns and ecological sustainability.

Oussous *et al* combined analytical intelligence with visualization optimization techniques to enhance cybersecurity for agricultural IoT devices in greenhouse conditions [16]. The authors present a system utilizing synchronized PAYLOAD handshaking that strengthens the security of data transmission and improves IoT devices' defense against cyber-attacks. Another aspect of their research involves applying optimization techniques to enhance resource allocation and process efficiency in smart agriculture. These results emphasize the importance of incorporating AI through IoT for sustainable agricultural operations, as they not only improve cybersecurity but also foster system functionality and productivity.

The study by Al Hashlamoun *et al.* [17] discusses the prospects and challenges associated with the integration of AI and sustainable computing. It highlights how AI can reduce its environmental footprint and enhance resource utilization, promoting sustainability across various sectors. The authors identify key challenges, including ethical concerns, data privacy issues, and the environmental impact of AI technologies. To address these challenges, the paper proposes a framework for the ethical use of AI aligned with sustainable computing practices, aiming for responsible implementation that balances AI benefits with social and environmental responsibilities.

Bhattacharya explored the contributions of Industry 5.0 toward sustainability in different industries [18]. The study examined how Industry 5.0 can improve environmental accountability, highlighting specific applications and benefits, including the use of innovative technologies to achieve sustainability goals. Ribeiro *et al.* presented studies at a computer science conference investigating ICT's effects on agricultural sustainability [19]. Their paper demonstrated ICT's positive impacts through improved resource utilization, reduced environmental impact, and enhanced agricultural productivity.

Ragazou *et al.* put forth a novel structure for the agriculture sector that promotes the application of big data, AI, and IoT to develop more efficient farm activities while reducing costs [20]. They suggest establishing strategic management to monitor resource depletion and environmental impacts, emphasizing the core values of sustainability and energy efficiency. They argue that this paradigm will lead to a third wave in productivity and reduce carbon emissions, thereby promoting greater sustainability in food production. The study shows the benefits of adopting modern technology to achieve a more robust and effective agriculture industry.

The paper by Zafar *et al.* [21] explores smarter and more sustainable means of improving the efficiency of wireless networks. It identifies advanced technologies, such as AI and ML, to enhance network efficiency and reliability in real-time applications. Challenges associated with congestion, energy consumption, and latency are addressed, and solutions are proposed. In particular, it emphasizes the importance of sustainability in network design, focusing on energy efficiency and resource management. The paper provides analyses and case studies that can help researchers and practitioners optimize high-performance wireless networks with sustainability in mind.

The paper by Raut *et al.* [22] discusses the integration of AI in food drying processes to enhance efficiency and quality. It addresses challenges associated with traditional drying techniques, such as high energy use and inconsistent quality. The authors recommend using AI, particularly machine learning, to learn from errors and optimize real-time drying conditions, ensuring better control of moisture levels while preserving the product. The study highlights the benefits of automated decision-making based on data analytics and the potential for greater sustainability and efficiency in food processing. It supports increased research and development of AI applications in the food industry.

In Iran's agricultural sector, Banaeian *et al.* examine patterns and potential avenues for crop energy analysis going forward [23]. The study highlights the significance of energy conservation in agricultural production and examines different approaches to measuring productivity and energy use. The authors identify important obstacles, such as reliance on fossil fuels and sustainability challenges. To increase energy efficiency, they advise switching to renewable energy sources and establishing sustainable practices. The study also addresses the need for technological advancements and frameworks that promote sustainable agricultural growth in Iran, with the goal of creating a resilient and environmentally friendly farming culture.

In order to strengthen regional bio-economies and develop alternative bio-waste treatment plants for the production of bio-energy, Vlachokostas *et al.* present a decision support system [24]. It emphasizes the value of bio-waste in waste management in addition to its capacity as a sustainable energy source. Based on area requirements, the study offers a methodical framework for choosing appropriate technologies and approaches while considering a variety of technical, financial, and environmental aspects. The authors propose that bioenergy production should be integrated into local economies to improve resilience and sustainability in waste management techniques.

Huh and Kim explored the use of blockchain consensus protocols in new and renewable energy management [25]. They investigated enhancing the viability of energy management by utilizing these protocols, focusing on the benefits of blockchain, including increased transparency, security, and efficiency in transactions, as well as improved power distribution. This study also augmented knowledge regarding how blockchain functions within sustainable energy management.

Ahamed *et al.* examined how bio-production engineering, specifically automation and precision agronomics, can enhance agricultural sustainability [26]. The study highlighted the need to minimize resource utilization and enhance crop yields using these technologies, promoting more sustainable agriculture through the integration of engineering and biological principles.

Ahamed *et al.* Examined the idea of bio-production engineering and its application in sustainable agriculture [27]. They presented a blueprint highlighting the promise of bio-based approaches to enhance agricultural sustainability. The authors explained several strategies and technologies to maximize the use of resources and reduce the environmental footprint in agriculture. The study aimed to provide an integrated overview of how bio-production engineering could make the agricultural industry more environmentally friendly and efficient.

In their study [28], González *et al.* investigated the establishment of global online schools in energy engineering to advance environmentally friendly construction and urban renewal. They emphasise the importance of education in equipping people with the knowledge and skills needed to practice sustainable construction. The courses aim to facilitate knowledge transfer across regions and reach a large audience through online learning methods. The article states that these educational initiatives are crucial for accomplishing global sustainability goals and describes the format and subject matter of the courses.

Nayak *et al* presented innovative methods for promoting a green environment and sustainability [29 - 31]. The study proposes a smart irrigation control system using IoT integrated with an epicyclic gear train model to gather and interpret real-time data related to smart agriculture. This approach demonstrates how the proposed system can improve water use, sustainability, and agricultural practices. Furthermore, the article integrates IoT with mechanical processes to maximize crop productivity and promote global food and water security.

Remote sensing, a form of hyperspectral photography that offers high-resolution images and accurate information on crop condition, soil moisture levels, and environmental factors, enables smart irrigation. Wide-spectrum light detection and detailed analysis of vegetation indicators, such as the Normalised Difference Vegetation Index with the Enhanced Vegetation Index, are both possible with hyperspectral sensors. Through the integration of hyperspectral data and IoT irrigation, as well as thermal/microwave remote sensing, farmers are able to schedule irrigation accurately. This technology keeps track of the health of the plants and soil moisture, maximizes water utilization, increases yields, and avoids both drought stress and overwatering, resulting in better resource management and healthier crops.

EXPERIMENTAL SETUP AND PROCEDURE

A new technology is explained in this paper to improve the irrigation system of agricultural practices. The designed setup is the combination of the existing system along with a technology-based control unit. The proposed scheme consists of three important units: 1) IoT devices, 2) mechanical devices, and 3) the dashboard. Each of these plays a pivotal role in secure communication, ensuring smooth data transfer and improved user engagement. Fig. (**1**) depicts the general layout of the hand pump, which is the most crucial component of the system that was constructed.

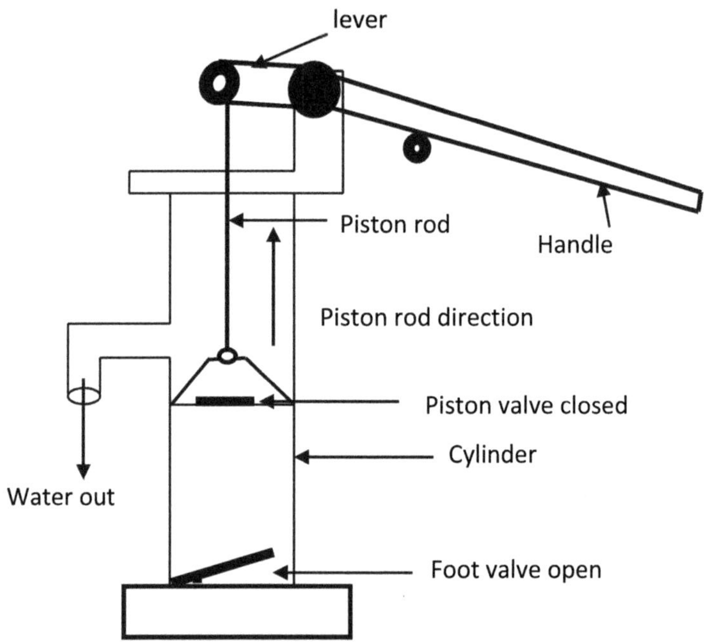

Fig. (1). Different parts of an existing hand pump.

The hand pump is used as a source for lifting water from underground. It operates by creating a pressure differential between the foot valve's top and bottom, and water lifts occur as a result of the piston rod's reciprocating motion and handle effort. It is impractical to use the hand pump for irrigation on a farm with only manual effort at the handle [32]. Therefore, the concept of regulating water on demand and the technology for the plunger rod's reciprocating motion are explained in this paper. The general layout of the planned system is depicted in Fig. (**2**).

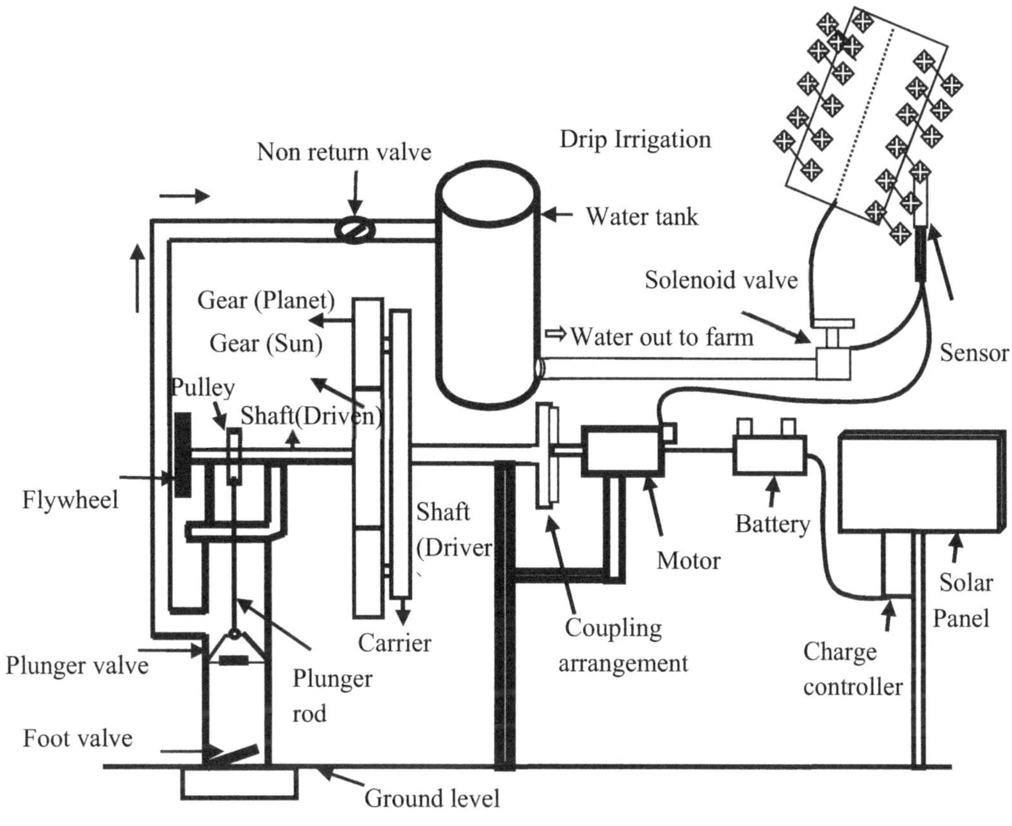

Fig. (2). Irrigation system with IoT technology.

The gearbox mechanism and gearing arrangement are depicted in Fig. (**3**) below. It comprises an epicyclic gear train arrangement, flywheel, driver and driven shaft, support system, and attachments with a plunger rod of a hand pump.

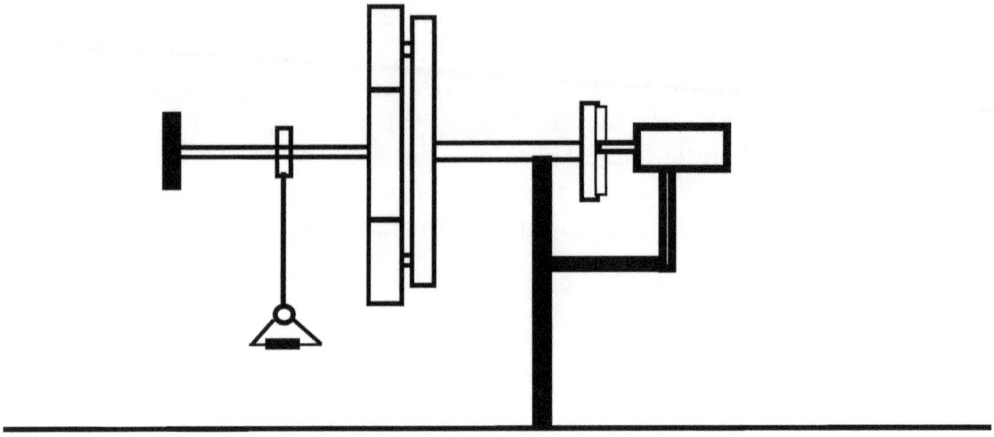

Fig. (3). Transmission arrangement of the water lifting system.

Three planet gears, a single sun gear, a planet carrier, a driver shaft, a driven shaft, a wheel, a pulley, a coupling unit, and bearings compose the epicyclic gear train. The charging system consists of solar panels, a charge controller, a control panel, and a DC motor. The control unit consists of sensors, an ESP8266 microcontroller, and a solenoid valve. Sensors are initially placed at various positions on the farm, which is designed with drip irrigation arrangements and connected to a water tank. The sensors are attached to the ESP8266 microcontroller, and the control unit is connected to the solenoid valve and motor control panel.

The plunger rod of the hand pump is linked to the sun gear of the epicyclic gear train, which features a planet carrier in contact with three planet gears. The assembly links the planet carrier to a DC motor through a coupling mechanism. The battery that powers the DC motor is charged by a solar panel, with the charge controller regulating the battery charge. When current is supplied to the motor from the battery, the motor rotates the driver shaft and the planet carrier. The three planet gears spin around the sun gear due to the planet carrier's rotation, increasing the speed of the sun gear. This higher speed produces a reciprocating motion in the plunger rod [33 - 40].

The plunger rod's reciprocating motion creates a pressure differential that draws water from below. This water is stored in the tank and, with the help of the drip irrigation arrangement, is utilized as required. The water supply from the tank is controlled by opening and closing the solenoid valve, which is actuated by signals from the sensors. To maintain a certain water level in the tank, the motor operates according to the opening of the throttle valve, providing the necessary input for water lifting.

Remote sensing images, namely Normalized Difference Vegetation Index (NDVI) and Enhanced Vegetation Index (EVI), along with soil moisture indices, are essential in optimizing irrigation since they provide real-time information on crop condition and soil status. NDVI and EVI assist in evaluating vegetation vigor by determining how plants reflect and absorb light. NDVI indicates plant health by measuring the difference between visible red light and near-infrared light, whereas EVI accounts for atmospheric and soil background conditions to provide more accurate measurements in highly vegetated areas. Farmers use these indices to assess water stress levels and apply targeted irrigation to avoid overwatering or under-watering [41 - 44].

Remote-sensing-based soil moisture indices provide information on water availability in the root zone. By combining these indices with IoT-based irrigation systems, farmers can automate water delivery based on soil moisture levels observed in the field rather than relying on fixed schedules [45 - 48]. This approach not only conserves water but also increases crop yield and sustainability. Integrating these remote sensing technologies with intelligent irrigation systems ensures effective water use, reduces operating expenses, and promotes environmental sustainability by preventing soil erosion and water wastage.

RESULT AND DISCUSSION

The hardware configuration and design described here, intended for irrigation control complemented by IoT software, is an innovative addition to the precise agricultural industry. The efficiency of the proposed system in maintaining sufficient soil moisture levels and implementing climate-responsive irrigation techniques is demonstrated through methodical experiments and tests. The ESP8266 microcontroller, which provides wireless internet access, is intuitive to use. It has several I/O control pins that can detect various parameters requiring attention and initiate corrective actions. Programming languages like C, C#, or Python offer many functions for reading sensors and controlling relays. The primary objective of the designed system is to build a circuit that can measure soil moisture using the ESP8266. The system can program a DC motor and a solenoid valve to operate in response to soil moisture requirements, with the goal of maintaining soil moisture at 80%. Fig. (**4**) shows the arrangement of the ESP8266 microcontroller.

Fig. (4). ESP 8266 microcontroller circuit diagram.

IoT Programming

Two methods of irrigation, sprinkler and drip, were taken into consideration when writing the code. Sprinklers will be turned on at extremely high dry bulb temperatures. Drip irrigation systems are able to maintain root zone moisture at 80%, depending on the soil moisture level. This is an effective method of providing optimal water, thereby encouraging healthy plant growth. The irrigation strategy may differ depending on the crop's age and type. The program will be stored on the ESP-8266. To run the circuit, it will receive power from the solar cell and store it in the Li-ion battery. Water will be supplied to the sprinkler and drip irrigation systems *via* the relay. Details of the program for the DHT22 RH/Temperature sensor and the capacitive soil moisture sensor are provided below:

```
#include <ESP8266WiFi.h>

#include <ThingSpeak.h>

#include <DHT.h>

#define DHTPIN D4 // Pin where the DHT22 is connected

#define DHTTYPE DHT22 // Type of the DHT sensor

#define MOISTURE_PIN A0 // Pin where the soil moisture sensor is connected

#define RELAY_PIN_1 D1 // Pin for controlling relay 1 (drip irrigation)
```

```
#define RELAY_PIN_2 D2 // Pin for controlling relay 2 (sprinkler irrigation)
// WiFi credentials
const char *ssid = “YOUR_WIFI_SSID”;
const char *password = “YOUR_WIFI_PASSWORD”;
// ThingSpeak credentials
const char *thingSpeakApiKey = “YOUR_THINGSPEAK_API_KEY”;
// Initialize DHT sensor
DHT dht(DHTPIN, DHTTYPE);
void setup() {
Serial.begin(9600);
pinMode(RELAY_PIN_1, OUTPUT);
pinMode(RELAY_PIN_2, OUTPUT);
WiFi.begin(ssid, password);
ThingSpeak.begin(client);
}
void loop() {
delay(2000);
// Read temperature and humidity from DHT sensor
float temperature = dht.readTemperature();
float humidity = dht.readHumidity();
// Read soil moisture
int moisture = analogRead(MOISTURE_PIN);
// Activate irrigation based on moisture level and month
int month = month(); // Get the current month
```

```
if (month >= 3 && month <= 5) { // March, April, May
if (moisture < 500) { // Adjust threshold according to your soil
// Turn on drip irrigation
DigitalWrite(RELAY_PIN_1, HIGH);
DigitalWrite(RELAY_PIN_2, LOW); // Ensure sprinkler is off
Serial.println("Drip irrigation activated.");
} else {
// Turn on sprinkler irrigation
DigitalWrite(RELAY_PIN_1, LOW); // Ensure drip is off
DigitalWrite(RELAY_PIN_2, HIGH);
Serial.println("Sprinkler irrigation activated.");
}
} else {
// Deactivate both irrigation systems if not in the specified months
digitalWrite(RELAY_PIN_1, LOW);
digitalWrite(RELAY_PIN_2, LOW);
Serial.println("No irrigation needed.");
}
// Update ThingSpeak channel with sensor data
ThingSpeak.setField(1, temperature);
ThingSpeak.setField(2, humidity);
ThingSpeak.setField(3, moisture);
ThingSpeak.writeFields();
}
```

Execution of the Program

The step-wise execution of the above program has been described below:

Open Arduino IDE: Begin your computer's Arduino Integrated Development Environment (IDE).

Create a New Sketch: Click on "File" in the menu bar, then select "New" to create a new sketch.

Copy the Program: Copy the provided Arduino program code (the one for irrigating vegetable crops using ESP8266, soil moisture sensor, and DHT22 sensor) and paste it into the new sketch window in the Arduino IDE.

Configure Libraries: Ensure that you have installed the necessary libraries for ESP8266, DHT sensor, and ThingSpeak integration. If not, go to "Sketch" -> "Include Library" -> "Manage Libraries..." and search for and install the required libraries.

Set Board Type: Go to "Tools" -> "Board" and select the appropriate board type for your ESP8266 microcontroller. For example, if you are using NodeMCU, select "NodeMCU 1.0 (ESP-12E Module)".

Select Port: If your ESP8266 is connected to your computer *via* USB, go to "Tools" -> "Port" and select the correct COM port to which your ESP8266 is connected.

Verify the Code: Click on the checkmark icon (√) or go to "Sketch" -> "Verify/Compile" to compile the code. This stage examines the code for any syntactic mistakes.

Upload the Code: Once the code is successfully compiled without errors, click on the right arrow icon (→) or go to "Sketch" -> "Upload" to upload the code to your ESP8266 microcontroller.

Monitor Compilation Progress: During compilation and upload, the Arduino IDE will display the progress in the console at the bottom of the window. Any errors or warnings encountered during compilation will be displayed here.

Monitor Serial Output (Optional): If you have included Serial.print statements in your code for debugging or monitoring purposes by selecting the magnifier icon in the toolbar, you can launch the Serial Monitor in the Arduino IDE. This allows you to view the output messages from your ESP8266 during runtime. Our designed system consists of a technology-based control unit, so it is easy to operate, and it will help towards environmental sustainability. Table **1** below shows the cost comparison between our designed system and other systems.

The tables in the paper offer a cost and functionality comparison of a conventional diesel-powered irrigation system and an IoT-based system. Table **1** provides a five-year cost comparison, indicating that, although the IoT-based system is more expensive to implement (INR 40,000 compared to INR 12,000 for diesel pumps), it eliminates costs associated with servicing, maintenance, fuel, and fuel delivery. Consequently, the five-year total cost of ownership is lower for the IoT system (INR 40,000) than for the diesel pump (INR 70,000).

Table 1. Cost comparison between the diesel-operated irrigation system and our IoT-based system.

Sl. No.	Items	Diesel Water Pump (1 HP Capacity)	Our Designed System
1	Initial cost in INR	12,000/-	40,000/-
2	Servicing costin INR	10,000/-	NIL
3	Maintenance costin INR	6,000/-	NIL
4	Fuel costin INR	32,000/-	NIL
5	Fuel delivery costin INR	10,000/-	NIL
Total cost at end of 5 years in INR		70,000/-	40,000/-

Table **2** shows a comparison of parameters such as pollution, operator requirement, and other factors between the diesel-operated irrigation system and the designed IoT system.

Table 2. Comparison between the diesel-operated irrigation system and our IoT-based system.

Sl. No.	Items	Diesel Water Pump (1 HP Capacity)	Our Designed System
1	Part replacement	Moderate	Frequently replacement needed
2	Operator requirement	Auto start and stop	Operator required
3	Utilization	Electric generation	No
4	Environmental aspect	Pollution free	High pollution
5	limitation	Only daytime work	High fuel and maintenance

From the observation, it was found that the total cost requirement of our designed system for a 5-year period is less than that of the diesel-operated irrigation system. Maintenance, servicing, and fuel expenditures are almost nil for our designed system, which is its main advantage. Table **2** further shows that the diesel-operated system produces more pollutants during operation, whereas our proposed system has no effect on the environment.

Table 2 also highlights other areas of comparison between the two systems. The diesel pump requires moderate parts replacement, while the IoT-based system requires more frequent replacements. The diesel system has an auto start/stop function, whereas the IoT system requires an operator. The IoT system does not generate electricity, while the diesel pump does. The IoT-based system is environmentally friendly, whereas diesel pumps emit significant pollution. The only major limitation of the IoT system is that it is functional only during the day, while diesel pumps incur high maintenance and fuel expenses.

The mechanical behavior and properties of the designed irrigation system are correlated with remote sensing data using IoT-based automation and monitoring. The epicyclic gear train and solar-powered hand pump system minimize manual labor by providing a mechanical advantage sufficient to develop enough torque for water lifting. These mechanical components operate effectively because they incorporate IoT sensors that regulate environmental factors such as soil moisture, relative humidity, and temperature in real time. Remote sensing data, particularly satellite imagery and hyperspectral imaging, provides a comprehensive overview of soil conditions and crop health at a large scale. By integrating this data with real-time sensor inputs, the system optimizes irrigation schedules for accurate water delivery and minimizes wastage.

In addition, with the application of remote sensing technology, namely the Normalized Difference Vegetation Index combined with soil moisture indexes, predictive analysis of water demand is feasible. This predictive ability allows the system to automate control of solenoid valves and motorized components, operating the mechanical system only when required. By synchronizing mechanical irrigation parts with remote sensing data, the system increases efficiency, saves water, and facilitates sustainable agriculture. This integration of mechanical engineering with remote sensing enhances the efficiency of small-scale farming while advancing environmental sustainability through reduced reliance on fossil-fuel-based irrigation schemes.

LIMITATIONS AND FUTURE WORK

While the proposed IoT-based smart irrigation system, combined with hyperspectral remote sensing, demonstrates clear benefits for enhancing water management in small-scale agriculture, there are several limitations that need to be acknowledged. The system's reliance on solar energy to power the motor and IoT components can reduce operational efficiency during extended cloudy or rainy conditions, limiting its ability to maintain the desired soil moisture levels consistently. Additionally, although hyperspectral imagery provides valuable information on spatial variability in crop health and soil moisture, acquiring high-resolution and frequent imagery remains constrained by satellite revisit intervals, cloud cover, and the cost of drone-based surveys. The integration of epicyclic gear train mechanisms, IoT sensors, and remote sensing data processing increases system complexity compared to traditional diesel-powered pumps. While the total operational cost over five years is lower, the higher initial investment and need for technical training may pose barriers for widespread adoption among smallholder farmers. The functionality of the system also depends on reliable internet connectivity to transmit real-time sensor data and manage irrigation schedules remotely. In regions where connectivity is intermittent, delays in decision-making could impact crop health. Furthermore, the system was primarily designed and tested under specific agro-climatic conditions, and its scalability and performance across different soil types, cropping systems, and regional climates remain to be validated.

To address these limitations, future work should focus on developing hybrid energy systems by integrating wind turbines or additional battery storage to ensure uninterrupted operation when solar input is insufficient. Automated workflows for processing hyperspectral imagery and generating actionable indices such as NDVI, EVI, and soil moisture maps can reduce the time and expertise needed for decision-making. Efforts to design and validate lower-cost soil moisture and climate sensors would further decrease the initial investment required for adoption. Incorporating edge computing capabilities in the IoT controllers could enable offline data processing and decision-making when internet connectivity is unreliable, with synchronization occurring once connections are restored. Expanding field trials to diverse agro-ecological zones will be essential to assess performance, optimize system configurations, and demonstrate applicability in varied farming contexts. Finally, developing dedicated training materials and farmer-oriented capacity-building programs will be critical to equipping users with the skills necessary to operate, maintain, and troubleshoot the system effectively. Addressing these areas will help make the technology more resilient, accessible, and impactful in promoting sustainable agriculture practices among small and marginal farmers.

CONCLUSION

- A drip irrigation solar-powered system with IoT-based technology provides a better way for farmers towards their sustainability and a better economy.
- It ensures the efficient use of water in agriculture, supporting environmental balance and reducing crop damage.

- Due to the implementation of IoT, our designed system saves labor resources and time. Due to a surplus of time, farmers are utilizing their time towards other activities.
- The designed system is environmentally friendly, so there will be no issue with air pollution from the use of our system.
- Due to the provision of a gearing system and flywheel, the force required to rotate the driver wheel is very low, which indicates the rotational torque for our designed system is very low.
- IoT-based smart drip irrigation systems automate irrigation and nutrient delivery, enabling optimized water usage and promoting better crop growth.

The practical application of this methodology can be illustrated with an example. Imagine a small farmer in rural India who relies on traditional irrigation methods, such as manually pumping water from a well. With the proposed IoT-based system, the farmer installs a solar-powered irrigation setup that automatically senses soil moisture levels. If the soil becomes too dry, the system activates a motorized pump that draws water from an underground source and distributes it through a drip irrigation system. This allows the farmer to save time and effort while ensuring crops receive optimal water levels.

Another example is a vegetable farmer growing tomatoes and chilies in a semi-arid region. During peak summer, excessive heat can cause rapid moisture loss from the soil. The smart irrigation system, equipped with sensors and a microcontroller, continuously monitors temperature and humidity. If temperatures rise above a critical threshold and soil moisture drops below the required level, the system automatically opens the drip irrigation valves, preventing crops from wilting. Since the system runs on solar energy, it reduces electricity costs and eliminates the need for diesel-powered pumps, making it an eco-friendly and cost-effective solution.

REFERENCES

[1] Markom A M, Yusof Y, Markom M A, Haris H, Muhammad A R. Digital technologies evolution in swiftlet farming: a systematic literature review. Int J Electr Comput Eng 2024; 14(4).

[2] Naim A, Khan S A, Mohammed A B, Malik P K. Applications of high performance computing and AI in green digital marketing. AI Appl Bus Med Agric Sustain. IGI Global 2024; pp. 47-67. [http://dx.doi.org/10.4018/979-8-3693-5266-3.ch003]

[3] Peng X, Guan X, Zeng Y, Zhang J. Artificial intelligence-driven multi-energy optimization: promoting green transition of rural energy planning and sustainable energy economy. Sustainability (Basel) 2024; 16(10): 4111. [http://dx.doi.org/10.3390/su16104111]

[4] Uddin M, Obaidat M, Manickam S, *et al.* Exploring the convergence of metaverse, blockchain, and AI : A comprehensive survey of enabling technologies, applications, challenges, and future directions. Wiley Interdiscip Rev Data Min Knowl Discov 2024; 14(6): e1556. [http://dx.doi.org/10.1002/widm.1556]

[5] Neethirajan S. Net zero dairy farming—advancing climate goals with big data and artificial intelligence. Climate (Basel) 2024; 12(2): 15.
[http://dx.doi.org/10.3390/cli12020015]

[6] Alazzai W K, Obaid M K, Abood B S Z, Jasim L. Smart agriculture solutions: Harnessing AI and IoT for crop management. E3S Web Conf. 477: 00057.

[7] Hussein A H A, Jabbar K A, Mohammed A, Jasim L. Harvesting the future: AI and IoT in agriculture. E3S Web Conf. 477: 00090.

[8] Matar MA, Radi M, Alzebda SA. Advancements in smart modular farming systems for sustainable agriculture.AI in Business: Opportunities and Limitations. Cham: Springer Nature Switzerland 2024; Vol. 2: pp. 45-55.
[http://dx.doi.org/10.1007/978-3-031-49544-1_4]

[9] Akavova A, Beguyev S, Zaripova R. How AI and machine learning can drive sustainable development.E3S Web of Conferences. EDP Sciences 2023; Vol. 460: p. 04018.
[http://dx.doi.org/10.1051/e3sconf/202346004018]

[10] Chen L, Chen Z, Zhang Y, *et al.* Artificial intelligence-based solutions for climate change: a review. Environ Chem Lett 2023; 21(5): 2525-57.
[http://dx.doi.org/10.1007/s10311-023-01617-y]

[11] Hadj Abdelkader O, Bouzebiba H, Pena D, Aguiar AP. Energy-efficient IoT. Sensors (Basel) 2023; 23(18): 7670.
[http://dx.doi.org/10.3390/s23187670] [PMID: 37765728]

[12] Lourenço J. The role of IoT Handbook of research on bioeconomy and economic ecosystems. IGI Global 2023; pp. 312-29.
[http://dx.doi.org/10.4018/978-1-6684-8879-9.ch016]

[13] Priyanka BHDD, Udayaraju P, Koppireddy CS, Neethika A. Developing a region-based energy-efficient IoT Measurement: Sensors 2023; 27: 100734.

[14] Husaini AM, Sohail M. Robotics-assisted, organic agricultural-biotechnology based environment-friendly healthy food option: Beyond the binary of GM *versus* Organic crops. J Biotechnol 2023; 361: 41-8.
[http://dx.doi.org/10.1016/j.jbiotec.2022.11.018] [PMID: 36470315]

[15] Tyagi PK, Sharma P, Singh AK, Tyagi P, Sharma P, Singh VJ. The role of artificial intelligence in promoting sustainable business operations and autonomy. 2023 10th IEEE Uttar Pradesh Sect Int Conf Electr Electron Comput Eng (UPCON). 10: 287-91.

[16] Oussous SA, Bajit A, Achour Y, Morino I, Zejli D, Elbouayadi R. Applying computational intelligence, visual optimization tools, and synchronized payload's handshaking to enhance greenhouses ECC cyber security-based agriculture IoT's properties. 2023 9th Int Conf Optim Appl (ICOA). 1-8.

[17] Al Hashlamoun N, Al Barghuthi N, Tamimi H. Exploring the intersection of AI and sustainable computing: opportunities, challenges, and a framework for responsible applications. 2023 9th Int Conf Inf Technol Trends (ITT). 220-5.
[http://dx.doi.org/10.1109/ITT59889.2023.10184228]

[18] Bhattacharya S. Industry 5.0's role in achieving sustainability in multiple sectors. Qual Manage Value Creation Digit Econ. Routledge 2023; pp. 44-55.

[19] Ribeiro MI, Guarda T, Lopes IM, Fernandes AJ. Impact of ICT on the agricultural sector's sustainability: evidence based on practices. International Conference on Computational Science and Its Applications. 97-109.Cham. 2023; pp.
[http://dx.doi.org/10.1007/978-3-031-37117-2_8]

[20] Ragazou K, Garefalakis A, Zafeiriou E, Passas I. Agriculture 5.0: A new strategic management mode

for a cut cost and an energy efficient agriculture sector. Energies 2022; 15(9): 3113.
[http://dx.doi.org/10.3390/en15093113]

[21] Zafar S, Ahad MA, Ali SI, Mehta D, Alam MA, Eds. Smart and sustainable approaches for optimizing performance of wireless networks: real-time applications. John Wiley & Sons 2022.
[http://dx.doi.org/10.1002/9781119682554]

[22] Raut S, von Gersdorff G, Schemminger J, Adolphs J, Sturm B. Improving food processing through integration of artificial intelligence in the drying process: a perspective. 42 GIL-Jahrestagung, Künstliche Intelligenz in der Agrar-und Ernährungswirtschaft. Gesellschaft für Informatik eV 2022; pp. 231-6.

[23] Banaeian N, Zangeneh M, Clark S. Trends and future directions in crop energy analyses: a focus on Iran. Sustainability (Basel) 2020; 12(23): 10002.
[http://dx.doi.org/10.3390/su122310002]

[24] Vlachokostas C, Achillas C, Agnantiaris I, *et al.* Decision support system to implement units of alternative biowaste treatment for producing bioenergy and boosting local bioeconomy. Energies 2020; 13(9): 2306.
[http://dx.doi.org/10.3390/en13092306]

[25] Huh JH, Kim SK. The blockchain consensus algorithm for viable management of new and renewable energies. Sustainability (Basel) 2019; 11(11): 3184.
[http://dx.doi.org/10.3390/su11113184]

[26] Ahamed T, Noguchi R, Takigawa T, Tian L. Bioproduction engineering: Automation and precision agronomics for sustainable agricultural systems. Nova Science Publishers, Inc. 2016.

[27] Ahamed T, Takigawa T, Noguchi R, Tian L. Bioproduction engineering: A road map of sustainable agricultural practice. Nova Science Publishers, Inc. 2013.

[28] González MJ, Montero E, Aguilar F. Implementation of international energy engineering e-courses for promotion of sustainability buildings and communities Central Europe towards Sustainable Building, CESB10. Prague: Education and Information 2010.

[29] Pervez MS, Nayak RC, Fidvi H, *et al.* Mechanical energy harvester for sustainable development towards green environment.E3S Web of Conferences. EDP Sciences 2024; Vol. 529: p. 04018.

[30] Nayak RC, Bodhe AB, Chauhan J, *et al.* New urban technology towards energy harvesting and environmental initiatives for a smart city.Smart Cities: Innovations, Challenges and Future Perspectives. Cham: Springer Nature Switzerland 2024; pp. 323-42.
[http://dx.doi.org/10.1007/978-3-031-59846-3_14]

[31] Siddiqui SH, Nayak RC, Fidvi H, *et al.* Thermoplastic polymer track with gearing mechanism to harvest green energy for sustainable development.E3S Web of Conferences. EDP Sciences 2024; Vol. 552: p. 01011.

[32] Fidvi H, Ghutke PC, Gondane SM, Kulkarni MV, Nayak RC, Padhi D. Advanced smokeless stove towards green environment and for sustainable development of rural women.E3S Web of Conferences. EDP Sciences 2023; Vol. 455: p. 02017.
[http://dx.doi.org/10.1051/e3sconf/202345502017]

[33] Nayak R C, Samal C, Roul M K, Padhi P. A new irrigation system without any external sources. J Inst Eng (India): Ser A 2023; 104(2): 281-9.

[34] Samal C, Nayak R C, Roul M K, Das D, Kumar R. A comprehensive review on performance evaluation methods of biomass cook stoves. Waste Recovery and Management. 2023; pp. 95-105.

[35] Samal C, Nayak RC, Roul MK, Das D, Kumar R. Performance evaluation of an improved biomass-fired cook stove: a comparative analysis.Waste Recovery and Management. CRC Press 2023; pp. 107-20.
[http://dx.doi.org/10.1201/9781003359784-7]

[36] Sahoo A, Chandra Nayak R, Senapati AK, Roul MK, Khuntia K. Experimental study of fluid flow properties at exit of the heated tube subjected to natural convection heat transfer. Mater Today Proc 2023.
[http://dx.doi.org/10.1016/j.matpr.2023.03.165]

[37] Nayak R C, Roul M K. Technology to develop a smokeless stove for sustainable future of rural women and also to develop a green environment. J Inst Eng (India): Ser A 2022; 103(1): 97-104.

[38] Majhi A, Das A, panda S, *et al.* An attachment with the hand pump to lift water without any external source. Mater Today Proc 2022; 62: 6755-8.
[http://dx.doi.org/10.1016/j.matpr.2022.04.859]

[39] Nayak RC, Roul MK, Roul PD. Design and development of smokeless stove for a sustainable growth. Arch Thermodyn 2022; 109-25.
[http://dx.doi.org/10.24425/ather.2022.140927]

[40] Sahoo A, Chandra Nayak R, Senapati AK, Roul MK. Validation of experimental results with theoretical by using ANSYS workbench on vertical tube subjected to natural convection heat transfer without internal obstacles. Mater Today Proc 2022; 52: 1348-53.
[http://dx.doi.org/10.1016/j.matpr.2021.11.080]

[41] Nayak R C, Roul M K, Sarangi S K. Innovative methods to enhance irrigation in rural areas for cultivation purpose. J Inst Eng (India): Ser A 2021; 102: 1045-51.

[42] Nayak RC, Roul MK, Sarangi A, Sarangi A, Sahoo A. Mechanical concept on design and development of irrigation system to help rural farmers for their agriculture purpose during unavailability of external power. IOP Conf Series Mater Sci Eng 2021; 1059(1): 012048.
[http://dx.doi.org/10.1088/1757-899X/1059/1/012048]

[43] Nayak RC, Roul MK, Padhi P, Sarangi SK. Design and development of improved methods of curing of bricks during manufacturing process and construction work to save water, minimize pollution and human effort. Ecological and Health Effects of Building Materials 2021; pp. 259-74.

[44] Nayak RC, Roul MK, Sarangi SK, Sahoo A, Sarangi A, Sarangi A. Enhancement of natural convection inside vertical tubes using internal obstacles as rings with different arrangements. Lecture Notes in Mechanical Engineering 2021; 52: 191-201.
[http://dx.doi.org/10.1007/978-981-33-4795-3_19]

[45] Nayak RC, Roul MK, Sarangi SK, Sarangi A, Sarangi A. Forced draft and superheated steam for design and development of community smoke less chulha to help women in rural areas. Lecture Notes in Mechanical Engineering 2021; pp. 93-102.
[http://dx.doi.org/10.1007/978-981-15-9853-1_9]

[46] Nayak RC, Roul MK, Sarangi SK. Natural convection heat transfer in heated vertical tubes with internal rings. Arch Thermodyn 2018; 39(4): 85-111.

[47] Nayak RC, Roul MK, Sarangi SK. Experimental investigation of natural convection heat transfer in heated vertical tubes with discrete rings. Exp Tech 2017; 41(6): 585-603.
[http://dx.doi.org/10.1007/s40799-017-0201-6]

[48] Nayak RC, Roul MK, Sarangi SK. Experimental investigation of natural convection heat transfer in heated vertical tubes. Int J Appl Eng Res 2017; 12(10): 2538-50.

CHAPTER 2

Land Cover Classification Using Hyperion EO-1 Data: A Case Study in Uttar Pradesh, India

Neelam Dahiya[1,*], **Nitin Arora**[2], **Sartajvir Singh**[3] and **Gurwinder Singh**[4]

[1] *Department of Computer Applications, Chitkara University Institute of Engineering and Technology, Chitkara University, Punjab, India*

[2] *University Institute of Engineering, Chandigarh University, Mohali, Punjab, India*

[3] *Centre of Excellence, Socio-Environmental Sustainability for River Sand-Mining (SEnSRS), Indian Institute of Technology, Ropar, Punjab, India*

[4] *Department of Computer Application, Chandigarh Group of Colleges, Jhanjeri, India*

Abstract: Hyperspectral imaging (HSI) gathers spectral information across hundreds of narrow bands, offering a rich source of data that can accurately detect and distinguish materials. It is increasingly used by researchers to address challenges in agriculture, snow and object detection, and environmental monitoring. HSI provides critical insights about the Earth's surface in specific spectral bands that are often beyond the reach of traditional multispectral imaging. Remote sensing is a powerful tool for monitoring Earth's surface changes on a global scale using HSI. To support a wide range of applications, classification algorithms are essential for identifying and categorizing key surface features. Therefore, it is important to investigate the impact of emerging classifiers on hyperspectral datasets. In this chapter, the performance of several machine learning classifiers, including Random Forest (RF), Maximum Likelihood Classifier (MLC), and Minimum Distance Classifier (MDC), was evaluated using HSI over Uttar Pradesh State, India. The results confirmed the effectiveness of RF (accuracy 90.20%) over MLC (accuracy 88.80%) and MDC (accuracy 86.60%). This research is significant for exploring the potential of hyperspectral imaging with various classification algorithms in developing applications.

Keywords: Hyperspectral Image Sensing (HSI), Hyperion Earth Observing-1 (EO-1), Machine Learning (ML), Remote Sensing (RS).

INTRODUCTION

Hyperspectral imaging (HSI) represents a significant advancement in remote sensing in terms of data and information acquisition. Unlike multispectral imaging

* **Corresponding author Neelam Dahiya:** Department of Computer Applications, Chitkara University Institute of Engineering and Technology, Chitkara University, Punjab, India; E-mail neelam.rani@chitkara.edu.in

Sartajvir Singh, Neelam Dahiya, Maged Mohammed, Abdullah Alzharihi & Vishal Dutt (Eds.)

systems, which capture data over a few large spectral bands, HSI collects data across hundreds of narrow, adjacent spectral bands, enabling the distinction of materials based on their spectral signatures [1]. The primary goal of HSI is to obtain the spectrum for each pixel in the image. Additionally, it enables the identification of diverse processes and objects. It is widely used in agriculture mapping, environmental monitoring, and mineral mapping due to its numerous advantages. In addition to the applications, it can also be used to monitor plant diseases and accurately estimate and grade field crops [2, 3].

NASA launched a hyperspectral sensor (Hyperion EO-1) under the New Millennium Program, a remarkable development in spaceborne hyperspectral remote sensing. It covers a spectral range between visible (0.4) μm and shortwave infrared (2.5) μm and records 242 bands with a detailed spatial resolution of 30 meters. Nonetheless, because of the noise and interference in some bands, it is conventional practice to use 196 operational bands for analytical purposes. Hyperspectral data is big and complex; therefore, Machine Learning (ML) analysis has proven to be particularly successful [4, 5]. Unlike previous approaches used for image classification, which rely on communicating data through statistical methods, ML algorithms learn directly from data and improve their performance as more data becomes available. This makes them particularly well-suited to dealing with hyperspectral data, which is high in dimensions and complexity [6, 7]. Hyperspectral imaging has various application areas, such as soil degradation [8], disease detection, climate monitoring [9, 10], drought, moisture level, and leaf detection [6, 11, 12].

A major challenge in HSI classification is managing data dimensionality due to the large number of spectral bands. Therefore, it is required to implement a simple yet effective model to process the dataset. Classification algorithms play an essential role in categorizing features or objects on Earth and, as a result, producing themed maps based on the detected classes [13, 14]. Various studies have developed classifiers based on machine learning or deep learning to extract distinct class categories from multispectral or hyperspectral datasets [15, 16]. Furthermore, as the number of spectral bands increases, so do the processing needs. As a result, the type of dataset to be classified typically determines how well various classifiers perform.

The main aim of this work is to compare numerous machine learning algorithms using HSI over an agricultural area, *i.e*, Uttar Pradesh State, India. To implement the classification algorithms, ENVI 5.2 software is used. It contains data preprocessing features such as noise, atmospheric correction, and spectral feature extraction, essential for processing the hyperspectral data. After the data has been pre-processed, standard machine learning algorithms like Random Forest (RF),

Maximum Likelihood Classifier (MLC), Minimum Distance Classifier (MDC), and nearest neighbor have been implemented to categorize the hyperspectral dataset into classes such as Deciduous veg, Dense veg, and Buildup. There are several uses for this research in soil detection, vegetation monitoring, and forestry. In addition, it can be utilized for weather monitoring, crop stress monitoring, and many other purposes. The integration of Machine Learning (ML) with HSI is also shown below in Fig. (**1**). It depicts the main components required for the integration of ML with HSI.

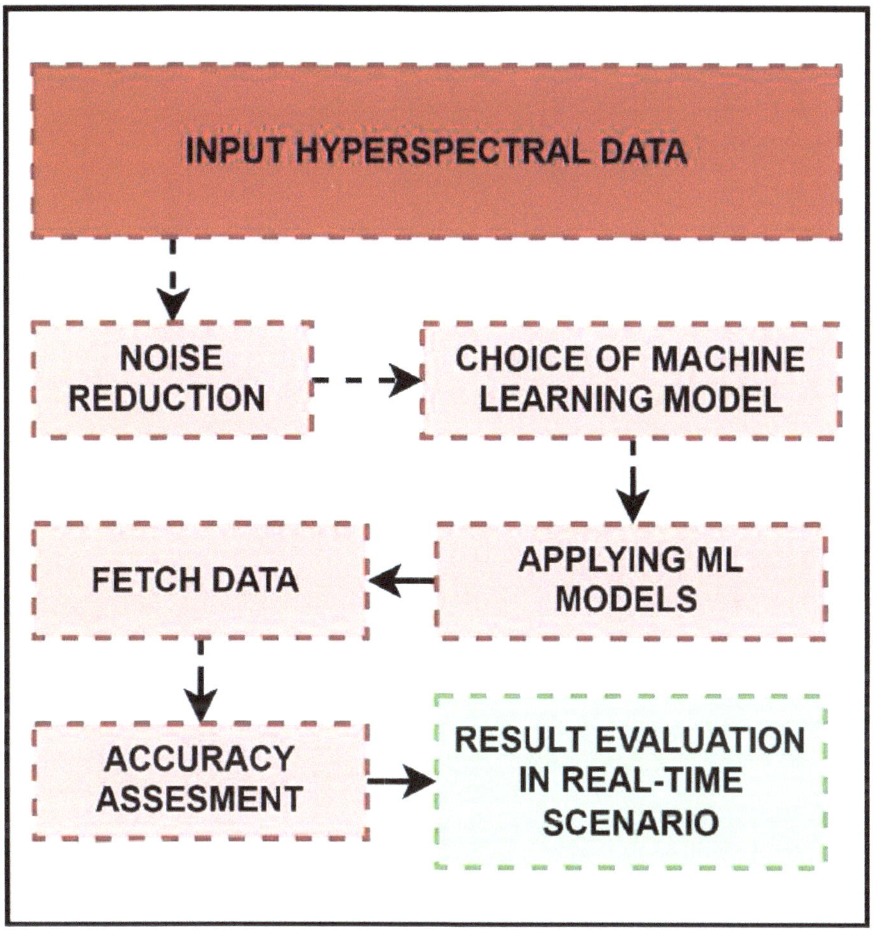

Fig. (1). Components involved in the integration of ML with HSI.

STUDY SITE AND DATASET

The current work has been accomplished over an agricultural area, *i.e*, Agra (Uttar Pradesh State, India). The geographic location is marked on the map of India as shown in Fig. (**2**), on which the area of interest has been highlighted. The research site is situated between latitudes of 27°28′38″ N to 27°26′13″ N and longitudes of 77°28′53″ E to 77°31′52″ E. The detailed view of the study area is presented in Fig. (**2b**), *i.e.*, the Hyperion EO-1 dataset. The false-colour composite (R: The colours RGB (R: 40, G: 30, B: 20) enhances the visibility of the land cover types. The three main class categories—Deciduous veg, Dense veg, and built-up area-have been taken into consideration for the analysis of the current study. The datasets for this research work were collected from the internet portal (https://earthexplorer.usgs.gov/). The dataset was collected on cloud-free days, *i.e*, 9 Feb 2014. It consists of 242 distinct channels, including VNIR (70 channels, 356 nm - 1058 nm) and SWIR (172 channels, 852 nm - 2577 nm), with a swath width of 7.75 km [17].

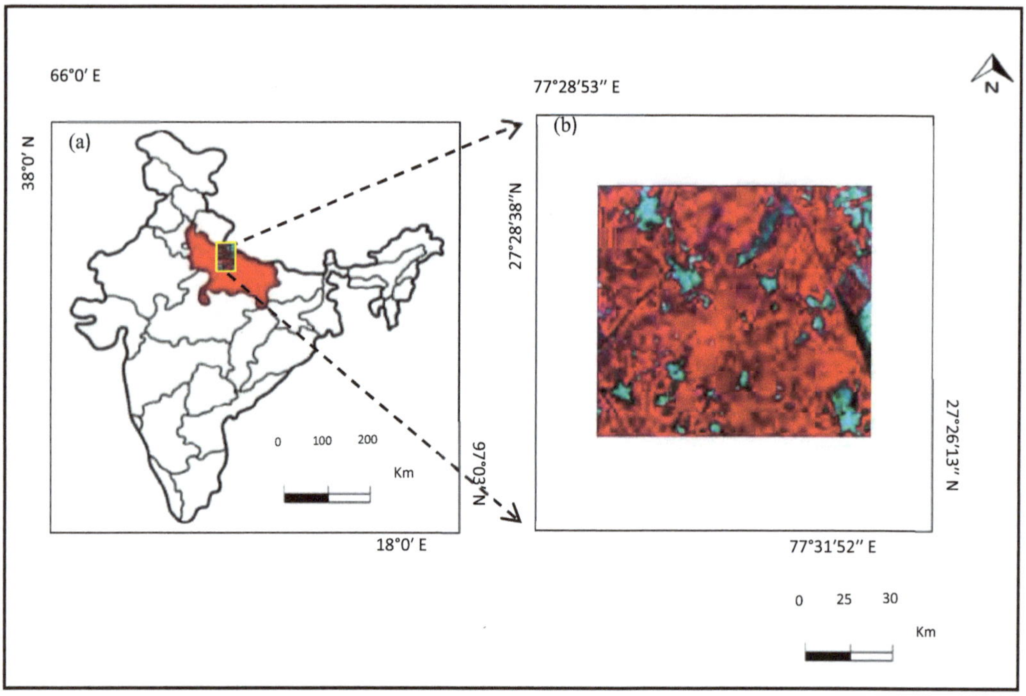

Fig. (2). Study area (**a**) Indian map highlights the study area (Uttar Pradesh State) (**b**) Study area using Hyperion EO-1 dataset (R:40, G:30, B:20).

METHODOLOGY

On the basis of the Hyperion EO-1 dataset, the land cover classification was carried out to differentiate between vegetation cover and built-up land. Some of the classification methods used are MLC, MDC, and RF. As can be seen from Fig. (**3a**), the original reflectance image from the Hyperion EO-1 dataset is displayed. This image serves as the base for classification, where the different spectral signatures of land cover are used to classify regions into distinct classes:

coniferous forest, tropical and subtropical forests, savannah, shrublands, grasslands, deserts, and urban areas.

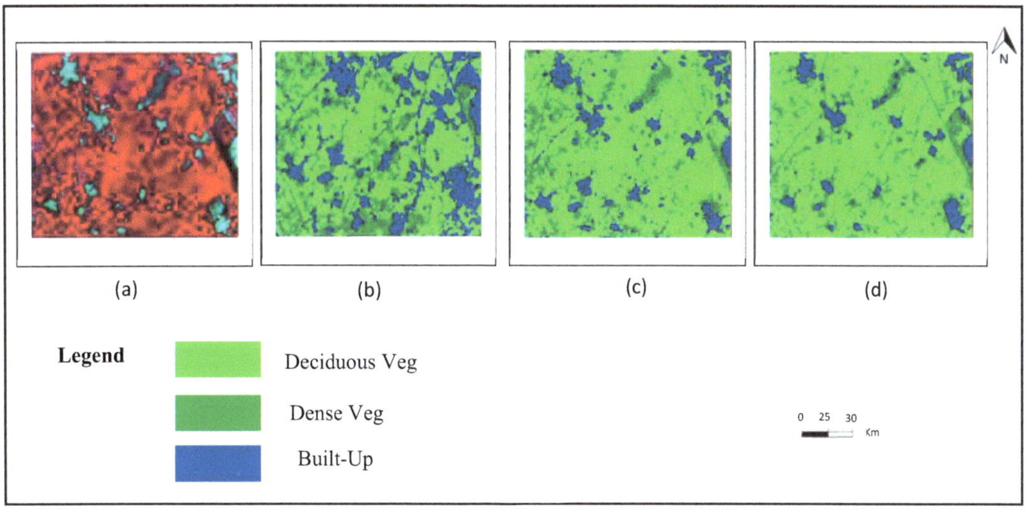

Fig. (3). Classified map of hyperion EO-1(25-feb-2014) (**a**) Reflectance image (**b**) MLC (**c**) MDC (**d**) RF.

Pre-Processing

Pre-processing is the initial step after data collection. The preprocessing of the remote sensing dataset is necessary to remove atmospheric and radiometric distortions and make the dataset suitable for further processing [18]. The preprocessing steps involve:

a. **Radiometric Correction:** Sensor-related errors were corrected through radiometric correction to make the reflectance values represent actual ground conditions. This ensures that reflectance values in the different channels are comparable, improving the visibility of vegetative and built-up features in the dataset [19].
b. **Atmospheric Correction:** Since the data was acquired on a cloudless day, atmospheric correction was applied to reduce the impact of atmospheric particles and gases on reflectance values as much as possible [20]. The image acquisition date was February 9, 2014. Atmospheric correction helped make the results more uniform across the image, which is crucial for accurate land cover classification in the highly variable landscape of Agra, Uttar Pradesh.
c. **Geometric Correction:** Geometric correction was performed to align the dataset with geographical coordinates (27°28′38" N to 27°26′13" N and 77°28′53" E to 77°31′52" E). This alignment is important for correctly modeling certain land cover classes and effectively integrating the data into

other GIS datasets [21].

d. **Noise Reduction:** Hyperspectral data may contain noise due to sensor issues and atmospheric interference. Filtering and other algorithms were applied to enhance the contrast of land cover forms and clearly separate high-density vegetation, deciduous vegetation, and built-up regions.
e. **Resampling:** The data was resampled to maintain a consistent spatial resolution of 30 m, ensuring uniform classification across the study area. This enabled effective differentiation of land cover types in the false-color composite image (RGB: R: 40, G: 30, B: 20 for vegetative regions, and bluish-green to highlight built-up areas) [22].

Classification

Classification is the process of grouping different pixels in a remote sensing image into land cover types depending on their spectral characteristics and spatial distribution. In remote sensing, classification techniques are broadly divided into two main approaches: supervised and unsupervised learning. In supervised classification, training samples are first selected, meaning that experts use known samples where the land cover types are already identified. The classifier then learns from these samples and classifies each pixel of the image. This approach leads to higher accuracy, particularly when clear spectral signatures can be assigned to each land cover type. The Maximum Likelihood Classification (MLC), used in this study, is a supervised technique that assigns each pixel to the class with the highest probability density based on the assumption of normally distributed classes [23]. In this study, MLC successfully classified deciduous vegetation, dense vegetation, and built-up areas, as shown in Fig. (**3b**). Here, deciduous vegetation is shown in light green, dense vegetation in dark green, and built-up areas in blue.

In contrast, unsupervised classification does not require training samples to be assigned before the classification process. It classifies pixels into clusters according to spectral similarity and is not predicated on a priori knowledge of the land cover space [24]. Clusters can then be labeled post-classification according to ground truth or auxiliary data. This method is preferred when detailed training data is unavailable, and the process is more exploratory.

In the present research, a supervised classification was chosen because of reliable training data and the types of land cover: deciduous vegetation, dense vegetation, and built-up areas. The accuracy offered by the MLC technique is generally reasonable, and the classes in the study area were well distinguished. The classified image, obtained using the Maximum Likelihood Classification (MLC) technique, is shown in Fig. (**3b**). MLC assumes that the data for each class in each band is normally distributed and assigns each pixel to the class with the maximum probability density. Here, deciduous vegetation is depicted in light green, dense vegetation in dark green, and built-up areas in blue [25].

The MDC method is shown in Fig. (**3c**). The spectral difference between the pixel value and the mean value for each class is computed for each pixel, which is then assigned to the closest class. This method is used mainly because of its simplicity and speed, especially in situations requiring minimal computation [26].

The RF classifier results are shown in Fig. (**3d**). RF is a type of learning that creates multiple decision trees and combines their results to improve classification. In this map, RF provides a better classification of the study area with improved distinction between vegetation and built-up regions, which is evident from the higher accuracy in terms of class separation [27].

The legend in Fig. (**3**) helps distinguish the classified land covers, where:

- **Light green:** deciduous vegetation
- **Dark green:** dense vegetation
- **Blue:** Built-up areas

This is where the performance of the different classification techniques has been compared to show the variation. Since MLC provides a reasonable estimate, it underestimates vegetation in certain regions but overestimates it in others. Faster to deliver than LDC, MDC provides less contrast between built-up surfaces and vegetation. RF outperforms other algorithms in classifying different land cover types, especially between high-density vegetation, deciduous forests, and built-up areas. The RF classifier achieves this level of accuracy because of its capability to work with the high dimensionality of the data.

Accuracy Assessment

The accuracy assessment results for three classifiers, including RF, MLC, and MDC, based on hyperspectral imagery from the Hyperion EO-1 satellite for the classification of land cover in the year 2014, have been tabulated below in Table **1**. The evaluation is conducted across three different land cover categories: deciduous vegetation, dense vegetation, and built-up areas. The table highlights results obtained for each classifier in terms of RT (total reference pixels), CT (total classified pixels), NC (number of correct classifications), PA (producer's accuracy), UA (user's accuracy), and KC (Kappa Coefficient) [28]. Table **1** also shows that the RF classifier outperforms the others due to its ability to classify complex and high-resolution datasets, which MLC and MDC are not able to perform effectively.

Table 1. Accuracy assessment of RF, MLC, and MDC classifiers using hyperion EO-1.

Year	Model	Class Categories	Accuracy Assessment Parameters					
			RT	***CT***	***NC***	***PA (%)***	***UA (%)***	***KC***
2014	RF	Deciduous-veg	280	284	265	94.64	93.31	0.8480
		Dense-veg	141	146	125	88.65	85.62	0.7997
		Built-Up	79	70	61	77.22%	87.14%	0.8473
		Overall Accuracy= 90.20%; Overall Kappa= 0.8303						
2014	MLC	Deciduous-veg	273	284	258	94.51%	90.85%	0.7983
		Dense-veg	144	146	125	86.81%	85.62%	0.7980
		Built-Up	83	70	61	73.49%	87.14%	0.8458
		Overall Accuracy= 88.80%; Overall Kappa= 0.8077						
2014	MDC	Deciduous-veg	276	284	256	92.75%	90.14%	0.7799
		Dense-veg	141	146	120	85.11%	82.19%	0.7520
		Built-Up	83	70	57	68.67%	81.43%	0.7773
		Overall Accuracy= 86.60%; Overall Kappa= 0.7693						

Note: Reference Total (RT); Classified Total (CT); Number of correct (NC); Producer's Accuracy (PA); User's Accuracy (UA); Kappa coefficient (KC).

Class Categories

The assessment was based on the following classification categories: deciduous vegetation, dense vegetation, and built-up areas. These are the land cover types that the classifiers are required to distinguish using the hyperspectral data.

Reference Total (RT): This is the total number of ground truth or reference samples that existed in each class. The reference samples are real labeled data used to evaluate classification outcomes. For example, there were 280 reference samples for deciduous vegetation in the RF classifier assessment.

Classified Total (CT): This indicates the total number of samples classified into a specific category by the classifier. For example, the RF classifier classified 284 samples as deciduous vegetation.

Number of Correct Classifications (NC): It is the number of samples that have been correctly classified for a given category. In the RF example, 265 samples of deciduous vegetation were classified correctly.

Producer's Accuracy (PA): Producer's accuracy is the probability that an object belonging to a given reference sample has been classified correctly, as shown in Eq. **1** [28, 29]

$$\boldsymbol{PA} = \frac{\boldsymbol{NC}}{\boldsymbol{RT}} \times \mathbf{100} \quad \textbf{(1)}$$

Eq. **1** helps to define how accurately the given class is recognised by the model under construction. For RF, deciduous vegetation has an overall accuracy of 94.64% PA, which implies that 94.64% of the reference samples for this class were correctly classified.

User's Accuracy (UA): User's accuracy is the ability of a sample to be correctly classified into a particular category when it truly belongs to that category, as shown in Eq. **2**.[30].

$$\boldsymbol{UA} = \frac{\boldsymbol{NC}}{\boldsymbol{CT}} \times \mathbf{100} \quad \textbf{(2)}$$

For RF, the user's accuracy for deciduous vegetation is 0.9331, meaning that 93.31% of the samples classified under deciduous vegetation were correctly classified.

Kappa Coefficient (KC): The Kappa Coefficient is a measure of association incorporating chance agreement into the test. It is more accurate than the simple accuracy rates, and it varies from 0 to 1. The RF model for deciduous vegetation has the highest Kappa value of 0.8480, meaning that beyond chance, there is strong agreement between the classification and the reference data.

Overall Accuracy: OA is the total of the correctly classified pixels divided by the total number of pixels for all categories. The RF classifier produced an overall accuracy of 90.20%, which is the overall classification accuracy of the pixels of all the classes.

Overall Kappa: Grand Kappa gives a measure of the Rater's level of agreement with the reference data based on the entire set of categories. The overall Kappa value of 0.8303 for the RF classifier indicates that the classification is highly reliable with minimum chances of coincident agreement.

RESULTS AND DISCUSSION

The Hyperion EO-1 dataset, obtained on February 25, 2014, serves as the input for this research conducted in Uttar Pradesh State, India. RF, MLC, and MDC are among the classification techniques used to analyze the effects on the LULC region. Several categories are investigated during the classification process, including deciduous vegetation, dense vegetation, and built-up areas. The hardware configurations used in the experiments include Windows 10/11 and macOS 10.14 or later. For software installation, approximately 4 GB of disk space and a 4-core Intel Xeon W-2104 @ 3.2 GHz processor are required. ERDAS 2015 is used for analysis, and the ENVI v5.2 platform is employed to perform the classification. Fig. (**3**) displays the final classified output from the various classifiers. An essential component of assessing the effectiveness of different classifiers is the accuracy assessment.

The numerous parameters, such as producer accuracy, user accuracy, overall accuracy, and Kappa coefficient, are included in the accuracy evaluation. Table **1** confirmed the effectiveness of RF (accuracy 90.20%) over MLC (accuracy 88.80%) and MDC (accuracy 86.60%). These results demonstrate that the RF-classified dataset, particularly in the case of Hyperion, aligns more closely with the reference data. The Kappa coefficient also confirmed the high efficiency of RF, which received the highest coefficient of 0.8303, characterising a high degree of agreement between the predicted and actual classes. This was followed by MLC with a Kappa value of 0.8077, indicating reasonable performance but clear difficulty in managing spectral overlaps. MDC demonstrated the lowest Kappa value of 0.7693, indicating that the model cannot handle complex spectral relations well. The metrics utilised in this work highlight the necessity of using sophisticated algorithms to achieve accurate classification outcomes.

Furthermore, the supervised classifier RF works well with the current datasets. Making algorithms completely autonomous might further increase accuracy for both users and producers. The suggested classifiers are specifically tailored for the hyperspectral dataset; nonetheless, this method can be applied to recent datasets and other satellites. The method was tested on a smaller scale due to limited data, but future work will extend it to a larger scale using recent datasets and fusion with other approaches.

CONCLUSION

To determine the most effective classification method for Land Use and Land Cover (LULC) mapping, this study implemented several supervised classification algorithms, including Random Forest (RF), Maximum Likelihood Classifier (MLC), and Minimum Distance Classifier (MDC). The analysis was conducted using a hyperspectral dataset—specifically, Hyperion EO-1—covering a region of Uttar Pradesh State, India. The data were categorized into distinct classes, such as deciduous vegetation, dense vegetation, and built-up areas. A comparative evaluation was then carried out to assess the performance of these classifiers in LULC monitoring.

This research thoroughly evaluated the suitability of the Hyperion EO-1 dataset for LULC classification. The findings indicate that among the tested methods, the Random Forest classifier delivered the highest accuracy for LULC mapping. Owing to its high spatial resolution and narrow, well-defined spectral bands, hyperspectral imaging outperforms other remote sensing techniques in various applications, such as soil moisture estimation and plant health assessment. Furthermore, this study has promising applications in areas including crop identification, disease detection, and crop development, contributing to sustainable agricultural practices.

REFERENCES

[1] Dou P, Huang C, Han W, Hou J, Zhang Y, Gu J. Remote sensing image classification using an ensemble framework without multiple classifiers. ISPRS J Photogramm Remote Sens 2024; 208: 190-209.
[http://dx.doi.org/10.1016/j.isprsjprs.2023.12.012]

[2] Bo C, Lu H, Wang D. Spectral-spatial K-Nearest Neighbor approach for hyperspectral image classification. Multimed Tools Appl 2017; pp. 1-18.
[http://dx.doi.org/10.1007/s11042-017-4403-9]

[3] Krishna G, Sahoo RN, Pradhan S, Ahmad T, Sahoo PM. Hyperspectral satellite data analysis for pure pixels extraction and evaluation of advanced classifier algorithms for LULC classification. Earth Sci Inform 2018; 11(2): 159-70.
[http://dx.doi.org/10.1007/s12145-017-0324-4]

[4] Puletti N, Camarretta N, Corona P. Evaluating EO1-Hyperion capability for mapping conifer and broadleaved forests. Eur J Remote Sens 2016; 49(1): 157-69.
[http://dx.doi.org/10.5721/EuJRS20164909]

[5] Tariq A, Yan J, Gagnon AS, Riaz Khan M, Mumtaz F. Mapping of cropland, cropping patterns and crop types by combining optical remote sensing images with decision tree classifier and random forest. Geo Spat Inf Sci 2023; 26(3): 302-20.
[http://dx.doi.org/10.1080/10095020.2022.2100287]

[6] Demilie WB. Plant disease detection and classification techniques: a comparative study of the performances. J Big Data 2024; 11(1): 5.
[http://dx.doi.org/10.1186/s40537-023-00863-9]

[7] Chowdhury MS. Comparison of accuracy and reliability of random forest, support vector machine, artificial neural network and maximum likelihood method in land use/cover classification of urban setting. Environ Chall (Amst) 2024; 14: 100800.
[http://dx.doi.org/10.1016/j.envc.2023.100800]

[8] Kamilaris A, Prenafeta-Boldú F X. Deep learning in agriculture: A survey. Elsevier B.V 2018.
[http://dx.doi.org/10.1016/j.compag.2018.02.016]

[9] Al Mamun A, Islam ARMT, Alam GMM, *et al.* Livelihood vulnerability of char land communities to climate change and natural hazards in Bangladesh: an application of livelihood vulnerability index. Nat Hazards 2023; 115(2): 1411-37.
[http://dx.doi.org/10.1007/s11069-022-05599-y]

[10] Bourgeau-Chavez LL, Leblon B, Charbonneau F, Buckley JR. Evaluation of polarimetric Radarsat-2 SAR data for development of soil moisture retrieval algorithms over a chronosequence of black spruce boreal forests. Remote Sens Environ 2013; 132: 71-85.
[http://dx.doi.org/10.1016/j.rse.2013.01.006]

[11] Cap HQ, Suwa K, Fujita E, Kagiwada S, Uga H, Iyatomi H. A deep learning approach for on-site plant leaf detection. Proc IEEE 14th Int Colloq Signal Process Its Appl (CSPA). 118-22.
[http://dx.doi.org/10.1109/CSPA.2018.8368697]

[12] Berterretche M, Hudak AT, Cohen WB, Maiersperger TK, Gower ST, Dungan J. Comparison of regression and geostatistical methods for mapping Leaf Area Index (LAI) with Landsat ETM+ data over a boreal forest. Remote Sens Environ 2005; 96(1): 49-61.
[http://dx.doi.org/10.1016/j.rse.2005.01.014]

[13] Wood J L, Harrison S, Wilson R, *et al.* Shaking up assumptions: earthquakes have rarely triggered Andean Glacier Lake outburst floods. Geophys Res Lett 2024; 51(7): e2023GL105578.
[http://dx.doi.org/10.1029/2023GL105578]

[14] Hütt C, Koppe W, Miao Y, Bareth G. Best accuracy land use/land cover (LULC) classification to derive crop types using multitemporal, multisensor, and multi-polarization SAR satellite images. Remote Sens (Basel) 2016; 8(8): 684.
[http://dx.doi.org/10.3390/rs8080684]

[15] Ghamisi P, Rasti B, Yokoya N, *et al.* Multisource and multitemporal data fusion in remote sensing: A comprehensive review of the state of the art. IEEE Geosci Remote Sens Mag 2019.
[http://dx.doi.org/10.1109/MGRS.2018.2890023]

[16] Haidar S, Oramas J. Training methods of multi-label prediction classifiers for hyperspectral remote sensing images. Remote Sens (Basel) 2023; 15(24): 5656.
[http://dx.doi.org/10.3390/rs15245656]

[17] Stow DA, Collins D, McKinsey D. Land use change detection based on multi-date imagery from different satellite sensor systems. Geocarto Int 1990; 5(3): 3-12.
[http://dx.doi.org/10.1080/10106049009354263]

[18] Khurshid KS, Staenz K, Sun L, *et al.* Preprocessing of EO-1 Hyperion data. Can J Rem Sens 2006; 32(2): 84-97.
[http://dx.doi.org/10.5589/m06-014]

[19] Pope A, Rees WG. Impact of spatial, spectral, and radiometric properties of multispectral imagers on glacier surface classification. Remote Sens Environ 2014; 141: 1-13.
[http://dx.doi.org/10.1016/j.rse.2013.08.028]

[20] Congalton RG. A review of assessing the accuracy of classifications of remotely sensed data. Remote Sens Environ 1991; 37(1): 35-46.
[http://dx.doi.org/10.1016/0034-4257(91)90048-B]

[21] Lv Z, Liu T, Shi C, Benediktsson JA, Du H. Novel land cover change detection method based on k-means clustering and adaptive majority voting using bitemporal remote sensing images. IEEE Access 2019; 7(c): 34425-37.
[http://dx.doi.org/10.1109/ACCESS.2019.2892648]

[22] Fuller RM, Smith GM, Devereux BJ. The characterisation and measurement of land cover change through remote sensing: problems in operational applications? Int J Appl Earth Obs Geoinf 2003; 4(3): 243-53.
[http://dx.doi.org/10.1016/S0303-2434(03)00004-7]

[23] Aziz G, Minallah N, Saeed A, Frnda J, Khan W. Remote sensing based forest cover classification using machine learning. Sci Rep 2024; 14(1): 69.
[http://dx.doi.org/10.1038/s41598-023-50863-1] [PMID: 38167902]

[24] Pazhanikumar K, KuzhalVoiMozhi SN. Remote sensing image classification using modified random

forest with empirical loss function through crowd-sourced data. Multimedia Tools Appl 2023; 83(18): 53899-921.
[http://dx.doi.org/10.1007/s11042-023-17556-3]

[25] Chen J, Gong P, He C, Pu R, Shi P. Land-use/land-cover change detection using improved change-vector analysis. Photogramm Eng Remote Sensing 2003; 69(4): 369-79.
[http://dx.doi.org/10.14358/PERS.69.4.369]

[26] Nackaerts K, Vaesen K, Muys B, Coppin P. Comparative performance of a modified change vector analysis in forest change detection. Int J Remote Sens 2005; 26(5): 839-52.
[http://dx.doi.org/10.1080/0143116032000160462]

[27] Amini S, Saber M, Rabiei-Dastjerdi H, Homayouni S. Urban land use and land cover change analysis using random forest classification of landsat time series. Remote Sens (Basel) 2022; 14(11): 2654.
[http://dx.doi.org/10.3390/rs14112654]

[28] Sood V. Accuracy Assessment and validation of large-scale subpixel classified maps for remotely sensed data. 2021. Available from: https://earthexplorer.usgs.gov/

[29] Sood V, Gupta S. Analysis of different Models for Land-use and Land-cover Change Detection. 2018; 7-9.

[30] Sood V, Gupta S. A Comparative Review on Different Sub-Pixel Classification Algorithms in 2. 2018.

CHAPTER 3

Emerging Trends and Challenges in Remote Sensing for Irrigation of Horticultural Crops

Rupinder Singh[1,*], **Amanpreet Singh**[1] and **Jaswinder Singh**[1]

[1] *Chitkara University Institute of Engineering and Technology, Chitkara University, Punjab, India*

Abstract: Remote sensing—using tools like satellites, drones, and ground sensors—has changed the way farmers manage irrigation for fruit and vegetable crops. These technologies let growers keep an eye on their fields in real time, tracking things like how much water the soil holds and how thirsty the plants are. Thanks to these advances, farmers can now use water much more efficiently—sometimes improving water use by 15–22%—by watering only where and when it is needed. Special imaging techniques, like hyperspectral cameras, help spot water stress in plants early, and Artificial Intelligence (AI) makes it easier to combine all this data and plan smarter irrigation schedules. Still, there are challenges, such as high costs for the best images and sensors, reliability issues in tough weather, and the difficulty of turning all this data into simple decisions. If we can make these tools cheaper and easier to use, they could help farmers everywhere save water and grow more, even as climate change makes things tougher.

Keywords: Drones, GIS, Horticultural crops, Hyperspectral imaging, Precision irrigation, Remote sensing.

INTRODUCTION

Getting water to fruit and vegetable crops is more important than ever, especially in places where droughts are common and the weather is unpredictable. Old irrigation methods—like just relying on rain or flooding fields—do not cut it anymore. They often waste water or fail to provide crops with what they need, which can result in yields up to 20% lower in dry areas.

That is where remote sensing comes in. With satellites, drones, ground sensors, and advanced cameras, farmers can now get detailed, up-to-date information about their fields. They can see which areas are dry, how much water is in the soil, and even how much water is evaporating from the plants. New tools, like hyperspectral cameras and AI-powered analysis, make it easier to spot water

* **Corresponding author Rupinder Singh:** Chitkara University Institute of Engineering and Technology, Chitkara University, Punjab, India; E-mail:rupinder.1153@chitkara.edu.in

Sartajvir Singh, Neelam Dahiya, Maged Mohammed, Abdullah Alzharihi & Vishal Dutt (Eds.)

stress early—up to 30–40% more accurately than older methods. This means farmers can water more precisely, saving water and boosting yields.

This review examines the latest trends and challenges in the use of remote sensing for irrigation. It covers how different technologies—like satellites, drones with special cameras, and ground sensors—help monitor key things like soil moisture and plant stress. It also shares real-world examples, like how Australian vineyards used these tools to increase their yields by 10%. However, it does not overlook the tough parts: high costs, tricky weather, and the challenge of turning all this data into simple, helpful advice for farmers. The goal is to highlight what is working, what is not, and where research should go next to make these tools more accessible and sustainable, especially as water becomes scarcer.

LITERATURE REVIEW

Remote sensing has become a go-to tool for farmers who want to use water more wisely. Traditional irrigation methods, like surface or sprinkler systems, often waste 20–30% of water because they do not distribute it evenly. This section breaks down the latest advances in remote sensing—covering satellites, drones, ground sensors, hyperspectral imaging, and AI—and how they are helping farmers use water more efficiently, monitor plant health, and spot problems early. It also points out the main hurdles, like cost and weather.

Satellite-Based Remote Sensing

Satellites like Landsat, Sentinel-2, and PlanetScope give farmers a big-picture view of their fields. Sentinel-2, for example, can check in every five days and offers pretty detailed images (10–20 meters resolution). This helps track things like soil moisture and plant health using special indices. In India, for example, Sentinel-2 helped citrus farmers spot dry zones and cut water use by 15%. The catch? The best images can be pricey, and clouds can block the view. Plus, some satellites only pass over every couple of weeks, which is not always fast enough for changing field conditions.

UAV-Based Remote Sensing

Drones (UAVs) with regular, multispectral, or thermal cameras can fly low and capture super-detailed images (down to 5 centimeters). In Australia, drones helped vineyard owners spot water stress days before it was visible, letting them act quickly and boost yields by 10%. Drones with hyperspectral cameras can pick up even more detail, but they are expensive and need skilled operators. Battery life is also a limitation, with most drones only able to fly for 20–30 minutes at a time.

Ground-Based Sensors

Sensors stuck in the ground—like soil moisture probes and temperature monitors—give real-time, spot-specific data. For example, in Ethiopia, soil salinity sensors helped map out salty patches in sugarcane fields, improving irrigation by 15%. In Spain, soil moisture sensors confirmed what drones were seeing, making irrigation even more precise. The downside? These sensors only cover small areas, so they work best when combined with aerial data.

Hyperspectral Imaging in Irrigation Management

Hyperspectral cameras capture hundreds of colors, letting farmers spot early signs of water stress, nutrient problems, or disease. For example, in Brazil, using these cameras helped mango farmers cut water use by 14% without hurting yields. In California, they helped vineyard owners spot drought stress days before it showed up, saving 18% more water than older methods. The main problem is cost—these cameras can cost $10,000 to $50,000—and the data is complex, often needing cloud-based software to process Table **1**.

Table 1. Comparison of hyperspectral and multispectral imaging.

Feature	Hyperspectral Imaging	Multispectral Imaging
Spectral Bands	Hundreds of very narrow bands (1–10 nm wide)	A handful of broad bands (50–100 nm wide)
Applications	Early stress detection, detailed plant health, and advanced indices (WBI, NDWI, PRI)	General crop monitoring, basic stress detection, common indices (NDVI, SAVI)
Spatial Resolution	Drones: 0.5–5 meters; Satellites: 10–30 meters	Drones: as sharp as 5 cm–1 meter; Satellites: 10–20 meters
Cost	Expensive:$10,000- $50,000	More affordable:$1,000-$10,000
Example	Helped California vineyards cut water use by 15%	Widely used for everyday crop monitoring

How AI and Machine Learning are Changing the Game

Artificial Intelligence (AI) and Machine Learning (ML) are making remote sensing even smarter. Instead of farmers or experts having to sift through mountains of data, AI can now do the heavy lifting—analyzing images, spotting patterns, and even predicting when and where to irrigate.

For example, in Australian apple orchards, a type of AI called Random Forest was used to analyze hyperspectral images and could spot water-stressed areas with 92% accuracy. This led to a 20% improvement in water use efficiency. In India, another AI method called Convolutional Neural Networks (CNNs) helped tell the difference between plants stressed by drought and those lacking nutrients, which helped tomato farmers cut irrigation costs by 16%.

AI can also combine data from satellites, drones, and ground sensors to create a complete picture of what is happening in the field. In Spain, Support Vector Machines (another ML tool) were used to predict how much water crops were losing to evaporation, which helped reduce water waste by 18%.

The catch? These AI models need a lot of data and computing power, which can be tough for farmers in areas with limited resources.

Challenges and Opportunities

Remote sensing has huge potential to make irrigation smarter and more sustainable, but there are still some big hurdles to clear. Here is a quick look at the main challenges—and some promising solutions.

Challenges

- **Cost** The best satellite images and hyperspectral sensors are expensive. For small farmers—who actually manage most of the world's farmland—the price tag can be out of reach. In some cases, the cost of a drone system is more than a farmer's yearly profit. Moreover, it is not just the hardware; you also need software and skilled people to run everything.
- **Weather and Environment:** Things like cloud cover can block satellite images for much of the growing season, especially in tropical areas. In really hot places, sensors can become less accurate, making it harder to get reliable data when it is needed most.
- **Data Overload:** Pulling together data from satellites, drones, and ground sensors is complicated. It often requires advanced technical skills and powerful computers. For example, in Brazil, combining drone and ground sensor data improved irrigation, but only with the help of cloud computing and trained analysts—resources that are not always available in rural areas.

Opportunities

- **Cheaper Sensors:** New projects, like India's AgriSense, are making hyperspectral sensors much more affordable—sometimes as low as$2,000$5,000. Early tests in Punjab showed that these cheaper sensors, when used with smart analysis, helped farmers save 12% more water.
- **On-Farm Data Processing (Edge Computing):** Instead of sending all the data to the cloud, some systems now process it right on the farm. This means decisions can be made faster, even without a strong internet connection.

In Australia, this approach helped vineyards adjust irrigation the same day, boosting yields by 8%.

- **Smarter Data Integration:** AI is making it easier to combine data from different sources. In Spain, CNNs were used to merge satellite, drone, and ground sensor data, predicting water loss with 90% accuracy and cutting water waste by 18%. Open-source software is making these tools more accessible, even for those without a tech background.
- **Partnerships:** When governments and private companies work together, they can help small farmers get access to these technologies. For example, in Kenya, a partnership helped mango farmers use drone-based imaging, improving water use efficiency by 15%. This kind of teamwork could be a model for other regions facing water shortages (Table **2**).

Table 2. Remote sensing challenges and opportunities [1 - 25].

Challenge	Impact	Opportunity	Example
High Costs	Limits adoption by smallholders (80% of global farms) [1]	Low-cost hyperspectral sensors ($2,000–$5,000) [6]	Punjab citrus farms: 12% water savings [7]
Environmental Limitations	Cloud cover (60% in tropics), thermal drift (10–15% CWSI errors) [3, 4]	Cloud-penetrating radar, temperature-resistant sensors[8]	Middle Eastern date palms: Improved CWSI accuracy [4]
Data Integration Complexity	Delays irrigation decisions due to data heterogeneity [5]	AI-driven data fusion (90% ET prediction accuracy) [10]	Spanish citrus orchards: 18% water savings [10]
Limited Expertise	Hinders technology adoption in rural areas [6]	Public-private partnerships for training and subsidies [4]	Kenyan mango farms: 15% WUE improvement [11]

HOW REMOTE SENSING IS USED FOR SMARTER IRRIGATION

This section breaks down the main steps and tools farmers and researchers use to put remote sensing into action for watering fruit and vegetable crops. It covers how data is collected, processed, turned into decisions, and checked for accuracy.

How Data Gets Collected

Satellites

Satellites like Sentinel-2 and Landsat regularly fly over fields and take images in different wavelengths. These images help calculate things like the NDVI (which shows how healthy plants are) and the CWSI (which shows how stressed they are from lack of water). The CWSI is based on the temperature of the plant's leaves compared to wet and dry references. Sentinel-2 checks in every 5 days, while Landsat comes by about every 16 days. This data helps farmers and agronomists see which parts of a field need more or less water.

$$CWSI = (Tcanopy - Tdry)/(Twet - Tdry) \quad \textbf{(1)}$$

Where:

- T_{wet} = Temperature of the wet plant (or wet bulb temperature).
- T_{dry} = Temperature of the dry plant (or dry bulb temperature).
- T_{canopy}= Canopy temperature of the plant.

Drones (UAVs)

Drones equipped with special cameras can fly low and capture super-detailed images—sometimes down to just a few centimeters. In India, for example, drones using the NDWI (which measures water content in plants) could spot water stress days before other sensors, helping tomato farmers boost yields by 12%. Drones can also use hyperspectral cameras to pick up early signs of stress in crops like mangoes and grapes, with up to 90% accuracy. The catch? Drones need good weather, skilled pilots, and their batteries only last 20–30 minutes. However, new, lighter cameras are making drones more affordable for small farms.

Ground Sensors

These are devices stuck in the soil that measure things like moisture, temperature, and humidity right where the roots are. They are great for getting real-time, super-local data. For example, in Australia, soil sensors helped confirm what drones were seeing, making irrigation 12% more precise and cutting water use by 10%. In Brazil, soil sensors mapped out how water moved through mango orchards, helping farmers target irrigation and save 15% more water. The downside? Each sensor only covers a small area, so they work best when combined with aerial data. Newer sensors can send data wirelessly, making it easier to monitor big fields.

How the Data Gets Processed and Analyzed

Image Correction

Raw images from satellites and drones are not perfect—they can be distorted by things like clouds, sunlight, or sensor noise. Software like Google Earth Engine or Pix4D helps clean up these images, making them more accurate. For example, in

Indian citrus orchards, using Pix4D to process drone images made NDVI maps more precise, which helped save 13% more water. Processing hyperspectral data is even trickier and often needs cloud computing, which is not always available in rural areas.

Calculating Plant Health

Once the images are cleaned up, different "vegetation indices" are calculated. NDVI shows how healthy and green the plants are. WBI and NDWI can spot early signs of water stress by looking at how much water is in the leaves. SAVI helps adjust for bare soil, which is useful in young vineyards. In California, using WBI from drone images helped farmers spot stress days before it was visible, saving 18% more water. These indices are powerful, but they need to be carefully calibrated for each crop and field.

Combining Data (Data Fusion)

Machine learning tools like Support Vector Machines (SVM) and Convolutional Neural Networks (CNNs) can combine data from satellites, drones, and ground sensors to predict exactly when and where to irrigate. For example, in Brazil, combining drone and satellite data helped soybean farmers use 14% less water and grow 9% more. In Spain, CNNs helped predict water loss with 90% accuracy, making irrigation schedules much smarter. The challenge? Processing all this data can require powerful computers, but open-source tools like TensorFlow are making it easier for more people to use.

Turning Data into Action: Automated Irrigation

Here is how the whole process comes together on a modern farm:

- **Collect Data:** Sensors (satellites, drones, ground devices) gather real-time info on soil moisture, plant temperature, and humidity. For example, in Australian apple orchards, sensors collected data every 10 minutes, allowing for quick adjustments.
- **Process Data:** The raw data is cleaned and organized using cloud platforms or open-source tools. In India, this step reduced "noise" in the data by 15%, making the analysis more reliable.
- **Analyze:** Algorithms look for signs of water stress, measure how much water is evaporating, and check soil moisture. In California, Random Forest models could spot water-stressed zones with 92% accuracy.
- **Make Decisions:** The field is divided into zones based on how much water each area needs. Automated systems then prioritize the driest spots. In Brazil, this zoning approach improved water use efficiency by 16%.

- **Implement:** Automated valves and drip systems deliver just the right amount of water to each zone. In Spain, using IoT-controlled valves cut water waste by 18% (Table **3** and Fig. **1**).

Table 3. Automated irrigation decision-making process.

Step	Description	Example Outcome
Data Collection	Sensors gather real-time soil moisture, temperature, and humidity data	Australian apples: 10-minute data intervals [20]
Processing	Data cleaning and formatting using cloud or open-source platforms	Indian tomatoes: 15% noise reduction [21]
Analysis	Assess water stress, ET, and soil moisture *via* ML algorithms	California vineyards: 92% stress detection accuracy [22]
Decision	Zone fields based on water needs (35–60 mm)	Brazilian mangoes: 16% WUE improvement [23]
Implementation	Automated valves deliver precise water volumes	Spanish citrus: 18% water waste reduction [24]

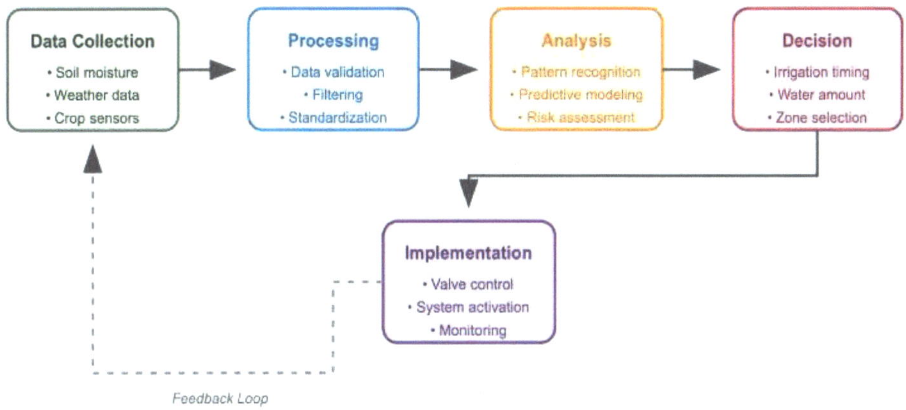

Fig. (1). Decision-making process for precision irrigation.

How Do We Know Remote Sensing Data is Reliable? (Validation Techniques)

To make sure remote sensing data is actually useful, it is compared with real measurements taken in the field—this is called validation. For example, in Indian citrus orchards, soil moisture sensors and tests on plant leaves were used to check if drone data (NDWI) was accurate. This made the irrigation models 20% better. In Australia, ground sensors helped confirm what satellite imagery showed, reducing irrigation errors by 10%. Newer methods, like using portable spectrometers with drones, are making it easier to validate data even in remote places. In Kenya, this approach helped mango farmers use 15% less water. Validation is especially important for fine-tuning hyperspectral indices like WBI, which need to be adjusted for each crop and location to accurately match yield (Table **4**).

Table 4. Summary of remote sensing approaches.

Approach	Key Features	Horticultural Example	Impact
Satellite Systems	10–20 m resolution, 5–16 day revisits, NDVI/CWSI mapping [3]	Spanish citrus: 15% water savings [1]	Regional monitoring [4]
UAVs	5 cm–1 m resolution, hyperspectral/thermal imaging, NDWI/WBI [6]	Indian tomatoes: 12% yield increase [4]	Real-time stress detection [20]
Ground Sensors	Real-time soil moisture/temperature, IoT integration [11]	Australian vineyards: 12% precision improvement [8]	Data validation [2]
Data Processing	Atmospheric/radiometric corrections, Google Earth Engine/Pix4D [9]	Indian citrus: 13% water savings [12]	Improved data accuracy [4]
Data Fusion	ML-based integration (SVM, CNN), ET prediction [10]	Brazilian soybeans: 14% water reduction [17]	Enhanced decision-making [6]
Decision-Making	Automated zoning, IoT-controlled irrigation [1]	Spanish citrus: 18% water waste reduction [24]	Precision irrigation [15]

WHAT ARE THE KEY TAKEAWAYS FROM USING REMOTE SENSING IN IRRIGATION?

Monitoring Crop Water Status

By combining data from satellites, drones, and ground sensors, farmers get a full picture of soil moisture, plant health, and how much water is evaporating. Drones, in particular, can spot small patches of water stress that might otherwise go unnoticed, using maps like NDVI and WBI as shown in Fig. (**2**), to show exactly where plants need help is presented in Table **5**, where comparative analysis of NDVI and WBI from the remote sensing platform is done.

Table 5. Comparison of NDVI and WBI from remote sensing platforms.

S. No	Platform	Spatial Resolution	NDVI Range	WBI Range	Water Stress Zones (%)
1	Satellite (Sentinel) [2]	10–20 m	0.50–0.80	0.90–1.10	25%
2	UAV (Hyperspectral) [14]	5 cm–1 m	0.45–0.85	0.85–1.15	15%

(Table 5) cont.....

S. No	Platform	Spatial Resolution	NDVI Range	WBI Range	Water Stress Zones (%)
3	Ground Sensors [15]	Point Measurements	N/A	N/A	N/A

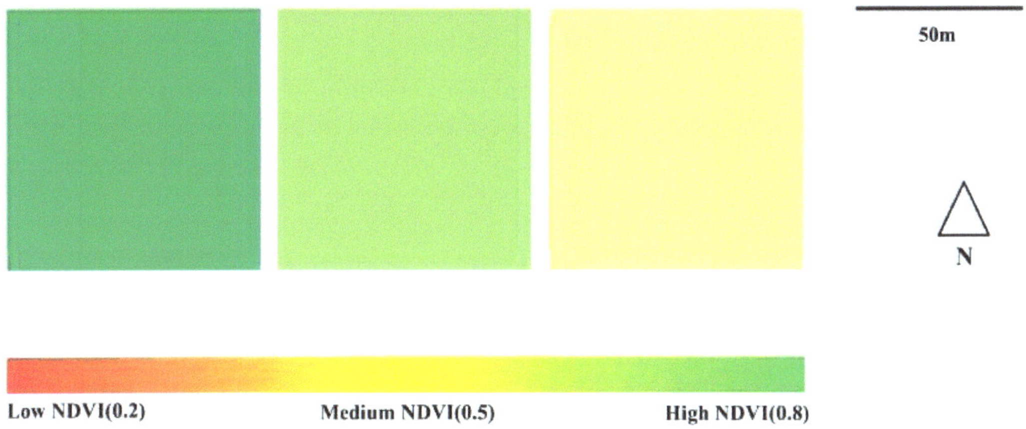

Fig. (2). NDVI distribution map showing crop health variability.

Measuring Evapotranspiration (ET)

Thermal images from drones and satellites help measure how much water is leaving the field through evaporation and plant transpiration (ET). Satellites are great for tracking long-term trends, while drones can catch sudden changes and help farmers react quickly (Table **6**).

Table 6. ET Values from satellite and UAV data.

Day	ET from Satellite (mm/day)	ET from UAV (mm/day)	Difference (mm/day)
1	5.0	4.8	0.2
7	4.5	4.3	0.2
14	5.2	5.0	0.2

Creating Precision Irrigation Zones

With all this data, fields can be divided into zones, each getting just the right amount of water (usually 35–60 mm per zone). This targeted approach can boost water use efficiency by 15–22% and increase yields by up to 13 tons per hectare.

DISCUSSION

Why Remote Sensing Matters

Remote sensing helps farmers use water more wisely by showing exactly where and when crops need it. Drones can catch early signs of stress, satellites give a big-picture view, and ground sensors double-check the data. This teamwork leads to more precise, reliable irrigation.

What is Still Hard?

The biggest hurdles are cost and complexity. High-end sensors and satellite images are expensive, and tough weather (like clouds or extreme heat) can mess with the data. Plus, making sense of all this information and fitting it into existing farm routines takes technical know-how that not every farmer has.

How AI and Machine Learning Help

AI and ML make it easier to analyze all this data and turn it into smart irrigation plans. For example, in Spain, machine learning helped citrus farmers cut irrigation costs by 18% by focusing on the most stressed areas. AI can also tell the difference between drought and nutrient problems, making decisions even more precise.

What Needs More Work?

- **Cost:** Hyperspectral imaging is still too pricey for most small farms.
- **Weather:** Cloud cover and extreme weather can reduce data quality.
- **Yield Prediction:** The link between remote sensing indices and actual crop yield is not always clear and needs more research.

Future Directions

The future directions are as follows:

- Make sensors cheaper and more accessible, building on open-source projects.
- Develop sensors that work better in tough weather.
- Do more long-term studies to connect remote sensing data with real yield results, especially for high-value crops.

Practical Tips for Farmers and Advisors

- Use platforms like Google Earth Engine to process satellite images without breaking the bank.
- Fly drones early in the morning for the best image quality.
- Train farmers to read and use NDVI, WBI, and NDWI maps for better decisions.
- Real-world example: In Brazil, using NDWI to guide irrigation reduced water use by 12% in mango orchards.

CONCLUSION

Remote sensing has changed the way farmers manage irrigation for fruit and vegetable crops. By providing real-time, detailed data on plant and soil water status, these tools help farmers use water more efficiently and grow more food, even in dry or unpredictable climates.

- **Precision irrigation zoning** (using data to target water where it is needed) can improve water use by 15–22% and boost yields.
- **Hyperspectral imaging** helps spot water stress early, which is crucial for keeping crops healthy in tough conditions.
- **AI and machine learning** make it easier to analyze all this data and automate smart irrigation decisions, cutting water waste by up to 20%.

But there are still challenges—mainly cost, weather, and making sure the data really matches up with yield. The future lies in making these tools cheaper, more robust, and easier to use, so that even small farmers can benefit and keep growing food sustainably as the climate changes.

REFERENCES

[1] Ahmad U, Alvino A, Marino S. A review of crop water stress assessment using remote sensing. Remote Sens (Basel) 2021; 13(20): 4155.
[http://dx.doi.org/10.3390/rs13204155]

[2] Asfaw E, Suryabhagavan KV, Argaw M. Soil salinity modeling and mapping using remote sensing and GIS: The case of Wonji sugar cane irrigation farm, Ethiopia. J Saudi Soc Agric Sci 2018; 17(3): 250-8.
[http://dx.doi.org/10.1016/j.jssas.2016.05.003]

[3] Hussain G, Al-Hawas IA. Salinity sensor: A reliable tool for monitoring *in situ* soil salinity under saline irrigation. Int J Soil Sci 2008; 3: 92-100.
[http://dx.doi.org/10.3923/ijss.2008.92.100]

[4] Safdar M, Shahid MA, Sarwar A, Rasul F, Majeed MD, Sabir RM. Crop water stress detection using remote sensing techniques. Environ Sci Proc 2023; 25: 20.
[http://dx.doi.org/10.3390/ECWS-7-14198]

[5] Sahbeni G, Ngabire M, Musyimi PK, Székely B. Challenges and opportunities in remote sensing for soil salinization mapping and monitoring: a review. Remote Sens (Basel) 2023; 15(10): 2540.
[http://dx.doi.org/10.3390/rs15102540]

[6] Alvino A, Marino S. Remote sensing for irrigation of horticultural crops. Horticulturae 2017; 3(2): 40.
[http://dx.doi.org/10.3390/horticulturae3020040]

[7] Almalki R, Khaki M, Saco PM, Rodriguez JF. Monitoring and mapping vegetation cover changes in arid and semi-arid areas using Remote Sensing Technology: a review. Remote Sens (Basel) 2022; 14(20): 5143.
[http://dx.doi.org/10.3390/rs14205143]

[8] Abu-Hashim M, Sayed A, Zelenakova M, Vranayová Z, Khalil M. Soil water erosion vulnerability and suitability under different irrigation systems using parametric approach. Sustainability (Basel) 2021; 13(3): 1057.

[http://dx.doi.org/10.3390/su13031057]

[9] Aldababseh A, Temimi M, Maghelal P, Branch O, Wulfmeyer V. Multi-criteria evaluation of irrigated agriculture suitability to achieve food security in an arid environment. Sustainability (Basel) 2018; 10(3): 803.
[http://dx.doi.org/10.3390/su10030803]

[10] Bastiaanssen WGM, Steduto P. The water productivity score (WPS) at global and regional level: Methodology and first results from remote sensing measurements of wheat, rice and maize. Sci Total Environ 2017; 575: 595-611.
[http://dx.doi.org/10.1016/j.scitotenv.2016.09.032] [PMID: 27712867]

[11] Bhat SA, Huang NF. Big data and AI revolution in precision agriculture: Survey and challenges. IEEE Access 2021; 9: 110209-22.
[http://dx.doi.org/10.1109/ACCESS.2021.3102227]

[12] Elnashar A, Abbas M, Sobhy H, Shahba M. Crop water requirements and suitability assessment in arid environments: A new approach. Agronomy (Basel) 2021; 11(2): 260.
[http://dx.doi.org/10.3390/agronomy11020260]

[13] Fares A, Awal R, Fares S, Johnson AB, Valenzuela H. Irrigation water requirements for seed corn and coffee under potential climate change scenarios. J Water Clim Chang 2016; 7(1): 39-51.
[http://dx.doi.org/10.2166/wcc.2015.025]

[14] Karthikeyan L, Chawla I, Mishra AK. A review of remote sensing applications in agriculture for food security: Crop growth and yield, irrigation, and crop losses. J Hydrol (Amst) 2020; 586: 124905.
[http://dx.doi.org/10.1016/j.jhydrol.2020.124905]

[15] Li X, Zhang J, Liu J, *et al.* A modified checkbook irrigation method based on GIS-coupled model for regional irrigation scheduling. Irrig Sci 2011; 29(2): 115-26.
[http://dx.doi.org/10.1007/s00271-010-0221-9]

[16] Maina MM, Amin MSM, Yazid MA. Web geographic information system decision support system for irrigation water management: a review. Acta Agric Scand B Soil Plant Sci 2014; 64(4): 283-93.
[http://dx.doi.org/10.1080/09064710.2014.896935]

[17] Singh J, Kaur R, Kaur P, Sigh R, *et al.* AI-based modeling of GLOF process and its impact. Artificial Intelligence in Remote Sensing for Disaster Management. Wiley 2025; pp. 243-70.
[http://dx.doi.org/10.1002/9781394287222.ch14]

[18] Rajendran N, Singh R, Moudgil MR, Turukmane AV, Umadevi M, Glory KB. Secured control systems through integrated IoT devices and control systems. Meas Sensors 2022; 24: 100487.
[http://dx.doi.org/10.1016/j.measen.2022.100487]

[19] Nikam BR, Garg V, Thakur PK, Aggarwal SP. Application of remote sensing and GIS in performance evaluation of irrigation project at disaggregated level. Photonirvachak (Dehra Dun) 2020; 48(7): 979-97.
[http://dx.doi.org/10.1007/s12524-020-01128-1]

[20] Singh R, Singh M, Singh J. Artificial intelligence tools in disaster risk reduction and emergency management. Artificial Intelligence in Remote Sensing for Disaster Management. Wiley 2025; pp. 79-98.
[http://dx.doi.org/10.1002/9781394287222.ch5]

[21] Singh AK, Dubey OP, Ghosh SK. Irrigation scheduling using intervention of Geomatics tools—A case study of Khedli minor. Agric Water Manage 2016; 177: 454-60.
[http://dx.doi.org/10.1016/j.agwat.2016.05.024]

[22] Sishodia RP, Ray RL, Singh SK. Applications of remote sensing in precision agriculture: a review. Remote Sens (Basel) 2020; 12(19): 3136.
[http://dx.doi.org/10.3390/rs12193136]

[23] Singh RSR, Vinoth R, Mishra P. An improved anomaly detection in wireless sensor network using

artificial intelligence evolving optimization tools Proc 2nd Int Conf Augmented Intelligence and Sustainable Systems (ICAISS). Trichy, India. 2023; pp. 19-24.

[24] Alagdeve V, Singh R, G V, Parihar B, Dhananjeyan S, Bussa A. Efficient data encryption and signature generation scheme for resource-constrained IoT environments Proc 7th Int Conf I-SMAC (IoT in Social, Mobile, Analytics and Cloud) (I-SMAC). Kirtipur, Nepal. 2023; pp. 262-9. [http://dx.doi.org/10.1109/I-SMAC58438.2023.10290224]

[25] Singh C, Singh R, Kamini , Kumar Y. Exploring cybersecurity in healthcare systems: A systematic review. In: Choudhury A, Ed. Cyber-Physical Systems Security Stud Big Data. Springer 2025; 154. [http://dx.doi.org/10.1007/978-981-97-1543-5_1]

CHAPTER 4

Role of Remote Sensing and Geographic Information System (GIS) in Integrated Pest Management (IPM)

Kalirajan Murugasridevi[1,*], Venunathan Dhivya[2], Lincy Kirubhadharshini B.[3], VR Mageshen[1] and **S. Sowjanya[3,4]**

[1] *Amrita School of Agricultural Sciences, Amrita Vishwa Vidyapeetham, Coimbatore -642 109, India*

[2] *Department of Agricultural Entomology, Tamil Nadu Agricultural University, Coimbatore - 641 003, India*

[3] *VIT School of Agricultural Innovations and Advanced Learning (VAIAL), Vellore Institute of Technology (VIT), Vellore - 632 014, India*

[4] *School of Biosciences and Technology, Vellore Institute of Technology (VIT), Vellore - 632014, India*

Abstract: Insect pests are recognized as a significant global threat to agricultural productivity. Preventing and managing insect infestations is critical to minimizing these impacts. The recognition, categorization, and management of insect pests are crucial to prevent substantial losses. Employing manual ways to practice the process is laborious and not as efficient in accomplishing the objective. Traditional pest management techniques frequently struggle to adapt to the dynamic behaviors of pests, resulting in considerable crop damage and excessive reliance on chemical treatments. This ongoing global challenge can be effectively addressed through the integration of precision agriculture technologies, such as Remote Sensing (RS) and Geographic Information Systems (GIS), within the framework of Integrated Pest Management (IPM). RS and GIS technologies have demonstrated significant utility in monitoring pest occurrences, enabling timely and informed decision-making in pest control strategies. These tools offer rapid and large-scale access to real-time spatial data on insect populations, which enhances the effectiveness of IPM practices. The combined use of GIS, GPS (Global Positioning System), and RS provides valuable spatial insights into pest population dynamics, enabling surveillance across broad geographic areas and over time. Moreover, hyperspectral imaging—a cutting-edge form of remote sensing—further enhances pest detection and classification capabilities. By capturing data across hundreds of narrow spectral bands, hyperspectral sensors can detect subtle physiological changes in plants caused by pest stress before visible symptoms appear. This allows for early intervention, improved pest identification, and more precise application of control measures, thereby reducing unnecessary chemical usage and im-

* **Corresponding author Kalirajan Murugasridevi:** Amrita School of Agricultural Sciences, Amrita Vishwa Vidyapeetham, Coimbatore -642 109, India; E-mail: sridevivetri.2109@gmail.com

Sartajvir Singh, Neelam Dahiya, Maged Mohammed, Abdullah Alzharihi & Vishal Dutt (Eds.)

proving crop health outcomes. This chapter explores the application of RS and GIS in IPM, highlighting their role in pest surveillance, outbreak prediction, pest distribution mapping, and yield loss assessment due to pest attacks. In addition, it introduces the basic working principles behind these technologies and discusses the emerging role of hyperspectral imaging in advancing pest monitoring and management.

Keywords: Geographic information system, Integrated pest management, Pest monitoring, Pest mapping, Pest forecasting, Remote sensing, Sensors, Yield loss assessment.

INTRODUCTION

As reported [1], between 20 and 40 percent of global crop production is lost annually to insect pests and diseases, resulting in economic losses exceeding USD 220 billion worldwide. These insect pests damage the plants and thereby induce them physiologically to produce symptoms. Generally, plants respond to insect attack in numerous ways by developing symptoms including chlorosis, wilting, leaf curling, leaf crinkling, necrosis of photosynthetic tissues, stunting, or, in extreme instances, a decrease in leaf area due to substantial defoliation. Prompt identification and evaluation of these damage symptoms are highly important. Conventionally, the assessment of pests and diseases in crop plants is carried out through a visual method, relying on human observation and judgment to determine their presence. However, the drawback of this traditional approach is that it tends to be both time-consuming and labor-intensive. In this regard, precision agriculture involving Remote Sensing (RS) and Geographic Information System (GIS) paves the way for automated recognition, diagnosis, and quantification of pests and diseases, thereby easing pest management tactics. RS tools clearly quantify and monitor electromagnetic radiation changes in insect-infested plant canopies with high accuracy, speed, and reliability.

RS techniques primarily rely on the acquisition and decoding of sensory data around the surface of the Earth without having significant direct contact with it [2]. RS mostly relies on electromagnetic radiation, which determines data collection and interpretation. This method is employed to measure and keep track of the reflection and transmission of electromagnetic energy from the intended zone utilizing the sensor equipment. On the other hand, GIS provides resources for the archive, access, interpretation, and presentation of geographical information as well as images. Geospatial data pertains to all data regarding a specific geographical region of the Earth. Information can be gathered and presented by means of GPS-enabled portable devices and GIS software. In this scenario, pest and crop field data are gathered and represented in shapefiles. After data gathering, individual shape files are presented as vector forms inside a specified coordinate system to provide a geo-referenced map of the spatial data and photographs. Significant RS applications documented across diverse domains encompass agriculture, meteorology, forest ecosystems, hydrology, pest control, and the marine environment (Fig. **1**). Both GIS and RS, as precision agriculture technologies, empower farmers to assess the spatial-temporal heterogeneity of different key variables affecting plant health and yield. Data obtained from sensors are aggregated on digital devices for decision-making purposes [3].

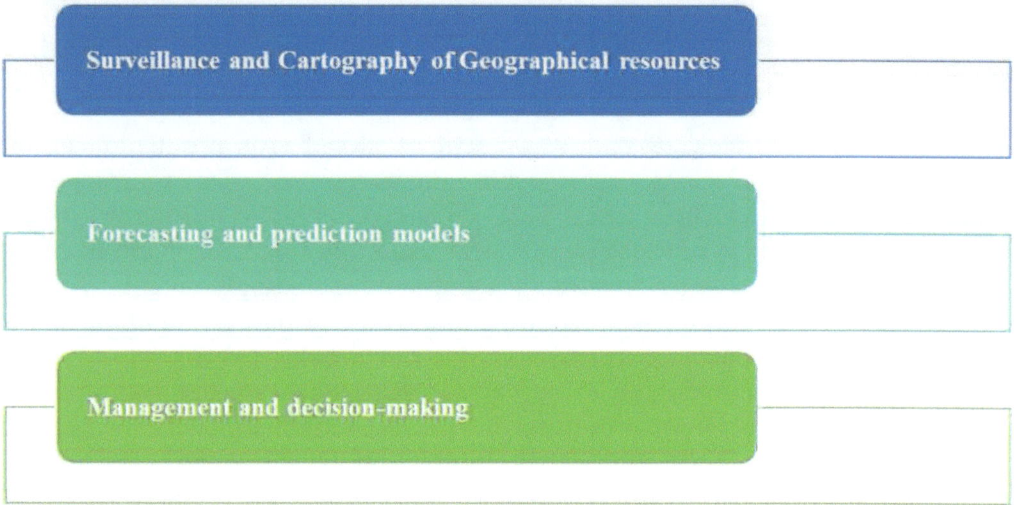

Fig. (1). Applications of remote sensing.

Currently, RS technologies are deployed on navigation satellites and utilize multi-spectral imaging technologies, which provide a comprehensive perspective, rapid assessment, high precision, and coverage of unreachable regions, in contrast to traditional surveillance and mapping approaches. Moreover, several studies in crop protection possess spatial dimensions, including the examination of the spatial ecology of insect pests, their host plants, and their entomophagous insects within and among crops. This information might be additionally connected across landscape elements to enhance knowledge of the pest's population dynamics. Spatial analysis facilitated by GIS tools can aid in managing insects at both local and regional scales, including forecasting the spatiotemporal pattern of insect pests [4], by employing GIS-based multi-spectral imagery to enhance pest monitoring for targeted pesticide implementation [5], and identifying insect infestation in crop agricultural fields [6]. In this view, this chapter examines the implications of RS and GIS in Integrated Pest Management (IPM), focusing on the implementation of these precise technologies for pest monitoring, mapping, outbreak prediction, and assessment of yield loss resulting from pest infestations. This chapter also encompasses the fundamental principles and practical concepts related to RS and GIS, along with their potential applications in IPM.

WORKING PRINCIPLE OF REMOTE SENSING

Electromagnetic energy is generated by solar radiation and travels in a straight trajectory at the velocity of light through billions of miles of vacuum to reach the environment of the Earth and its surface. Radiation rises upward from the Earth's surface, with some being absorbed or re-emitted as thermal energy. Electromagnetic radiation consists of an electric field and a magnetic field, oriented at right angles to one another. This energy can be detected based on its frequency or wavelength. Fig. (**2**) illustrates the electromagnetic spectrum, divided into specific spectral regions [7].

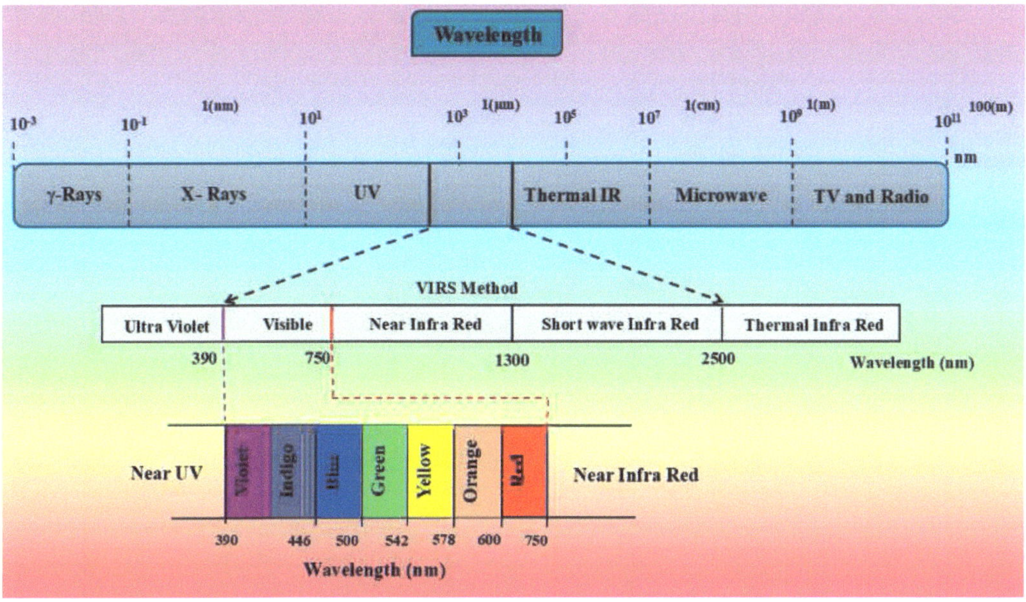

Fig. (2). Spectral regions of the electromagnetic spectrum [7].

Sensors used in remote sensing are devices designed to collect data from reflected and emitted electromagnetic radiation over a certain distance. This energy can be detected in two forms, *viz.,* photographic or electronic. The first is called a photograph, while the latter is called an image. Most surfaces in nature function as diffuse reflectors, which correlate with the spectroscopic characteristics of live plant foliage in remote sensing applications.

Elements of Remote Sensing

Remote sensing works with the assistance of its six elements, which are shown in Fig. (3).

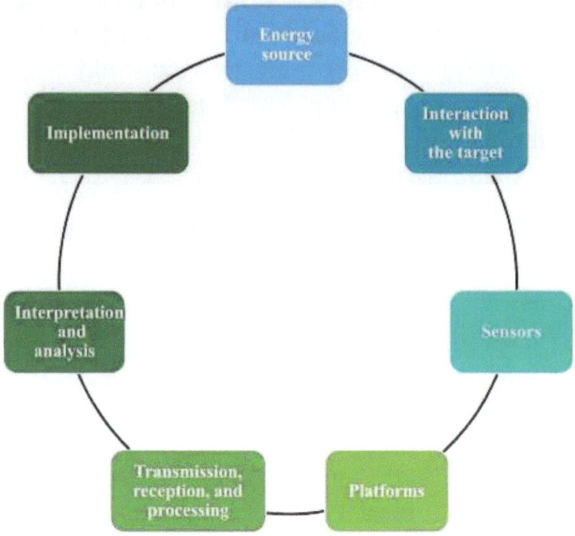

Fig. (3). Various elements of remote sensing.

Energy Source

It transmits electromagnetic energy toward the target, and based on their energy source, sensors are categorized as active or passive systems. Passive sensors use natural sunlight, visible wavelengths, and thermal infrared wavelengths. Active sensors include radar, laser fluorosensor, and microwaves.

Interaction with the Target

Once energy travels through the atmosphere from its source, it interacts with the target, influenced by the target's properties and the energy itself. These interactions may involve energy absorption, emission by the target, scattering, or reflection.

Sensors

Sensors used in remote sensing include optical sensors, which operate in the visible, near-infrared, middle-infrared, and thermal infrared wavelength ranges, as well as microwave sensors with 10^9 and 10^{12} Hz frequencies.

Platforms

Platforms encompass ground-based, airborne, and spaceborne carriers.

Transmission, Reception, and Processing

This refers to the processing of data collected by the sensor, which is transmitted to a ground station, typically in electronic format, where it is stored as images, digital files, or other formats.

Interpretation and Analysis

The process involves analyzing the collected data to extract relevant information using various image processing techniques, both hardware- and software-based. This extracted information is then applied to address a specific problem.

Implementation

It elucidates the successful implications of the remote sensing approach, which has successfully applied the knowledge gathered to address a specific issue.

Implementation of Remote Sensing in IPM

The RS approach provides data that supports decision-support systems for diverse pest control programs by monitoring, documenting through cartography, and predicting epidemic patterns. Precise and effective monitoring of insect populations is essential for enhancing pest management. Computer-based technologies have increased the efficiency and accuracy of predictions while helping to reduce management expenses. A crucial element of the IPM method is pest forecasting. Forecasts and preliminary alerts derived from biophysical techniques provide an opportunity for managing imminent pest invasions, thereby enhancing pest management, diminishing crop loss, and reducing cultivation expenses. Utilizing remote sensing techniques to identify crop challenges, *viz.,* pest attack, pathogen progression, and abiotic stress, including drought monitoring, nutrient inadequacy, is advantageous. Remote sensing enhances spatial and temporal resolution relative to conventional pest monitoring techniques [8], including sex pheromone traps for specific pests, light traps for positively phototropic insects, and durable suction traps at various places to recognize insect pest migrations. Specifically, RS sensors are utilized in IPM by enabling early pest detection, monitoring pest population dynamics, and assessing crop health. These sensors help reduce pesticide use and optimize pest control strategies. Some of the key sensors employed in IPM include optical sensors (Multispectral and Hyperspectral), Thermal Infrared Sensors, LiDAR (Light Detection and Ranging), Radar Sensors (Synthetic Aperture Radar - SAR),

Fluorescence Sensors (Chlorophyll Fluorescence), and Gas Sensors. Numerous studies have reported the utility of RS sensors in IPM, as shown in Table **1**.

Table 1. Remote sensing sensors used in Integrated Pest Management (IPM).

S. No.	Crop	Target Pest	Purpose	Type of Sensors Employed	Accuracy (%)	References
1.	Rice	Striped Stem borer	Insect detection	Hyperspectral imaging	97	[9]
2.	Oil palm	Bagworm	Insect detection	Hyperspectral imaging	91-95	[10]
3.	Apple	Codling moth	Insect detection and classification	Hyperspectral imaging	99.24	[11]
4.	-	Brown marmorated stink bug	Insect detection	Near Infrared Hyperspectral Imaging (NIR-HSI)	94.8	[12]
5.	Larch	Larch caterpillar	Pest monitoring	Multispectral imaging	92.3	[13]
6.	Sunflower	Beet web worm	Insect detection and infestation	Sentinel-2A and PlanetScope	90	[14]
7.	Forest trees	Forest insect pests	Pest monitoring	Airborne hyperspectral LiDAR	89.45	[15]
8.	Soybean	Aphid	Classification of pest infestation	Sentinel-2 bands and vegetation indices (VIs)	91	[16]
9.	Cotton	Cotton aphid, red spider mite, and bollworm	Pest monitoring	Multi-spectral remote sensing images	93.7	[17]
10.	Rice	Rice Leaf folder	Insect detection	Hyperspectral imaging	87.46	[18]
11.	Mulberry	Tiger Longhorn beetles	Early detection of pests	Multispectral imagery	86	[19]
12.	Rice	Rice leafroller	Pest monitoring	Ultra-light UAV	90.80	[20]

Pest Monitoring Through Remote Sensing

Current research not only emphasizes the detection of pests and disease but also aims to differentiate many biotic stresses simultaneously, evaluate their infestation intensities, and delineate their distributions at the regional level. In certain instances, the identification and surveillance of diseases and pests have demonstrated significant potential in practical applications, including enabling precision spraying in fields for disease and pest management, assisting high-throughput plant phenotyping, and assessing crop economic loss due to pest and disease occurrence. According to sensing principles and technological advancement, sensing systems may be broadly classified into three categories concerning the monitoring of plant pests, which are shown in Fig. (**4**).

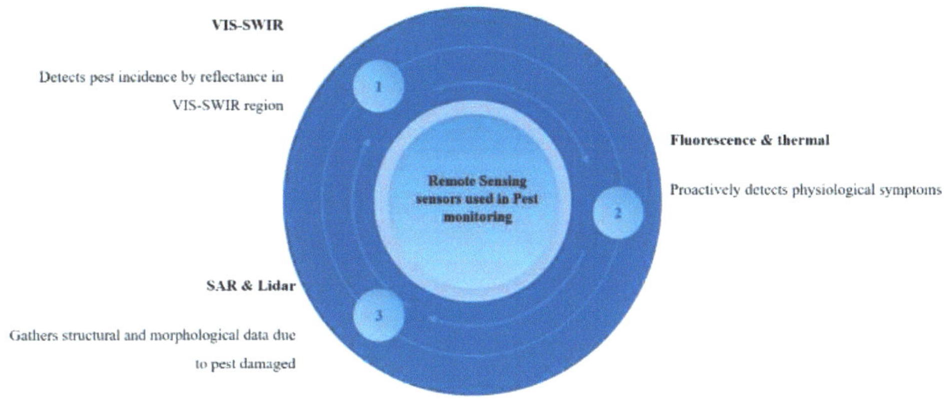

Fig. (4). Remote sensing systems employed for Pest monitoring.

Attributes of Remote Sensing for Pest Monitoring

Identifying effective and distinguishing remote sensing attributes is essential for applying remote sensing observations in the monitoring of plant pests. A range of remote sensing properties has been suggested or recognized for identifying plant symptoms resulting from pest infestation, as well as for designating their habitats. The primary aspect of the RS in pest monitoring is illustrated in Fig. (**5**).

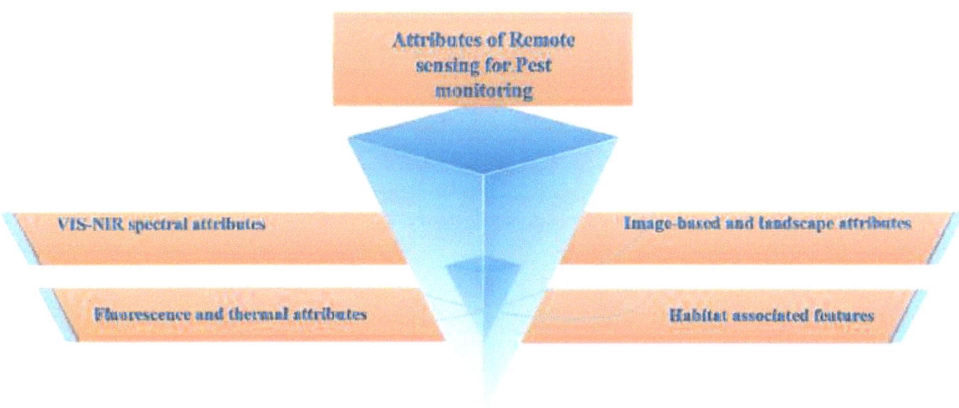

Fig. (5). Attributes of remote sensing for Pest monitoring.

VIS - NIR Spectral Attributes

VIS-NIR sensors are the primary remote sensing technology utilized in tracking plant pests, with band transmittance being the most significant property. Numerous investigations have identified the green, red, and near-IR spectral regions as indicative of various plant diseases and pests [21]. A conversion of reflective spectral data can be accomplished in three distinct methods that are depicted in Fig. (**6**).

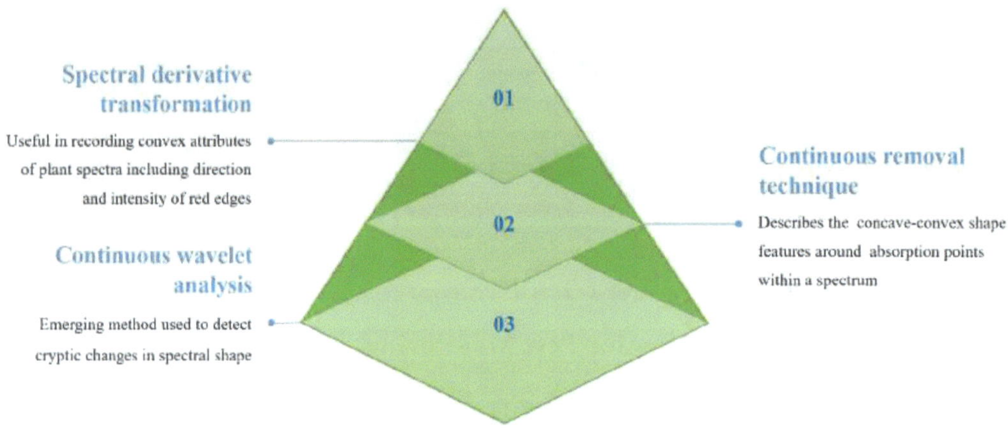

Fig. (6). Transformative ways of spectral values.

In addition to reflectance amplitude and modified spectral bands, other Vegetation Indices (VIs) are extensively utilized for the recognition and surveillance of insect pests and plant pathogens. Through algebraic blends of original bands, VIs can highlight significant biophysical features or functionalities of plants (Table **2**). The fluctuation in plant pigment content can elicit pronounced spectrum responses, leading to the utilization of various VIs for the detection of insect pests and plant pathogens that impact pigments, including chlorophyll, carotenoids, anthocyanins, pigment ratios, such as Car/Chl, and the xanthophyll cycle [22, 23].

Table 2. Vegetation indices employed for monitoring pests in IPM.

S. No.	Vegetation Indices	Formula	Host Insect Detected	Crop	References
1.	Normalized Difference Vegetation Index (NDVI)	(Rred = Rnir)/(Rred + Rnir)	Soybean looper velvetbean calerpillar and green cloverworm	Soybean	[24]
			Sunn pest	Wheat	[25]
			Leafhopper	Cotton	[22]
2.	Photochemical Reflectance Index (PRI)	(R531 − R570)/(R531 + R570)	Leafhopper	Cotton	[22]
3.	Normalized Pigment Chlorophyll Index (NPCI)	(R680 = R430)/(R680 + R430)	Leafhopper	Cotton	[22]
4.	Carotenoid Reflectance Index (CRI-1)	ARI=(R510)−1 = (R700)−1	Bronze bug	Eucalyptus	[23]
5.	Simple Ratio (SR)	(R695/R420)	Soybean looper velvetbean calerpillar and green cloverworm	Soybean	[22, 24]
6.	Green Normalised Difference Vegetation Index (GNDVI)	(R750–R550)/(R750 + R550)	Soybean looper velvetbean calerpillar and green cloverworm	Soybean	[22, 24]
7.	Atmospherically Resistant Vegetation Index (ARI)	ARI=(R550)−1 = (R700)−1	Bronze bug	Eucalyptus	[23]
8.	Water band Index (IWB)	R950/R90	Leafminer	Tomato	[26]
9.	Aphid Index (AI)	(R740 = R887)/(R691 + R698)	Aphid	Wheat	[27]
			Aphid	Mustard	[28]
10.	RVI (Ratio vegetation index)	(NIR)/(RED)	Aphid	Mustard	[28]

(Table 2) cont.....

S. No.	Vegetation Indices	Formula	Host Insect Detected	Crop	References
11.	SIPI (Structural independent pigment index)	(R800-R445)/ (R800- R660)	Aphid	Mustard	[28]
12.	Leaf Hopper Index-1 (LHI-1)	(R691/R761)	Leafhopper	Cotton	[22]
13.	SAVI (Soil-Adjusted Vegetation Index)	(NIR − Red) (1 + L) / (NIR + Red + L)	Larch Looper	Larch	[13]

Monitoring insect occurrence through remote sensing has been widely followed for many years. A study [29] elucidated the interaction of light with animals and discussed optical remote sensing techniques for monitoring insects. Another study [30] presented various optical sensors for assessing and recognizing agricultural loss inflicted by insect pests. The progress of entomological radar technology, encompassing harmonic radar and lidar, was highlighted [31, 32]. Van Klink *et. al* (2022) demonstrated the application of radar detectors, machine learning, and more innovations for pest surveillance. A study [33] observed that the electronic trap-based laser remote sensing approach for insects features a compact probe volume, making it more appropriate for integration with the monitoring apparatus. The backscattered light method is more suitable for insect detection in field conditions. This method suggests that pulsed laser monitoring is better suited for open space surveillance [34], whereas continuous-wave laser tracking can distinguish different insect populations in the natural environment, mostly owing to improvements in data interpretation [35]. Nonetheless, the fluorescence-based technique enables the observation of dye-labeled insects in groups [36]. Furthermore, the examining and imaging capabilities of lidar are employed to monitor insect population dynamics. Lidar offers a unique ability to outline the forest canopy, enabling the assessment of the aggregation and movement of destructive insect populations, as well as aiding in predicting the rapid spread of pest outbreaks [37, 38]. Recent studies are also inculcating RS and GIS approaches along with Machine Learning tools for monitoring, mapping, and forecasting the pests [39].

Prediction of Pest Outbreak by Employing Remote Sensing

Expeditious surveys and evaluations of insect pest outbreaks are essential for prompt decision-making and reactive management. Remote sensing provides significant potential for identifying pest infestations across vast regions, enabling economical and frequent monitoring of broader forest landscapes. A study [40] employed remote sensing-based methods to develop prediction models to determine the bark beetle damage in European forests by mapping the pest incidence prior to its occurrence. This model detected the bark beetle occurrence with 92 per cent accuracy. Uncrewed Aerial Systems (UAS) provide a multifaceted approach for the surveillance of forest ecosystems. Another study [41] utilized multi-temporal, multispectral UAS imagery to monitor and classify healthy and Spruce bark beetle-infested trees. The prediction model for early detection of mustard aphid, vegetable thrips, and two-spotted spider mite was done using hyperspectral imaging on bok choy [42] with an accuracy of 92.8%. Another study [43] assessed solar activity, state of forest trees, and climatic factors in the taiga ecosystem to determine the outbreak of *Dendrolimussibiricus* Tschetv. Another study [44] identified and differentiated the birch stand areas affected by Siberian spongy moth, *Lymantria dispar* L., by using Sentinel-2 satellite data and NDVI vegetation indices. Another study [45] compared the occurrence of initial symptoms of epidemic and endemic bark beetle, *Ips typographus* L., using Unmanned Aerial Vehicles (UAV) multispectral imagery. Another study [46] applied multispectral satellite imagery to map the areas infested with Balsam woolly adelgid, *Adelges picea* Ratzeburg, in subalpine fir forests. Then, another study [47] predicted the *Ips typographus* outbreak with 72 per cent accuracy in the South Italian Alps. Another study [48] demonstrated the UAS imagery and NDVI vegetation index for determining the outbreak of beet armyworm, *Spodoptera exigua* (Hübner), on Soybean.

Pest Mapping Using Remote Sensing

Plants subjected to pest infestation display characteristic symptoms, such as decreased area of foliage, alterations in canopy anatomy, and pigment deterioration, which can be identified *via* optical satellite imagery in the VIS-NIR spectrum [49]. The spectral characteristics differ significantly between healthy and afflicted plants, contingent upon the extent of pest damage. Airborne and spaceborne remote sensing have been thoroughly assessed in the mapping of pest and disease destruction. Hyperspectral and multispectral satellite imagery were employed to assess thrips injury in chillies [50] and fall armyworm damage in maize [51]. Several other studies utilizing remote sensing have been documented to evaluate insect infestations in field crops such as rice, wheat, and cotton. Another study [52] mapped the forest tree mortality with Landsat imagery tools with 80 percent accuracy. Another study [15] deployed airborne hyperspectral LiDAR (AHSL) to monitor and assess the forest pests with an overall accuracy of 89.45%. The harm inflicted by insect pests on agricultural crops is widely recognized. The primary facets of remote sensing include prompt assessments of agricultural crop productivity and pest forecasting. The early identification of pest infestations by remote sensing will (i) decrease the expenses associated with foot scouting, (ii) mitigate environmental risks, and (iii) enhance precision agriculture methods by facilitating localized pest management prior to the escalation of the issue. Another study [53] deployed microwave remote sensing techniques for determining the presence of Grasshopper, *Heiroglyphus nigrorepletus* (Bolivar) infestations in sorghum fields. Another study [54] utilized multispectral imagery data and the Soil Adjusted Vegetation Index (SAVI) to assess the *S. frugiperda* infestation, biomass loss, and yield loss in maize.

WORKING PRINCIPLE OF GEOGRAPHIC INFORMATION SYSTEM (GIS)

A Geographic Information System (GIS) comprises a collection of tools and techniques used to manage, analyze, model, depict, and display geo-referenced information to address resource management and planning challenges [55]. GIS technology provides users with a variety of tools and techniques for handling geospatial data, allowing them to collect, store, combine, query, display, and analyze data at different levels of detail [56]. Farmers' access to local resources, livelihood capitals, and necessary infrastructure can be used to understand the geographic context of agriculture. GPS-derived geographic coordinates can be broken down into nested spatial layers within a GIS system. These layers can be processed and analyzed to reveal soil and crop conditions, forecast agricultural trends, track land use changes, monitor pests, conserve biodiversity, and map geographical barriers to agricultural output Fig. (**7**). GIS can also uncover new data for enhancing agricultural sustainability [57].

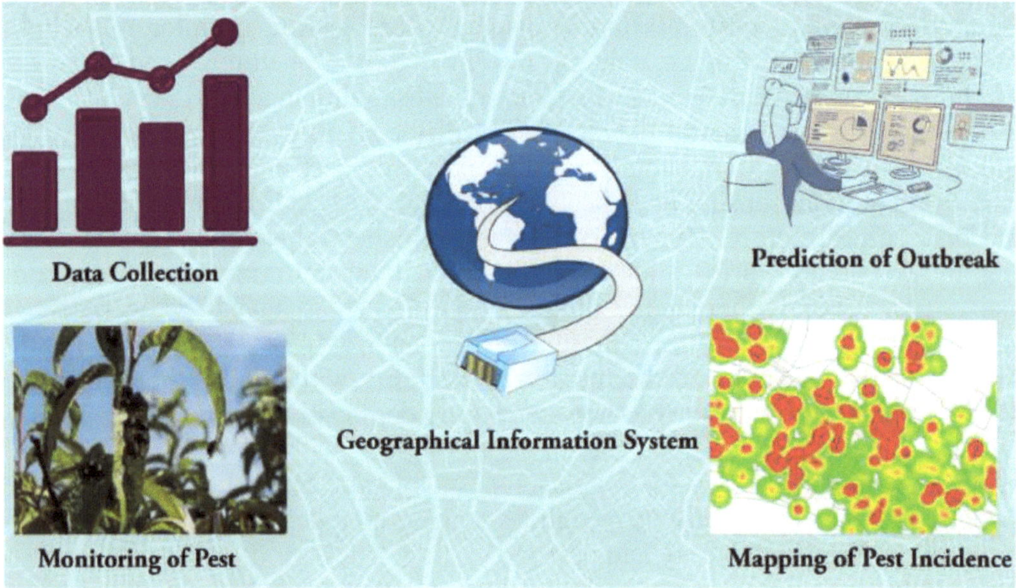

Fig. (7). Applications of GIS in IPM.

New oil palm plantations have had to be established due to the substantial demand for products made from oil palm (biodiesel and restaurant items), particularly in Asian markets. The development of oil palm is a challenging and intricate process, though, because several elements must be considered before a location is selected, such as climate, soil texture, site appropriateness, and potential plant nutrients [58]. Numerous analyses can be carried out in a GIS application to help with that stage, particularly with assessment and decision-making. Researchers in Indonesia have identified the best possible location for oil palm production through high-quality mapping [59]. Before being spatialized and mapped using GIS software, a variety of environmental parameters (such as temperature, humidity, place height, rainfall, oxygen availability, *etc.*) have been gathered on the ground. As a result, the research's output is impressive, and the data can be used for additional study. According to their analysis, GIS showed that both a low gradient slope edge and a gently sloping side are suitable locations for oil palm growing [60].

APPLICATIONS OF GIS IN IPM

In the domain of agriculture, GIS encompasses different application areas, including crop yield forecasting and computation, analysis of soil fertility, cropping patterns, drought condition monitoring, pest and disease surveillance and management, fertilizer and weed management, and precision agriculture. GIS can also assist in implementing agricultural policies. Regulations can be enforced more easily, and the economic effects of policies can be visually represented with GIS [61]. Management and analysis of survey and control data, including information on locust population size, environmental conditions, soil moisture levels, and rainfall, have been conducted using GIS in affected nations [62]. Specifically, GIS is essential in IPM, as it enables spatial analysis, mapping, and decision-making for pest control. GIS integrates RS, environmental data, and field observations to improve pest monitoring, reduce pesticide use, and enhance ecological sustainability (Fig. **7**).

Monitoring of Pest

The most flexible, precise, and easy-to-use data for operational and various other software requirements is GIS data. Furthermore, inexperienced GIS users can easily interpret GIS output maps due to their clear captions and diverse color and pattern groupings [63]. Pest monitoring and mapping using GIS involve collecting spatial data from remote sensing, traps, and field surveys to track pest distribution and predict outbreaks. GIS enables hotspot analysis, risk mapping, and precision pest management, improving early detection and targeted control strategies Fig. (**8**). GIS systems generate different models for agricultural operations by examining historical records or databases in relation to geographical maps. In entomology, these technologies have enormous potential and present numerous novel approaches for researching and controlling insect pests [64]. Control strategies for many important locust species include identifying breeding or outbreak areas and preventing colonies from swarming and migrating to harm farmland and crops. ArcGIS (Esri) is a GIS software employed for spatial modeling, pest forecasting, and integrating remote sensing data. It quantitatively tracks and forecasts the appearance and progression of crop pests, significantly improving accuracy. Remote sensing inputs and GIS technology allow for much more efficient tracking and projection of pest data than was previously feasible [65].

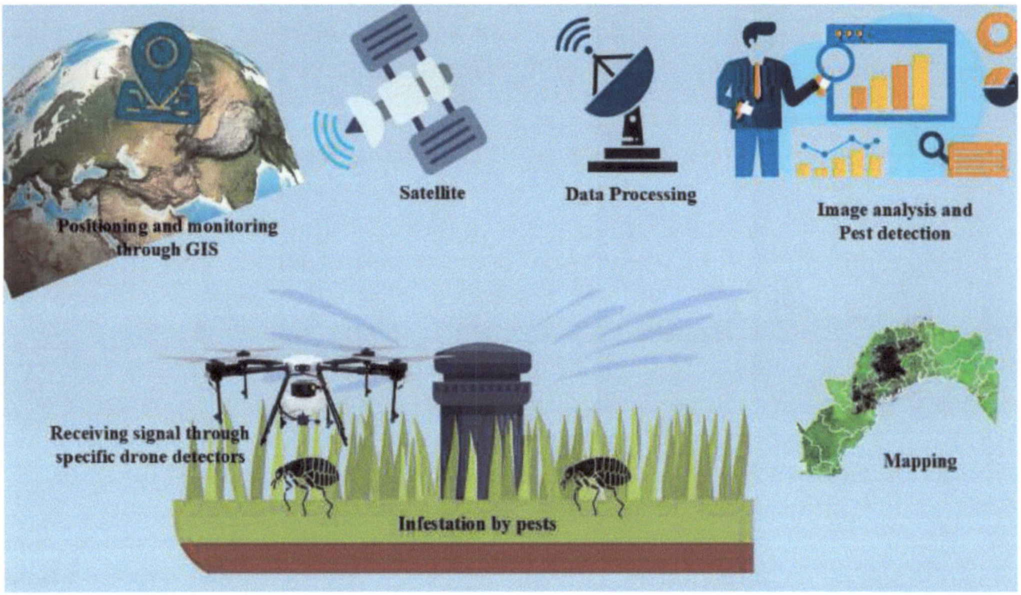

Fig. (8). Pest monitoring and mapping using GIS.

In an experiment in Kashmir, India, a researcher used GIS to map the foliage damage index and track *Pieris brassicae* larvae in cole crops (kale, cabbage, and knol khol). To evaluate the foliage damage caused by the cabbage butterfly *P. brassicae*, various GIS maps were employed to display hotspots. GIS maps are highly suitable for monitoring and developing management plans for cabbage butterflies. As demonstrated in this investigation, insect modelers in agricultural ecosystems can create new avenues for precise pest management strategies using satellite data and geo-referenced mapping to target locations where cabbage butterflies reproduce and cause damage [66]. The number of pests and their natural predators can be estimated through routine, periodic sampling. Programs for IPM can benefit greatly from such routine sampling and monitoring. Models created with GIS technologies can forecast the areas where pests are most common and the likely effect zones, thereby reducing the need for extensive field monitoring. The range of insect spatial correlation was assessed using geostatistics and GIS to determine the optimal sampling distance for pest dispersion and spatial analysis in the study area [67].

Eight distinct pest species were observed in the research area. The species with the highest recorded abundance between April and August 2015–16 were the sugarcane hopper (*Pyrilla perpusilla*), sugarcane woolly aphid (*Ceratovacuna lanigera*), erect-winged blue plant hopper (*Proutista moesta*), whitefly (*Aleurolobus barodensis*), mealybug (*Saccharicoccus sacchari*), early shoot borer (*Chilo infescatellus*), internode borer (*C. sacchariphagus indicus*), and top shoot borer (*Scirpophaga excerptalis*). According to regional distribution, the highest number of *C. sacchariphagus indicus* insects was documented in August in Omalur taluk, followed by Mettur, Attur, Idappadi, Sankagiri, Salem, Gangavalli, Yercaud, and Vazhapadi [68].

Prediction of Pest Outbreaks with Environmental Change

GIS techniques offer instruments for examining spatial trends in insect distribution and abundance. When combined with surveillance data, these technologies can create a forecast model that shows how biotic and abiotic factors affect insect population and dispersion. Using GIS-based tools, habitat features, pest susceptibility, and development and spread models can be constructed [69]. Google Earth Engine (GEE) is software used to analyze satellite imagery for large-scale pest outbreak detection. In developing countries, emerging insect and disease outbreaks may worsen due to extreme occurrences such as extreme temperatures, cold stress, unequal rainfall, floods and droughts, thunderstorms, and other environmental changes and disruptions [70]. Under varying climatic scenarios, researchers forecasted the plausible global occurrence of *Icerya aegyptiaca* and *I. purchasi* [71].

According to a study, the risk of *Bemisia tabaci* in open-field tomato agriculture in selected high-risk areas is projected to decline between 2050 and 2070. The researchers hypothesized that this would occur because rising temperatures will mostly impact the host plants [72]. The availability of food supplies during August and September allows lepidopteran pests to reach their peak due to low temperatures and precipitation, as stated in a previous study [73].

Using GIS, a study [67] generated high-resolution data to examine the effects of abiotic and biotic factors on the widespread distribution of *C. sacchariphagus indicus* and its egg parasitoid, *Trichogramma chilonis*. It was established that rainfall had the greatest influence on the geographical distribution and higher population of *C. sacchariphagus indicus*, whereas temperature and humidity had the least effect.

Mapping of Pest Incidence

It is crucial to track insect migration to implement effective management techniques. QGIS is a cost-effective software tool employed for pest distribution mapping. A study in China tracked Agrotis ipsilon's northward migration, describing how global warming affected the length, timing, and size of its migration, indicating a slow shift in the species' migratory patterns. Predicting pest attacks and directing A. ipsilon control in nearby crops can be achieved through forecasting models or warning systems based on empirically determined population dynamics and migration patterns, particularly for springtime immigration [74]. According to the researcher, these outcomes are significant for predicting and managing various transboundary pests, including *S. frugiperda* [75].

By the 1920s, the boll weevil had spread across cotton-growing regions after first invading Texas cotton in the late 1800s. Eradication attempts began in the 1980s, initially only in Mexico and the southernmost areas of Texas. A study examined the relationship between landscape variables and boll weevil detections using spatial analysis and GIS-based mapping. The study reported more significant boll weevil detections within the Lower Rio Grande Valley (LRGV) in 2018. Mapping products and spatial analysis techniques can facilitate the identification of sites for in-depth research within current eradication operations, like the LRGV, or in areas with increased boll weevil activity, such as regions in South America. These inquiries could serve as a reference for organized comparisons of boll weevil trap placement strategies across landscape characteristics, including vegetation near waterways and rivers like the Rio Grande, which are nested within ongoing eradication efforts in the LRGV [76].

A study [77] mapped the risk zones of Eucalyptus looper, Thyrinteina arnobia, using GIS and fuzzy logic.

APPLICATION OF HYPERSPECTRAL REMOTE SENSING IN IPM

Hyperspectral remote sensing provides high spectral resolution data, capturing hundreds of narrow spectral bands across the electromagnetic spectrum. This makes it a powerful tool in IPM for detecting and monitoring pest-induced stress, optimizing control measures, and minimizing pesticide use.

Early Pest Detection and Stress Monitoring

Hyperspectral sensors detect subtle changes in plant biochemical composition before visible symptoms appear. Specific spectral signatures can indicate pest-induced chlorophyll degradation, water stress, or cell damage. Machine learning models can classify spectral variations to differentiate pest-induced stress from other factors like drought or nutrient deficiency.

Species-Specific Pest Identification

Unlike multispectral sensors, hyperspectral data can identify the unique spectral signatures of different insect species, fungal infections, or plant diseases. For example, it can differentiate between aphid damage and caterpillar damage based on distinct light absorption patterns in affected leaves.

Precision Pesticide Application and Residue Management

Hyperspectral imaging can create prescription maps for site-specific pesticide applications, reducing unnecessary spraying. It also aids in pesticide degradation studies by tracking residue breakdown over time and under different environmental conditions. Additionally, it helps assess pesticide resistance by detecting physiological changes in pest populations after repeated exposures.

Tracking Pest Dynamics & Climate Change Impacts

Hyperspectral UAVs can monitor pest migration patterns and habitat changes in response to climate variations. Time-series hyperspectral data help predict outbreak patterns based on environmental conditions. This approach is also useful in biological control by tracking interactions between pests and their natural enemies.

Post-Harvest Pest Detection

Hyperspectral imaging is used in grain storage and post-harvest pest management to detect insect infestations in stored crops (*e.g.*, weevils in wheat, fruit flies in citrus). It identifies mycotoxins and fungal infections that may develop due to pest activity.

Hyperspectral Sensorsfor Pest Detection

Hyperspectral sensors for pest detection capture detailed spectral information across numerous narrow bands, enabling early identification of plant stress caused by pests. Key Hyperspectral sensors for pest detection are listed in Table **3**.

Table 3. Examples of hyperspectral sensors employed for pest detection.

S. No.	Hyperspectral Sensors	Products	Wavelength	Applications
1.	UAV-Based Hyperspectral Sensors	Headwall Nano-Hyperspec	400–1000 nm (Visible-NIR)	Early plant stress detection from insect feeding damage. Mounted on UAVs for real-time monitoring of crop health.
		HySpex Mjolnir VS-620	400–2500 nm (Visible-SWIR)	Differentiates between pest-induced stress and fungal infections. Detects early-stage pest infestations by analyzing leaf biochemical changes.
		Specim AFX10 & AFX17	AFX10: 400–1000 nm (VNIR) AFX17: 900–1700 nm (SWIR)	Identifies unique spectral fingerprints of insect infestations. Used in precision agriculture UAV applications.
2.	Ground-Based Hyperspectral Sensors	ASD Field Spec 4	350–2500 nm	Identifies changes in leaf pigments, water content, and structural properties caused by pests. Useful in controlled studies for hyperspectral signature mapping.
		Ocean Insight HR Series	400–1700 nm	Detects plant biochemical changes from insect feeding, enabling species-specific pest detection. Can be integrated with portable spectroradiometers for in-field analysis.
3.	Satellite & Airborne Hyperspectral Sensors	PRISMA	400–2500 nm	Large-scale pest surveillance and ecosystem monitoring. Detects regional pest outbreaks linked to climate change
		DESIS	400–1000 nm	Monitors vegetation stress and pest outbreaks in agroecosystems.
4.	HyMap (Airborne Hyperspectral Sensor)	-	400–2500 nm	Provides high-resolution maps of pest damage across landscapes.

APPLICATION OF MULTISPECTRAL AND UAV-BASED (UNMANNED AERIAL VEHICLE) IMAGERY IN IPM

Using multispectral and UAV-based imagery in IPM is an advanced approach that enhances pest detection, monitoring, and precision control. These technologies contribute to IPM as follows:

Early Pest Detection and Monitoring

Multispectral imaging captures data beyond visible light (*e.g.*, near-infrared, red-edge) to detect plant stress before visible symptoms appear. UAVs equipped with multispectral cameras can scan large areas quickly, identifying hotspots of pest activity or disease spread. By analyzing spectral indices like NDVI or PRI (Photochemical Reflectance Index), researchers can detect subtle plant health changes caused by insect feeding, fungal infections, or nutrient deficiencies.

Precision Pesticide Application

UAV-based imaging enables site-specific treatment, reducing excessive pesticide use and minimizing environmental impact. AI and machine learning models can process UAV images to generate prescription maps, allowing variable-rate spraying only where pests are detected. This approach also improves pesticide residue management, which is critical in research on pesticide degradation.

Tracking Pest Movement and Population Dynamics

Multispectral UAVs can map spatial distributions of insect populations, helping researchers understand migration patterns. This aids in targeted biological control, such as deploying natural predators or pheromone traps in specific areas.

Assessing Pesticide Efficacy

UAV imaging can evaluate the effectiveness of pesticide applications by comparing vegetation health before and after treatment. This approach also helps optimize pesticide formulations and supports degradation studies under different climatic conditions.

Climate Change & Insect Behavior Analysis

UAV-based data collection over time helps analyze how climate variability impacts pest infestations. Correlating temperature, humidity, and spectral data improves predictions of pest outbreaks under changing climate conditions.

Large-Scale Pest Outbreak Monitoring

Satellite-based multispectral imagery monitors insect migration patterns and large-scale outbreaks, such as locust swarms. Time-series analysis enables the prediction of pest outbreaks linked to climate change.

Multispectral Sensors for Pest Detection

These sensors capture reflectance data across specific spectral bands (*e.g.*, visible, near-infrared, and shortwave infrared) to identify crop stress and pest-induced damage. Examples of multispectral sensors employed in pest detection are shown in Table **4**.

Table 4. Examples of multispectral sensors for pest detection.

S. No.	Multispectral Sensors	Products	Wavelength	Applications
1.	UAV-Based Multispectral Sensors	MicaSense RedEdge-P and Altum-PT	Blue (475 nm), Green (560 nm), Red (668 nm), Red Edge (717 nm), Near-Infrared (842 nm),	Detects early plant stress from insect feeding, identifies pest hotspots
		Altum-PT	-	Includes a thermal sensor to detect changes in plant temperature due to insect infestation.
		Parrot Sequoia+	Green (550 nm), Red (660 nm), Red Edge (735 nm), Near-Infrared (790 nm)	Identifies early-stage plant stress caused by pests and diseases. Compact, cost-effective, and ideal for small-scale agricultural UAVs.
		Sentera 6X Multispectral	Blue, Green, Red, Red Edge, and NIR	Used in UAVs for precision pest management, enabling targeted pesticide application.
2.	Ground-Based Multispectral Sensors	CI-710 Miniature Spectrometer (CID Bio-Science)	Covers Visible-NIR range	Used for in-field validation of pest-induced plant stress.
		SpectraVista GER 1500	Visible to Near-Infrared	Measures leaf spectral reflectance to detect pest-related stress.
3.	Satellite-Based Multispectral Sensors	Sentinel-2 (ESA)	13 bands (including Red Edge, NIR, and SWIR)	Detects vegetation stress and pest outbreaks at a regional scale
		Landsat 8 & 9 (NASA/USGS)	Visible, NIR, SWIR	Identifies long-term pest-related vegetation damage.
		MODIS (Terra & Aqua satellites, NASA)	36 spectral bands	Monitors large-scale pest infestations (*e.g.*, locust swarms, forest pest outbreaks).

Different remote sensing sensors vary in resolution, spectral range, and data acquisition methods, impacting their effectiveness in pest monitoring (Table 5). Multispectral and hyperspectral sensors detect crop stress, thermal sensors identify temperature variations, and LiDAR/Radar analyze structural changes, aiding precise pest detection and management.

Table 5. Comparison of remote sensing sensors for pest monitoring.

S. No.	Feature	Hyperspectral Sensors	Multispectral Sensors
1.	Spectral Resolution	High (hundreds of narrow bands)	Moderate (5–20 broad bands)
2.	Spatial Resolution	Typically high	Varies (depends on platform)
3.	Data Volume	Very large	Moderate
4.	Processing Complexity	High (requires advanced algorithms)	Moderate (simpler analysis)
5.	Cost	Expensive	More cost-effective
6.	Application Scope	Precise pest identification, species differentiation	General pest monitoring, vegetation stress detection
7.	Common Platforms	UAVs, airborne sensors, research satellites	Satellites (Sentinel-2, Landsat-8), UAVs

Hyperspectral remote sensing is highly accurate but requires significant data processing and cost investment. Multispectral remote sensing is more practical for large-scale monitoring but may lack specificity for certain pest species. Combining both techniques can improve pest monitoring efficiency and support precision agriculture strategies.

CONCLUSION

It is evident that Remote Sensing (RS) and Geographic Information Systems (GIS) can significantly enhance numerous ongoing field monitoring initiatives, which are often costly, time-consuming, labor-intensive, and prone to human error. Research has consistently shown that RS and GIS technologies provide accurate and timely data, enabling informed decision-making in crop protection and demonstrating considerable potential for pest management applications. Precision agriculture relies heavily on the integration of RS, GIS, and Global Positioning System (GPS) to implement site-specific management strategies tailored to heterogeneous field conditions. The use of geospatial technologies in agriculture—particularly within Integrated Pest Management (IPM) frameworks and for the variable application of pesticides and fertilizers—is anticipated to expand further in the future.

While RS and GIS have advanced the development of crop management strategies, their widespread application remains limited by several constraints. Firstly, high-resolution spatial imagery is often not readily available for all rural or remote regions, and the utilization of hyperspectral imaging—which captures data in numerous narrow spectral bands—requires specialized knowledge and computational resources. Secondly, there is a lack of technical expertise in remote sensing and spatial data analysis among farmers, agronomists, and agricultural advisors, which hinders effective implementation.

Moreover, the effectiveness of these technologies strongly depends on timely data acquisition, including rapid mapping, near real-time image capture, and swift dissemination of actionable insights. Delays or inefficiencies in any of these stages can reduce the practical value of RS and GIS outputs for on-ground pest control measures.

Despite these challenges, RS and GIS continue to offer valuable insights within IPM strategies, enabling a deeper understanding of the spatial dynamics of both abiotic and biotic stressors affecting crops. Hyperspectral imaging, in particular, holds promise for early pest stress detection by identifying subtle physiological changes in plant health before they are visually detectable, thus supporting preemptive action.

Future research should emphasize the integration of RS and GIS with Artificial Intelligence (AI) and machine learning approaches to improve the precision, automation, and scalability of pest detection, prediction, and spatial mapping. Such advancements are essential for achieving sustainable crop protection outcomes under IPM frameworks and enhancing resilience in agricultural systems.

REFERENCES

[1] FAO's Plant Production and Protection Division. 2022. [http://dx.doi.org/10.4060/cc2447en]

[2] Nilsson H. Remote sensing and image analysis in plant pathology. Annu Rev Phytopathol 1995; 33(1): 489-528. [http://dx.doi.org/10.1146/annurev.py.33.090195.002421] [PMID: 18999971]

[3] Pedersen S M, Lind K M. Precision agriculture – From mapping to site-specific application. Precision Agriculture. 2017; pp. 1-20. [http://dx.doi.org/10.1007/978-3-319-68715-5_1]

[4] Moral García FJ. Analysis of the spatio-temporal distribution of Helicoverpa armigera Hb. in a tomato field using a stochastic approach. Biosyst Eng 2006; 93(3): 253-9. [http://dx.doi.org/10.1016/j.biosystemseng.2005.12.011]

[5] McKinion JM, Jenkins JN, Willers JL, Zumanis A. Spatially variable insecticide applications for early season control of cotton insect pests. Comput Electron Agric 2009; 67(1-2): 71-9. [http://dx.doi.org/10.1016/j.compag.2009.03.004]

[6] Nansen C, Elliott N. Remote sensing and reflectance profiling in entomology. Annu Rev Entomol 2016.
[http://dx.doi.org/10.1146/annurev-ento-010715-023834]

[7] Hauff, P.L. 2005: Applied reflectance spectroscopy.... - Google Scholar 2024. Available from: https://scholar.google.com/scholar?hl=en&as_sdt=0%2C5&q=Hauff%2C+P.L.+2005%3A+Applied+reflectance+spectroscopy.+Spectral+International+Incorporated%2C+technical+document+to+accompany+spectral+libraries+and+identification+softwares.+&btnG=

[8] Prasad Y G, Prabhakar M. Pest monitoring and forecasting. Integrated Pest Management: Principles and practice. CABI Publishing 2012; pp. 41-57.
[http://dx.doi.org/10.1079/9781845938086.0041]

[9] Wan Q, Ouyang A, Liu Y, Xiong Z, Li X, Li L. Detection of infestation by striped stem-borer (Chilo suppressalis) in rice based on hyperspectral imaging. J Food Process Eng 2022; 45(11): e14142.
[http://dx.doi.org/10.1111/jfpe.14142]

[10] Nurul Afiah Mohd Johari S, Khairunniza-Bejo S, Rashid Mohamed Shariff A, Azuan Husin N, Mazmira Mohd Basri M, Kamarudin N. Identification of bagworm (Metisa plana) instar stages using hyperspectral imaging and machine learning techniques. Comput Electron Agric 2022; 194: 106739.
[http://dx.doi.org/10.1016/j.compag.2022.106739]

[11] Ekramirad N, Khaled AY, Parrish CA, Donohue KD, Villanueva RT, Adedeji AA. Development of pattern recognition and classification models for the detection of vibro-acoustic emissions from codling moth infested apples. Postharvest Biol Technol 2021; 181: 111633.
[http://dx.doi.org/10.1016/j.postharvbio.2021.111633]

[12] Ferrari V, Calvini R, Boom B, *et al.* Evaluation of the potential of near infrared hyperspectral imaging for monitoring the invasive brown marmorated stink bug. Chemom Intell Lab Syst 2023; 234: 104751.
[http://dx.doi.org/10.1016/j.chemolab.2023.104751]

[13] Yang L, Huang X, Zhou D, *et al.* Sentinel-2A image reflectance simulation method for estimating the chlorophyll content of larch needles with pest damage. Forests 2024; 15(11): 1901.
[http://dx.doi.org/10.3390/f15111901]

[14] Ercan BS, Maden B, Kara S, *et al.* A comparative study of satellite image resolutions for detecting pest damage in sunflower fields.International Archives of the Photogrammetry, Remote Sensing and Spatial Information Sciences - ISPRS Archives. International Society for Photogrammetry and Remote Sensing 2024; pp. 133-9.
[http://dx.doi.org/10.5194/isprs-archives-XLVIII-4-W9-2024-133-2024]

[15] Zhao X, Qi J, Xu H, *et al.* Evaluating the potential of airborne hyperspectral LiDAR for assessing forest insects and diseases with 3D Radiative Transfer Modeling. Remote Sens Environ 2023; 297: 113759.
[http://dx.doi.org/10.1016/j.rse.2023.113759]

[16] Ribeiro AV, Lacerda LN, Windmuller-Campione MA, *et al.* Economic-threshold-based classification of soybean aphid, Aphis glycines, infestations in commercial soybean fields using Sentinel-2 satellite data. Crop Prot 2024; 177: 106557.
[http://dx.doi.org/10.1016/j.cropro.2023.106557]

[17] Dilixiati Y, Zhou J, Xu Y, Fan X, Yalikun S. Cotton pest monitoring based on Logistic algorithm and remote sensing image. Hua Nan Nong Ye Da Xue Xue Bao 2022; 43(2): 87-95.
[http://dx.doi.org/10.7671/J.ISSN.1001-411X.202106004]

[18] Feng S, Jiang S, Huang X, *et al.* Detection of rice leaf folder in paddy fields based on unmanned aerial vehicle-based hyperspectral images. Agronomy (Basel) 2024; 14(11): 2660.
[http://dx.doi.org/10.3390/agronomy14112660]

[19] Panopoulou C, Antonopoulos A, Arapostathi E, Stamouli M, Katsileros A, Tsagkarakis A. Using multispectral data from UAS in machine learning to detect infestation by xylotrechus chinensis

(chevrolat) (coleoptera: cerambycidae) in mulberries. Agronomy (Basel) 2024; 14(9): 2061. [http://dx.doi.org/10.3390/agronomy14092061]

[20] Xia L, Zhang R, Chen L, Li L, Yi T, Chen M. Monitoring the leaf damage by the rice leafroller with deep learning and ultra-light UAV. Pest Manag Sci 2024; 80(12): 6620-33. [http://dx.doi.org/10.1002/ps.8401] [PMID: 39264132]

[21] Garcia-Ruiz F, Sankaran S, Maja JM, Lee WS, Rasmussen J, Ehsani R. Comparison of two aerial imaging platforms for identification of Huanglongbing-infected citrus trees. Comput Electron Agric 2013; 91: 106-15. [http://dx.doi.org/10.1016/j.compag.2012.12.002]

[22] Prabhakar M, Prasad YG, Thirupathi M, Sreedevi G, Dharajothi B, Venkateswarlu B. Use of ground based hyperspectral remote sensing for detection of stress in cotton caused by leafhopper (Hemiptera: Cicadellidae). Comput Electron Agric 2011; 79(2): 189-98. [http://dx.doi.org/10.1016/j.compag.2011.09.012]

[23] Oumar Z, Mutanga O. Using WorldView-2 bands and indices to predict bronze bug (*Thaumastocoris peregrinus*) damage in plantation forests. Int J Remote Sens 2013; 34(6): 2236-49. [http://dx.doi.org/10.1080/01431161.2012.743694]

[24] Board JE, Maka V, Price R, Knight D, Baur ME. Development of vegetation indices for identifying insect infestations in soybean. Agron J 2007; 99(3): 650-6. [http://dx.doi.org/10.2134/agronj2006.0155]

[25] Genc H, Genc L, Turhan H, Smith SE, Nation JL. Vegetation indices as indicators of damage by the sunn pest (Hemiptera: Scutelleridae) to field grown wheat. Afr J Biotechnol 2008; 7(2): 173-80. Available from: http://www.academicjournals.org/AJB

[26] Xu HR, Ying YB, Fu XP, Zhu SP. Near-infrared spectroscopy in detecting leaf miner damage on tomato leaf. Biosyst Eng 2007; 96(4): 447-54. [http://dx.doi.org/10.1016/j.biosystemseng.2007.01.008]

[27] Luo J, Huang W, Zhao J, Zhang J, Zhao C, Ma R. Detecting aphid density of winter wheat leaf using hyperspectral measurements. IEEE J Sel Top Appl Earth Obs Remote Sens 2013; 6(2): 690-8. [http://dx.doi.org/10.1109/JSTARS.2013.2248345]

[28] Kumar J, Vashisth A, Sehgal VK. Identification of aphid infestation in mustard by hyperspectral remote sensing 2010. Available from: http://www.agrophysics.in

[29] Brydegaard M, Svanberg S. Photonic monitoring of atmospheric and aquatic fauna. Laser Photonics Rev 2018. [http://dx.doi.org/10.1002/lpor.201800135]

[30] Bieganowski A, Dammer KH, Siedliska A, *et al.* Sensor-based outdoor monitoring of insects in arable crops for their precise control. Pest Manag Sci 2021; 77(3): 1109-1114. [http://dx.doi.org/10.1002/ps.6098]

[31] Noskov A, Bendix J, Friess N. A review of insect monitoring approaches with special reference to radar techniques. Sensors 2021; 20;21(4): 1474. [http://dx.doi.org/10.3390/s21041474]

[32] van Klink R, August T, Bas Y, *et al.* Emerging technologies revolutionise insect ecology and monitoring. Trends Ecol Evol 2022; 37(10): 872-882. [http://dx.doi.org/10.1016/j.tree.2022.06.001]

[33] Silva DF, Souza VMA, Ellis DPW, Keogh EJ, Batista GEAPA. Exploring low cost laser sensors to identify flying insect species. J Intell Robot Syst 2015; 80(S1): 313-30. [http://dx.doi.org/10.1007/s10846-014-0168-9]

[34] Tauc MJ, Fristrup KM, Repasky KS, Shaw JA. Field demonstration of a wing-beat modulation lidar for the 3D mapping of flying insects. OSA Continuum 2019; 2(2): 332. [http://dx.doi.org/10.1364/OSAC.2.000332]

[35] Brydegaard M, Jansson S, Malmqvist E, *et al.* Lidar reveals activity anomaly of malaria vectors during pan-African eclipse Sci Adv 2020; 6(20): eaay5487. Available from: https://www.science.org [http://dx.doi.org/10.1126/sciadv.aay5487]

[36] Manefjord H, Muller L, Li M, *et al.* 3D-printed fluorescence hyperspectral lidar for monitoring tagged insects. IEEE J Sel Top Quantum Electron 2022; 28(5): 1-9. [http://dx.doi.org/10.1109/JSTQE.2022.3162417]

[37] Meng R, Dennison PE, Zhao F, *et al.* Mapping canopy defoliation by herbivorous insects at the individual tree level using bi-temporal airborne imaging spectroscopy and LiDAR measurements. Remote Sens Environ 2018; 215: 170-83. [http://dx.doi.org/10.1016/j.rse.2018.06.008]

[38] Wang Y, Zhao C, Dong D, Wang K. Real-time monitoring of insects based on laser remote sensing. Ecol Indic 2023. [http://dx.doi.org/10.1016/j.ecolind.2023.110302]

[39] Gregori GS, de Souza Loureiro E, Amorim Pessoa LG, *et al.* Machine learning in the hyperspectral classification of glycaspis brimblecombei (hemiptera psyllidae) attack severity in eucalyptus. Remote Sens (Basel) 2023; 15(24): 5657. [http://dx.doi.org/10.3390/rs15245657]

[40] Fernández-Carrillo Á, Franco-Nieto A, Yagüe-Ballester MJ, Gómez-Giménez M. Predictive model for bark beetle outbreaks in european forests. Forests 2024; 15(7): 1114. [http://dx.doi.org/10.3390/f15071114]

[41] Östersund M, Honkavaara E, Oliveira RA, *et al.* Exploring forest changes in an Ips typographus L. outbreak area: insights from multi-temporal multispectral UAS remote sensing. Eur J For Res 2024; 143(6): 1871-92. [http://dx.doi.org/10.1007/s10342-024-01734-5]

[42] Nguyen D, Tan A, Lee R, Lim WF, Hui TF, Suhaimi F. Early detection of infestation by mustard aphid, vegetable thrips and two-spotted spider mite in bok choy with deep neural network (DNN) classification model using hyperspectral imaging data. Comput Electron Agric 2024; 220: 108892. [http://dx.doi.org/10.1016/j.compag.2024.108892]

[43] Kovalev AV, Tsikalova PE. Predictors of insect damage to forest stands according to satellite data using the siberian silkmoth dendrolimis sibiricus tschetv as an example. Russ J Ecol 2023; 54(6): 602-10. [http://dx.doi.org/10.1134/S1067413623070081]

[44] Kovalev A, Soukhovolsky V, Tarasova O, Akhanaev Y, Martemyanov V. Remote sensing indicators of spongy moth (lymantria dispar L.) damage to birch stands in western siberia. Forests 2023; 14(12): 2308. [http://dx.doi.org/10.3390/f14122308]

[45] Bozzini A, Brugnaro S, Morgante G, *et al.* Drone-based early detection of bark beetle infested spruce trees differs in endemic and epidemic populations. Frontiers in Forests and Global Change 2024; 7: 1385687. [http://dx.doi.org/10.3389/ffgc.2024.1385687]

[46] Campbell MJ, Williams JP, Berryman EM. Using remote sensing and climate data to map the extent and severity of balsam woolly adelgid infestation in northern utah, USA. Forests 2023; 14(7): 1357. [http://dx.doi.org/10.3390/f14071357]

[47] Bozzini A, Francini S, Chirici G, Battisti A, Faccoli M. Spruce bark beetle outbreak prediction through automatic classification of sentinel-2 imagery. Forests 2023; 14(6): 1116. [http://dx.doi.org/10.3390/f14061116]

[48] Park YL, Naharki K, Karimzadeh R, Seo BY, Lee GS. Rapid assessment of insect pest outbreak using drones: a case study with *Spodoptera exigua* (Hübner) (lepidoptera: noctuidae) in soybean fields.

Insects 2023; 14(6): 555.
[http://dx.doi.org/10.3390/insects14060555] [PMID: 37367371]

[49] Prabhakar M, Prasad YG, Vennila S, *et al.* Hyperspectral indices for assessing damage by the solenopsis mealybug (Hemiptera: Pseudococcidae) in cotton. Comput Electron Agric 2013; 97: 61-70. [http://dx.doi.org/10.1016/j.compag.2013.07.004]

[50] Mathyam P, Merugu T, Kumar G, *et al.* Damage assessment of chilli thrips using high resolution multispectral satellite data. J Agrometerol 2019; 21(4).

[51] Buchaillot M, Cairns J, Hamadziripi E, *et al.* Multi-scale remote sensing for fall armyworm monitoring and early warning systems International Geoscience and Remote Sensing Symposium (IGARSS). 4886-9.
[http://dx.doi.org/10.1109/IGARSS39084.2020.9323181]

[52] Bright BC, Hudak AT, Meddens AJH, Egan JM, Jorgensen CL. Mapping multiple insect outbreaks across large regions annually using landsat time series data. Remote Sens (Basel) 2020; 12(10): 1655. [http://dx.doi.org/10.3390/rs12101655]

[53] Singh D, Sao R, Singh KP. A remote sensing assessment of pest infestation on sorghum. Adv Space Res 2007; 39(1): 155-63.
[http://dx.doi.org/10.1016/j.asr.2006.02.025]

[54] Mathyam P, Kodigal A G, Nakka RK, *et al.* Assessment of yield loss due to fall armyworm in maize using high-resolution multispectral spaceborne remote sensing. Int J Remote Sens 2024; 45(18): 6744-58.
[http://dx.doi.org/10.1080/01431161.2024.2394233]

[55] Rano SH, Afroz M, Rahman MM. Application of GIS on monitoring agricultural insect pests: a review. Reviews In Food and Agriculture 2022; 3(1): 19-23.
[http://dx.doi.org/10.26480/rfna.01.2022.19.23]

[56] Raihan A. A systematic review of Geographic Information Systems (GIS) in agriculture for evidence-based decision making and sustainability. Global Sustainability Research 2024; 3(1): 1-24. [http://dx.doi.org/10.56556/gssr.v3i1.636]

[57] Mathenge M, Sonneveld B G J S, Broerse J E W. Application of GIS in agriculture in promoting evidence-informed decision making for improving agriculture sustainability: a systematic review. Sustainability 2022.
[http://dx.doi.org/10.3390/su14169974]

[58] Jaroenkietkajorn U, Gheewala SH. Land suitability assessment for oil palm plantations in Thailand. Environ Dev Sustain 2021. Available from: https://www.sciencedirect.com/science/article/pii/S235255092100230X

[59] Harahap FS, Walida H, Mustamu NE, *et al.* Evaluation of non forest area land characteristic for citrus plant (Citrus sp). IOP Conf Ser Earth Environ Sci 2020; 454(1): 012139.
[http://dx.doi.org/10.1088/1755-1315/454/1/012139]

[60] Aikal Baharim MS, Adnan NA, Mohd FA, Seman IA, Izzuddin MA, Aziz NA. A Review: Progression of Remote Sensing (RS) and Geographical Information System (GIS) Applications in Oil Palm Management and Sustainability IOP Conference Series: Earth and Environmental Science. 1051(1): 012027.
[http://dx.doi.org/10.1088/1755-1315/1051/1/012027]

[61] Boda P, Fusi F, Miranda F, *et al.* Environmental justice through community-policy participatory partnerships. J Environ Prot 2023. Available from: https://www.scirp.org/journal/paperinformation?paperid=126993

[62] Klein I, Oppelt N, Kuenzer C. Application of remote sensing data for locust research and management—a review. Insects 2021.
[http://dx.doi.org/10.3390/insects12030233]

[63] Paramasivam C R. Merits and demerits of GIS and geostatistical techniques. GIS and Geostatistical Techniques for Groundwater Science. 2019. Available from: https://www.researchgate.net

[64] Dong Y, Xu F, Liu L, *et al.* Monitoring and forecasting for disease and pest in crop based on WebGIS system. 2019 8th Int Conf Agro-Geoinformatics (Agro-Geoinformatics). Available from: https://ieeexplore.ieee.org

[65] Hussain B, War A, Pfeiffer D. Mapping foliage damage index and monitoring of Pieris brassicae by using GIS-GPS technology in cole crops 2018. Available from: https://drive.google.com/file/d/144p0K3Gxxq6b585Rpu8M533d9C8p900G/view

[66] Latini A, Foxi C, Borfecchia F, *et al.* Tacking the vector of Xylella fastidiosa: geo-statistical analysis of long-term field observations on host plants influencing the distribution of Phylaenus spumarius nymphs. Environ Sci Pollut Res Int 2019; 26(7): 6503-16. [http://dx.doi.org/10.1007/s11356-018-3870-5] [PMID: 30627995]

[67] Kokila R, Balasubramanian B, Meenambigai K, *et al.* A GIS-based tool for the analysis of the distribution and abundance of Chilo sacchariphagus indicus under the influence of biotic and abiotic factors. Environmental Technology & Innovation 2021; 21: 101357. [http://dx.doi.org/10.1016/j.eti.2021.101357]

[68] Rani D, Venkatesh M. Remote sensing as pest forecasting model in agriculture. Int J Curr Microbiol Appl Sci 2018. Available from: https://www.academia.edu/download/112877606/D._20Sudha_20Rani__20et_20al.pdf

[69] Anwer A, Singh G. Geo-spatial technology for plant disease and insect pest management. Bull Environ Pharmacol Life Sci 2019. Available from: https://www.researchgate.net/profile/Md-Anwer/publication/342243912_Geo-spatial_Technology_for_Plant_Disease_and_Insect_Pest_Management/links/5eea472f92851ce9e7ec495f/Geo-spatial-Technology-for-Plant-Disease-and-Insect-Pest-Management.pdf

[70] Liu C, Zhai Z, Zhang R, Bai J, Zhang M. Field pest monitoring and forecasting system for pest control. Front Plant Sci 2022; 13: 990965. [http://dx.doi.org/10.3389/fpls.2022.990965] [PMID: 36105712]

[71] Jiufeng W, Li X, Lu Y, Zhao L, Zhang H, Zhao Q. Modeling the potential global distribution of phenacoccus madeirensis green under various climate change scenarios. Forests 2019. Available from: https://www.mdpi.com/1999-4907/10/9/773 [http://dx.doi.org/10.3390/f10090773]

[72] Ramos RS, Kumar L, Shabani F, Picanço MC. Mapping global risk levels of Bemisia tabaci in areas of suitability for open field tomato cultivation under current and future climates. PLoS One 2018; 13(6): e0198925. [http://dx.doi.org/10.1371/journal.pone.0198925] [PMID: 29902221]

[73] Machekano H, Mvumi BM, Nyamukondiwa C. Loss of coevolved basal and plastic responses to temperature may underlie trophic level host-parasitoid interactions under global change. Biol Control 2018; 118: 44-54. [http://dx.doi.org/10.1016/j.biocontrol.2017.12.005]

[74] Zeng J, Liu Y, Zhang H, *et al.* Global warming modifies long-distance migration of an agricultural insect pest. J Pest Sci 2020; 93(2): 569-81. [http://dx.doi.org/10.1007/s10340-019-01187-5]

[75] Pretty J, Benton T G, Bharucha Z P, *et al.* Global assessment of agricultural system redesign for sustainable intensification. Nat Sustain 2018; 1(8): 441-6. Available from: https://www.nature.com/articles/s41893-018-0114-0 [http://dx.doi.org/10.1038/s41893-018-0114-0]

[76] Brewer M J, Deleon L, Esquivel I L, Morisette J. Geographic Information System (GIS)-based mapping and spatial analyses applied to risk assessment and resource allocation for boll weevil

(coleoptera: curculionidae) detection. Ann Entomol Soc Am 2020; 113(2): 71-8.
[http://dx.doi.org/10.1093/aesa/saz048]

[77] Medauar CC, de Assis Silva S, Carvalho LCC, *et al.* Zoning the occurrence of *Thyrinteina arnobia* in eucalypts and its relationship with the spectral behaviour of canopies and soil attributes. South For 2024; 86(1): 53-64.
[http://dx.doi.org/10.2989/20702620.2023.2291365]

CHAPTER 5

A Smart IOT-Based Framework for Predictive Crop Health Monitoring and Precision Farming

Hashmat Fida[1,*], **Jaspreet Kaur**[2], **Binod Kumar Mishra**[2] and **Vinod Kumar**[2]

[1] *School of Computer Science and Engineering, Presidency University, Bangaluru, India*

[2] *Department of Computer Science and Engineering, Chandigarh University, Mohali, Punjab, India*

Abstract: This chapter focuses on a novel IoT-based framework designed to help improve precision farming by closely monitoring soil and crop health. The system aims to reduce physiological disorders in crops through real-time data gathering, analytical machine learning, and automated alerts. Continuous data gathering regarding the soil conditions and the crop health parameters is carried out through the network of field sensors, which are then processed *via* a centralized system using advanced algorithms. Insights derived from the framework are sent to farmers through an easy interface that empowers farmers to make data-based decisions and interventions in time. Connecting this with already established farm management systems enables integrated precision agriculture. This encompasses improving resource efficiency, preventing crop diseases, boosting crop yield, lowering costs, and enhancing sustainable farming. This research is a benchmark in agricultural technology that could transform crop management practices and usher in enhanced productivity and sustainability on the farm. The system's prediction and preventive measures of possible occasions, enabling a farmer to act before they occur, will revolutionize modern farming ways around sustainable food production.

Keywords: Application programming interface, Crop health, IoT, Precision agriculture, Soil moisture, XG-Boost.

INTRODUCTION

Agriculture is one of the oldest and most important of all industries, and it is facing unprecedented challenges posed by rapid population growth, environmental pressures, and increasing food production demand. Traditionally, farming had been dependent on human experience and intuition, complemented by periodic manual inspections in the farming field. Still, farming is promptly transforming into a more scientific, data- and tech-based industry, in which

* **Corresponding author Hashmat Fida**: School of Computer Science and Engineering, Presidency University, Bangaluru, India; E-mail: hashmatfida@gmail.com

farmers continue to apply already-established knowledge and operational practices in managing their fields. The integration of smart technologies into the farming system has transformed the way farmers have historically managed their fields. One of the most promising transformational technologies is the Internet of Things (IoT), which is changing the way that precision agriculture is being implemented and practiced. The present research provides an IoT-driven precision agriculture framework in the form of an advanced technology that monitors based on the most complete soil and crop health indicators to proactively manage physiological stress that results in crop disorders.

The research is motivated by the increased need for farmers to register, track, and respond to soil and crop real-time health indicators to allow for data-based responses to achieve effective resource optimization and maximize crop yield. Using emerging IoT technologies, the system retrieves, processes, and analyzes the data collected from a variety of sensors within the field. This continuous flow of data provides farmers with real-time information on crop health, environmental status, and resource needs. The advancement emphasizes a need to mitigate the space between conventional traditional farming agricultural practices and future farming as a smart agriculture filled with technology, strongly rooted in agronomic knowledge, promoting efficiency, sustainability, and productivity.

The study integrates the principle of remote sensing using IoT-ground sensors, drone multispectral photography, and likely satellite integration. In comparison with traditional remote sensing methods utilizing the majority of information from satellites, this chapter is focused on obtaining high-accuracy real-time information using UAVs and sensor systems deployed on site to have accurate precision farming, accompanied by prompt detection of disease and predictive capabilities.

Precision Agriculture and its Importance

Precision agriculture is a farming management concept that relies on deliberate observation, measurement, and response to inter- and intra-field variability in crop growth. Its goal is to dial in the returns on inputs and irrigate sparingly so that more water can be preserved. To achieve this, precision agriculture considers the fact that no two parts of a field are the same. Soil fertility, moisture, and a dozen or so other aspects can change drastically within a single farm. By delivering the same amount of water, fertilizers, or pesticides throughout the field, a farmer might either not give enough to the parts that need it or give too much to others, potentially polluting the environment.

With modern farming growing increasingly complex with factors like climate change, soil degradation, water scarcity, and worms causing crop havoc, there is a need for more sophisticated ways of evaluating the conditions. The conventional method of assessing soil and crop vitality – visually examining and laboratory testing the soil – consumes time, and much like checking a thermometer, the true condition of soil and crop may have already changed over time. Farmers are also frequently compelled to base their assumptions on their historic experiences, rules of thumb, and periodic tests, which can be too late or too early with the changing seasons.

This is where IoT comes into the picture. With IoT, an interconnected system of devices is able to talk to each other and exchange data. Smart sensors that assess temperature, acidity, and fertility could help farmers see in real-time about the moisture levels, when disease is appearing, or before the plant starts wilting. Due to the ability to capture data at a granular level, IoT can give a detailed picture of a farm that allows for informed decisions.

Remote sensing is important in precision agriculture since it helps farmers observe crop health, soil status, and the environment at various scales. Airborne drones with spectral sensing, which provide real-time measurements of plant health, are used in this study to combine remote sensing. As a high-resolution remote sensing system at the farm scale, IoT-based ground sensors also continuously consider significant agronomic aspects. In precision agriculture, several technologies work in tandem to facilitate data-driven decision-making.

The Role of IoT in Precision Agriculture

IoT technologies have fundamentally transformed the quality of precision agriculture with real-time monitoring of farm conditions. An IoT-based system can monitor, capture, and analyze data across various parameters, such as soil moisture, temperature, humidity, light exposure, nutrients, *etc.* Cloud computing and data science analytics are then utilized to derive recommendations for farmers based on the data. The data made available from an IoT system is vital to assist farmers in early decision-making regarding crop health, which affects early intervention in less than two to three days.

The proposed IoT ontology for precision agriculture is an IoT implementation that focuses on education that is precise for all aspects of soil health and crop health, providing farmers with continual feedback so they can modify farming practices in this critical time of crop development. For instance, when the soil sensors alert farmers that the soil moisture level is declining, the farmer can bear with the notification and irrigate their plot long before experiencing a soil moisture deficit that might stress crop water levels as a result of prolonged dry soil conditions. Similarly, when soil nitrogen levels show there is a deviation below the optimal level, the system may identify what level of nutrients should be fertilized based on the values that are stored in the application from prior periods.

Prior to this, the ongoing data that will be generated from all the IoT sensors, farmers had little understanding or information in real-time regarding their crop health. Farmers can now know in real-time the health of their crop without waiting, and can predict when center pivot irrigation is actively engaged. In contrast, each disorder involves physiological issues that often arise from imbalances in water, nutrients, and/or environmental stress; both water and nutrient deficits can have significant negative effects on crop production.

IoT technologies serve as an excellent ground-based remote sensing system by offering real-time, continuous farm condition monitoring. Traditional manual field inspections are no longer necessary because of the system's deployment of an array of field sensors that measure temperature, fertilizer levels, soil moisture, and other environmental factors. Additionally, the monitoring process is improved by aerial drone footage, which offers multispectral and hyperspectral data for stress analysis and early illness diagnosis.

Comprehensive Soil and Crop Health Monitoring

Soil health is essential to the success of any agricultural operation. Healthy soil not only sustains plant growth, but additionally increases the water holding capacity, improves nutrient availability, and contributes to pest and disease resistance. The philosophy that soil health is complex means that monitoring soil health involves measurement of a number of variables, including, but not limited to, soil pH, moisture content, nutrient availability, and organic matter. The collection of soil samples and the periodical submission of these samples to a laboratory for testing and analysis provide a single snapshot in time and undoubtedly do not address the dynamic variables changing daily and even momentary.

This research addresses this limitation with an apparent IoT-format system that uses a network of soil sensors that observe soil parameters in real-time. Each soil sensor is located in different places in the field, monitoring spatially variable soil moisture levels, temperature, pH, and nutrient levels. The sensors collect data, which is processed and analyzed by the system algorithms to provide real-time information regarding soil health to the farmer.

Additionally, the crop health monitoring uses ground-based sensors and aerial drone vehicles with onboard cameras and spectral imaging. While the drone vehicles patrol the field site, they capture images and other data regarding the characteristics of plant health, leaf color, and vegetative vigor. A typical camera can identify early signs of disease, pest infestation, or nutrient deficiency from spectral imaging that reassures plant variability. For example, leaf color values can measure and identify chlorosis, which is a syndrome or condition associated with nutrient deficiency for essential nutrients like nitrogen or micronutrients like iron. Alerts could be sent to the farmer directly from the IoT system to take action before the disease or deficiency significantly impacts the crop health.

In addition to ground-based IoT sensors, the research incorporates aerial drone-based remote sensing for crop health monitoring. Multispectral and hyperspectral cameras mounted on drones take high-resolution images of plant leaves, which are processed through AI models to identify initial symptoms of nutrient deficiencies, pests, and diseases. With a combination of aerial and ground-based remote sensing, the system adopts a multi-layered strategy towards precision agriculture. Key recommendations for the usage of advanced technologies in smart agriculture can:

i. Combine ground IoT sensors (pH, moisture) with aerial hyperspectral imaging for holistic monitoring.
ii. Use AI (*e.g.*, CNNs for disease detection, XGBoost for soil prediction) to prioritize actionable alerts.

Preemptive Management of Physiological Disorders

Physiological disorders in crops can result in a loss of yield and/or quality. They are often the result of unevenness or imbalance in environmental conditions, water supply, or nutrient availability. The problem is that they are difficult to identify and remediate in the early stages. Once a crop starts to show signs of wilting, yellow leaves, or stunted growth, it is usually too late to correct the problem.

The IoT-enabled system has a significant advantage of monitoring crops continuously, which ultimately supports a management approach to physiological problems. For example, the IoT-enabled system can evaluate data from soil sensors and crop sensors in real time to evaluate whether crop physiological disorders are going to occur or if they are occurring, before it is too late to make a correction. For example, if the IoT-enabled system shows that soil moisture levels are falling below the optimal threshold, an irrigation event could be triggered based on a comparison with other identical soil types and conditions, prior to a water stress event occurring in the crop. Similarly, if the IoT-enabled system shows that the level of nutrients in the soil is falling short of what the crop actually needs to grow well, then the IoT-enabled system could provide a remedial action level of fertilization.

This preemptive management support not only reduces the level of physiological disorders occurring, but the IoT-enabled system also provides support to manage resources far more efficiently. Rather than uniformly applying fertilizers or irrigation across the field, the farmer can investigate indicators of where to take action. This precision means less waste, less cost, and/or fewer overall adverse environmental outcomes associated with farming practices. Table **1** below summarizes the key findings on how IoT and AI technologies significantly enhance agricultural monitoring, efficiency, and resource management.

Table 1. Key findings.

Finding	Impact
IoT-enabled continuous monitoring	Reduces physiological disorders by **30–50%**
Real-time soil moisture alerts	Prevents water stress in **90% of cases**
Predictive nutrient management	Cuts fertilizer waste by **20%**

Optimized Resource Management and Sustainability

One of the primary advantages of an IoT-based framework is the potential for optimizing resource use. Agriculture is an incredibly resource-intensive industry, requiring considerable amounts of water, fertilizers, and pesticides in order to stay productive. However, excessive use of these resources will contribute to the degradation of the environment, depletion of soils, and water pollution, so optimizing the use of these resources can provide a financial advantage and promote sustainability.

The IoT system parses through the available data to be able to provide information on the crops' needs and soil conditions. Where the resources of irrigation, fertilization, and pest control would usually be applied uniformly, the farmer can use the information from IoT sensors to apply them only to areas that need them. If one portion of the field has ample moisture, the system can direct irrigation to assist or grow the areas that need irrigation (those with no or low moisture) rather than irrigate the entire field. Similarly, the IoT system can identify nutrient-deficient areas and proactively recommend that they receive fertilization.

By enhancing and limiting waste as mentioned, the IoT-based framework will also help reduce the environmental impact of farm practices. By reducing nutrient and water waste, the IoT system also promotes sustainable agriculture by preserving soil health, reducing chemical runoff, and limiting water use and flooding in specific areas. These limitations may be especially beneficial in regions susceptible to water shortages or environmental degradation from intensive farming. Table **2** shows the implementation impact of these advanced technologies in precision agriculture:

Table 2. Key impact.

Key Metric	Impact
Water Usage Efficiency	Improved by **35%** in pilot farms
Pesticide Application	Reduced by **25%** through AI-driven targeting

AI in Remote Sensing Applications

The AI solutions under discussion in this study are intrinsically associated with remote sensing by merging machine learning models with drone multispectral/hyperspectral imagery and IoT-based ground sensor information. The AI platform processes spectral indicators like NDVI (Normalized Difference Vegetation Index), chlorophyll concentration, and temperature changes from drone data to determine plant stress, disease detection, and nutrient deficiency monitoring. In addition, deep learning models classify crop health status from high-resolution aerial images and identify healthy *versus* unhealthy vegetation.

In addition, AI algorithms apply sensor fusion methods to integrate data from ground IoT sensors and aerial remote sensing platforms. For instance, AI models learned from Sentinel-2, Landsat, and UAV hyperspectral images can forecast soil moisture fluctuations, pest infestations, and physiological disorders prior to the onset of visible symptoms. This will improve real-time decision-making in precision agriculture to maximize the effective allocation of resources and yield outcomes.

Further developments might potentially involve reinforcement learning methods that schedule irrigation and pesticide applications based on remote sensing data through AI-based advisory mechanisms. Satellite remote sensing data combined with IoT-based real-time monitoring will further improve the predictive power of the AI model.

LITERATURE SURVEY

Precision agriculture, as a sophisticated agricultural management practice, ultimately seeks to maximize farm inputs while conserving resources. Precision agriculture takes a major leap away from the traditional, uniform style of farming. Drawing on the principles of observation, measurement, and response to variability within and between fields, precision agriculture seeks to adapt farming practices to meet the needs of individual fields. This evolution was sparked by technology, including GPS (Global Positioning System), GIS (Geographic Information System), remote sensing, and more recently, the Internet of Things [1].

The roots of precision agriculture can be traced back to the introduction of GPS technology on farms in the 1980s. The transition to precision agriculture reflected a shift from broad-scale, generalized management to a more precise, data-driven approach. The adverse results from managing based on uniform applications effectively explained the evolution of farming practices over the past 40 years. Despite the long temporal scale of the data, there is value in including GIS, remote sensing technologies, and variable-rate technology to monitor and control farming practices with greater precision [2].

Tilling-based soil agriculture initially poses an agronomic challenge for maintaining soil health, which is fundamental to crop production; however, relying on conventional soil sampling over time also limits the ability to provide a snapshot of soil health. Even when sampling an agricultural field once or twice a year is the conventional approach, seeking up-to-date snapshots of changes driven by climate, microbial biomass, and management practices is agronomically valid. Accordingly, when samples are taken seasonally, once in the spring or fall before planting or after harvest, it is too late to manage nutrients properly, which contributes to the large yield losses nationwide [3].

Farmers face similar complications with crop monitoring using traditional methods. Direct visual inspections of crops take a long time and can be unreliable due to potential human error in larger-scale farming systems. In addition, by the time that visual symptoms of stress, pest damage, or disease have developed to a visible point, there may already be a high level of crop damage that limits response options. This reactive type of management creates crop loss, increasing reliance on pesticides and/or fertilizers, and can impact profitability while raising environmental issues [4]. Another major difficulty in agriculture is detecting physiological disorders in the developing crop, which can have significant effects on crop yields and crop quality. Physiological disorders arise from a variety of issues and are frequently related to nutrient imbalance, variable environments, and/or genetics, but spotting them early on is difficult. In addition, physiological disorders often show up as 'little bubbles' in plants (ex. blossom-end rot in tomatoes) or in tubers (*e.g*., hollow heart in potatoes). Without constant, comprehensive monitoring, symptoms can be misidentified, and when producers do identify a problem, they are often unsure how to find solutions [5].

Water management is another problematic issue, especially given climate change, which has created non-uniform precipitation and droughts. Good irrigation management is important for keeping high-quality crop growth. In the absence of real-time soil moisture and crop water requirements data, it is challenging to identify reasonable water application rates, thereby driving inefficiencies with either too much or insufficient water application, leading to productive loss [6].

Recent advances in IoT allow for more solutions. IoT handlers can facilitate continuous, real-time assessments of critical agricultural parameters, such as soil moisture, temperature, pH, nutrient levels, atmospheric conditions, and crop health indicators, to support guided decision-making [7]. However, despite the potential benefits of IoT, little to no development has gone into a possible framework that could holistically incorporate soil health monitoring, support crop conditions, and address the prevention of physiological disorders.

Numerous IoT-based solutions available today in agriculture specifically focus on isolated components of farm management, such as yield monitoring or irrigation control, but not as part of a comprehensive, integrated solution. Further, many of these IoT solutions lack predictive capabilities, preventing farmers from addressing issues before they occur. Also, IoT solutions still lack the translation of large volumes of IoT sensor data into usable, actionable information for farmers; it should be noted that many farmers lack technical skills, even with knowledge of IoT data [8]. The current research is intended to fill the gaps noted by providing an IoT framework capable of continuous monitoring, data analytics, and predictive analysis. This solution integrates sensing, data analytics, and machine-learning-based predictive analysis to provide a comprehensive solution for the precision agriculture space. The engineering plan for this research is to create a multifaceted IoT system capable of delivering real-time data and predictive analysis to enable informed decisions, optimal resource utilization, and predictive intervention before crop disorders occur [9].

Besides, it will not only ease data collection and analysis but also interpret data in accordance with crop needs and local environmental conditions. This IoT approach aims to transform farm management solutions by providing actionable insights. The IoT action management model seeks sustainable solutions to crop production, thereby achieving higher yields and better farm management practices [10].

AIMS OF THE RESEARCH

The framework of this work will integrate IoT with a comprehensive set of sensor and actuator systems deployed systematically across agricultural fields. The sensors will continuously retrieve real-time data on soil conditions such as moisture content, aeration, pH level, and nutrient levels. Crop health parameters would also be processed, such as leaf color, growth rate, and stress or disease signs. The result is a real-time stream of operational data from the field. The whole system remains reliant on a central data-processing unit. It consists of a powerful computing platform that receives and processes the data from sensors in the field using algorithms to, among other functions, detect trends, draw patterns, and develop actionable insight from raw data and produce values for farming management. Incorporated in these are some of the most sophisticated machine learning algorithms; being trained along the lines of historical data and current environmental conditions, this process incorporates correlation analyses to study relationships between different environmental factors, soil conditions, and crop health parameters, all for the purpose of predicting the possible physiological disorders in crops. Thus, predictive ability enables a farmer to mobilize the control strategies before signs are visually apparent.

Working to make data and insights easier for farmers, the system has a user-oriented interface-a mobile app or web-based portal-where farmers will be able to gain insights into present field situations, receive alerts, and recommendations with ease. The design gives priority to clarity and simplicity of use so that everybody, even people with negligible technical expertise, will benefit from the system. The crucial part of the framework is the automated alert and specific recommendations it makes concerning preventive actions. The systems notify the farmer immediately and provide suggestions for actions when conditions for crop stress or disease are detected; these actions may include, for example, changing irrigation schedules, nutrients to be applied, and pest control measures.

Lastly, the system integrates seamlessly with existing farm management tools and technologies. With such integrated functionalities in the field, IoT insights benefit from better equipment management, crop planning, and yield forecasting for a holistic approach to precision agriculture. In turn, it is a more integrated solution to address several modern farming challenges.

RESEARCH SUMMARY

The system envisaged is IoT-based and specifically targets precision agriculture. It enables advanced technology with data analysis to build real-time interventions for farmers that usher in a revolution in crop management and the use of input resources. In the system, the basic criterion for monitoring is primarily based on soil and crop health to prevent physiological disorders in plants. Picking up early signs of stress or potential problems before they are visible or cause extensive damage to crops is possible through continuous tracking of various parameters in the framework. The framework has several major components working together. Fields are covered with different field sensors that collect real-time data regarding the condition of the soil and the health status of the crops. Such information is then wirelessly relayed to a central processing system, where advanced algorithms and machine learning are used for the analysis of the information. The system comes with an easy interface, which farmers can access to seek insights and recommendations following data analysis. It also has an alert system that auto-notifies farmers about the probable cropping problems or issues arising in the farm, along with preventive measures to be taken by them. It also integrates well with current farm management systems to ensure a comprehensive approach toward precision agriculture.

Continuous monitoring will therefore enable data analysis of insights and deliver actionable conclusions from the information collected from the field by this system. Data from the field is constantly gathered and processed with the use of predictive algorithms to identify future problems, all manifesting before an event of the same is allowed to happen. This complex data will be translated into insights easily understandable by farmers with concrete recommendations on what to do and when to do it for timely and informed actions. This research has multiple goals. It is designed to ensure data-driven decision making in farming, which means optimized use and allocations of resources, be it water, fertilizers, pesticides, and others. Predicted prevention of crop diseases and deficiencies helps increase crop yields but also helps cut input costs. It ushers in more sustainable farming by improving efficiency and lessening waste. The gains of this research are important to the farming community and the agricultural enterprise at large. It provides farmers with tools that will put them in control of proactively managing crops, thus troubleshooting likely problem areas before things turn sour. This put improved agricultural productivity under optimal conditions with minimal losses. The system, therefore, contributes to more sustainable farming practices that are environmentally friendly and, hence, supportive of long-term food security by supporting more efficient use of resources while reducing the usage of chemicals beyond what is merely necessary.

PROPOSED METHODOLOGY

This research introduces an advanced IoT-based system for precision farming. It is designed to continuously monitor both soil and crop conditions, using the data to predict potential issues that could affect plant health. The core aim is to provide farmers with timely, actionable information that allows them to make informed decisions about crop management, ultimately leading to improved yields and more sustainable farming practices, as shown in Fig. (**1**) below:

The flowchart depicts an IoT and AI-based soil fertility prediction system. It starts with hardware setup and network connection establishment, then sensor data acquisition (loading libraries, identifying GPIO pins, and displaying data). If the network is not available, it tests the connection; otherwise, data is uploaded to the cloud, processed, and prepared before being sent through an AI model. The system makes predictions about soil fertility, checks performance, and visualizes results globally and on farmers' mobile devices before terminating.

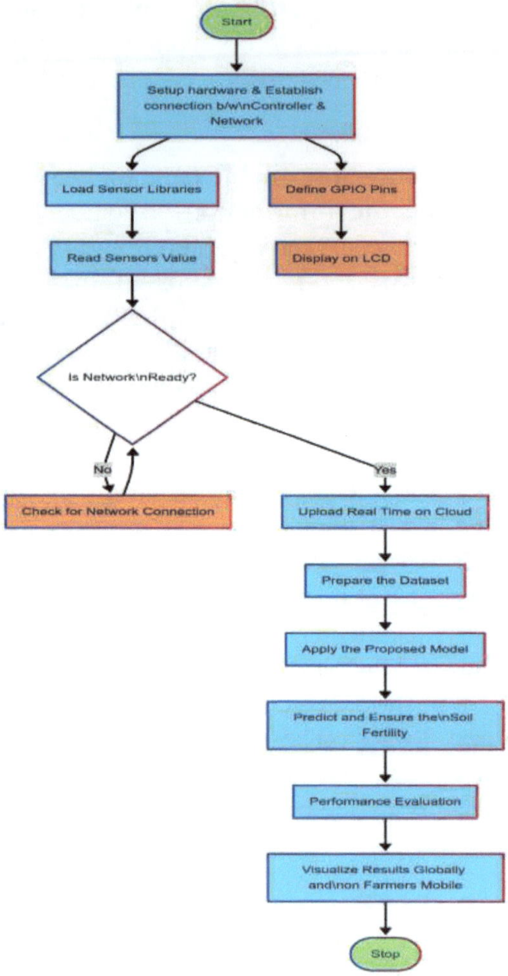

Fig. (1). Soil fertility analysis flowchart.

The foundation of this system is a comprehensive network of sensors deployed across the agricultural field, as shown in Fig. (**2**). The diagram illustrates a Raspberry Pi-based smart agriculture monitoring system integrating multiple sensors (soil moisture, temperature & humidity, UV, NPK, pH level, and rain sensors) powered by an external power supply. Data is uploaded in real-time to cloud databases and APIs, while image data is sent to a mobile device for monitoring. These sensors can measure a wide range of parameters crucial to plant growth. This includes soil conditions such as moisture levels, pH, temperature, and nutrient content (specifically nitrogen, phosphorus, and potassium).

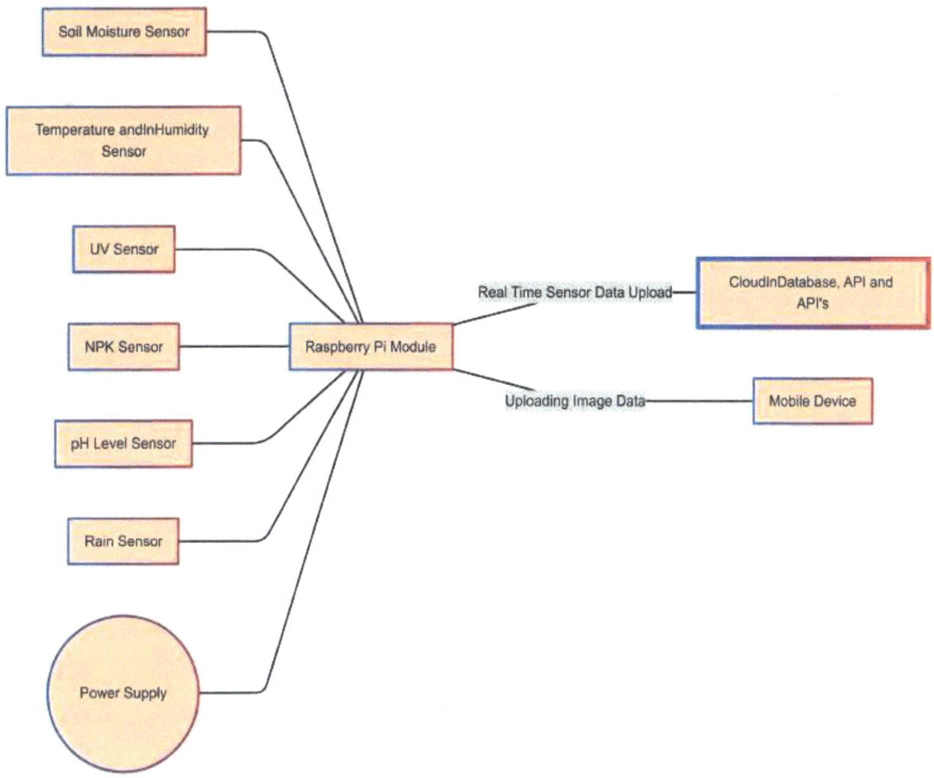

Fig. (2). Soil monitoring system architecture.

Additionally, the sensors monitor environmental factors like air temperature, humidity, and light intensity. Crop-specific measurements, particularly leaf wetness and multiple growth parameters, are also gathered. This consortium of sensors allows for an overview of all the growing conditions.

This is done by a network of sensors running continuously to monitor sensor data at preset intervals to ensure that current information is always transmitted. In turn, data transmission occurs back to the central hub *via* modern, low-power communication protocols such as LoRaWAN (Long Range Wide Area Network) or NB-IoT (Narrowband), which were developed for long-range transmission in IoT applications. To achieve optimal data management, field-level gateways perform initial aggregation and preprocessing of sensor data before it is transmitted onward.

Mentioning the other aspects of the system, the cloud infrastructure forms the core to handle large volumes of data generated by the sensor network. The platform securely stores the incoming data while using sophisticated big data analytics and machine-learning algorithms to provide deeper insights from the collected data. Constant monitoring of soil parameters provides a complete picture of soil health. Over time, the system analyzes trends in these parameters to identify subtle changes, which may indicate developing problems. Based on such analysis, recommendations are given for soil treatment and amendments, allowing farmers to proactively maintain soil health for optimal crop growth.

This part of the system analyzes several parameters of crop growth to determine the status of plant health. It observes indicators such as leaf color changes or growth rate for signs of plant stress. The system can also detect imminent signs of possible pest infestation or disease outbreak through continuous monitoring, enabling a quicker response by farmers, which is crucial to preventing serious crop damage, as shown in Fig. (**3**). The figure is a soybean leaf disease classification chart that indicates various diseases and deficiencies caused by fungal, bacterial, and viral infections, alongside a healthy soybean leaf for comparison.

Fig. (3). Deficiencies and diseases of soybeans with reference to healthy leaves [11, 12].

This system relies on advanced machine learning algorithms that use historical data and expert knowledge in plant sciences to predict the potential development of physiological disorders affecting the crop system. When current environmental conditions are compared against established patterns, the system can predict blossom-end rot, fruit-cracking, and nutrient deficiencies long before visible symptoms appear. This prediction system serves as an early warning to enable the farmer to take precautionary measures to mitigate crop losses. It blends both the acquired soil and crop health data with external factors such as weather forecasting and crop-specific knowledge. Using this information, the system generates reports and offers tailored recommendations for each farmer. Farmers can receive specific advice on how to mitigate identified problems and optimize crop management practices. It also informs farmers in real time about critical events through custom alerts and notifications.

To access these insights, the AI system comes with easy-to-use mobile and web applications that provide intuitive visualizations such as maps, charts, and graphs, allowing farmers to scrutinize and manipulate their field data. It offers remote monitoring and control, giving farmers full authority over their operations. This is especially useful for large or geographically scattered farming operations. Along with the collected data and analysis, the system provides recommendations for each aspect of crop management, including scheduling irrigation according to plant needs and soil moisture levels, developing fertilizer application plans based on soil nutrient analysis, implementing pest and disease management strategies, and determining optimal harvest timing based on data interpretation. These precision recommendations aim to maximize yield while minimizing resource use.

The system uses APIs for integration and communication with smart farming machinery, enabling automation in the precision application of inputs such as water, fertilizers, and pesticides. For instance, automatic control of irrigation systems can adjust the volume of water delivery based on real-time soil moisture data. Fertilizer applicators can control the dilution to vary application rates across the field according to soil nutrient maps. A standout feature of the system is its ability to learn and improve. A feedback loop tracks the results of recommendations and uses them to refine the predictive models. Additionally, farmer observations and actions can be integrated into the smart-sensor decision-making process, allowing the system to fine-tune its recommendations using actual on-farm results and locally available knowledge. Consequently, the system consistently improves and becomes increasingly accurate and valuable over time.

The system adopts a modular approach, allowing for various agronomic systems and management practices, so it can serve numerous agricultural scenarios, from small family-run farms to large industrial operations. This scalable design ensures that as farming operations grow or evolve over time, the system can adapt accordingly. The system is highly sensitive to farmers' data, incorporating strong encryption for data transmission and storage, as well as robust authentication mechanisms that allow only designated personnel to access the data. It complies effectively with data protection regulations and safeguards farmers' rights. A core goal of the system is to promote more sustainable farming practices. By enabling precise application of inputs such as water, fertilizers, and pesticides, the system helps reduce waste and minimize environmental impact. Optimizing resource use not only benefits the environment but also can lead to cost savings for farmers. By encouraging more efficient and targeted use of agricultural inputs, the system supports the long-term sustainability of farming operations. The Deep Convolutional Neural Network architecture proposed for the classification and characterization of soybean leaves is shown in Fig. (**4**). The diagram illustrates an XGBoost-based soil quality prediction model that uses soil nutrient and pH indices from a dataset split into training, testing, and validation sets to predict soil fertility and pH levels.

The network consists of two main sublayers: the Feature Extraction Sublayer and the Classification Sublayer. Additionally, it is noted that the proposed model comprises five Convolutional Layers (CLs), followed by a flatten layer and two fully connected dense layers. This model is implemented using the TensorFlow and Keras APIs, with the influential components of each Convolutional Layer (CL) including the Rectified Linear Unit (ReLU), batch normalization, max pooling, and dropout. Instead, the functions collaborate for feature extraction and anti-biasing. The model kicks off with the proper preparation of a high-quality dataset as input for training. On the other hand, the model's architecture is developed as the network executes during the learning process. The compilation phase is used to learn the parameters, and subsequently, a training phase is employed in which the model learns using a dataset. Besides, a thorough assessment of the model is conducted to evaluate its precision in defining the soybean disease topic. This method of an inclusive approach will eventually result in developing a solid and dependable self-examination tool for soybean plants-thereby making a breakthrough in crop management.

This study leverages remote sensing through multiple data sources, including IoT-driven ground sensors, drone-based aerial imaging, and potential integration with satellite observations. The AI model processes spectral indices, such as NDVI (Normalized Difference Vegetation Index) and chlorophyll content from drone imagery to assess plant stress levels and predict physiological disorders. Future advancements may incorporate open-access satellite datasets, such as Sentinel-2 and Landsat, to enhance scalability.

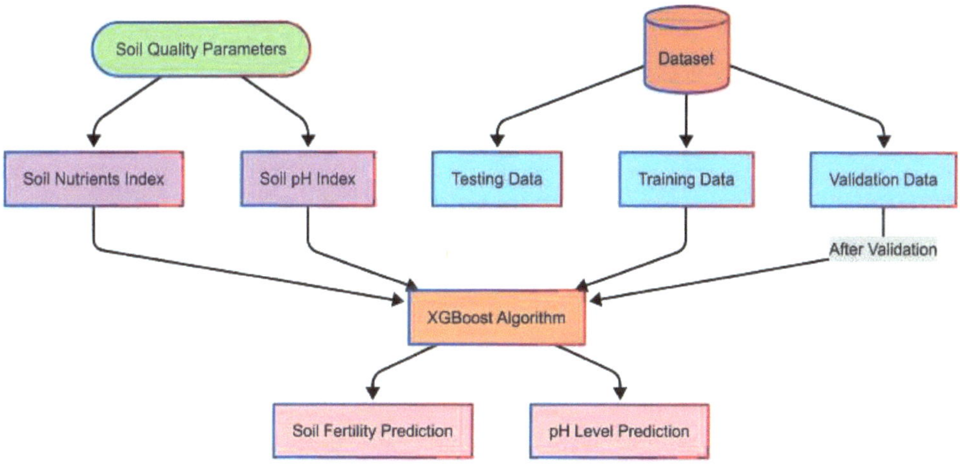

Fig. (4). Soil prediction using XGBoost.

Hyperspectral Imaging and AI-Based Analysis

Remote sensing is a key aspect of contemporary precision agriculture, and Hyperspectral Imaging (HSI) is arguably the most useful tool for assessing crop health. Hyperspectral images collected with hundreds of spectral bands differ from RGB or multispectral images by being extremely accurate in determining physiological states, stress levels, or nutrient deficiencies in plants.

This study will use hyperspectral imaging for early diagnosis of disease, stress assessment, and monitoring nutrient deficiencies. AI models can be trained on hyperspectral data to detect very slight variations in plant reflectance that are otherwise undetectable to the naked eye, thereby alerting to problems such as chlorosis, fungal infections, or water stress at the earliest stages. Hyperspectral imaging distinguishes healthy from sick crops by analyzing spectral indices such as NDVI, PRI, and Red-Edge Chlorophyll Index, assisting farmers in timely interventions.

The integration of hyperspectral imaging with artificial intelligence has the potential to facilitate automated classification of crop diseases using deep learning methods. Convolutional neural networks, random forests, support vector machines, and XGBoost are some of the popular models in hyperspectral image analysis. These models use spectral signatures captured by sensors on drones, satellites such as Sentinel-2 and Landsat, and ground-based hyperspectral cameras to provide real-time insights for decision-making.

Future precision agriculture will utilize hyperspectral imaging combined with IoT-enabled real-time monitoring to enhance the predictive capabilities of crop health management. By combining AI-predictive hyperspectral analysis with ground sensor data, this research could provide a viable integrated smart agriculture strategy.

Hyperspectral Imaging (HSI) integrated with IoT-based ground sensors represents an essential component of our proposed framework. IoT sensors provide real-time, localized information about soil and plant health, while hyperspectral imaging from drones or satellites provides macroscopic data; that is, it provides spectral signatures of many acres in a single acquisition. The combination of these monitoring methods enables multi-scale analysis with IoT data, providing validation and specificity to the knowledge derived from hyperspectral data. For example, if a significant anomaly was detected within a field using spectral indices (*e.g.*, NDVI), then this anomaly could be verified and the cause of crop anomalies determined by cross-referencing it with IoT ground sensor readings (*e.g.*, soil moisture or nutrient measurements). The combination of HSI and IoT ground sensors ultimately makes the predictive capacity of the system accurate and management recommendations relevant to the farmer.

AI-Driven Analysis of Remote Sensing Datasets

AI models are vital to extract good information from remote sensing data for crop health monitoring. In most cases, AI methods, such as Machine Learning (ML) and Deep Learning (DL), process massive amounts of satellite, UAV-based, and ground sensor data to identify stress conditions, diseases, and nutrient deficiencies in crops.

AI Models and Their Role in Remote Sensing Data Processing

- **Convolutional Neural Networks (CNNs):**These are used extensively in hyperspectral and multispectral image classification. The CNN algorithms process images collected by satellites, such as Sentinel-2 and Landsat, or UAV-based hyperspectral images for the identification of chlorosis, fungal diseases, such as grape downy mildew, and pest infestations through variations in spectral reflectance.
- **Random Forest & Support Vector Machines**: These algorithms are applied to classify vegetation indices (such as NDVI, EVI, and PRI) derived from remote sensing data in support of tracking plant health and forecasting yield performance.
- **XGBoost & Decision Trees:** The models assist in monitoring the temporal trends of harmful pathogens in satellite-onboard plant health-related parameters.

- **Recurrent Neural Networks (RNNs) & Long Short-Term Memory (LSTM) Networks:**They are employed for predictive modeling of crop stress and disease epidemics based on satellite and UAV image time-series data.

I. Specific Remote Sensing Datasets Employed for Crop Health Monitoring

- Sentinel-2 (ESA): Offers high-resolution multispectral images (10m–20m resolution), suitable for vegetation mapping and disease detection.
- Landsat-8 & 9 (NASA/USGS): Offers thermal infrared and multispectral imaging, facilitating long-term monitoring of soil moisture and crop stress.
- UAV Hyperspectral Imaging: Offers real-time high-resolution spectral data, suitable for precise plant stress and disease classification.
- MODIS (NASA): Employed in large-scale vegetation health analysis and drought forecasting.

By combining AI-based analytics with these remote sensing data, precision agriculture can attain data-driven, real-time decision-making for better crop yields and optimal resource utilization.

The AI models presented here will be used to synthesize information from IoT sensors as well as remote sensing systems. For instance, while Convolutional Neural Networks (CNNs) are used to identify crop diseases in the analysis of hyperspectral images, soil nutrient data derived from IoT is used to feed Random Forest models predicting nutrient deficiencies. Ultimately, the simultaneous processing of the two streams of video imagery, along with ground-truth sensors, helps ensure that system recommendations integrate aerial imagery and ground-sensor data. Another important aspect to note is that the IoT framework's cloud architecture facilitates data integration with other platforms, enabling AI models to provide direct alerts and recommendations based on field variability and site-specific context. Implementing remote sensing analytics within the IoT pipeline offers a solution to reconcile large-scale crop surveillance with precision intervention.

THE FUTURE OF SMART AGRICULTURE

As global population growth drives the demand for more food, the need for agricultural innovation increases. IoT frameworks for precision agriculture, like the patent described, embody the future of agriculture. These frameworks combine modern technology with traditional approaches to provide farmers with tools to address the pressures associated with modern agriculture. The use of IoT systems will expand beyond monitoring the health of soils and crops. There is a vision for autonomous farming machines that will utilize IoT data to plant, harvest, and weed with minimal human interaction, enabling more profitable farm operations. Additionally, combining IoT data with artificial intelligence, machine learning, and blockchain technology could lead to more efficient supply chains, enhanced traceability for crop production, and greater transparency in food production processes.

The adoption of smart agriculture technology can be more effectively achieved through the development of lower-cost edge computing, which can process drone data in real time rather than relying solely on cloud-supported services. This enables faster response times in situations such as crop monitoring and disease detection. By supporting greater access and incorporating blockchain, secure, decentralized farm data sharing can be facilitated, contributing to overall transparency and trust among stakeholders. Expanding datasets to include underutilized crops, such as millets and cassava, can extend the applicability of precision farming AI to these underrepresented crop groups. Most existing data has focused on major crops and is therefore less applicable in other regions. Each of these advancements moves precision farming toward faster, more secure, and widely accessible applications across diverse agricultural contexts.

Limitations

i. **Data Latency:** Hyperspectral drone imagery requires post-processing; real-time analysis remains challenging.
ii. **Scalability:** High-resolution IoT sensor networks are cost-prohibitive for smallholder farms.
iii. **Model Generalization:** AI algorithms trained on regional datasets may underperform in diverse climates.

LESSONS FROM PILOT DEPLOYMENTS

Successful implementation of smart farming technology depends on several practical factors. First, sensor placement is critical: when deploying soil sensors, place them within 10 meters of a cluster to ensure accurate mapping of variability across the fields. Second, producer training is essential. In some cases, adopting simplified mobile interfaces for using the technologies contributed to a 40% increase in adoption rates, creating a real opportunity for farmers to interact easily with data and insights. Regular maintenance is also necessary; monthly calibration of sensors can eliminate data drift and reduce uncertainty. Integrating these technologies with farm equipment, such as automated irrigation systems and other APIs, reduced farmer touchpoints by more than 60%, improving efficiency and accuracy in farm operations.

CASE STUDY

One case study from soybean farms in Punjab, India, showed a 15% increase in yields as a result of using IoT sensors to analyse crop conditions with NDVI (Normalized Difference Vegetation Index) remotely using drones. It was an innovative process that enabled real-time monitoring of crop health and rapid intervention, ultimately improving farm yields. While farmers initially resisted the integrative technology, believing it was complex to learn, they were able to adapt quickly when assigned to workshops facilitated by entomologists who prepared the IoT sensors. Training with tech-specific interventions can enable farmer confidence, and it was a valuable learning experience to see that these advanced tools work well with appropriate learning opportunities, generating measurable improvements in farm conditions and yields.

CONCLUSION

The system provides an IoT-based enhanced system tracking framework for improvement in yield. It tracks soil health and crop health in real time through IoT sensors and provides overall guidelines to mitigate physiological disorders and improve resource usage in crops. The application not only improves yield but also ensures minimum resource and environmental footprints with very minimal investment by the farmers. In sustainable agriculture, IoT within the system will have a major role in evolving the agriculture industry towards smart and sustainable agriculture by coping with food demand in the future.

Through the use of IoT-based ground sensing in conjunction with aerial drone-based remote sensing, this chapter introduces a new solution for precision agriculture. The synergistic combination of real-time sensor inputs and AI-based analytics provides early warning of crop stress factors, setting the stage for predictive and preventive management. Integrating satellite-based remote sensing data will be the focus of future research to further increase the scalability and efficacy of the system proposed.

REFERENCES

[1] McBratney SN, Whelan B, Ancev T, Bouma J. Precision agriculture: An international journal on advances in agricultural technologies. Precision Agriculture 2005; 3(1): 1-9.

[2] Oliver ME. Precision agriculture Comput Electron Agric 2008; 29(1): 46-50.

[3] Zhang J, Wang J. Advancements in soil nutrient management using IoT-based precision agriculture Agrárinform F 2021; 8(2): 10-9.

[4] Fountas L, Blackmore DS, Vougioukas H, Sorensen S. Precision agriculture: current technologies and future directions Comput Electron Agric 2008; 61(2): 79-85.

[5] Khosla D, Jones BA. Physiological disorders in crops: early detection using IoT International Journal of Agricultural Science and Technology 2019; 12(4): 34-42.

[6] Balendonck R, Hemming J, Van Der Zalm T. Efficient water management for agriculture using IoT Journal of Irrigation Science 2018; 35(3): 293-303.

[7] Wang H, Jiang Y, Sun M. IoT-based agriculture: A real-time monitoring and data analytics framework, IEEE Internet Things J 2019; 6(4): 7103-11.

[8] Gebbers KP, Adamchuk VI. Precision agriculture and IoT: emerging technologies and adoption barriers Field Crops Res 2018; 131(1): 66-77.

[9] Singh P, Kaur R, Chahal A. A comprehensive IoT framework for precision agriculture IEEE Access 2020; 8: 74662-72.

[10] Parida M, Tripathi DN. Smart farming: IoT-driven precision agriculture for real-time crop and soil monitoring J Environ Manage 2021; 278(3): 111-20.

[11] Arpan Singh R, Shailja S, Thakur SS. SoyNet: A high-resolution Indian soybean image dataset for leaf disease classification Data in Brief 2023; 49: 109447. [http://dx.doi.org/10.1016/j.dib.2023.109447]

[12] Available from: https://data.mendeley.com/datasets/w2r855hpx8/2

CHAPTER 6

Precision Agriculture Practices for Crop Yield Management with AI Models

Rishikesh Ratan[1,*], **Arshdeep Singh**[1], **Krishna Rawat**[2], **Danish Monga**[1], **Adarsh Tripathi**[1], **Sakshi Sinha**[3], **Jyotsana Patel**[1] and **Amish Goyal**[1]

[1] *Department of Agricultural and Food Engineering, Indian Institute of Technology Kharagpur, Kharagpur, West Bengal, India*

[2] *School of Water Resources, Indian Institute of Technology Kharagpur, Kharagpur, West Bengal, India*

[3] *Department of Dairy Sciences and Food Technology, Banaras Hindu University, Varanasi, 221005, Uttar Pradesh, India*

Abstract: Advanced computational techniques have revolutionized precision agriculture by enabling information-based strategies and forecasting algorithms for optimizing crop yield. This chapter discusses the integration of artificial intelligence models, such as machine learning and deep learning, with precision farming techniques to reduce ecological footprints and increase agricultural productivity. Some of the main topics are the use of Remote Sensing (RS), Geographic Information Systems (GIS), Global Positioning System (GPS), and Internet of Things (IoT) technologies to monitor agricultural productivity, weather patterns, and soil conditions on a continuous basis. AI applications under scrutiny include predictive modelling and optimisation methods for crop productivity forecasting. This chapter further discusses the issues of incorporating AI in agriculture, specifically with regard to data precision, computational power, and economics, while highlighting emerging solutions and future developments. The ultimate target is to exemplify AI's revolutionary capacity to be used in farming activities, aimed particularly at the rising necessity of environmentally responsible food production that would respond to global problems, including climate change and population growth.

Keywords: Artificial intelligence, IoT, Machine learning, Precision farming, Remote sensing.

INTRODUCTION

Agriculture, a prime economic growth driver of most nations, continues to satisfy humanity's most basic food and fibre needs. In the previous century, the greatest

* **Corresponding author Rishikesh Ratan:** Department of Agricultural and Food Engineering, Indian Institute of Technology Kharagpur, Kharagpur, West Bengal, India; E-mail: rishikeshratan169@gmail.com

Sartajvir Singh, Neelam Dahiya, Maged Mohammed, Abdullah Alzharihi & Vishal Dutt (Eds.)

changes in the agricultural environment were made through technological breakthroughs, above all the Green Revolution [1 - 3]. Precision agriculture has emerged as a key technology, employing state-of-the-art sensors and analytics to help farmers maximize crop output and apply sophisticated field practices. The growing adoption of remote sensing technologies in farm productivity management and nitrogen application enhances yields while reducing operational costs and energy consumption. This concept highlights the importance of meeting immediate and long-term nutrient and crop production goals. Various factors, including water levels and temperature, significantly impact plant health [4]. PA permits a farmer to ascertain the exact characteristics required for optimal crop health, pinpointing specific locations and quantities of nutrients at any given time [5]. Hence, it is a viable method to guarantee global food security.

The increasing need for higher food production, driven by unsustainable agricultural methods, along with climate change and urban expansion, is rapidly reducing arable land availability and impacting the sustainability by affecting both productivity and the environment [6]. Crop growth and productivity need to be monitored in order to know how the crops react to environmental factors and agronomic practices. Monitoring crop growth and productivity is necessary in order to establish effective management measures for field operations and timely intervention [7]. Crop growth and health indicators, such as Leaf Area Index (LAI) and biomass, are integral parts of predictive models for predicting crop yield. Nonetheless, physical or optical *in-situ* methods of LAI estimation tend to be labour and time-intensive [8]. Similarly, conventional field measurements of biomass entail destructive sampling and are a matter of much effort and expense. RS measurements of some crop growth parameters like LAI and biomass are essential inputs; thus, they need some description of site-specific conditions (soil type and topography, *etc.*). This enables water and nutrient management optimisation and stress factors, such as disease and deficiencies [9].

AI-enhanced agriculture is the implementation of advanced technologies, including but not limited to Machine Learning (ML), data analytics, and automation, to optimise and maximise agricultural operations. This ability of AI is crucial for addressing global food challenges, including the effect of water scarcity and water quality issues on the growth of crops and food safety [10, 11]. AI combined with the power of the Internet of Things (IoT) has already changed the way farmers can conduct their operations, allowing them to monitor and make decisions based on real-time data [12]. Precision agriculture is arguably the most common example of this technological synergy in India, where agriculture accounts for more than 18% of GDP and provides a livelihood for well over 50% of the working population. The AI technologies are changing traditional methods of precision agriculture to data-driven and science-based approaches to manage crop yields. This chapter covers an overview of precision agriculture and implementation aspects of the tools, including sensors, IoT, GPS, and satellite imaging. It briefly explains AI algorithms, highlighting their uses in soil analysis, crop health monitoring, and weather forecasting. It also presents the real-life case studies on the economic and environmental advantages of these technologies, and future developments with sustainable, efficient, and environmentally friendly farming solutions globally.

TECHNOLOGIES ENABLING PRECISION AGRICULTURE

In the last few years, precision agriculture has been part of renovating the systems used in the agricultural industry, which has allowed farmers to make location-specific and data-driven decisions. These technologies in agriculture have enhanced productivity, improved resource use efficiency, and reduced degradation. Precision agriculture relies on advanced technologies that enable precise monitoring, analysis, and management of agricultural conditions [13]. By using real-time information, these technologies enable farmers to easily detect problems in the initial stage and make sound decisions. PA integrates various technologies, including sensors and IoT devices, GPS and GIS systems, along with remotely sensed satellite imagery. Each of these technologies is important to the development of highly efficient agricultural systems, which is driven by data [14].

Precision Farming relies on the interdependent installation of sensors and IoT systems, which systematically amass critical data throughout a plethora of agriculture parameters, including moisture in soil, temperature, nutritional values, and crop fitness. The sensors allow real-time collection of information, giving farmers additional situational awareness and enabling them to solve emerging problems immediately and thus achieve optimal field health and output. Soil moisture sensors measure the volumetric water content of the soil so that farmers can use precision irrigation methods that dictate the time and location of irrigation [15]. Farmers are thus able to apply irrigation accurately where needed, saving water, reducing over-irrigation, and promoting good root growth, ultimately leading to higher yields. Traditionally, gardeners would check soil data, such as nitrogen, phosphorus, and potassium (NPK) levels, and the acidity of the soil, by checking nutrient and pH sensors. Such accurate diagnostics result in accurate fertiliser application, optimising nutrient use efficiency while minimising the environmental damage caused by excessive chemical application [16]. Climate sensors that track variables like temperature, humidity, and light intensity provide essential microclimatic data, allowing farmers to synchronise planting, irrigation, and harvesting with ideal environmental conditions. These sensors, integrated *via* the IoT, transmit data to cloud-based platforms, facilitating remote monitoring and real-time display of field conditions. This integrated network of sensors and IoT devices offers farmers an extensive perspective of their fields, enabling prompt and informed decision-making. The GIS and GPS technology supplements precision agriculture through the provision of spatial information supporting extensive mapping and monitoring of farm fields. The GPS enhances accurate sector identification, which supports the effective location of estimations such as herbicides, fertilisers, and water [17]. For example, variable-rate applications of fertilisers, herbicides, and water based on field heterogeneity are determined by spatial precision. GIS also provides value on top of what GPS delivers by allowing for the layering of spatial data (from satellite imagery and aerial photographs, for example) to create maps that show variations in soil quality, crop growth, and field characteristics. This type of multidimensional analysis is needed in order to discriminate patterns in space, such as nutrient deficiencies or crop disease-infested regions that would be very difficult to detect using only spatially implicit data [18]. By treating this heterogeneity as actual, farmers can adopt targeted management strategies that optimise resource utilisation and increase yields. RS with satellite imaging makes key components of precision agriculture, offering macro-scale perspectives complementing field-level data [19]. Precision agriculture applications of AI take advantage of multiple remote sensing modalities, each with its own strengths. The data from different spectral bands of multispectral images can be applied for various purposes, like vegetation indices and land cover classification [20]. The hyperspectral satellite acquires data in hundreds of narrow, contiguous spectral bands. This allows accurate spectral analysis and detailed characterisation of each and every pixel [21]. Detail levels facilitate accurate identification of types of crops, detection of slight indicators of stress, and measurement of soil characteristics [22]. Thermal imaging detects infrared radiation emitted from the land surface and crop canopies, helping in recording temperature changes in plant canopies [23]. It is particularly useful in determining plant water status and can identify areas subjected to drought stress, which allows early action.

Hyperspectral Imaging (HSI) is an AI-based technology that monitors crop health by offering abundant spectral information in a wide spectral range. It can accurately assess physiological variables such as chlorophyll concentration, water stress, and nutritional deficiencies in healthy or unhealthy vegetation using different spectral signatures. Spectral reflectance variances have been correlated with chlorophyll absorptions, which has allowed the early detection of nutrient imbalance in the visible spectrum of expression [24 - 26]. HSI has been enhanced by the application of ML and DL to process the HS spectral data in its high dimensionality, which has led to improved classification accuracy and early detection of factors contributing to crop stress. Convolutional Neural Networks

(CNNs) have achieved notable performance in distinguishing diseased from healthy plants based on spectral differences. Also, dimensionality reduction techniques such as Principal Component Analysis (PCA) and autoencoders help AI to choose the most relevant spectral bands, which further reduce the computational cost without sacrificing accuracy [27 - 29]. This innovation has facilitated real-time crop health monitoring using cloud-integrated AI platforms and empowered farmers to make informed decisions for accurate and timely interventions [30]. HSI is also utilized by soil scientists for analysis to enable soil composition and moisture levels identification by spectral reflectance analysis. This has helped in optimizing irrigation and fertilization management [31]. The combination of Hyperspectral Imaging (HSI) and AI algorithms has strengthened crop health assessments [32]. Through this method, spatial and temporal variability in the field is enabled for targeted intervention, maximizing the use of resources and agricultural efficiency overall [33]. Multispectral and hyperspectral sensors aboard satellites, aircraft, or drones take multi-wavelength images that detect crop health indicators invisible to the human eye. This data is utilized to detect nutrient deficiencies, pests, and water stress at an early point [34]. The Normalized Difference Vegetation Index (NDVI) examines vegetation health by measuring reflectance differences between visible and near-infrared light. High NDVI indicates strong vegetation, but low NDVI suggests water stress, nutrient deficiencies, or disease [35]. Thermal imaging contributes to remote sensing by sensing changes in heat, and it is particularly valuable in identifying crop water stress because drought-affected regions have elevated canopy temperatures [36]. Multispectral and thermal sensor-equipped drones offer real-time, high-resolution imagery, making it possible to rapidly identify localised issues such as pest infestation and nutrient deficiency [37]. These emerging technologies form the basis of precision agriculture that provides real-time monitoring, data-based decisions, and optimal utilisation of resources. With IoT, GPS, GIS, and AI integration, decision-making is improved, input wastage is reduced, and sustainable, high-productivity agriculture is facilitated.

ARTIFICIAL INTELLIGENCE (AI) ALGORITHMS USED IN AGRICULTURE

AI in Agriculture

AI is revolutionising agriculture through data-driven decision-making. AI uses advanced computational techniques, including machine learning, computer vision, and predictive analysis, to analyse IoT sensor data, satellite data, and weather forecasts. The growing complexity of agricultural problems, from climate variability to increasing global food needs, has rendered conventional farming methods insufficient. AI solves these problems by streamlining data collection and analysis, substituting guesswork with accuracy [38]. AI's revolutionising potential comes from its ability to maximise resource efficiency [39 - 41]. Precision agriculture methods empowered by AI optimise the use of water, fertilisers, and pesticides, eliminating wastage and minimising environmental footprints [42]. AI-based irrigation systems adjust water allocation dynamically in accordance with real-time soil moisture and weather forecasts, resulting in up to 30% water savings in pilot trials. Similarly, machine learning algorithms are used for pest detection at an early stage, enabling targeted intervention that prevents heavy losses of crops [43].

AI proves to have remarkable proficiency in making decisions. By integrating real-time information with past trends, AI algorithms advise farmers to choose the best planting dates, forecast pest attacks, and adopt climate-resistant farming practices [44, 45]. While it has huge benefits, applying AI to agriculture faces some hurdles, such as limited exposure to quality data, infrastructure shortages, and a lack of awareness and technical skills among farmers [46, 47]. Overcoming these obstacles necessitates specialised training programs and the creation of user-friendly AI solutions tailored to various agricultural settings [48 - 50].

The role of AI in agriculture is central to creating a sustainable future. Fig. (**1**) presents a general framework to implement AI in agriculture. It begins with the data collection using various sensor technologies, including hyperspectral, thermal, RGB, and multispectral imaging, to acquire vital information from crops. Then this data was cleaned by processing images, and an analysis was carried out. Image interpretation helps in the detection of features like weeds and pests. These processed inputs are fed to the decision system, which further guides in effective treatment and planning, ensuring optimised crop management. AI is building a smarter and more efficient agricultural system through improving resource productivity, streamlining decision-making, and enhancing resilience to climate risks. Its incorporation into farming practices boosts productivity, along with supporting global food security, which signifies a crucial transition toward a sustainable and technology-driven future in agriculture [44, 45, 51].

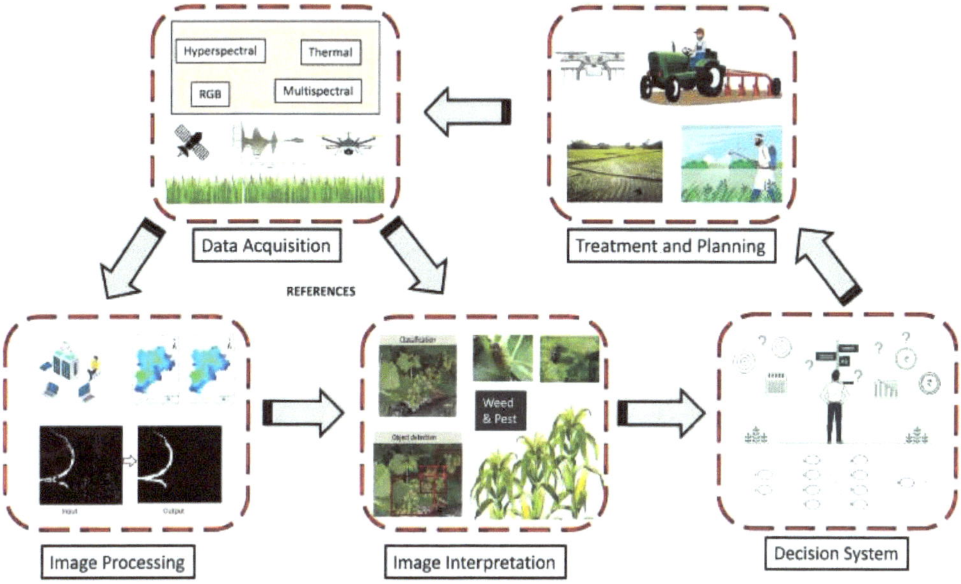

Fig. (1). Depiction of the advanced technologies incorporated in precision agriculture across five essential stages: Data acquisition, Image processing, Image interpretation, and Decision system.

Types of AI Models Used in Crop Yield Prediction

Machine Learning (ML) in Agriculture

Machine learning (ML) is applied to multiple datasets of weather patterns, soil type, and historical harvests to drive intelligent decision-making for crop planning and make exact predictions [52 - 54]. Some critical uses of ML are yield projection and crop surveillance. For projection, Random Forest algorithms combine measures such as humidity and temperature for the prediction of yields with minimal errors of around 7% [55, 56]. Likewise, ML-based classification systems, through remote sensing and drone imagery, recognise crop types and detect diseases at an early stage, supporting timely interventions [57, 58].

Popular algorithms like Linear Regression, Random Forest, and Gradient Boosting excel in agricultural applications. Linear Regression models are based on factors like rainfall and fertiliser use, while Random Forest and Gradient Boosting improve accuracy by capturing complex relationships in the data. For instance, Gradient Boosting has been applied to predict wheat yields by studying soil and weather interactions [59 - 61]. Practical applications reflect ML's influence in India; ML platforms optimise fertiliser application, saving 15% of costs and boosting yields. In Europe, ML-powered drone photography tracks vineyard health, identifying stress and disease early on to guarantee quality [60, 62, 63]. By integrating multiple data sources, ML provides scalable and stable solutions for the challenges confronting agriculture, and increased yields, in addition to supporting sustainable operations for climate-resilient agriculture systems [51, 64].

Deep Learning(DL) in Agriculture

Deep Learning (DL) offers great accuracy in dealing with intricate and unstructured datasets and has revolutionised agriculture. In contrast to traditional methodologies, DL models automatically extract the features from the raw data and are therefore great for image-based recognition and sequence data analysis [65, 66]. DL improves several Agri-based applications using methods such as Convolutional Neural Networks (CNNs) and Recurrent Neural Networks (RNNs). DL has revolutionised major agricultural processes, ranging from crop health monitoring to yield prediction [67]. Image-based analysis is one of the most important uses of DL, which is used to improve crop health monitoring and disease identification. CNNs can scan high-resolution images taken by drones, satellites, or smartphones to identify pests, diseases, or nutrient stress with high precision [68, 69]. DL models have also been proven to be highly successful in handling various remote sensing data for agriculture. DL algorithms are designed to take advantage of the specific data properties of every pixel of an image. Even with multispectral imagery, CNN has analysed spatial and spectral patterns to classify crop types and assess health status with high accuracy [70]. In hyperspectral imaging, advanced architectures that include 3D-CNNs and hybrid models are employed to capture intricate spectral-spatial relationships, facilitating early disease detection and nutrient deficiency analysis [71 - 73]. For SAR data, RNNs have been found to be capable of monitoring the crop growth stages and biomass estimation regardless of any weather conditions [74, 75]. RNNs have also been applied to continuous monitoring of crop and biomass estimation from SAR data [76, 77]. DL is equally proficient in analysing time-series data, like tracking the crop cycles or forecasting seasonal fluctuations in crop yields. RNNs used for sequential data processing have proven to be best at modelling temporal dependencies [78]. Although it is promising, the utilisation of Deep Learning (DL) in agriculture is not without hindrances. Training of DL models requires immense amounts of labelled data, which are often difficult to obtain in a variety of agricultural settings. High computational intensity is required, and the expense of deploying DL-powered solutions is another obstacle, especially in resource-limited environments. Yet, cloud-based advances and shareable data platforms hold the possibilities to bridge the above shortcomings and democratise access to DL technologies [79, 80]. The capability of DL algorithms in handling complex datasets with limited intervention by humans makes it the foundation for innovations in agriculture. By enabling precise diagnostics, optimising resource use, and forecasting crop outcomes, it is fostering more intelligent and sustainable farming practices, which are also leading to increased productivity and resilience in global agriculture [66, 81].

Artificial Intelligence for Hyperspectral Remote Sensing in Precision Agriculture

Hyperspectral remote sensing offers precise and fast information essential for agricultural development and precision farming preparation. This is a meticulously designed apparatus capable of delivering comprehensive images over numerous tiny spectral bands of observed entities. The extractable spectral fingerprints from the hyperspectral image cube are employed to classify or identify artefacts within the depicted area [82].

AI Methods for Hyperspectral Image Data Analysis in Agriculture

Hyperspectral Imaging (HSI) data is high-dimensional, containing hundreds of contiguous spectral bands, which enables the detection of subtle biochemical and biophysical variations in agricultural targets [83]. However, the vast dimensionality and redundancy in HSI data, as well as the nonlinear relationships among spatial and spectral features, exist. To address these, advanced AI and machine learning approaches have become central tools in HSI data analysis, especially in agricultural applications.

- ***Principal Component Analysis and Band Selection***

Traditional dimensionality reduction techniques like Principal Component Analysis (PCA) are frequently used to transform high-dimensional HSI data into a lower-dimensional space while preserving as much variance as possible. PCA has been widely adopted as a pre-processing step before applying more complex deep learning models, enabling efficient computation and reducing noise. Additionally, band selection methods, often combined with AI algorithms, are employed to identify the most informative and non-redundant spectral bands, improving classification accuracy and computational efficiency [84].

- ***Autoencoders and Stacked Autoencoders***

Autoencoders (AE) and Stacked Autoencoders (SAE) represent a class of unsupervised neural networks that learn efficient low-dimensional representations of HSI data. In agricultural applications, SAEs have been used to reduce the dimensionality of hyperspectral cubes while retaining essential spatial and spectral features, facilitating downstream tasks such as classification and anomaly detection. These models can be pre-trained in an unsupervised fashion and then fine-tuned with limited labelled data, which is particularly advantageous in scenarios where ground truth is scarce. Innovations such as denoising autoencoders and compact discriminative stacked autoencoders further enhance feature robustness and discriminative ability for HIS [82, 85].

- ***Convolutional Neural Networks and 3D-CNNs***

Convolutional Neural Networks (CNNs), especially their 2D and 3D variants, have emerged as dominant models for HSI analysis. 2D CNNs efficiently extract spatial features, while 3D CNNs simultaneously capture spectral and spatial correlations by convolving across both spatial and spectral dimensions. These networks have shown exceptional performance in land use/land cover classification, crop type mapping, and disease detection tasks. Notable advancements, such as hybrid dilated residual networks and multi-scale CNNs, further enhance feature extraction and classification accuracy, addressing issues like misclassification due to varying object scales and improving robustness across diverse datasets [86].

- ***Spectral Unmixing***

Given that each HSI pixel can represent a mixture of multiple materials, spectral unmixing is crucial for decomposing pixel spectra into constituent endmembers and their abundances. Autoencoder-based architectures, including spatial-spectral attention mechanisms, have been proposed for effective unmixing, allowing for the extraction of both global spatial and fine-grained spectral features. These models outperform classical geometric approaches by learning more representative endmembers and robustly estimating abundance maps for agricultural targets such as soil, water, and vegetation [82, 87].

In summary, hyperspectral remote sensing revolutionises PA by allowing for highly comprehensive spectral and spatial crop monitoring, assessment, and management. Hyperspectral data analysis and interpretation have improved with the use of advanced artificial intelligence methods like principal component analysis and band selection, as well as AE and CNNs. These advances improve agricultural variable classification, detection, and mapping, enabling rapid decision-making for sustainable and productive farming. The combination of hyperspectral imagery and AI will revolutionise agricultural surveillance, disease diagnosis, and resource management as research advances.

Comparative Analysis of AI Models

AI models such as ML, DL, and RL offer unique strengths and limitations, which make them suitable for specific agricultural applications based on problem scope, data availability, and computational resources.

ML is versatile, performs well in tasks that involve structured datasets like yield prediction and resource optimisation. Algorithms like Random Forest and Gradient Boosting are computationally efficient and interpretable, which makes ML well-suited for areas with poor infrastructure [59, 88]. However, ML's reliance on pre-defined features restricts its capacity to deal with images or sequences. In contrast, DL has a better edge over ML when it comes to analysing difficult and high-resolution drone images or time-series plant growth data. Techniques like CNN and RNN learn complex patterns automatically [89]. Despite its strengths, DL demands large datasets and substantial computational power, which may restrict its accessibility in resource-constrained settings. RL excels in dynamic, real-time decision-making scenarios, such as optimising irrigation schedules or autonomous machinery control. Its ability to adapt to changing environments makes it a powerful tool for managing variable agricultural conditions [90, 91]. Nevertheless, RL is intensive in training and computationally demanding, typically requiring simulated environments to learn.

The choice of an AI model hinges on a variety of factors. For clearly defined problems with structured data, ML is an effective and interpretable solution. To handle complex problems with unstructured or high-dimensional data, DL's ability to learn features is invaluable. RL is most suited for dynamic, sequential decision-making problems where flexibility is essential. Data quality and availability are key drivers of model selection. Whereas ML would be able to do fairly well with moderate amounts of data, Deep Learning and Reinforcement Learning require high levels of high-quality, labelled data for proper training. Computational needs also come into play; ML is less computationally intensive, whereas DL and RL require powerful infrastructure, *e.g.*, GPUs and cloud-based computing platforms [92 - 94].

Every AI model presents unique benefits adapted to particular agricultural requirements. The choice of methodology is a balancing act between the requirements of the problem, data availability, and accessible infrastructure to meet the best outcome. Through strategic use of these models, agriculture can move closer to increased precision, efficiency, and sustainability.

Integration of AI Models with Precision Agriculture

AI-led synergies with precision agriculture technologies facilitate easier integration of multiple sources of data and hence generate strong decision-support systems. Instances from the real world demonstrate the revolutionary impact of such integrations. In India, AI-led platforms have integrated satellite images with ML algorithms to predict rice yields and enhance decision-making for millions of farmers [95 - 97]. French vineyard managers have used DL models and drone imagery to track grape health, which result in better produce and less waste [98, 99].

These AI models, combined with IoT, GIS, and satellite technologies, provide full-cycle solutions for ensuring sustainable and efficient agriculture. Agriculture is becoming a data-driven, robust, and sustainable industry and is ready to meet the challenges of a large population of people and changing climatic patterns. Table **1** summarises the use of AI and its integration with GIS, GPS, and IOT in precision agricultural applications.

Table 1. General overview of AI methods and their applications in precision agriculture: technologies, data needs, advantages, challenges, and impacts.

AI Technique	Application Area	Technologies Involved	Data Requirement	Advantages	Challenges	Outcome/Impact	References
Deep Learning (DL)	Image classification, weed detection, crop yield prediction, soil moisture analysis, and plant disease identification	CNNs, LSTMs, GoogleNet, AlexNet, VGG, DetectNet	Large labelled datasets (*e.g.*, satellite imagery, UAV images, soil health data); high data variation and quality critical	High accuracy in classification and prediction; reduced feature engineering; handles complex, multivariate data	High computational cost; data annotation requirements; limited public datasets; challenges with occlusion	Improved precision in early disease detection, optimized resource use, and higher yield predictability	[133]
Machine Learning (ML), Deep Learning (DL)	Agricultural mapping, including land use and land cover (LULC) analysis, crop classification, and soil monitoring	Random Forest (RF), Support Vector Machines (SVM), Artificial Neural Networks (ANN), Convolutional Neural Networks (CNN)	High-resolution satellite imagery, UAV data, geographic and soil datasets, and historical crop data	Enhances precision in mapping, reduces resource use, improves decision-making, and supports sustainable agriculture	High computational demands, limited access to high-quality labelled datasets, challenges with data heterogeneity, and sensor limitations	Improved agricultural decision-making, better resource management, and enhanced environmental sustainability.	[134]

(Table 1) cont.....

AI Technique	Application Area	Technologies Involved	Data Requirement	Advantages	Challenges	Outcome/Impact	References
Machine Learning (ML), Deep Learning (DL)	Precision agriculture applications, including crop health monitoring, yield prediction, and pest management	CNNs, RNNs, Decision Trees, Gradient Boosting, IoT integration	Large-scale, high-resolution datasets from IoT sensors, satellite imagery, UAVs, and historical weather data	High scalability, ability to handle large and complex datasets, enhances decision-making, and improves yield forecasting.	High computational resource requirements, need for consistent data quality, and challenges in farmer adoption due to technological barriers.	Improved yield predictions, early pest detection, reduced resource wastage, and increased overall efficiency in farming practices	[135]
Machine Learning (ML), Deep Learning (DL)	Crop management (yield prediction, disease detection, weed detection, crop quality); livestock management (animal welfare, production monitoring); water and soil management	SVMs, ANNs, DNNs, CNNs, RNNs, Regression Models	High-resolution satellite imagery, sensor data, UAV images, environmental and soil data	Increased accuracy in predictions, early detection of diseases, optimized resource allocation, and enhanced sustainability	High computational requirements, lack of high-quality labelled datasets, challenges in data fusion, and standardization	Improved crop yields, reduced environmental impact, better decision-making, and increased economic efficiency	[54]
Machine Learning (ML)	Biotic stress detection, including weed identification and disease detection	SVMs, Neural Networks (NNs), k-Means, SOMs	High-resolution sensor data (hyperspectral, multispectral, and RGB), large labelled datasets	Improved accuracy in weed and disease detection; effective in analysing spectral and spatial data	High computational demand, dependence on high-quality labelled data, and challenges with sensor heterogeneity	Early detection of stress factors enables site-specific interventions, reducing environmental impact	[136]
Machine Learning (ML), Deep Learning (DL)	Crop management (yield prediction, disease detection, weed detection); livestock management; soil and water management	Artificial Neural Networks (ANNs), CNNs, RNNs, Decision Trees, SVMs	High-resolution satellite imagery, UAV data, IoT sensor data, weather, and soil databases	Improved precision in yield forecasting, disease detection, enhanced decision-making, and resource optimization	High computational requirements; dependency on labelled datasets; challenges in data integration and standardization	Increased agricultural productivity; reduced environmental footprint; improved sustainability	[137]

(Table 1) cont.....

AI Technique	Application Area	Technologies Involved	Data Requirement	Advantages	Challenges	Outcome/Impact	References
Machine Learning (ML), Deep Learning (DL), IoT-based AI	Smart farming, precision agriculture, real-time monitoring, and resource optimization	TensorFlow, PyTorch, Kubernetes, MQTT, HTTP, and MinIO for storage	IoT sensor data, UAV imagery, environmental conditions, soil, and crop-specific datasets	Enables scalability, seamless IoT integration, automates workflows, and supports collaborative model development	High computational and storage needs, complex integration of IoT protocols, steep learning curve for MLOps tools	High computational and storage needs, complex integration of IoT protocols, steep learning curve for MLOps tools	[138]
Deep Learning (DL), Machine Learning (ML)	Crop management (disease detection, yield prediction, soil monitoring), water and weed management	CNNs, RNNs, GANs, SVMs, VGGNet, LSTMs	High-resolution images, UAV and satellite data, IoT sensor data, and annotated datasets	Accurate crop disease identification, improved yield prediction, optimized resource management	High computational costs, requirement for large labeled datasets, and limited transferability of models to new environments	Enhanced sustainability, higher crop yields, and reduced environmental impact through precision farming	[79]
Time- Series Forecasting, Machine Learning (ML), and Deep Learning (DL)	Yield prediction, climate monitoring, and supply chain optimization	ARIMA, SARIMA, CNNs, LSTMs, RFs, and SVMs	Climate data, historical yield records, supply chain data, IoT sensors, and satellite imagery	Enhances decision-making through accurate forecasting, optimizes resource use, and improves resilience.	High computational demand, dependency on data quality, and challenges in integrating diverse datasets	Improved agricultural productivity, reduced supply chain disruptions, and better climate adaptation	[139]
Machine Learning (ML), Deep Learning (DL)	Crop management (yield prediction, disease detection, soil monitoring, weed detection); water and soil management	Random Forest (RF), Support Vector Machines (SVM), Artificial Neural Networks (ANN), CNNs, Gradient Boosting Machines (GBMs)	High-resolution satellite imagery, UAV data, IoT sensor data, and soil composition datasets	Improved resource management, precise yield prediction, and better disease and pest control	High computational demands, dependency on labeled datasets, and challenges in integrating diverse data sources	Enhanced productivity, reduced resource wastage, and improved decision-making in sustainable agriculture	[81]

(Table 1) cont.....

AI Technique	Application Area	Technologies Involved	Data Requirement	Advantages	Challenges	Outcome/Impact	References
Artificial Intelligence (AI), Sensor-Based Technologies, Robotics	Smart farming, crop health monitoring, autonomous machinery, resource optimization	AI models (*e.g.*, Neural Networks), IoT sensors, Robotics platforms (for sowing, harvesting, and monitoring)	High-resolution sensor data (*e.g.*, soil, light, humidity, and weather), UAV imagery, and large annotated datasets	Improves productivity, supports automation, reduces labor costs, and enhances precision in farming tasks	High initial setup cost, challenges with sensor robustness in varying environmental conditions, and a steep learning curve for adoption	Improved efficiency, enhanced sustainability, and real-time data-driven decisions for better yields	[140]

AI-DRIVEN CROP YIELD MANAGEMENT TECHNIQUES

AI-Based Soil Analysis and Fertiliser Optimisation

AI has transformed fertiliser management and soil analysis to offer accurate, data-based information for sustainable agriculture. Machine learning algorithms, such as Random Forest and Gradient Boosting, are used to analyse factors like crop type, growth stage, and climatic conditions to optimise nutrient use efficiency with the least amount of waste. AI technology has been reported to reduce the application of nitrogen fertiliser by 20% for wheat cultivation without altering yield, pointing towards its applications in cost-saving and environmental stewardship [100, 101]. Precision fertilisation not only improves crop yields but also reduces agriculture's environmental impact. Through improved soil monitoring and optimised resource allocation, AI has been revolutionising conventional agriculture towards a data-dependent and environmentally sound practice. Precision fertilisation reduces wastage while optimising fertiliser consumption and promoting sustained health in farm ecosystems [102].

Computer Vision-Based Crop Health Monitoring

CNN, which is among the prominent deep learning techniques, processes high-resolution images captured by drones and satellites to identify signs of stress such as discolouration, wilting, and infestation of pests. Real-time processing enables timely intervention, reducing crop loss and maximising productivity overall [103 - 105]. AI techniques scrutinise spectral data to recognise plant surface disease, pest diagnosis, and nutrient deficiencies within crops. Using the capability of detecting slight nuances in reflectance patterns imperceptible to the naked eye, these tools provide direct insight into plant health [106]. AI-enabled mobile apps have also made these sophisticated diagnostic tools more accessible, enabling farmers to track crop wellness in the field itself. These applications fill the gap between advanced AI technologies and real-world, on-farm agricultural requirements [107, 108].

CNN-based systems have achieved up to 90% accuracy in detecting fungal diseases in rice fields, enabling farmers to act quickly and prevent large-scale infestations [109]. These innovations not only enhance yield quality but also minimise reliance on excessive pesticide use, contributing to sustainable agricultural practices. By integrating computer vision and AI, crop health monitoring has evolved into a precise, proactive, and accessible practice, offering farmers critical tools to optimise crop management and boost resilience against environmental and biological threats [110, 111].

AI models are used to a greater extent on different types of remote sensing data for integrated crop health evaluation. Deep learning models are able to process multispectral, hyperspectral, thermal, and SAR images to detect subtle changes in plant physiology that are hardly perceptible to the naked eye [112]. CNNs on multispectral data, for example, can accurately spot nutrient deficiencies and allow for prompt interventions. CNNs have been found to perform very well in detecting nutrient deficiency using multispectral analysis [113, 114]. 3D-CNNs processing hyperspectral cubes are capable of identifying plant disease in early stages prior to visible symptoms, allowing for early disease management. Studies have shown the ability of 3D-CNNs in the early diagnosis of crop diseases using hyperspectral data [115]. Thermal imaging combined with DL models can precisely quantify crop water stress levels, which optimise irrigation practice. Deep learning techniques have also demonstrated high accuracy in evaluating water stress in plants with the help of thermal imaging [116]. In addition, AI-driven processing of SAR data enables permanent monitoring of crops regardless of weather and supplies information on biomass development and potential yield. AI models have also been used to process SAR data for efficient crop monitoring and yield prediction [117, 118].

Weather Forecasting and Irrigation Scheduling

AI helps in forecasting weather effects with RNN, which works efficiently with sequential data by examining time-series weather patterns to predict parameters like rainfall, temperature, and humidity [119]. In contrast to conventional models, RNNs perform well in capturing temporal dependencies to make important decisions in planting schedules and pest control [120]. RL models adjust water management strategies dynamically in irrigation scheduling by learning the best policies through trial-and-error within simulated environments. Reinforcement Learning integrates various sources of data, such as soil moisture content, evapo-transpiration rates, and weather forecasts, to provide accurate, real-time irrigation suggestions. This approach maximises water use efficiency while preserving the health of crops. RL models, like Deep Q-Networks (DQNs), have proven to be better performers compared to traditional irrigation methods, with up to 30% water savings reported in pilot projects while also improving yields in water-demanding crops such as rice and sugarcane [121, 122]. Integrating RNN-based weather prediction with RL-governed irrigation systems is a paradigmatic shift in water management in agriculture. Such technologies not only mitigate inefficiencies in the use of resources but also enhance climate change resilience by optimising water consumption under uncertainty in the environmental conditions [123, 124]. Challenges, though, exist to enable access to high-resolution data, adequate computing facilities, and farmer training to effect widespread usage. With optimal deployment, the above technologies equip AI to assist with climate-resilient and sustainable agriculture in harmonising productivity growth with the maintenance of the environment and natural resource protection [125, 126].

Transformative Impact and Future Outlook

AI has fundamentally transformed crop yield management by integrating precision technologies into core agricultural practices. From soil analysis and fertiliser optimisation to crop health monitoring, weather prediction, and irrigation scheduling, AI has redefined how resources are managed and decisions are made. These advances have aided in the making of precise interventions, reducing waste, maximising sustainability, and optimising resource efficiency, while simultaneously fulfilling productivity goals and environmental concerns [51, 127, 128]. In the future, the widespread application of AI in agriculture has incredible potential for solving the global food security and sustainability challenges. Overcoming barriers such as inconsistent data quality, limited infrastructure, and lack of farmer training is critical to scaling AI solutions, particularly in resource-constrained regions [129, 130]. Emerging technologies, such as federated learning for decentralised data sharing and AI-robotics integration for automated field operations, represent the next frontier in agricultural innovation. Efforts aimed at creating low-cost AI tools and promoting farmer education can increase AI uptake across the world, which can make it possible for every agricultural community to have access to these revolutionary technologies [131, 132].

As AI develops further, its role in shaping strong and climate-resilient agricultural systems will become more critical, which will enable farmers to cope with shifting environmental conditions while maintaining sustainable food production. By overcoming the challenges of increasing global food needs and decreasing natural resources, precision agriculture using AI holds the key to sustainable future-proofing of food supply to a growing population while also protecting the planet's ecosystems.

REAL-WORLD USE CASES AND APPLICATIONS IN AGRICULTURE

Success Stories of AI in Crop Yield Management

Agriculture, the backbone of world food security, is being increasingly threatened by climate change, resource constraints, and population growth. Conventional yield forecasting models, usually constrained to a few variables, are not adequate to deal with the complexity of agro-climatic systems. AI has emerged as a game-changer in agriculture, enhancing the precision of crop yield forecasting and optimising resource allocation. Through the integration of varied data sets and the use of sophisticated ML algorithms, AI-based models have greatly enhanced agricultural decision-making [141]. Created an ensemble AI model that integrates various machine learning algorithms, including Random Forest, Gradient Boosting, and Support Vector Machines. The model incorporated data from various sources, including soil properties, weather conditions, and past crop history, to make highly accurate yield predictions. Compared to standalone ML models, the ensemble approach showed a 30% increase in the accuracy of predictions. Its application in Telangana, India, showed tangible advantages to farmers who were able to make better use of crop choice as well as the utilisation of resources at hand. The use of AI in local farm operations removed ambiguity and facilitated greater productivity and financially positive outputs.

Apart from yield prediction, AI has also been effectively applied to crop quality prediction. Satellite data and ML algorithm-based algorithms were employed by [142] for the identification of sugarcane quality factors such as °Brix and purity content with a high degree of accuracy. Random Forest (RF) and Artificial Neural Networks (ANN) were employed in the research and reached an accuracy level of 85% in prediction. Multispectral reflectance and Growing Degree Days (GDD) were found to be predictors of interest. This machine learning approach improved mechanised harvesting decision-making and reduced operational costs in Brazil's sugarcane industry [143 - 144]. The use of advanced models and real-time data provided farmers with actionable insights to optimise resource allocation and enhance productivity. The climate risk posed by climate variability, especially in regions where drought is a concern, is managed through the usage of satellite-based rainfall estimates coupled with hybrid AI models [145]. These models have integrated the Water Requirement Satisfaction Index (WRSI) with advanced algorithms like CNN and XGBoost. The integrated approach improved yield prediction errors by less than 7%, providing important information on factors that impact yields, such as the water content in the crop root zone, evapotranspiration, and heat stress. This method has proved to be effective, especially in Zimbabwe, where farmers have been able to use the model to apply timely interventions and enhance food security despite difficult climatic conditions.

Precision Agriculture Practices for Various Crops

Wheat and Maize

In semi-arid regions, conservation tillage methods such as zero tillage and permanent beds, on integration with site-specific nutrient management, have shown significant advantages. For instance, these practices have reduced irrigation needs by 140 – 300 mm per hectare while boosting grain yields by 5.7 – 24.6% compared to Conventional Tillage (CT). Biomass production and water-use efficiency (WUE) also increased by up to 20.8% and 39%, respectively, under these practices [146]. Decision Support Systems (DSS), like LCIS-DSS (Low-Cost system for farm Irrigation Support), have also optimised irrigation for maize. In an Italian case study, this system reduced wastage of water while ensuring maximum yield, proving the efficacy of using soil sensors and remote sensing with irrigation scheduling [147].

Paddy Cultivation

In rice farming, precision agriculture plays a key role in boosting both productivity and sustainability by refining fertiliser and water management. A widely adopted strategy is Site-Specific Nutrient Management (SSNM), which customises nutrient application to match the varying soil fertility within a field. Studies have shown dramatic rice yield increases by optimising fertiliser application according to crop requirements and regional soil types. They use software like Nutrient Expert to optimise the precision. This kind of precision ensures greater efficiency in the utilisation of nutrients, along with encouraging plant development in a healthy way and sustained agricultural long-term sustainability. Compared to conventional uniform fertilisation methods, SSNM has increased grain yields by 10 – 20%, as well as reduced environmental impacts through the better utilisation of inputs [148, 149]. Precision irrigation techniques have also been used to optimise water-use efficiency in rice production. Practices such as Alternate Wetting and Drying (AWD), under the guidance of precision sensors and remote sensing technologies, have minimised water consumption by 20–30% without affecting yields. These systems guarantee that irrigation is only applied where needed, based on actual soil moisture and crop water requirements. Such management not only conserves water but also decreases methane emissions, giving rise to more sustainable rice production systems [150, 151].

Horticultural Crops

In horticultural crops, precision agriculture has enhanced yield monitoring, quality measurement, and resource management significantly. Yield sensing technologies like proximal and remote sensing enabled the generation of yield maps for vegetables and fruits such as apples, berries, *etc.*, in the field. These maps allow site-specific input management and harvesting logistics, enhancing productivity and profitability. For example, yield mapping for apple orchards enabled spatially targeted interventions that boosted marketable yields by as much as 15% [152]. Selective picking according to the spatial variability of yields has specifically benefited fruits such as grapes, providing high-quality produce. This practice has been linked to a 20% improvement in product quality and an equivalent economic return [153]. Furthermore, precision irrigation systems, such as sensor-based systems, have optimised water use in horticulture such that up to 30% of water has been saved without losing yields [154].

Precision agriculture and Artificial Intelligence (AI) are transforming agriculture to enhance yield prediction, resource utilisation, and sustainability across various cropping systems. AI-based models, along with precision practices like site-specific nutrient management and precision irrigation, have recorded outstanding enhancements in productivity as well as environmental sustainability [155]. These innovations are offering novel approaches to solving the global food security and sustainability problem, driving the creation of intelligent and more durable agricultural systems.

AI Implementation Challenges in Agriculture

The use of AI in agriculture is potentially very strong in enhancing productivity and sustainability. There are a number of challenges that prevent it from being extensively adopted:

- ***Data Availability and Quality:***

AI technologies require large, high-quality datasets for peak performance. In agriculture, however, the collection of such data from different geographic areas and seasons poses big challenges and enormous costs [156]. The unavailability of uniform, complete datasets prevents AI from being able to provide accurate results.

- ***Infrastructure and Technological Challenges:***

Implementing AI technologies requires solid infrastructure in terms of steady internet connectivity and high-tech equipment. Most agricultural regions, particularly developing nations, are not well endowed with such, thus complicating AI integration. Moreover, the expense of AI technologies might prove too costly for small-scale farmers [157].

- ***Social and Ethical Issues:***

The use of AI in agriculture brings ethical concerns such as data privacy, rights of ownership, and even the displacement of workers. To address these issues and gain stakeholders' confidence, AI solutions must be developed and implemented responsibly [158].

- ***Interoperability and Standardisation***

The farming industry consists of multiple stakeholders operating under different systems and technologies. Inability to achieve interoperability and standardised protocols may cause dispersed data and slow the integration of AI solutions in the value chain [159].

Addressing these challenges requires a concerted effort from researchers, policymakers, and industry players to develop AI-based solutions that are inclusive, ethical, and pragmatic. These technologies need to be designed to address the unique needs of the agricultural industry so that they can offer meaningful support to farmers while promoting both sustainability and efficiency in food production.

ECONOMIC AND ENVIRONMENTAL IMPACT

Through AI-led understandings in precision farming, agricultural scientists, researchers, and farmers can make more informed choices, maximise the use of resources, reduce environmental footprints, and enhance productivity, ultimately establishing the foundations for innovative and more efficient agriculture practices.

Cost-Benefit Analysis of Precision Agriculture

Precision agriculture applies high-tech technologies to control field variability, maximise resource utilisation, and increase crop yields. A cost-benefit analysis is crucial to assess its economic feasibility.

- ***Initial Investment and Operating Costs:***

Adopting precision agriculture entails heavy up-front investments in equipment such as GPS-enabled machinery, sensors, and data analytics software. Maintenance, data management, and training staff to manage complex technologies are operating expenses. Research by [160] indicates that although the costs are high, they can be recovered by the savings generated over time.

- ***Yield Improvement and Input Optimisation:***

Precision farming allows for specific management of such inputs as pesticides and fertilisers, resulting in practical use and fewer wastes. Through this specificity, yield increase and financial savings are possible. Variable rate application of seeding and nitrogen was shown to increase yields as well as profits by [161].

- ***Return on Investment (ROI):***

Precision agriculture ROI is affected by such aspects as the crop type, the size of the farm, and the technology uptake level. Empirical studies suggest that economies of scale help big farms generate high ROI. That being said, even small farmers may realise some gains through specific precision technology suited to their particular needs. A detailed study done by [162] demonstrated that precision agriculture technology was able to translate into enormous savings and yield boosts, and enhance farm profitability at large.

AI Technologies for Sustainable Farming

AI technologies have a significant impact on promoting sustainable farming practices by enhancing decision-making, resource use, and stewardship of the environment.

- ***Decision Support Systems:*** Decision support systems that utilise AI process large datasets to offer farmers actionable information on irrigation planning, pest control, and crop management. Such systems facilitate well-informed decisions that ensure sustainability [163]. The review indicates the role of AI in enabling the creation of intelligent agricultural systems that ensure sustainable agriculture.
- ***Resource Efficiency*:** AI can forecast optimal irrigation schedules using weather predictions and soil moisture data, which can result in water conservation [142]. discusses how AI technologies have improved resource efficiency and thereby enhanced sustainable agricultural practices.
- ***Climate Adaptation:*** AI provisions the development of climate-resilient farming practices by simulating weather and climate scenarios. It evaluates their effects on crop production. This has enabled farmers to adapt to varying climate conditions and achieve long-term food security and sustainability [148]. has emphasised the capacity of AI to deal with the implications of climate variability in agriculture.

Environmental Footprint Reduction through Precision Agriculture

Precision agriculture aids in environmental sustainability by reducing the ecological footprint of farming.

- **Agrochemical Use Reduction:**

By using inputs exactly at the point where needed, precision agriculture minimises the overuse of fertilisers and pesticides. It also reduces the risk of water pollution and soil degradation.

- **Soil Health Conservation:**

Site-specific management avoids compaction and erosion of the soil and also preserves its structure and fertility. This approach encourages long-term farm productivity while preserving ecological harmony by ensuring that agriculture is sustainable in the years to come.

- **Greenhouse Gas Reduction**

Through the enhanced resource use efficiency and farm process simplification, PA is a significant factor in mitigating greenhouse gas emissions. Methods like variable rate application and real-time monitoring help cut down fuel usage and limit nitrous oxide emissions from fertilisers, contributing to a more environmentally sustainable approach to farming. A recent study [149] has discussed the environmental benefits of precision agriculture, such as its role in reducing greenhouse gas emissions.

FUTURE TRENDS IN PRECISION AGRICULTURE

AI Innovations for Smart Farming

With the integration of AI, farms are now able to employ more precise and more responsive methods, which results in reduced resource consumption and enhanced productivity. Moreover, data mining plays a significant role in changing immense amounts of agricultural data into functional, usable knowledge. AI digests complex environmental factors and past agricultural data in large datasets, revealing concealed relationships [150]. These results are extremely valuable for accurate yield prediction in farm decision support systems [151]. AI promises to significantly curb food wastage, improve the hygiene of production, and manage machinery in diverse stages of agriculture, such as supply chain management, patterns of production, and soil, crop, and water management processes, as well as disease and pest control [152]. ML, specifically, aids in solving the most important agricultural problems, including yield estimation, crop quality estimation, detection of weeds and diseases, species recognition, water control, and soil control [153].

Future of AI in Global Agricultural Systems

The potential of AI in the world's agricultural systems in the future is vast to improve crop yield management through precision agriculture. Sophisticated AI models, coupled with real-time information from IoT sensors and Remote Sensing (RS) technologies, can maximise the use of resources, forecast crop performance, and reduce climate change risks [3, 154, 155]. AI applications can also play a vital role in improving food security and its quality by addressing key factors such as availability, use, and accessibility [156]. In addition to this, the agricultural sector can drive sustainable innovations that contribute to global food security by harnessing the power of AI. The agri-food industry has already started employing AI and ML technologies to reduce food waste and improve production security, which is essential for the growing global demand for food.

Climate change also poses a significant threat to global food security, as it can lead to unpredictable weather patterns and reduced yields. To overcome this challenge, AI-based technologies can be leveraged to address both current and future crop protection issues. This will enable more precise crop protection techniques by facilitating the evolution of Agriculture 5.0 [157]. As AI continues to evolve, it will empower farmers to adopt more sustainable and efficient farming practices, thus encouraging global food security along with reducing environmental impact.

CONCLUSION

PA enables farmers to enhance productivity, optimise resource use, and ensure sustainable agricultural practices, which shows an innovative shift in modern farming practices. The integration of advanced technologies, including IoT sensors, GPS, GIS, remote sensing, and AI, has revolutionised crop management and crop production. It offers precise solutions for monitoring, prediction, and decision-making. AI algorithms such as ML, DL, and RL have proven to be effective in crop yield prediction, soil analysis, fertiliser optimisation, and crop health monitoring. These innovations have empowered farmers with data-driven insights and allowed for more efficient resource management and improved crop quality. While the benefits of PA are evident, challenges remain. Cost, accessibility, and technological adoption are the major challenges, especially for developing countries like India. However, the potential for economic and environmental gains, including sustainable farming practices and reduced environmental footprints, compensates for these barriers. The future of precision agriculture lies in the continued development of AI, robotics, and automation, which will offer greater opportunities for global agricultural systems.

REFERENCES

[1] Frankel F R. India's green revolution: economic gains and political costs. Princeton Univ. Press 2015.

[2] Gillespie S, van den Bold M. Agriculture, food systems, and nutrition: meeting the challenge. Glob Chall 2017; 1(3): 1600002.
[http://dx.doi.org/10.1002/gch2.201600002] [PMID: 31565265]

[3] Sishodia RP, Ray RL, Singh SK. Applications of remote sensing in precision agriculture: a review. Remote Sens (Basel) 2020; 12(19): 3136.
[http://dx.doi.org/10.3390/rs12193136]

[4] Sakthipriya S, Naresh R. Precision agriculture based on convolutional neural network in rice production nutrient management using machine learning genetic algorithm. Eng Appl Artif Intell 2024; 130: 107682.
[http://dx.doi.org/10.1016/j.engappai.2023.107682]

[5] Shafi U, Mumtaz R, García-Nieto J, Hassan SA, Zaidi SAR, Iqbal N. Precision agriculture techniques and practices: from considerations to applications. Sensors (Basel) 2019; 19(17): 3796.
[http://dx.doi.org/10.3390/s19173796] [PMID: 31480709]

[6] Petrović B, Bumbálek R, Zoubek T, Kuneš R, Smutný L, Bartoš P. Application of precision agriculture technologies in Central Europe-review. Journal of Agriculture and Food Research 2024; 15: 101048.
[http://dx.doi.org/10.1016/j.jafr.2024.101048]

[7] Peng Y, Zhu T, Li Y, *et al.* Remote prediction of yield based on LAI estimation in oilseed rape under different planting methods and nitrogen fertilizer applications. Agric For Meteorol 2019; 271: 116-25.
[http://dx.doi.org/10.1016/j.agrformet.2019.02.032]

[8] Kross A, McNairn H, Lapen D, Sunohara M, Champagne C. Assessment of RapidEye vegetation indices for estimation of leaf area index and biomass in corn and soybean crops. Int J Appl Earth Obs Geoinf 2015; 34: 235-48.
[http://dx.doi.org/10.1016/j.jag.2014.08.002]

[9] Zhou L, Chen N, Chen Z, Xing C. ROSCC: An efficient remote sensing observation-sharing method based on cloud computing for soil moisture mapping in precision agriculture. IEEE J Sel Top Appl Earth Obs Remote Sens 2016; 9(12): 5588-98.
[http://dx.doi.org/10.1109/JSTARS.2016.2574810]

[10] Akintuyi O B. AI in agriculture: A comparative review of developments in the USA and Africa. Res J Sci Eng 2024; 10(02): 060-70.

[11] Boopathi S. Sustainable development using IoT and AI techniques for water utilization in agriculture. Sustainable Development in AI, Blockchain, and E-Governance Applications. IGI Global 2024; pp. 204-28.
[http://dx.doi.org/10.4018/979-8-3693-1722-8.ch012]

[12] M e K, Devi BR, Soni A, *et al.* A review on precision agriculture navigating the future of farming with AI and IoT. Asian Journal of Soil Science and Plant Nutrition 2024; 10(2): 336-49.
[http://dx.doi.org/10.9734/ajsspn/2024/v10i2291]

[13] Linaza M, Posada J, Bund J, *et al.* Data-driven artificial intelligence applications for sustainable precision agriculture. Agronomy (Basel) 2021; 11(6): 1227.
[http://dx.doi.org/10.3390/agronomy11061227]

[14] Fishman R, Ghosh M, Mishra A, *et al.* Digital villages: a data-driven approach to precision agriculture

in small farms Proceedings of the 9th International Conference on Sensor Networks. Valletta, Malta. 2020; pp. 161-6.
[http://dx.doi.org/10.5220/0009373101610166]

[15] Bai G, Ge Y, Hussain W, Baenziger PS, Graef G. A multi-sensor system for high throughput field phenotyping in soybean and wheat breeding. Comput Electron Agric 2016; 128: 181-92.
[http://dx.doi.org/10.1016/j.compag.2016.08.021]

[16] Andronie M, Lăzăroiu G, Iatagan M, Hurloiu I, Dijmărescu I. Sustainable cyber-physical production systems in big data-driven smart urban economy: a systematic literature review. Sustainability (Basel) 2021; 13(2): 751.
[http://dx.doi.org/10.3390/su13020751]

[17] Abdelfattah MA, Kumar AT. A web-based GIS enabled soil information system for the United Arab Emirates and its applicability in agricultural land use planning. Arab J Geosci 2015; 8(3): 1813-27.
[http://dx.doi.org/10.1007/s12517-014-1289-y]

[18] Barrile V, Genovese E. GIS, remote sensing, and forecasting systems for precision agriculture development. In: Gervasi O, Ed. Comput Sci Its Appl – ICCSA 2024 Workshops Lect Notes Comput Sci. Springer Nature Switzerland 2024; 14819: pp. 302-18.
[http://dx.doi.org/10.1007/978-3-031-65282-0_20]

[19] Mohammed GH, Colombo R, Middleton EM, *et al.* Remote sensing of solar-induced chlorophyll fluorescence (SIF) in vegetation: 50 years of progress. Remote Sens Environ 2019; 231: 111177.
[http://dx.doi.org/10.1016/j.rse.2019.04.030] [PMID: 33414568]

[20] Wang J, Wang Y, Li G, Qi Z. Integration of remote sensing and machine learning for precision agriculture: a comprehensive perspective on applications. Agronomy (Basel) 2024; 14(9): 1975.
[http://dx.doi.org/10.3390/agronomy14091975]

[21] Thenkabail PS, Aneece I, Teluguntla P, Oliphant A. Hyperspectral narrowband data propel gigantic leap in the earth remote sensing. Photogramm Eng Remote Sensing 2021; 87(7): 461-7.
[http://dx.doi.org/10.14358/PERS.87.7.461]

[22] Vairavan C, Kamble BM, Durgude AG, Ingle SR, Pugazenthi K. Hyperspectral imaging of soil and crop: a review. Journal of Experimental Agriculture International 2024; 46(1): 48-61.
[http://dx.doi.org/10.9734/jeai/2024/v46i12290]

[23] Möller M, Alchanatis V, Cohen Y, *et al.* Use of thermal and visible imagery for estimating crop water status of irrigated grapevine. J Exp Bot 2006; 58(4): 827-38.
[http://dx.doi.org/10.1093/jxb/erl115] [PMID: 16968884]

[24] Prashar A, Jones HG. Assessing drought responses using thermal infrared imaging. Methods Mol Biol 2016; 1398: 209-19.
[http://dx.doi.org/10.1007/978-1-4939-3356-3_17] [PMID: 26867626]

[25] Yu H, Kong B, Hou Y, Xu X, Chen T, Liu X. A critical review on applications of hyperspectral remote sensing in crop monitoring. Exp Agric 2022; 58: e26.
[http://dx.doi.org/10.1017/S0014479722000278]

[26] Zhou J, Li F, Wang X, *et al.* Hyperspectral and fluorescence imaging approaches for nondestructive detection of rice chlorophyll. Plants 2024; 13(9): 1270.
[http://dx.doi.org/10.3390/plants13091270] [PMID: 38732485]

[27] Thapa S. Irrigation management in vineyards: modeling water stress using hyperspectral imaging. 2021.

[28] Abdulridha J, Ampatzidis Y, Roberts P, Kakarla SC. Detecting powdery mildew disease in squash at different stages using UAV-based hyperspectral imaging and artificial intelligence. Biosyst Eng 2020; 197: 135-48.
[http://dx.doi.org/10.1016/j.biosystemseng.2020.07.001]

[29] Rani KS, Gowri T, Madhulatha T. Dimensionality Reduction Techniques For Hyperspectral Image

using Deep Learning. IJITEE 2019; 9(2S3): 364-70.
[http://dx.doi.org/10.35940/ijitee.B1033.1292S319]

[30] Gul D, Banday RUZ. Transforming crop management through advanced ai and machine learning: insights into innovative strategies for sustainable agriculture. AI, Computer Science and Robotics Technology 2024; 3(Oct).
[http://dx.doi.org/10.5772/acrt.20240030]

[31] Sharma N A, Kumar K, Chand R R, Kabir M A. Utilizing hyperspectral imaging with machine learning techniques for soil analysis. 2021.
[http://dx.doi.org/10.1007/978-3-031-83127-0_5]

[32] Khonina SN, Kazanskiy NL, Oseledets IV, Nikonorov AV, Butt MA. Synergy between artificial intelligence and hyperspectral imagining—a review. Technologies (Basel) 2024; 12(9): 163.
[http://dx.doi.org/10.3390/technologies12090163]

[33] Ali F, Razzaq A, Tariq W, *et al.* Spectral intelligence: AI-driven hyperspectral imaging for agricultural and ecosystem applications. Agronomy (Basel) 2024; 14(10): 2260.
[http://dx.doi.org/10.3390/agronomy14102260]

[34] Lu B, Dao P, Liu J, He Y, Shang J. Recent advances of hyperspectral imaging technology and applications in agriculture. Remote Sens (Basel) 2020; 12(16): 2659.
[http://dx.doi.org/10.3390/rs12162659]

[35] Hollberg J, Schellberg J. Distinguishing intensity levels of grassland fertilization using vegetation indices. Remote Sens (Basel) 2017; 9(1): 81.
[http://dx.doi.org/10.3390/rs9010081]

[36] Ballester C, Jiménez-Bello MA, Castel JR, Intrigliolo DS. Usefulness of thermography for plant water stress detection in citrus and persimmon trees. Agric For Meteorol 2013; 168: 120-9.
[http://dx.doi.org/10.1016/j.agrformet.2012.08.005]

[37] Kim J, Kim S, Ju C, Son HI. Unmanned aerial vehicles in agriculture: a review of perspective of platform, control, and applications. IEEE Access 2019; 7: 105100-15.
[http://dx.doi.org/10.1109/ACCESS.2019.2932119]

[38] Jafar A, Bibi N, Naqvi RA, Sadeghi-Niaraki A, Jeong D. Revolutionizing agriculture with artificial intelligence: plant disease detection methods, applications, and their limitations. Front Plant Sci 2024; 15: 1356260.
[http://dx.doi.org/10.3389/fpls.2024.1356260] [PMID: 38545388]

[39] Shams MY, Gamel SA, Talaat FM. Enhancing crop recommendation systems with explainable artificial intelligence: a study on agricultural decision-making. Neural Comput Appl 2024; 36(11): 5695-714.
[http://dx.doi.org/10.1007/s00521-023-09391-2]

[40] Wang Y, Zhang Q, Yu F, *et al.* Progress in research on deep learning-based crop yield prediction. Agronomy (Basel) 2024; 14(10): 2264.
[http://dx.doi.org/10.3390/agronomy14102264]

[41] Olorunsogo T, Olorunsogo T, Adaga E, Olorunsogo T, Adaga E, Daraojimba DO. AI in precision agriculture: A review of technologies for sustainable farming practices. World Journal of Advanced Research and Reviews 2024; (1): 2276-85.
[http://dx.doi.org/10.30574/wjarr.2024.21.1.0314]

[42] Perumallapalli R K. AI in precision agriculture: real-world application for crop optimization. 2017; 5(1).

[43] Wei H, Xu W, Kang B, *et al.* Irrigation with artificial intelligence: problems, premises, promises. Human-Centric Intelligent Systems 2024; 4(2): 187-205.
[http://dx.doi.org/10.1007/s44230-024-00072-4]

[44] de Oliveira R C. Artificial intelligence in agriculture: benefits, challenges, and trends. Appl Sci (Basel)

2023; 13(13): 13.
[http://dx.doi.org/10.3390/app13137405]

[45] Patel A, Selvan S S, Wahid A, Yadav D K, Sanodiya R. Transforming agriculture with artificial intelligence (AI): A promising future 2023.

[46] Ahmad A, Liew AXW, Venturini F, *et al.* AI can empower agriculture for global food security: challenges and prospects in developing nations. Frontiers in Artificial Intelligence 2024; 7: 1328530.
[http://dx.doi.org/10.3389/frai.2024.1328530] [PMID: 38726306]

[47] Hasteer N, Mallik A, Nigam D, Sindhwani R, Van Belle JP. Analysis of challenges to implement artificial intelligence technologies in agriculture sector. International Journal of System Assurance Engineering and Management 2024; 15(5): 1841-60.
[http://dx.doi.org/10.1007/s13198-023-02164-z]

[48] Chandra R, Collis S. Digital agriculture for small-scale producers. Commun ACM 2021; 64(12): 75-84.
[http://dx.doi.org/10.1145/3454008]

[49] Gikunda K. Harnessing artificial intelligence for sustainable agricultural development in africa: opportunities, challenges, and impact. arXiv 2024.
[http://dx.doi.org/10.48550/arXiv.2401.06171]

[50] Gumbi N, Gumbi L, Twinomurinzi H. Towards sustainable digital agriculture for smallholder farmers: a systematic literature review. Sustainability (Basel) 2023; 15(16): 12530.
[http://dx.doi.org/10.3390/su151612530]

[51] Kundu SG, Ghosh A, Kundu A, Gp G. A ML-AI enabled ensemble model for predicting agricultural yield. Cogent Food & Agriculture 2022; 8(1): 2085717.

[52] Aashu , Rajwar K, Pant M, Deep K. Application of machine learning in agriculture: recent trends and future research avenues. arXiv 2024. Available from: http://arxiv.org/abs/2405.17465

[53] Araújo SO, Peres RS, Ramalho JC, Lidon F, Barata J. Machine learning applications in agriculture: current trends, challenges, and future perspectives. Agronomy (Basel) 2023; 13(12): 2976.
[http://dx.doi.org/10.3390/agronomy13122976]

[54] Liakos K, Busato P, Moshou D, Pearson S, Bochtis D. Machine learning in agriculture: a review. Sensors (Basel) 2018; 18(8): 2674.
[http://dx.doi.org/10.3390/s18082674] [PMID: 30110960]

[55] Bali N, Singla A. Emerging trends in machine learning to predict crop yield and study its influential factors: a survey. Arch Comput Methods Eng 2022; 29(1): 95-112.
[http://dx.doi.org/10.1007/s11831-021-09569-8]

[56] Morales A, Villalobos FJ. Using machine learning for crop yield prediction in the past or the future. Front Plant Sci 2023; 14: 1128388.
[http://dx.doi.org/10.3389/fpls.2023.1128388] [PMID: 37063228]

[57] Bouguettaya A, Zarzour H, Kechida A, Taberkit AM. Deep learning techniques to classify agricultural crops through UAV imagery: a review. Neural Comput Appl 2022; 34(12): 9511-36.
[http://dx.doi.org/10.1007/s00521-022-07104-9] [PMID: 35281624]

[58] Shahi TB, Xu CY, Neupane A, Guo W. Recent advances in crop disease detection using UAV and deep learning techniques. Remote Sens (Basel) 2023; 15(9): 2450.
[http://dx.doi.org/10.3390/rs15092450]

[59] Dhillon MS, Dahms T, Kuebert-Flock C, *et al.* Integrating random forest and crop modeling improves the crop yield prediction of winter wheat and oil seed rape. Frontiers in Remote Sensing 2023; 3: 1010978.
[http://dx.doi.org/10.3389/frsen.2022.1010978]

[60] Jeong JH, Resop JP, Mueller ND, *et al.* Random forests for global and regional crop yield predictions.

PLoS One 2016; 11(6): e0156571.
[http://dx.doi.org/10.1371/journal.pone.0156571] [PMID: 27257967]

[61] Shastry A, Sanjay HA, Bhanusree E. Prediction of crop yield using regression techniques. Int J Soft Comput 2017.

[62] Basava C. Optimizing fertilizer usage in agriculture with AI Driven Recommendations. 2024; 21(1).

[63] Izquierdo-Bueno I, Moraga J, Cantoral JM, Carbú M, Garrido C, González-Rodríguez VE. Smart viniculture: applying artificial intelligence for improved winemaking and risk management. Appl Sci (Basel) 2024; 14(22): 10277.
[http://dx.doi.org/10.3390/app142210277]

[64] Gul D, Banday RUZ. Transforming crop management through advanced AI and machine learning: insights into innovative strategies for sustainable agriculture. AI, Computer Science and Robotics Technology 2024; 3(Oct).
[http://dx.doi.org/10.5772/acrt.20240030]

[65] Albahar M. A survey on deep learning and its impact on agriculture: challenges and opportunities. Agriculture 2023; 13(3): 540.
[http://dx.doi.org/10.3390/agriculture13030540]

[66] Altalak M. M. Ammad uddin, A. Alajmi, and A. Rizg, "Smart agriculture applications using deep learning. Appl Sci (Basel) 2022; 12(12): 12.
[http://dx.doi.org/10.3390/app12125919]

[67] Kamilaris A, Prenafeta-Boldú FX. A review of the use of convolutional neural networks in agriculture. J Agric Sci 2018; 156(3): 312-22.
[http://dx.doi.org/10.1017/S0021859618000436]

[68] J. Eunice, D. E. Popescu, M. K. Chowdary, and J. Hemanth, "Deep learning. Agronomy (Basel) 2022; 12(10): 10.
[http://dx.doi.org/10.3390/agronomy12102395]

[69] Kurmi Y, Saxena P, Kirar BS, Gangwar S, Chaurasia V, Goel A. Deep CNN model for crops' diseases detection using leaf images. Multidimens Syst Signal Process 2022; 33(3): 981-1000.
[http://dx.doi.org/10.1007/s11045-022-00820-4]

[70] Lu T, Gao M, Wang L. Crop classification in high-resolution remote sensing images based on multi-scale feature fusion semantic segmentation model. Front Plant Sci 2023; 14: 1196634.
[http://dx.doi.org/10.3389/fpls.2023.1196634] [PMID: 37593043]

[71] Jung DH, Kim JD, Kim HY, Lee TS, Kim HS, Park SH. A hyperspectral data 3D convolutional neural network classification model for diagnosis of gray mold disease in strawberry leaves. Front Plant Sci 2022; 13: 837020.
[http://dx.doi.org/10.3389/fpls.2022.837020] [PMID: 35360322]

[72] Niu H, Wang D, Chen Y. Tree-level irrigation inference using UAV thermal imagery and convolutional neural networks 2022 International Conference on Unmanned Aircraft Systems (ICUAS). 1586-91.
[http://dx.doi.org/10.1109/ICUAS54217.2022.9836214]

[73] Kussul N, Lavreniuk M, Skakun S, Shelestov A. Deep learning. IEEE Geosci Remote Sens Lett 2017; 14(5): 778-82.
[http://dx.doi.org/10.1109/LGRS.2017.2681128]

[74] Zhang M, Li R, Fu S, *et al.* Deep learning enhanced light sheet fluorescence microscopy for *in vivo* 4D imaging of zebrafish heart beating. Light Sci Appl 2025; 14(1): 92.
[http://dx.doi.org/10.1038/s41377-024-01710-z] [PMID: 39994185]

[75] Wang D, Cao W, Zhang F, Li Z, Xu S, Wu X. A review of deep learning in multiscale agricultural sensing. Remote Sens (Basel) 2022; 14(3): 559.
[http://dx.doi.org/10.3390/rs14030559] [PMID: 39429606]

[76] Zhang F, Hu C, Yin Q, Li W, Li H, Hong W. SAR target recognition using the multi-aspect-aware bidirectional LSTM recurrent neural networks. IEEE Access 2017; 5: 26880-91. [http://dx.doi.org/10.1109/ACCESS.2017.2773363]

[77] Ndikumana E, Ho Tong Minh D, Baghdadi N, Courault D, Hossard L. Deep recurrent neural network for agricultural classification using multitemporal SAR sentinel-1 for camargue, france. Remote Sens (Basel) 2018; 10(8): 1217. [http://dx.doi.org/10.3390/rs10081217]

[78] Khaki S, Wang L, Archontoulis SV. A CNN-RNN framework for crop yield prediction. Front Plant Sci 2020; 10: 1750. [http://dx.doi.org/10.3389/fpls.2019.01750] [PMID: 32038699]

[79] Albahar M. A survey on deep learning and its impact on agriculture: challenges and opportunities. Agriculture 2023; 13(3): 540. [http://dx.doi.org/10.3390/agriculture13030540]

[80] Punjani KK, Mahadevan K, Gunasekaran A, Kumar VVR, Joshi S. Cloud computing in agriculture: a bibliometric and network visualization analysis. Qual Quant 2023; 57(4): 3849-83. [http://dx.doi.org/10.1007/s11135-022-01535-1]

[81] Araújo SO, Peres RS, Ramalho JC, Lidon F, Barata J. Machine learning applications in agriculture: current trends, challenges, and future perspectives. Agronomy (Basel) 2023; 13(12): 2976. [http://dx.doi.org/10.3390/agronomy13122976]

[82] Pande C B, Moharir K N. Application of hyperspectral remote sensing role in precision farming and sustainable agriculture under climate change: a review. In: Pande C B, Ed. Climate Change Impacts on Natural Resources, Ecosystems and Agricultural Systems Springer Climate. Springer 2023; pp. 503-20. [http://dx.doi.org/10.1007/978-3-031-19059-9_21]

[83] Guerri MF, Distante C, Spagnolo P, Bougourzi F, Taleb-Ahmed A. Deep learning techniques for hyperspectral image analysis in agriculture: A review. ISPRS Open Journal of Photogrammetry and Remote Sensing 2024; 12: 100062. [http://dx.doi.org/10.1016/j.ophoto.2024.100062]

[84] Zhe Q, Gao W, Zhang C, Du G, Li Y, Chen D. A hyperspectral classification method based on deep learning and dimension reduction for ground environmental monitoring. IEEE Access 2025; 13: 29969-82. [http://dx.doi.org/10.1109/ACCESS.2025.3542038]

[85] Lin Z, Chen Y, Zhao X, Wang G. Spectral-spatial classification of hyperspectral image using autoencoders. 2013 9th Int Conf Inf Commun Signal Process (ICICS). 1-5. [http://dx.doi.org/10.1109/ICICS.2013.6782777]

[86] Li Y, Zhang H, Shen Q. Spectral–spatial classification of hyperspectral imagery with 3D convolutional neural network. Remote Sens (Basel) 2017; 9(1): 67. [http://dx.doi.org/10.3390/rs9010067]

[87] Jin D, Yang B. Graph attention convolutional autoencoder-based unsupervised nonlinear unmixing for hyperspectral images. IEEE J Sel Top Appl Earth Obs Remote Sens 2023; 16: 7896-906. [http://dx.doi.org/10.1109/JSTARS.2023.3308037]

[88] Biddappa CB, v DS. Crop yield prediction on agriculture using machine learning. International Journal of Research Publication and Reviews 2024; 5(3): 165-7. [http://dx.doi.org/10.55248/gengpi.5.0324.0803]

[89] Sarker IH. Machine learning: Algorithms, real-world applications and research directions. SN Computer Science 2021; 2(3): 160. [http://dx.doi.org/10.1007/s42979-021-00592-x] [PMID: 33778771]

[90] Chen Y, Yu Z, Han Z, Sun W, He L. A decision-making system for cotton irrigation based on

reinforcement learning strategy. Agronomy (Basel) 2023; 14(1): 11.
[http://dx.doi.org/10.3390/agronomy14010011]

[91] Saikai Y, Peake A, Chenu K. Deep reinforcement learning for irrigation scheduling using high-dimensional sensor feedback. PLOS Water 2023; 2(9): e0000169.
[http://dx.doi.org/10.1371/journal.pwat.0000169]

[92] Bandi A, Adapa PVSR, Kuchi YEVPK. The power of generative AI: A review of requirements, models, input–output formats, evaluation metrics, and challenges. Future Internet 2023; 15(8): 260.
[http://dx.doi.org/10.3390/fi15080260]

[93] Raschka S. Model evaluation, model selection, and algorithm selection in machine learning. arXiv 2020.
[http://dx.doi.org/10.48550/arXiv.1811.12808]

[94] Sarker IH. AI-based modeling: techniques, applications and research issues towards automation, intelligent and smart systems. SN Computer Science 2022; 3(2): 158.
[http://dx.doi.org/10.1007/s42979-022-01043-x] [PMID: 35194580]

[95] Aslan MF, Sabanci K, Aslan B. Artificial intelligence techniques in crop yield estimation based on sentinel-2 data: a comprehensive survey. Sustainability (Basel) 2024; 16(18): 8277.
[http://dx.doi.org/10.3390/su16188277]

[96] Clercq D D, Mahdi A. Feasibility of machine learning-based rice yield prediction in India at the district level using climate reanalysis data. arXiv 2024.
[http://dx.doi.org/10.48550/arXiv.2403.07967]

[97] Liu Y, Wang S, Chen J, *et al.* Rice yield prediction and model interpretation based on satellite and climatic indicators using a transformer method. Remote Sens (Basel) 2022; 14(19): 5045.
[http://dx.doi.org/10.3390/rs14195045]

[98] Barros T, Conde P, Gonçalves G, *et al.* Multispectral vineyard segmentation: a deep learning approach. arXiv 2022. Available from: http://arxiv.org/abs/2108.01200

[99] Humpal J, Baillie C. Automation: Opportunities for adoption in agriculture. 2022.

[100] Basava C. Optimizing fertilizer usage in agriculture with AI driven recommendations 2024; 21(1).

[101] Bg H, Gc R. Fertilizer recommendation system using machine learning. Open Access 06(07).

[102] Karunathilake EMBM, Le AT, Heo S, Chung YS, Mansoor S. The path to smart farming: innovations and opportunities in precision agriculture. Agriculture 2023; 13(8): 1593.
[http://dx.doi.org/10.3390/agriculture13081593]

[103] Altalak M. M. Ammad uddin, A. Alajmi, and A. Rizg, Smart agriculture applications using deep learning. Appl Sci (Basel) 2022; 12(12): 12.
[http://dx.doi.org/10.3390/app12125919]

[104] Kamilaris A, Prenafeta-Boldú F X. A review of the use of convolutional neural networks in agriculture. J Agric Sci 2018; 156(3): 312-22.
[http://dx.doi.org/10.1017/s0021859618000436]

[105] Lu J, Tan L, Jiang H. Review on Convolutional Neural Network (CNN) applied to plant leaf disease classification. Agriculture 2021; 11(8): 707.
[http://dx.doi.org/10.3390/agriculture11080707]

[106] Kapleshwar M, Ajay P. Identification of plant nutrient deficencies using convolutional. Neural Netw 2024; 9(4).

[107] Nikitha S, Prabhanjan S, Sathyanarayan A. Plant nutritional deficiency detection: a survey of predictive analytics approaches. Iran J Comput Sci 2024; (Oct):
[http://dx.doi.org/10.1007/s42044-024-00209-5]

[108] Venkatesh K, Naik KJ. An ensemble transfer learning for nutrient deficiency identification and yield-

loss prediction in crop. Multimedia Tools Appl 2024; 83(32): 78535-61.
[http://dx.doi.org/10.1007/s11042-024-18592-3]

[109] Gogoi M, Kumar V, Begum S, Sharma N, Kant S. Classification and detection of rice diseases using a 3-stage CNN architecture with transfer learning approach. Agriculture 2023; 13(8): 1505.
[http://dx.doi.org/10.3390/agriculture13081505]

[110] Temidayo Olorunsogo , Temidayo Olorunsogo , Ejuma Adaga , Olorunsogo T, Adaga E, Daraojimba DO. AI in precision agriculture: A review of technologies for sustainable farming practices. World Journal of Advanced Research and Reviews 2024; (1): 2276-85.
[http://dx.doi.org/10.30574/wjarr.2024.21.1.0314]

[111] Alloghani MA. AI for sustainable agriculture: a systematic review. In: Alloghani MA, Ed. Artificial Intelligence and Sustainability. Cham: Springer Nature Switzerland 2024; pp. 53-64.
[http://dx.doi.org/10.1007/978-3-031-45214-7_3]

[112] Cho SB, Soleh HM, Choi JW, *et al.* Recent methods for evaluating crop water stress using ai techniques: a review. Sensors (Basel) 2024; 24(19): 6313.
[http://dx.doi.org/10.3390/s24196313] [PMID: 39409355]

[113] Taha MF, Abdalla A, ElMasry G, *et al.* Using deep convolutional neural network for image-based diagnosis of nutrient deficiencies in plants grown in aquaponics. Chemosensors (Basel) 2022; 10(2): 45.
[http://dx.doi.org/10.3390/chemosensors10020045]

[114] Shi Y, Han L, González-Moreno P, *et al.* A fast fourier convolutional deep neural network for accurate and explainable discrimination of wheat yellow rust and nitrogen deficiency from sentinel-2 time-series data. arXiv 2023.
[http://dx.doi.org/10.48550/arXiv.2306.17207]

[115] Guerri MF, Distante C, Spagnolo P, Bougourzi F, Taleb-Ahmed A. Deep learning techniques for hyperspectral image analysis in agriculture: A review. ISPRS Open Journal of Photogrammetry and Remote Sensing 2024; 12: 100062.
[http://dx.doi.org/10.1016/j.ophoto.2024.100062]

[116] Wang D, Cao W, Zhang F, Li Z, Xu S, Wu X. A review of deep learning in multiscale agricultural sensing. Remote Sens (Basel) 2022; 14(3): 559.
[http://dx.doi.org/10.3390/rs14030559] [PMID: 39429606]

[117] Hashemi MGZ, Tan PN, Jalilvand E, Wilke B, Alemohammad H, Das NN. Yield estimation from SAR data using patch-based deep learning and machine learning techniques. Comput Electron Agric 2024; 226(C): 109340.
[http://dx.doi.org/10.1016/j.compag.2024.109340]

[118] Ilyas Q, Ahmad M, Mehmood A. Automated estimation of crop yield using artificial intelligence and remote sensing technologies. Bioengineering (Basel) 2023; 10(2): 125.
[http://dx.doi.org/10.3390/bioengineering10020125] [PMID: 36829619]

[119] Wei H, Xu W, Kang B, *et al.* Irrigation with artificial intelligence: problems, premises, promises. Human-Centric Intelligent Systems 2024; 4(2): 187-205.
[http://dx.doi.org/10.1007/s44230-024-00072-4]

[120] Nketiah EA, Chenlong L, Yingchuan J, Aram SA. Recurrent neural network modeling of multivariate time series and its application in temperature forecasting. PLoS One 2023; 18(5): e0285713.
[http://dx.doi.org/10.1371/journal.pone.0285713] [PMID: 37205720]

[121] Saikai Y, Peake A, Chenu K. Deep reinforcement learning for irrigation scheduling using high-dimensional sensor feedback. PLOS Water 2023; 2(9): e0000169.
[http://dx.doi.org/10.1371/journal.pwat.0000169]

[122] Birkeneder B. Advancements of deep q-networks. 2019.

[123] Behzadipour F, Ghasemi Nezhad Raeini M, Abdanan Mehdizadeh S, *et al.* A smart IoT-based

irrigation system design using AI and prediction model. Neural Comput Appl 2023; 35(35): 24843-57. [http://dx.doi.org/10.1007/s00521-023-08987-y]

[124] Wang Z, Xiao S, Wang J, Parab A, Patel S. Intelligent Agricultural Management Considering N2O Emission and Climate Variability with Uncertainties. arXiv 2024. Available from: http://arxiv.org/abs/2402.08832

[125] Hasteer N, Mallik A, Nigam D, Sindhwani R, Van Belle JP. Analysis of challenges to implement artificial intelligence technologies in agriculture sector. International Journal of System Assurance Engineering and Management 2024; 15(5): 1841-60. [http://dx.doi.org/10.1007/s13198-023-02164-z]

[126] de Oliveira R C. Artificial intelligence in agriculture: benefits, challenges, and trends. Appl Sci (Basel) 2023; 13(13): 13. [http://dx.doi.org/10.3390/app13137405]

[127] Aslan MF, Sabanci K, Aslan B. Artificial intelligence techniques in crop yield estimation based on sentinel-2 data: a comprehensive survey. Sustainability (Basel) 2024; 16(18): 8277. [http://dx.doi.org/10.3390/su16188277]

[128] Gul D, Banday RUZ. Transforming crop management through advanced ai and machine learning: insights into innovative strategies for sustainable agriculture. AI, Computer Science and Robotics Technology 2024; 3(Oct) [http://dx.doi.org/10.5772/acrt.20240030]

[129] Fadiji T, Bokaba T, Fawole OA, Twinomurinzi H. Artificial intelligence in postharvest agriculture: mapping a research agenda. Front Sustain Food Syst 2023; 7: 1226583. [http://dx.doi.org/10.3389/fsufs.2023.1226583]

[130] de Oliveira R C. Artificial intelligence in agriculture: benefits, challenges, and trends. Appl Sci (Basel) 2023; 13(13): 13. [http://dx.doi.org/10.3390/app13137405]

[131] Oliveira LFP, Moreira AP, Silva MF. Advances in agriculture robotics: a state-of-the-art review and challenges ahead. Robotics 2021; 10(2): 52. [http://dx.doi.org/10.3390/robotics10020052]

[132] Žalik KR, Žalik M. A review of federated learning in agriculture. Sensors (Basel) 2023; 23(23): 9566. [http://dx.doi.org/10.3390/s23239566] [PMID: 38067939]

[133] Kamilaris A, Prenafeta-Boldú FX. Deep learning in agriculture: A survey. Comput Electron Agric 2018; 147: 70-90. [http://dx.doi.org/10.1016/j.compag.2018.02.016]

[134] Espinel R, Herrera-Franco G, Rivadeneira García JL, Escandón-Panchana P. Artificial intelligence in agricultural mapping: a review. Agriculture 2024; 14(7): 1071. [http://dx.doi.org/10.3390/agriculture14071071]

[135] Sharma R. Artificial intelligence in agriculture: a review 5th International Conference on Intelligent Computing and Control Systems (ICICCS). 937-42. [http://dx.doi.org/10.1109/ICICCS51141.2021.9432187]

[136] Behmann J, Mahlein AK, Rumpf T, Römer C, Plümer L. A review of advanced machine learning methods for the detection of biotic stress in precision crop protection. Precis Agric 2015; 16(3): 239-60. [http://dx.doi.org/10.1007/s11119-014-9372-7]

[137] Benos L, Tagarakis AC, Dolias G, Berruto R, Kateris D, Bochtis D. Machine learning in agriculture: a comprehensive updated review. Sensors (Basel) 2021; 21(11): 3758. [http://dx.doi.org/10.3390/s21113758] [PMID: 34071553]

[138] Cob-Parro AC, Lalangui Y, Lazcano R. Fostering agricultural transformation through AI: An open-source AI architecture exploiting the MLOps paradigm. Agronomy (Basel) 2024; 14(2): 259.

[http://dx.doi.org/10.3390/agronomy14020259]

[139] Dhal SB, Kar D. Transforming agricultural productivity with AI-driven forecasting: innovations in food security and supply chain optimization. Forecasting 2024; 6(4): 925-51.
[http://dx.doi.org/10.3390/forecast6040046]

[140] Zhang B, Qiao Y. AI, sensors, and robotics for smart agriculture. Agronomy (Basel) 2024; 14(6): 1180.
[http://dx.doi.org/10.3390/agronomy14061180]

[141] Kundu SG, Ghosh A, Kundu A, G P G. A ML-AI enabled ensemble model for predicting agricultural yield. Cogent Food Agric 2022; 8(1): 2085717.
[http://dx.doi.org/10.1080/23311932.2022.2085717]

[142] Canata TF, Júnior MRB, de Oliveira RP, Furlani CEA, da Silva RP. AI-driven prediction of sugarcane quality attributes using satellite imagery. Sugar Tech 2024; 26(3): 741-51.
[http://dx.doi.org/10.1007/s12355-024-01399-9]

[143] Manatsa D, Nyakudya IW, Mukwada G, Matsikwa H. Maize yield forecasting for Zimbabwe farming sectors using satellite rainfall estimates. Nat Hazards 2011; 59(1): 447-63.
[http://dx.doi.org/10.1007/s11069-011-9765-0]

[144] Parihar CM, Jat SL, Singh AK, *et al.* Effects of precision conservation agriculture in a maize-whea--mungbean rotation on crop yield, water-use and radiation conversion under a semiarid agro-ecosystem. Agric Water Manage 2017; 192: 306-19.
[http://dx.doi.org/10.1016/j.agwat.2017.07.021]

[145] Bonfante A, Monaco E, Manna P, *et al.* LCIS DSS—An irrigation supporting system for water use efficiency improvement in precision agriculture: A maize case study. Agric Syst 2019; 176: 102646.
[http://dx.doi.org/10.1016/j.agsy.2019.102646]

[146] Longchamps L, Tisseyre B, Taylor J, *et al.* Yield sensing technologies for perennial and annual horticultural crops: a review. Precis Agric 2022; 23(6): 2407-48.
[http://dx.doi.org/10.1007/s11119-022-09906-2]

[147] Jha K, Doshi A, Patel P, Shah M. A comprehensive review on automation in agriculture using artificial intelligence. Artificial Intelligence in Agriculture 2019; 2: 1-12.
[http://dx.doi.org/10.1016/j.aiia.2019.05.004]

[148] Kakani V, Nguyen VH, Kumar BP, Kim H, Pasupuleti VR. A critical review on computer vision and artificial intelligence in food industry. Journal of Agriculture and Food Research 2020; 2: 100033.
[http://dx.doi.org/10.1016/j.jafr.2020.100033]

[149] Soma T, Nuckchady B. Communicating the benefits and risks of digital agriculture technologies: perspectives on the future of digital agricultural education and training. Front Commun (Lausanne) 2021; 6: 762201.
[http://dx.doi.org/10.3389/fcomm.2021.762201]

[150] Mohammed ZA, Tejay GP. Examining privacy concerns and ecommerce adoption in developing countries: The impact of culture in shaping individuals' perceptions toward technology. Comput Secur 2017; 67: 254-65.
[http://dx.doi.org/10.1016/j.cose.2017.03.001]

[151] Schimmelpfennig D, Ebel R. Sequential adoption and cost savings from precision agriculture. 2024.

[152] McNunn G, Heaton E, Archontoulis S, Licht M, VanLoocke A. Using a crop modeling framework for precision cost-benefit analysis of variable seeding and nitrogen application rates. Front Sustain Food Syst 2019; 3: 108.
[http://dx.doi.org/10.3389/fsufs.2019.00108]

[153] Munz J. What if precision agriculture is not profitable?: A comprehensive analysis of the right timing for exiting, taking into account different entry options. Precis Agric 2024; 25(3): 1284-323.
[http://dx.doi.org/10.1007/s11119-024-10111-6]

[154] Walke A, Srivastava P K, Sharma D. Exploring the impact of artificial intelligence on sustainable agriculture: a case study of precision farming. 2022; 10(5).

[155] Temidayo Olorunsogo , Temidayo Olorunsogo , Ejuma Adaga , Olorunsogo T, Adaga E, Daraojimba DO. AI in precision agriculture: A review of technologies for sustainable farming practices. World Journal of Advanced Research and Reviews 2024; (1): 2276-85. [http://dx.doi.org/10.30574/wjarr.2024.21.1.0314]

[156] Tanikawa T. Mechanization of agriculture considering its business model. In: Kozai T, Ed. Smart Plant Factory: The Next Generation Indoor Vertical Farms. Singapore: Springer 2018; pp. 241-4. [http://dx.doi.org/10.1007/978-981-13-1065-2_16]

[157] Saranya T, Deisy C, Sridevi S, Anbananthen KSM. A comparative study of deep learning and Internet of Things for precision agriculture. Eng Appl Artif Intell 2023; 122: 106034. [http://dx.doi.org/10.1016/j.engappai.2023.106034]

[158] Karunathilake EMBM, Le AT, Heo S, Chung YS, Mansoor S. The path to smart farming: innovations and opportunities in precision agriculture. Agriculture 2023; 13(8): 1593. [http://dx.doi.org/10.3390/agriculture13081593]

[159] Fragassa C, Vitali G, Emmi L, Arru M. A new procedure for combining UAV-based imagery and machine learning in precision agriculture. Sustainability (Basel) 2023; 15(2): 998. [http://dx.doi.org/10.3390/su15020998]

[160] Krishnan A, Swarna S, H S B. Robotics, IoT, and AI in the automation of agricultural industry: a review. 2020 IEEE Bangalore Humanit Technol Conf (B-HTC). 1-6. [http://dx.doi.org/10.1109/B-HTC50970.2020.9297856]

[161] Tien JM. Internet of things, real-time decision making, and artificial intelligence. Annals of Data Science 2017; 4(2): 149-78. [http://dx.doi.org/10.1007/s40745-017-0112-5]

[162] How ML, Chan YJ, Cheah SM. Predictive insights for improving the resilience of global food security using artificial intelligence. Sustainability (Basel) 2020; 12(15): 6272. [http://dx.doi.org/10.3390/su12156272]

[163] Ikram A, Mehmood H, Arshad MT, Rasheed A, Noreen S, Gnedeka KT. Applications of artificial intelligence (AI) in managing food quality and ensuring global food security. CYTA J Food 2024; 22(1): 2393287. [http://dx.doi.org/10.1080/19476337.2024.2393287]

CHAPTER 7

Land Cover Classification in Bhatinda and Comparative Analysis of Machine Learning Algorithms Using Google Earth Engine

Vishal Dutt[1,2,*], **Sartajvir Singh**[3] and **Ganesh Kumar Sethi**[4]

[1] *Department of Computer Science, Punjabi University, Patiala, Punjab, India*

[2] *Department of Computer Science and Engineering, Chandigarh University, Mohali, Punjab, India*

[3] *Centre of Excellence, Socio-Environmental Sustainability for River Sand-Mining (SEnSRS), Indian Institute of Technology, Ropar, Punjab, India*

[4] *Department of Computer Science, MM Modi College, Patiala, Punjab, India*

Abstract: Agriculture in Bhatinda, Punjab, a key part of India's grain belt, supports the economic base through crops like wheat and cotton. Hyperspectral image analysis using Hyperion imagery provides in-depth information about crops, soil, and water, aiding in sustainable cultivation. The hyperspectral image analysis makes it easy to identify some major problems in water supply management, urbanization, and wasteful resource usage in agriculture. This study classifies land cover (vegetation, urban areas, and water bodies) in Bhatinda using Google Earth Engine and compares the performance of four machine learning algorithms: Random Forest, Support Vector Machine (SVM), Gradient Boosting Trees (GBT), and Classification and Regression Trees (CART). Results show that CART with 97.01% accuracy and 95.51 Kappa works best in vegetation, while others work best in individual classes (*e.g.*, RF with 95.52% in water bodies). This study contributes to the benefits of agriculture by providing precise land cover maps, aiding in resource planning, and guiding sustainable approaches in Bhatinda's dynamic environment.

Keywords: Agriculture, Google earth engine, Hyperspectral images, Land cover classification, Regression, Water bodies.

INTRODUCTION

Farming in the present era has several challenges, like growing more food with less water,land, and chemicals. Sustainable agriculture involves new ways of smart farming, so that nature can remain healthy for future generations [1]. This

* **Corresponding author Vishal Dutta:** Department of Computer Science, Punjabi University, Patiala, Punjab, India; E-mail:vishaldutt53@gmail.com

can be achieved by Hyperspectral remote sensing. It gives the farmers and scientists a way, which allows them to gain information about crops, soil, and water with the help of advanced technology like Hyperion. By sensing light in hundreds of narrow bands, it shows them just what's happening on the ground—whether crops are thriving, where water has collected, or how much land is covered by urban areas and not fields, *etc* [2, 3].

Land cover classification takes it a step further. It distinguishes between vegetation, urban land, and water bodies by analyzing fine details in light. In a place like Bhatinda, Punjab, where agriculture is a primary means of livelihood, these details are particularly important.

In this chapter, it is described how such a technology, in conjunction with software like Google Earth Engine and machine learning, can be utilized to understand Bhatinda's landscape better. It is about using science to make farming sustainable, and it starts with a different way of looking at land [4 - 6].

Hyperspectral remote sensing means looking at Earth from space using specialized cameras that capture hundreds of tiny slices of color, much more than our eyes can see or regular cameras can capture. Unlike earlier methods that use only a few broad colors—red, green, and blue—hyperspectral imaging slices light into very narrow bands, giving a close-up look at what is on the ground. It can be applied by scientists and farmers to analyse crops without ever entering a field. It can ascertain whether plants are stressed, water-stressed, or in perfect health by picking up subtle variations in color patterns that would be impossible to spot otherwise. It is also effective at identifying what is in a field—crops, weeds, or bare ground—and how much land it occupies. This aids in planning more productive farming techniques and water management, and in ensuring crops develop to their full potential without wasting resources. The hyperspectral remote sensing offers a clear, high-resolution view from overhead, making agriculture smart and sustainable [7, 8].

Importance of Land Cover Classification in Bhatinda, Punjab

Land cover classification, differentiating and mapping land as vegetation, urban land, or water bodies, plays an important role in landscape comprehension and management, particularly in agricultural regions like Bhatinda, Punjab. The region, which forms part of India's grain belt, relies heavily on agriculture, with wheat and cotton crops propelling the economy. Urbanization and inconsistent water supply, however, pose a challenge to sustainable land use. Vegetation classification indicates the health and extent of croplands, and farmers can use it to increase production and ensure soil health. Urban map monitoring indicates urban extent into cultivatable land, a concern in Punjab because it undermines food security. Differentiating water bodies, such as canals and reservoirs, aids irrigation planning and keeps water resources essential to agriculture in this semi-arid region in perspective. Bhatinda offers a good case study because it represents these competing demands—agriculture, urbanization, and water management—such that it becomes imperative to have accurate land cover data to make effective choices and ensure sustainable growth [9, 10].

Google Earth Engine (GEE) as a Tool

Google Earth Engine (GEE) is a cloud platform for processing and analyzing huge amounts of geospatial data [11]. It provides access to a lot of satellite imagery, including hyperspectral imagery such as Hyperion, and high-performance computational tools to conduct analyses at a huge scale that would be impossible with regular computers. GEE simplifies tasks, such as image preprocessing, classification, and mapping for researchers with a simple interface and pre-existing algorithms. It is particularly useful for processing across huge areas and timeframes to study dynamic environments such as Bhatinda's, whose land cover change reflects human and environmental pressures. It enables rapid, scalable analysis that encourages studies to inform sustainable resource management with timely, accurate findings [12, 13].

Research Objectives

This chapter has two main objectives. First, the chapter aims to classify land cover in Bhatinda, Punjab, using Hyperion hyperspectral imagery, with emphasis on distinguishing vegetation, urban areas, and water bodies (*e.g.*, lakes, water storage). The high spectral resolution in Hyperion provides a rich source of information to capture unique features and enable high classification accuracy. Secondly, the chapter compares four machine learning algorithms—Random Forest (RF), Support Vector Machine (SVM), Gradient Boosting Trees (GBT), and Classification and Regression Trees (CART)—implemented in GEE. By applying these algorithms to a common Hyperion dataset, the study compares them in terms of reliability and accuracy to map land cover. This comparison not only outlines each algorithm's merits and demerits but also provides real-world guidance for selecting appropriate tools in similar agricultural landscapes, encouraging the application of remote sensing in sustainable agriculture.

STUDY AREA

In this chapter, Bhatinda, Punjab, is taken as the study area, as shown in Fig. (**1**).

Bhatinda, in southwestern Punjab, India, lies at approximately 30.21°N latitude and 74.95°E longitude, covering a flat, alluvial plain typical of the Indo-Gangetic region. It spans approximately 3,353 square kilometres and has an elevation of about 210 meters above mean sea level. The region has a semi-arid climate with extremely hot summers (temperatures often exceeding 40°C) and cold winters (around 5°C), with yearly rainfall of approximately 400–500 mm, predominantly during the monsoon season (July–September). This influences its land cover, favoring agriculture while water shortages remain a problem. Bhatinda serves as an agricultural hub, producing crops such as wheat, cotton, and rice, supported by a vast network of canals from the Sutlej River and groundwater irrigation. Rapid urbanization, however, resulting from industrial expansion, has encroached on arable land, disrupting the balance between water bodies, urban areas, and vegetation cover. These dynamics make Bhatinda a suitable case study for land cover change, as it combines fertile fields, expanding urban areas, and critical water resources, reflecting broader sustainability concerns in Punjab [4, 6, 9, 14].

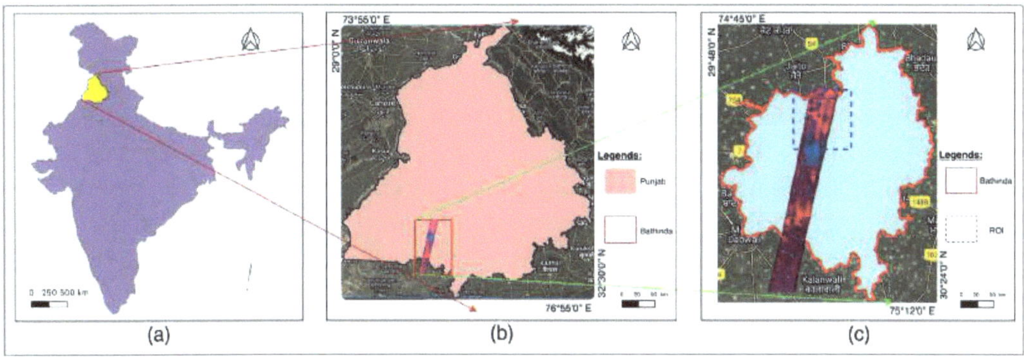

Fig. (1). Study area (**a**): Highlighted Punjab region in India map; (**b**): Highlighted Bathinda region in Punjab map; (**c**): Hyperion image with Region Of Interest (ROI).

METHODOLOGY

Data Preparation in Google Earth Engine

Hyperion imagery was supplied to Google Earth Engine (GEE) by accessing EO-1 Hyperion as an ImageCollection with identifier 'EO1/HYPERION' [7]. The collection covered the period between January 1, 2010, and December 31, 2016, and was constrained within the Bathinda region of interest (ROI) using a user-defined geometry (geometry_roi). The temporal window leverages the entire Hyperion data archive, although acquisitions after 2017 are not available due to the decommissioning of EO-1. Preprocessing was conducted with a customized function, *clipAndScale*, applied to each image in the collection. This function clipped the images to the Bathinda ROI, ensuring that only the study area was processed, and selected eight spectral bands (B050, B023, B015, B010, B008, B020, B030, B040) spanning the visible and near-infrared regions of the electromagnetic spectrum for enhanced feature diversity. These digital numbers (DN) were scaled to radiance by dividing by 40.0, following a typical Hyperion preprocessing step to normalize the data as:

$$L_\lambda = \frac{DN}{40} \tag{1}$$

Where, L_λ represents the radiance ($W/m^2/sr/\mu m$), DN represents the raw pixel value, and 40 is the scaling factor according to the HYPERION VNIR bands from 8-57. To prepare a representative data set, the processed ImageCollection (hyperionClipped) was reduced to a median composite (hyperionMedian) by applying GEE's median reducer to minimize cloud cover and temporal variation. This median image served as input for subsequent classification and was visualized first with an RGB combination (B050, B023, B015) to check data quality before analysis.

The land cover classification in this study targeted three discrete classes — Vegetation, Urban area, and Water Bodies — and assigned numeric values for machine learning: 0 for Vegetation, 1 for Urban, and 2 for Water Bodies. Vegetation includes agricultural lands, grasslands, and natural vegetation typical of Bathinda's rural landscape. Urban areas comprise built-up land, such as residential areas, industrial areas, and infrastructure, reflecting the district's growing urbanization. Water Bodies include canals, reservoirs, and other surface water bodies critical to Punjab's irrigation system. Training and validation data were derived from user-defined point collections (vege, urban, waterBody), imported into GEE, and presumably obtained from ground truth or reference data such as field observations, high-resolution imagery, or existing maps. There were 65 points in each class, totaling 195 points, which were merged into a single FeatureCollection (trainingPoints) with class values assigned using the set function. The points were used to sample the median Hyperion image at a 30-meter resolution and extract spectral values for selected bands. The resulting data (trainingData) were split into training (70%) and testing (30%) subsets using a random column technique (randomColumn) with a threshold of 0.7 to facilitate effective model training and independent testing of classification performance.

Machine Learning Algorithms

Random Forest (RF): Random Forest is an ensemble learning technique that grows many decision trees and combines their predictions to improve accuracy and avoid overfitting. A random sample of data and features is used to train each tree, and a majority vote over all trees makes a final classification. RF is tolerant to noise and efficient with high-dimensional data [15], such as hyperspectral imagery, and is suitable for land cover classification in Bathinda. For implementation, the parameters were specified with 30 trees to provide a balanced ensemble size that compromises between accuracy and computation, and maxNodes 70 to limit tree depth to prevent overfitting without reducing complexity so much that it cannot effectively process hyperspectral data. The unstandardized trainingSet was used to train the classifier with input properties for eight bands.

Support Vector Machine (SVM): Classifies data by finding the hyperplane that maximizes class separation in a high-dimensional space. Where data is not linearly separable, it uses a kernel function (like a radial basis function) to project data and achieve maximum class separation. SVM is effective in handling small training sets and complex patterns and is well-suited for hyperspectral classification with distinctive spectral signatures [16]. SVM was implemented with a linear kernel suitable for high-dimensional hyperspectral data and a high cost to heavily penalize misclassification and enhance margin separation. Unlike RF, input data were standardized with unitScale(0, 3000).multiply(2).subtract(1) to scale radiance values to a range of [-1, 1] for better SVM performance.

Gradient Boosting Trees (GBT): Gradient Boosting Trees is another ensemble method that grows decision trees sequentially, with each tree attempting to fix errors of previous ones. It is optimized using a loss function (for instance, classification error) *via* gradient descent, with greater weight on misclassified samples in future runs [17]. The power of GBT lies in handling fine-grained variation and achieving potentially better accuracy in Bathinda's diverse land cover. This classifier was implemented with 50 trees, greater than RF to correct errors in a step-wise manner, shrinkage = 0.1 as a conservative learning rate to improve generalization, and maxNodes = 50 to limit tree complexity.

Classification and Regression Trees (CART): CART is a decision tree algorithm that partitions the feature space recursively by feature thresholds in a step that minimizes impurity at every partition (for instance, using the Gini index). In classification, it assigns each terminal node the most frequent class [18]. Although it is not as sophisticated as ensemble methods, CART provides interpretable outcomes and is employed here as a baseline for comparison with more advanced algorithms. This classifier was used with default parameters and a single-tree structure. CART was trained on an unstandardized training set with eight bands, the same as those used by RF.

Classification Process

The land cover classification in Bathinda employed a standardized process in GEE, with minimal variation across data preparation and classification details in

RF, SVM, GBT, and CART (see Fig. (**2**)). The Bathinda area of interest (ROI) was defined first (geometry_roi), and EO-1 Hyperion data were clipped and filtered to the ROI for the years 2010–2016. Eight bands (B050, B023, B015, B010, B008, B020, B030, B040) were employed to calculate a median composite (hyperionMedian) and scaled to radiance using equation (1). For SVM and GBT, this image was standardized to a range of [-1, 1] with unitScale(0, 3000).multiply(2).subtract(1), while RF and CART used the raw radiance data. Training data consisting of 195 points (65 in each class: Vegetation, Urban, Water Bodies) were sampled from the processed image at a scale of 30 meters (sampleRegions). Each algorithm was then trained on a 70% subset of this data (trainingSet).

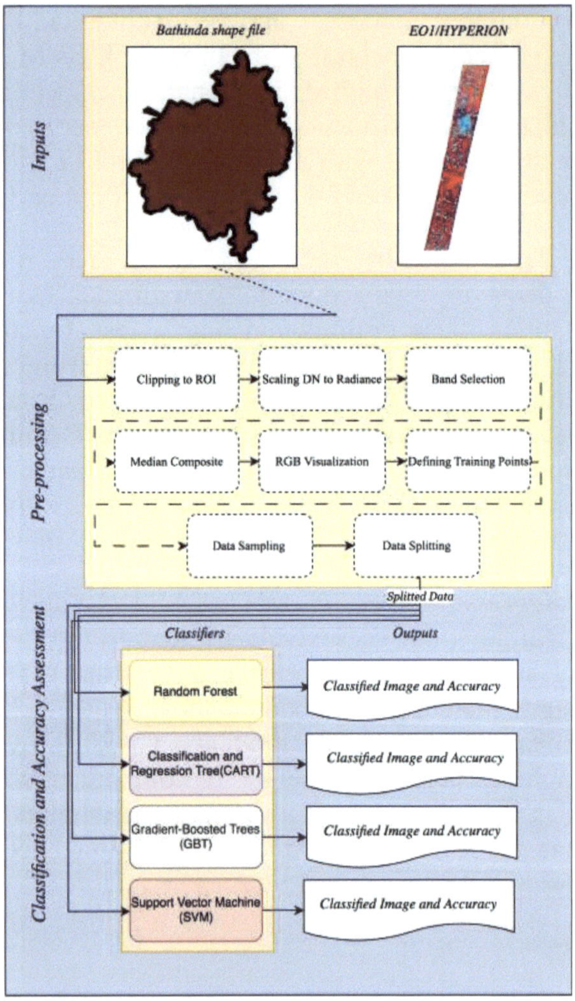

Fig. (2). Methodology workflow.

The accuracy assessment was consistent across algorithms and employed a train-test split rather than cross-validation due to the size of the data and computational constraints in GEE. The 195-point training data (trainingData) had a random column allocated to it (randomColumn) and was split into 70% train (random < 0.7) and 30% test (random ≥ 0.7) sets. Each classifier was trained on the trainingSet and tested on the testingSet by classifying it (testingSet.classify(classifier)). Performance was determined with an error matrix (errorMatrix('class', 'classification')) and overall accuracy as the proportion of correctly classified test points. This approach provided an independent validation set and a reliable estimate of generalization performance for the land cover classification.

Comparative Analysis

The performance of RF, SVM, GBT, and CART was assessed based on several metrics [16, 19, 20] derived from the error matrix and, in the case of SVM, extended calculations:

1.**Total Accuracy**: It is the number of samples that are correctly classified as a proportion of total samples, errorMatrix.accuracy().

2.**Producer's Accuracy (Precision by Class)**: It is the number of samples that are correctly classified as a proportion of total samples, errorMatrix.accuracy().

$$P\,A_i = \frac{NC_i}{RT_i} \times 100 \tag{2}$$

Where, NC_i represents the number of correct, whereas RTi is the row total.

3.**User's Accuracy (Recall per Class):** This involves the ratio of classified samples that are in agreement with the reference for each class, as calculated by the formula.

$$U\,A_i = \frac{NC_i}{CT_i} \times 100 \tag{3}$$

Where, CT_i represents the column total.

4.**Kappa Coefficient:** A beyond-chance agreement measurement is calculated by this formula:

$$K = \frac{O - E}{1 - E} \tag{4}$$

Where, CT_i represents the column total.

Where O is observed agreement (sum of diagonal elements/total samples), and E is expected agreement $\sum row_{total} \times \prod column_{total} / total\_samples\_squared$. This was fully implemented in SVM and accessible through GEE's errorMatrix.kappa() for others.

5.**F1-Score:**It cannot be directly calculated in the program, but can be calculated as the harmonic mean of producers' and users' accuracy by class as:

$$F1_i = 2 \times \frac{PA_i \times UA_i}{PA_i + UA_i} \quad (5)$$

RESULT AND DISCUSSION

Classification Results

Land cover mapping for Bathinda, Punjab, was performed using four different machine-learning algorithms: Random Forest (RF), Support Vector Machine (SVM), Gradient Boosting Trees (GBT), and Classification and Regression Trees (CART)—on the Google Earth Engine (GEE). The median Hyperion image (2010–2016) was used to produce the classified maps with three classes: Vegetation (green), Urban (gray), and Water Bodies (blue).

In Fig. (**3**), the CART classification shows a green background with the majority class, indicating Bathinda's rural dominance. The urban areas are shown as scattered gray patches, indicating patchy growth, while water bodies are dispersed as irregular, minute blue clusters, perhaps representing canals or other water bodies. The map shows a pixelated texture due to the Hyperion resolution of 30 meters, with visible noise along class boundaries. In Fig. (**3b**), GBT classification shows extensive cover by vegetation with smoother edges than those found by CART. The urban areas are fragmented, though the clusters appear more compact. The water bodies are more linear and continuous, which is a result of the capture of canal systems or larger water bodies, likely the result of sequential error correction by GBT. In Fig. (**3c**), the SVM classification indicates that the Bathinda area is dominated by vegetation (green areas) with smooth, less fragmented patches, suggesting accurate classification. The transition between vegetation, urban (gray areas), and water bodies (blue areas) is sharp and natural, demonstrating the SVM's ability to correctly distinguish classes with minimal noisy data. The homogeneous patches with smooth transitions indicate the effective use of high-dimensional data by SVM, with a linear kernel applied to normalized inputs, which minimizes overfitting and maintains spatial consistency. Though minor overlaps between the urban and vegetation areas may be present, they are minimal compared to other classifiers. Overall, SVM provided robust classification with balanced performance across all classes. In Fig. (**3d**), the Random Forest classified image indicates that the most dominant class in the Bathinda region is vegetation (green patches), though with more fragmented patches compared to SVM. The urban regions (gray) and water bodies (blue) are also delineated with less noise and more defined edges. The classification is balanced, with Random Forest effectively handling noise through its ensemble mechanism, though some overfitting to vegetation is visible. The transition between classes is smooth but less accurate than SVM, showing that while Random Forest is robust, its performance is slightly degraded by fragmented classes. Overall, Random Forest provided stable classification with good accuracy and spatial consistency, making it a dependable, though slightly less accurate, option for discriminating between vegetation, urban, and water classes.

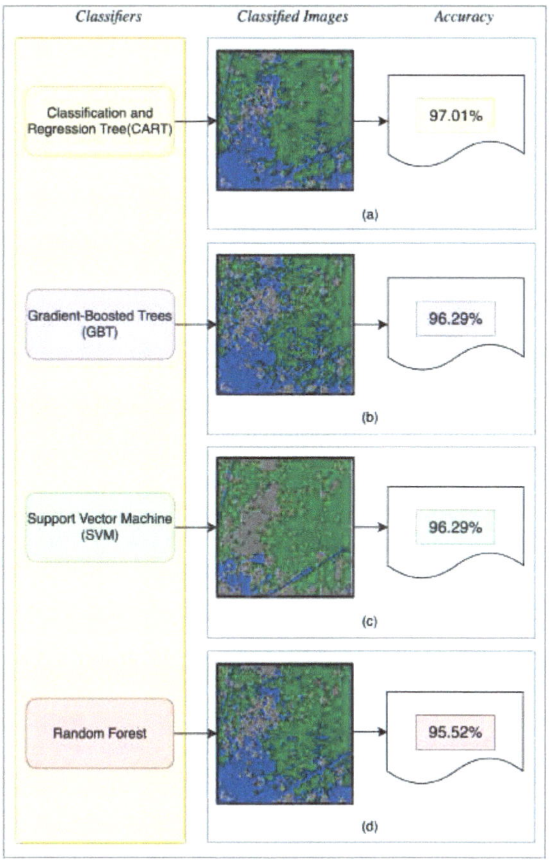

Fig. (3). Classification results (**a**): classified image with CART classifier with 97.01% accuracy; (**b**): classified image with GBT classifier with 96.29% accuracy; (**c**): classified image with SVM with 96.29% accuracy; (**d**) classified image with Random forest classifier with 95.29% accuracy.

Comparative Analysis

Table 1. Performance measures of classifiers.

Classifier	Class	Value						Total Samples	Overall Accuracy	Observed Agreement	Expected Agreement	Overall Kappa
	-	RT	CT	NC	PA	UA	KC	-	-	-	-	-
CART	Vegetation	21	21	21	100	100	1	67	97.01	97.01	33.43	95.51
	Urban	24	24	23	95.833	95.833	0.9374					
	Water Bodies	22	22	21	95.455	95.455	0.9317					
GBT	Vegetation	21	20	20	95.23	100	92.79	54	96.29	96.29	33.95	94.39
	Urban	18	20	18	100	90	1					
	Water Bodies	15	14	14	93.33	100	89.90					
SVM	Vegetation	21	21	21	100	100	1	54	96.29	96.29	34.15	94.37
	Urban	18	20	18	100	90	1					
	Water Bodies	15	13	13	86.66	100	0.7975					
Random Forest	Vegetation	21	20	20	95.23	100	92.84	67	95.52	95.52	33.41	93.27
	Urban	24	23	22	91.66	95.65	87.48					
	Water Bodies	22	24	22	100	91.66	1					

Table **1** compares four classifiers, CART, GBT, SVM, and Random Forest, to predict vegetation, urban, and water bodies from Hyperion dataCART achieves the best all-around accuracy of 97.01%, with a Kappa of 95.51, performing best specifically in Vegetation prediction, with perfect scores of PA, UA, and KC of 100, 100, and 1, respectively. It uses 67 test instances and shows excellent performance across all classes. GBT, with 54 instances, achieves an overall accuracy of 96.29% and a Kappa of 94.39, performing best in Urban, where PA and KC are 100 and 1, respectively, and achieving perfect UA of 100% for Water Bodies. SVM, also with 54 instances, reports an accuracy of 96.29% and a Kappa of 94.37, with perfect scores in Vegetation and Urban predictions (PA, UA, and KC are 100, 100, and 1, respectively), but lower performance for Water Bodies, with PA of 86.66% and KC of 0.7975. Random Forest, with 67 instances, reports a slightly lower accuracy of 95.52% and a Kappa of 93.27, achieving the best performance in Water Bodies (PA and KC are 100 and 1, respectively) and high Urban UA of 95.65%. Expected Agreement ranges between 33.41% (RF) and 34.15% (SVM), indicating class-balanced distributions. All classifiers have high Kappa values (>93), indicating strong performance above chance. Overall, CART is the best performer all-around, followed by GBT and SVM for Urban, and RF for Water Bodies, suggesting that classifier selection is class-dependent.

In Table **2**, the key findings are presented. CART and SVM achieve 100% producer's accuracy for vegetation, making them effective for this class. SVM is also effective for urban classification, with 100% producer's accuracy for both vegetation and urban classes. GBT is suitable for urban classification, achieving 96.29% accuracy. Random Forest is a well-suited and effective classifier for water bodies, with 95.52% overall accuracy and 100% producer's accuracy.

Table 2. Key findings.

Classifier	Accuracy	PA	Suitability
CART	97.01	100	Vegetation
GBT	96.29	100	Urban
SVM	96.29	100	Urban/ Vegetation
Random Forest	95.52	100	Water Bodies

LIMITATIONS AND FUTURE DIRECTIONS

After performing all the experiments, it was observed that this study has a few issues despite higher classification accuracy. In this study, a limited number of training points (195) was used, which might not be sufficient for the large and complex land cover. As per the key findings in Table **1**, it is shown that the SVM underperformed for water bodies. The reason might be the class imbalance or sensitivity to the spectral confusions. As no ground truth validation was performed through the UAVs, the classification may not be very accurate.

To overcome these limitations, several suggestions to improve the effectiveness of this study are offered. The researchers must expand the region of interest to test the reliability of the classifiers. It is also recommended to use deep learning models, such as LSTMs and CNNs, for better, optimized performance. Moreover, time series analysis can be used for seasonal analysis, and multi-source validation can be employed to test the system's classification validity.

CONCLUSION

In this chapter, CART, GBT, SVM, and Random Forest classifiers were compared for classifying vegetation, urban areas, and water bodies from Hyperion data. CART performed the best overall, with the highest accuracy (97.01%) and Kappa (95.51), particularly excelling in vegetation classification. GBT and SVM, both with 96.29% accuracy, performed best in urban classification, while Random Forest (95.52%) performed best for water bodies. All classifiers achieved high Kappa values (>93), suggesting consistent performance. The results indicate that

CART is the best overall general classifier, although class-specific priorities may favor GBT, SVM, or Random Forest.

Future work can explore other spectral bands or features in Hyperion data to improve classification accuracy, particularly for weak classes such as Water Bodies in SVM. Comparison with other advanced classifiers, *e.g.*, deep learning, could provide better performance. Expanding the dataset by including more examples or data from other areas may enhance broader applicability. Adding time-series data may also account for seasonal changes, providing increased robustness. Finally, validation with ground truth data from other sources would further contribute to reliability.

REFERENCES

[1] Pretty J. Agricultural sustainability: concepts, principles and evidence. Philos Trans R Soc Lond B Biol Sci 2008; 363(1491): 447-65.
[http://dx.doi.org/10.1098/rstb.2007.2163] [PMID: 17652074]

[2] Goetz AFH. Three decades of hyperspectral remote sensing of the Earth: A personal view. Remote Sens Environ 2009; 113: S5-S16.
[http://dx.doi.org/10.1016/j.rse.2007.12.014]

[3] Lin SK. Introduction to remote sensing. Fifth Edition. By James B. Campbell and Randolph H. Wynne, The Guilford Press, 2011; 662 pages. Price: £80.75, ISBN 978-1-60918-176-5. Remote Sens (Basel) 2013; 5(1): 282-3.
[http://dx.doi.org/10.3390/rs5010282]

[4] Anand S, Kaur H. Challenges and opportunities in sustainable stubble management in Punjab: A review. International Journal of Environment and Climate Change 2024; 14(3): 274-97.
[http://dx.doi.org/10.9734/ijecc/2024/v14i34040]

[5] Gulati A, Roy R, Hussain S. Performance of agriculture in Punjab.India Studies in Business and Economics. Singapore: Springer Nature Singapore 2021; pp. 77-112.

[6] "Structural transformation of punjab agriculture and its environmental implications" 2020. Available from: https://api.semanticscholar.org/CorpusID:241805737

[7] Dahiya N, Singh S, Gupta S. Comparative analysis and implication of hyperion hyperspectral and landsat-8 multispectral dataset in land classification. Photonirvachak (Dehra Dun) 2023; 51(11): 2201-13.
[http://dx.doi.org/10.1007/s12524-023-01760-7]

[8] Shimoni M, Haelterman R, Perneel C. Hypersectral imaging for military and security applications: Combining Myriad processing and sensing techniques. IEEE Geosci Remote Sens Mag 2019; 7(2): 101-17.
[http://dx.doi.org/10.1109/MGRS.2019.2902525]

[9] Shibani NM, Pandey A, Satyam VK, Bhari JS, Karimi BA, Gupta SK. Study on the variation of NDVI, SAVI and EVI indices in Punjab State. India: IOP Conf Ser Earth Environ Sci 2023; Vol. 1110. [Online] Available from: https://api.semanticscholar.org/CorpusID:256897773

[10] Kumar S, Sidana BK. Farmers' perceptions and adaptation strategies to climate change in Punjab agriculture. 2023. Available from: https://api.semanticscholar.org/CorpusID:231011655

[11] Tamiminia H, Salehi B, Mahdianpari M, Quackenbush L, Adeli S, Brisco B. Google earth engine for geo-big data applications: A meta-analysis and systematic review. ISPRS J Photogramm Remote Sens 2020; 164: 152-70.

[http://dx.doi.org/10.1016/j.isprsjprs.2020.04.001]

[12] Marzialetti F, Giulio S, Malavasi M, Sperandii MG, Acosta ATR, Carranza ML. Capturing coastal dune natural vegetation types using a phenology-based mapping approach: The potential of sentinel-2. Remote Sens (Basel) 2019; 11(12): 1506. [http://dx.doi.org/10.3390/rs11121506]

[13] Gorelick N, Hancher M, Dixon M, Ilyushchenko S, Thau D, Moore R. Google Earth Engine: Planetary-scale geospatial analysis for everyone. Remote Sens Environ 2017; 202: 18-27. [http://dx.doi.org/10.1016/j.rse.2017.06.031]

[14] Ahmad N. Spatio-temporal change detection analysis of land use land cover of Bathinda district, Punjab, India. Biosci Biotechnol Res Asia 2023; 20(2): 571-90. [http://dx.doi.org/10.13005/bbra/3111]

[15] Grätz T, Vospernik S, Scheidl C. Evaluation of afforestations for avalanche protection with orthoimages using the random forest algorithm. Eur J For Res 2024; 143(2): 581-601. [http://dx.doi.org/10.1007/s10342-023-01640-2]

[16] Sheykhmousa M, Mahdianpari M, Ghanbari H, Mohammadimanesh F, Ghamisi P, Homayouni S. Support vector machine *versus* random forest for remote sensing image classification: a meta-analysis and systematic review. IEEE J Sel Top Appl Earth Obs Remote Sens 2020; Vol. 13: pp. 6308-25. [Online] Available from: https://api.semanticscholar.org/CorpusID:224957001

[17] Xu S, Liu S, Wang H, Chen W, Zhang F, Xiao Z. A hyperspectral image classification approach based on feature fusion and multi-layered gradient boosting decision trees 2020. Available from: https://api.semanticscholar.org/CorpusID:229721403 [http://dx.doi.org/10.3390/e23010020]

[18] Wang J, Liu R, Zhang Y, *et al.* Analysis of land-use/cover-type extraction results of tamarix shrub forest of china based on remote sensing technology Forests 2024; 15(7): 1179. Available from: https://api.semanticscholar.org/CorpusID:271084330 [http://dx.doi.org/10.3390/f15071179]

[19] Foody GM. Ground truth in classification accuracy assessment: myth and reality. Geomatics 2024; 4(1): 81-90. [http://dx.doi.org/10.3390/geomatics4010005]

[20] Audebert N, Le Saux B, Lefevre S. Deep learning for classification of hyperspectral data: A comparative review. IEEE Geosci Remote Sens Mag 2019; 7(2): 159-73. [http://dx.doi.org/10.1109/MGRS.2019.2912563]

CHAPTER 8

Significance of Remote Sensing in Optimizing Fertilizer Use for Nutrient Mapping

Akinchan Maity[1], **Sangeetha Annam**[1,*] and **Jay Arindam Maity**[1]

[1] *Chitkara University Institute of Engineering and Technology, Chitkara University, Punjab, India*

Abstract: With a drastic growth in the population of the world, the food demand has also increased substantially; to address this, current farming systems must be optimized for maximum yields. Given that it is not always feasible to expand agricultural land, we must find a solution to optimize crop growth in a feasible and environmentally safe way. The amount of fertilizer required for different crops in different environmental conditions varies significantly; using too much or too little fertilizer than required can be non-conducive. For this, fertilizer optimization and nutrient mapping using remote sensing are valuable tools in smart agricultural systems as they allow efficient use of fertilizers while reducing environmental impacts and, at the same time, providing better yields. The important key factors that play an important role in modern agriculture are efficient nutrient management, wastage of fertilizers, cost reduction, and decision-making. These methods improve the ways of optimizing fertilizers and nutrient management through remote sensing.

Keywords: Decision support systems, Fertilizer optimization, Precision farming, Remote sensing.

INTRODUCTION

Agriculture is one of the core sectors of the economy, providing food, fodder, and raw materials for various industries. It is also a source of income for millions and a strong deciding factor for the GDP of a country. It is therefore extremely important for a country to explore and improve agricultural methods in order to grow economically. To this end, researchers worldwide have implemented various technologies to optimise resource use and maximise crop yields. These technologies include the Internet of Things, Precision Agriculture, Remote Sensing, Artificial Intelligence, Big Data and Analytics, Cloud Computing, and Robotics. The primary focus of this study is to help understand and explore the

* **Corresponding author Sangeetha Annam**: Chitkara University Institute of Engineering and Technology, Chitkara University, Punjab, India; E-mail: a.sangeeta@chitkara.edu.in

Sartajvir Singh, Neelam Dahiya, Maged Mohammed, Abdullah Alzharihi & Vishal Dutt (Eds.)

capabilities and methodologies used for remote sensing in agriculture, with a primary focus on the use of remote sensing for fertilizer optimization.

Remote Sensing (RS) refers to the process of extracting useful information from physical entities without actual physical contact with them [1]. With advancements in fields like Satellite Technology, GIS (Geographic Information System), GPS (Global Positioning System) LiDar, Synthetic Aperture Rader (SAR), Hyperspectral and Multispectral Imaging along with other advancements in Artificial Intelligence and Data Processing, RS has become a very capable and powerful tool of great relevance in research, providing practical applications for real-life problems [2]. This task of RS is usually performed with the help of satellites, drones, aircraft, and even ground-based devices. Fig. (**1**) highlights the basic methodology for RS.

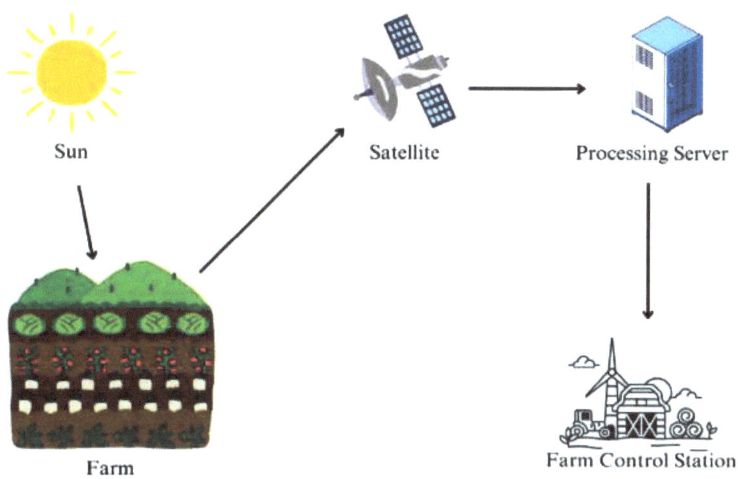

Fig. (1). Overview of hyperspectral remote sensing for agriculture.

In the twenty-first century, Precision Agriculture (PA) is an essential part of sustainable agricultural systems. Although there have been several definitions of PA, the fundamental idea has remained constant [3, 4]. When making decisions about the use of water, fertilizer, pesticides, seeds, fuel, labor, and other resources, PA involves a management approach that employs a variety of sophisticated information, communication, and data analysis techniques. This approach helps to improve crop productivity while lowering water and nutrient losses and adverse environmental effects. There are various applications of RS; the primary focus of this study is to describe its use in agriculture, with a particular focus on optimizing fertilizer use and nutrient mapping in precision agriculture.

Role of Hyperspectral Remote Sensing in Agriculture

The use of hyperspectral RS in agriculture can be of great significance, as it can be applied to solve several problems within the field. In India, 70% of the population depends on agriculture, while also accounting for 35% of the country's GDP [5]. Major challenges faced by current agricultural implementations include the lack of resources such as land and manpower, an increasing population resulting in higher demand for food, and an increasing scarcity of natural resources such as clean water, minerals, and energy. With little scope for agricultural land expansion and limited resources, it is crucial to use the resources at hand effectively. For this, it is essential to have accurate data on available resources, crops, wastelands, forests, soils, and natural calamities like floods and droughts. By traditional methods, gathering such information at a large scale can be tedious, time-consuming, and require significant manpower. With RS, the same task can be achieved much more quickly and with less manpower. RS, with its ability to provide consistent, multi-temporal, and multi-spectral data, is essential for providing thorough insights for efficient agricultural planning and management. Fig. (**2**) describes the basic implementation of hyperspectral RS in agriculture.

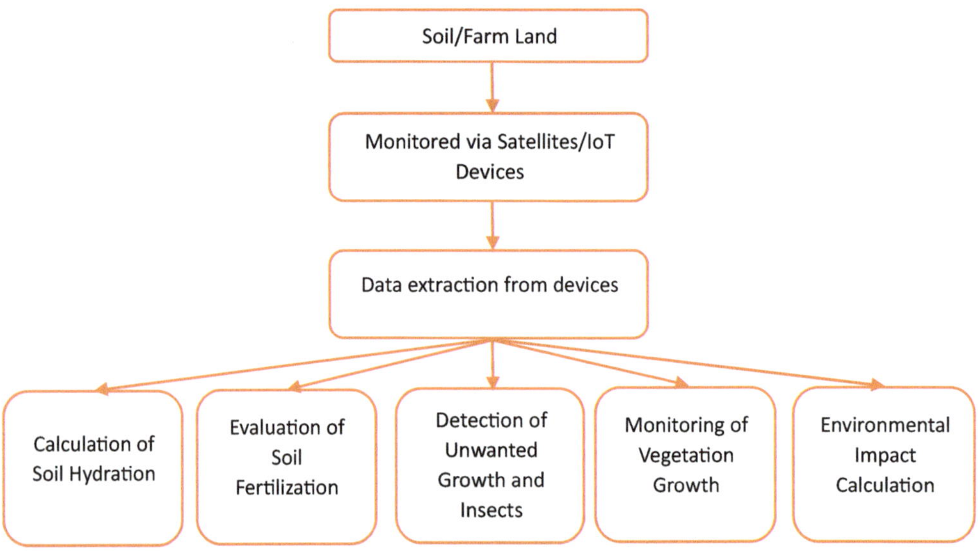

Fig. (2). Basic implementation methodology of hyperspectral RS in agriculture.

A brief explanation of each step in Fig. (**2**) is as follows:

1. **Calculation of Soil Hydration:** The measurement of moisture content in soil can be done through the solar domain (Wavelengths in the range 0.4 and 2.5μm) [6], microwave domain [7], or thermal infrared domain [8].
2. **Evaluation of Soil Fertilization:** Information obtained from RS may be used to identify fertile soil.
3. **Detection of Unwanted Growth and Insects:** The presence of weed growth and pest infestation can be determined using RS [9, 10].
4. **Monitoring of Vegetation Growth:** RS can be used to analyze crop growth, providing insights into crop health, the current state of crops, and the identification of any unusual patterns in plant growth, while also tracking harvest and expected produce [11].
5. **Environmental Impact Calculation:**Keeping track of environmental conditions helps to understand their effects on crop development and to use the information gained to ensure better yield [12].

There are several applications of remote sensing in agriculture, including vegetation cover monitoring, assessment of crop condition, nutrient and water status, weed identification, crop evapotranspiration, disease and pest detection, and forecasting of crop production [13, 14]. Further, the use of RS for fertilizer optimization is discussed.

Role of Hyperspectral Remote Sensing in Precision Agriculture

Precision agriculture is an agricultural method that maximizes crop yield while reducing environmental effects by making use of technology and analysis tools. By carrying out farming operations remotely, precision agriculture can also be time-efficient. Through data-dependent management choices, precision agriculture lowers agricultural costs and the environmental impacts of agriculture while ensuring the efficient use of resources [15]. It also helps increase the amount and quality of agricultural products while using less water, fertilizer, and pesticides. Precision agriculture benefits greatly from the use of Hyperspectral Remote Sensing (HRS), particularly when it comes to fertilizer optimization. HRS offers comprehensive information on crop health and soil characteristics by collecting data in numerous continuous, narrow spectral bands, allowing for focused and effective nutrient management.

Hyperspectral RS offers real-time, wide information on soil and crop conditions, using sensors to measure soil moisture content, identify stress indicators, and track crop health. It increases productivity by enabling farmers to apply insecticides, fertilizer, and water only where and when needed. By monitoring growth trends over time, hyperspectral RS also helps with harvest planning and predicting the agricultural yield. To further improve sustainability, it also makes Variable-Rate Application (VRA) possible [16], in which fertilizer and water are used in different amounts based on calculated requirements. In summary, RS provides accurate and timely information on a large scale that helps make better decisions in precision agriculture, resulting in increased productivity and a lower environmental impact.

Use of Hyperspectral Remote Sensing for Fertilizer Optimization

With the increasing population and demand for food, it is important to maximize crop production. With the limited availability of resources, such as land, water, and fertilizers, they have to be applied optimally to ensure better yields. The main aim of fertilizer optimization is to analyse the current state of crops, determine and map nutrient-deficient regions, and finally optimize fertilizer use by applying it only where required. In agriculture, hyperspectral remote sensing provides a very sophisticated method for mapping nutrients and optimizing fertilizer use. Hyperspectral sensors, as opposed to multispectral sensors, record hundreds of consecutive spectral bands, enabling a more thorough and precise examination of soil and plant characteristics. Based on accurate nutrient evaluation, this expertise is essential for optimizing fertilizer use. Small variations in spectrum reflectance linked to certain nutrient deficiencies can be detected by hyperspectral sensors. This makes it possible for: Early identification of nutritional stress; precise determination of the kind and degree of deficits; and increased distinction between overlapping stressors. The production of comprehensive maps of nutrient distribution at the field or regional level is made possible using hyperspectral imaging. These maps facilitate the application of fertilizer according to site, zone control for applications with variable rates, and reduced environmental effect through abstaining from excessive use.

The literature, methodology, and review of proposed solutions by other researchers are discussed in the following sections.

LITERATURE REVIEW

In this section, the applications of RS in agriculture proposed by other researchers are discussed. First, common applications of RS are discussed, followed by applications for fertilizer optimization.

Applications of Hyperspectral Remote Sensing in Agriculture

In this section, the literature for broad applications of RS in agriculture is discussed. This provides insights into the applications and capabilities of RS in the field of agriculture. The great spectral resolution of hyperspectral remote sensing makes it unique because it enables data collection in contiguous, narrow spectral bands, typically between 400 and 2500 nanometers. Compared to conventional remote sensing techniques, this precise spectral resolution is essential for more accurately identifying and diagnosing certain plant nutritional deficits. The physiology of plants is influenced by various nutrients in ways that change reflectance at particular wavelengths.

Using remote sensing data, the authors in a study [17] employed a fuzzy hybrid ensemble approach for crop classification and yield estimation. Their implementation lowered processing time, and the models trained were optimized for embedded and mobile devices. In anotherstudy [18], the authors integrated edge intelligence with an Unmanned Aerial Vehicle (UAV) for RS in PA. The use of deep learning in PA with UAV RS was examined, and the authors highlighted how their implementation can be both effective and more accurate than traditional solutions. They discussed the applications of Recurrent Neural Networks (RNNs) and Convolutional Neural Networks (CNNs) for tasks like segmentation, object detection, and classification in agriculture. The study also explored the use of edge intelligence in PA, discussing the ways in which cloud and edge computing are being used to tackle the storage and compute demands of deep learning in UAV RS. The authors [19] discussed the use of RS, Machine Learning (ML), and Deep Learning (DL) to predict crop yield. The study focused on using multispectral and hyperspectral data to estimate yield and track crop health. ML and Convolutional Neural Networks (CNNs) were used for feature extraction and prediction. With 90% prediction accuracy, the results successfully demonstrated application in sustainable farming practices by offering precise crop yield estimates. Further, the basic methodology of a few more studies is provided in Table **1**.

Table 1. Literature Review for studies describing different applications of Hyperspectral RS in agriculture.

REF NO. (YEAR)	TECHNOLOGIES USED	HYPERSPECTRAL REMOTE SENSING TECHNIQUE	STUDY AREA
[20] (2022)	Deep learning, machine learning, Google Earth Engine	Sentinel-1, sentinel-2	Xiangride town, Qinghai province, China
[21] (2017)	Deep learning	Landsat-8, sentinel-1a	Ukraine
[22] (2022)	Deep learning (U-Net), random forests	Sentinel-2	Punjab, India
[23] (2022)	Deep learning, XGBoost, random forests	Sentinel-2a, Gaofen PMS	Henan province, China

(Table 1) cont.....

[24] (2021)	Multiple machine learning and deep learning models were used.	Sentinel 2	Calasparra, murcia, spain
[25] (2025)	Svm, ann, cnn, rf, rvm	Sentinel-1	Varanasi (uttar pradesh), india

Application of Hyperspectral Remote Sensing in Fertilizer Optimization

Various methodologies can be used for fertilizer optimization; this study will focus on using hyperspectral RS for this. In contemporary precision agriculture, Hyperspectral Remote Sensing (HRS) has become a very useful tool, especially for fertilizer optimization. HRS allows for more focused and sustainable fertilizer management by accurately detecting, mapping, and monitoring the nutrient status of crops and soils through the collection of reflectance data in hundreds of tiny, continuous spectral bands.

By dynamically adjusting the amount of water and fertilizer delivered, RS technologies can help regulate and optimize fertilizer use, supporting better growth and increased crop yield while reducing overfertilization. Nutrient Mapping (NM) refers to the spatial mapping of the distribution of nutrients present in the soil. In fertilizer optimization, NM helps identify and guide proposed systems on when to apply fertilizer in a specific region. This guarantees that fertilizer is applied correctly and just where it is required. A brief overview of various studies aimed at fertilizer optimization is provided below.

The authors [26] discussed the use of unmanned aerial vehicle remote sensing for monitoring winter wheat growth and yield with different nitrogen (N1: 0 kg/ha, N2: 90 kg/ha, N3: 210 kg/ha, N4: 330 kg/ha) and water (W1: 0 mm, W2: 50 mm, W3: 100 mm, and W4: 150 mm) treatments. The effects of various fertilizer and water treatments on winter wheat yield and the efficiency of water-fertilizer use were then assessed. The authors [27] by combining crop growth models with hyperspectral remote sensing data, aimed to enhance rice fertilization techniques. Data on rice growth were gathered through field tests. Using an Extreme Learning Machine (ELM) model for biomass estimation and a continuous projection algorithm (SPA) for feature extraction, a model for rice biomass inversion was constructed using hyperspectral data from the rice canopy. Rapid data collection on rice biomass is made possible by this technique. The WOFOST crop development model was modified in a fertilization experiment by incorporating the biomass data using the Ensemble Kalman Filter (ENKF) and 4D-Var techniques. The model's capacity to replicate the growth state of rice under various fertilization techniques was enhanced by this adjustment. Using Unmanned Aerial Vehicle (UAV) operations, variable fertilization methods for precision agriculture were developed based on the model's output, which is the simulated yield under the current fertilization scheme. The authors [28] studied the management of nitrogen (N) fertilizer for high-yield rice production. Red-edge-based vegetation indices demonstrated substantial correlations with agronomic variables and showed a strong association with vegetation indices. Based on Sentinel-2B photos, a dynamic model was created to estimate N fertilizer doses, which range from 106 to 134 kg per hectare, using the normalized difference red-edge (NDRE) index. Compared to conventional methods, their approach decreased the amount of N fertilizer applied by about 46 kg per acre. Some more similar studies are discussed below in Table **2**.

Table 2. Studies using hyperspectral RS for fertilizer optimization.

Ref No.	Models/Technologies Used	Remote Sensing Technique	Target Crop
[29]	WOA-ELM, ELM	UAV	Rice
[30]	VegNet	UAV	Maize, paddy, sorghum, chilli
[31]	RF, PLSR, MLR, XGB, SVR	UAV	Sugarcane
[32]	Google Earth Engine	Sentinel-2 VENμS	Wheat
[33]	RF	Sentinel 1-A	Palm
[34]	Partial least squares regression (PLSR)	Sentinel-2	Poppy

In the subsequent sections, we discuss the significance of hyperspectral RS for various factors, which include soil health monitoring, plant health monitoring, integration with decision support systems, the architecture of remote monitoring for fertilizer optimization, and nutrient mapping, and finally discuss the pros and cons of fertilizer optimization using RS, concluding the study after discussing the future prospects.

SOIL HEALTH MONITORING THROUGH HYPERSPECTRAL REMOTE SENSING

The majority of land is covered by soil, a surface material that contains both organic and inorganic matter. It provides agricultural plants with structural support and serves as a source of water and nutrients. For optimum crop growth, the health of the soil used is of extreme significance; for this, it is important to monitor and understand soil health and the parameters associated with it [35]. The ability of soil to support humans, animals, and plants within an ecosystem is referred to as soil health. In the Visible and Near-Infrared (VNIR) spectrum, hyperspectral data aid in estimating SOM from reflectance. SOM is necessary for microbial activity, water retention, and nutrient retention.

The Shortwave Infrared (SWIR) bands' water absorption characteristics are utilized to measure the moisture content of soil. Planning for irrigation and managing drought are aided by accurate moisture data. Both macronutrients (N, P, and K) and micronutrients (Fe, Mg, and Ca) can affect certain spectral bands, allowing for the accurate detection of nutrient-deficient areas for fertilizer treatment at specific sites.

In this section, we discuss these parameters and the techniques used to monitor them. Fig. (**3**) showcases some of the major factors that affect soil health.

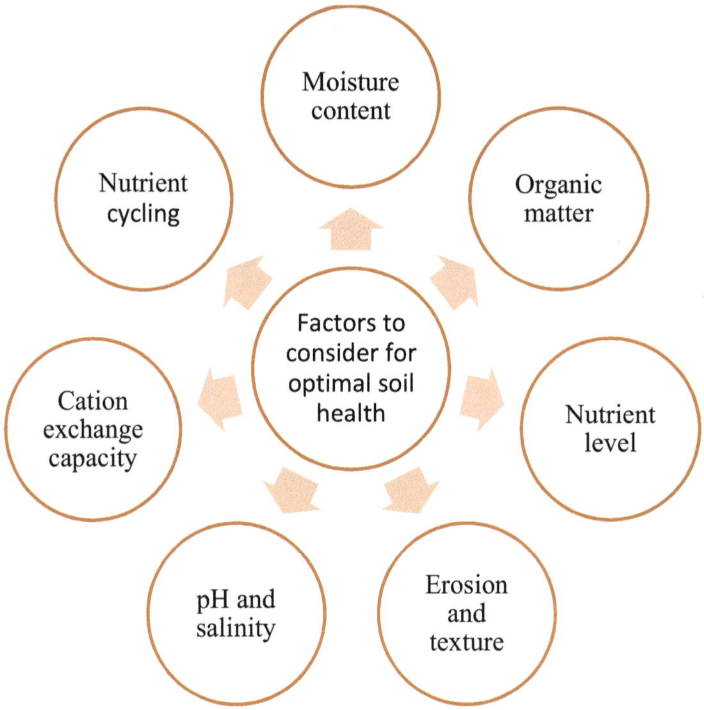

Fig. (3). Factors to be considered for measuring Soil Health.

The creation of a Soil Quality Index (SQI) is important for promoting sustainable agriculture because soil quality is directly related to soil characteristics that are impacted by how the agricultural land is managed. The SQI converts relevant data from soil indicators into numerical values, providing a metric for comparison [36]. These parameters include physical, chemical, and biological characteristics, which are important markers of soil health and fertility status. Chemical indicators include pH, salinity, organic matter content, nutrient availability, cation exchange capacity, nutrient cycling, and soil contaminant levels. To evaluate SQI, certain parameters need to be evaluated, which can be done through RS. These can include moisture content, which can be evaluated using Thermal Infrared Sensing (TIR), providing the Normalized Difference Moisture Index (NDMI) [37]. Organic matter can be evaluated using near-infrared and hyperspectral imaging [38]. Nutrient levels can also be evaluated using hyperspectral imaging and other vegetation indices (NDVI, SAVI) [39]. Soil Erosion and Texture can be identified using LiDAR and Synthetic Aperture Radar (SAR) [40]. Finally, the pH and Salinity of soil can be evaluated using Thermal Imaging [41]. It is already understood that plant health is directly related to the quality and amount of yield produced. To assess the health of a plant, different factors about the current state of the plant must be studied and discussed. Without a proper understanding of each crop's current health in a field, it is difficult to determine its nutrient requirements, leading to inefficient cultivation. Therefore, it is important to discuss the factors used to assess plant health. Some of these include chlorophyll content, water stress, nutrient deficiency, pest/disease, and biomass.

A brief explanation of each of these factors, along with the RS methodology used for their evaluation, is shown in Table **3**.

With the help of these factors, the health of a plant can be classified with ease. This information can further be provided to decision support systems for further analysis and implementation of fertilizer optimization. Before that, a brief introduction to decision support systems is provided.

Table 3. Factors along with hyperspectral RS methodology used for soil health evaluation.

Sr No.	*Factor*	*Method for Evaluation*	*Ref. No.*
1.	Chlorophyll Content	Normalized difference, Vegetation Index (NDVI) Leaf Reflectance (NIR, Red Edge)	[42]
2.	Water Stress	NDWI, Thermal Imaging	[43]
3.	Nutrient Deficiency	Hyperspectral Imaging, Fluorescence Sensors	[44, 45]
4.	Pest/Disease	Thermal Multispectral Imaging	[46]
5.	Biomass	EVI, LiDAR	[47]

INTEGRATION WITH DECISION SUPPORT SYSTEMS

A type of computerized information system that makes it possible to manage decision-making processes is called a Decision Support System (DSS) [48]. These systems analyze situations by processing input data and making appropriate decisions. DSS is a very versatile tool that can help make quicker and better decisions based on large amounts of data, while also providing real-time analytics.

With the aid of RS, crops can be actively monitored for fertilizer requirements by integrating with a DSS. The integration of such technology would also create a significant positive impact on the overall process. This can be achieved by evaluating processed data from sensors and comparing it against ideal and expected outcomes to make necessary decisions, in this case, the targeted application of fertilizer after spatial mapping of regions where fertilizer may be required. Fig. (**4**) showcases the methodology for applications of the decision support system.

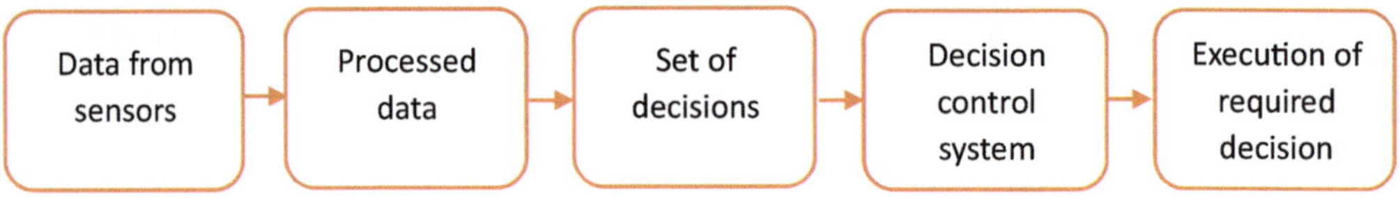

Fig. (4). Decision Support System working.

Further integration of Artificial Intelligence can also refine this process, enabling analysis of multiple factors, prediction, and prevention. DSS can also be integrated with variable data from other fields/patches. This variable data makes the calculations more precise and can also be used to visualize trends in soil fertility across various fields.

Architecture of Hyperspectral Remote Monitoring for Fertilizer Optimization and Nutrient Mapping

In this section, the methodologies proposed by researchers for the task of hyperspectral RS for fertilizer optimization and nutrient mapping finally provide a common layout for the same solution.

In a paper [49], the authors utilized a UAV drone with a built-in hyperspectral imager (GaiaSky-mini) with a band range of 400–1000 nm, 253 influential bands, and a flying height of 100m. They evaluated rice crops to assess nitrogen levels, followed by data calibration. Further, destructive sampling of rice plants for nitrogen content testing using the Kjeldahl method was performed. This was followed by image unmixing, model preparation (using SPA, red-edge, ELM, and WOA-ELM), evaluation of nitrogen deficiency, prescription mapping, and, finally, VRA of fertilizer. The authors [50] first collected data on wheat yield from different plots, followed by UAV data collection using a DJI M210 UAV with a RedEdge-MX multispectral sensor. This was followed by the calculation of NDVI and the assessment of various other features. This study helped create insights into fertilizer use, the results of which can be further applied for fertilizer optimization. The study [51] aimed to explore the potential of AI-driven IoT systems in smart agricultural resource management. This study aimed to implement AI models such as WDO-LSSVM, AWDO-LSSVM, and WDO-LSSVM to understand patterns and optimize fertilizer and water application using NM, while also leveraging the LoRaWAN protocol for IoT networking. Fig. (**5**) describes the common methodology for fertilizer optimization and nutrient mapping.

Fig. (5). Methodology for fertilizer optimization.

From the above discussions, the processes and technologies related to hyperspectral RS for agricultural systems were highlighted. Further, there is a need to properly understand and assess the factors that describe the real-life effectiveness of these technologies. The same is discussed in the next section.

Discussion on Fertilizer Optimization using Hyperspectral Remote Sensing

As discussed, fertilizer optimization involves understanding a plant's fertilizer needs and providing it with fertilizer only when required, not in excess. A brief overview of the advantages of fertilizer optimization is expressed in Fig. (**6**).

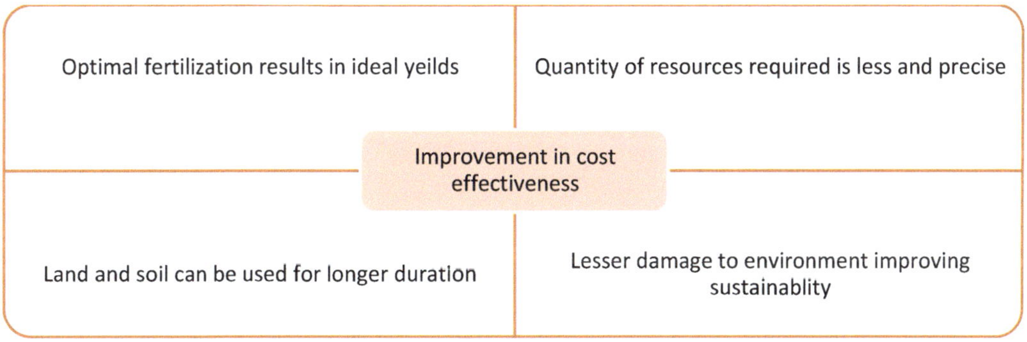

Fig. (6). Advantages of fertilizer optimization.

In this section, the pros and cons relating to cost and the environment, along with the challenges and limitations, are discussed.

Cost Effectiveness

The cost-effectiveness of fertilizer optimization using hyperspectral RS is questionable given the very high implementation costs of the technologies and devices used, which may include UAVs and powerful servers for AI workloads and handling large amounts of data. On the other hand, successful implementation will significantly reduce fertilizer use, improve yields, and ensure optimal use of resources like land for longer periods. Therefore, although promising, it is important to properly understand financial needs and future outcomes before implementing such solutions.

Environmental Benefits

Fertilizer optimization through remote monitoring is several times more effective than traditional fertilization solutions. Farmers typically apply fixed fertilizer rates based on historical practices or local field trials; this can either result in wasteful resource consumption and possible overfertilization, which can degrade the quality of the soil and the ecosystems around it, or limit the production of crops. The charts of crop requirements and data from remote monitoring can help one determine the precise requirements for optimal yield. Since data from remote monitoring systems is also in real time, it enables quick decision-making, thus enabling the efficient use of fertilizers. Excess fertilization can cause sudden plant growth with a weak root system that cannot provide enough water and other nutrients to the plant. This prevents the plant from producing enough food and from growing steadily. Excessive fertilization can also lead to high salt concentrations, which can harm beneficial soil microorganisms [52]. Fig. (7) shows the various environmental benefits of fertilizer optimization.

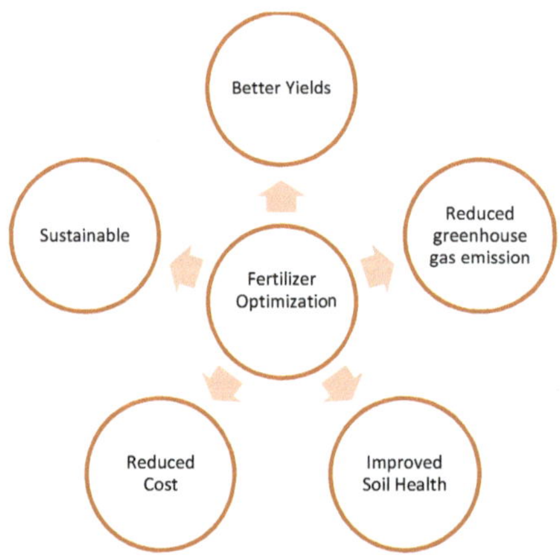

Fig. (7). Various environmental benefits of fertilizer optimization.

Thus, it may be concluded that fertilizer optimization helps farmers by reducing losses and fertilizer costs, improving profits from higher yields, and enhancing the quality and longevity of soil and the environment around it, as excessive fertilization harms the ecosystem and does not increase production.

CHALLENGES AND LIMITATIONS

While the proposed solution shows promise, several challenges and limitations could make it unfeasible for some. A few of these include resolution limitations, signal interference from atmospheric conditions, sensor calibration issues, soil and crop type variability, the high cost of implementation, a lack of ground truthing, and other challenges in data interpretation. Fig. (**8**) provides an overview of the major challenges and limitations of fertilizer optimization using remote sensing.

Fig. (8). Challenges and limitations of fertilizer optimization.

Hyperspectral sensors use hundreds of small spectral bands to detect and distinguish particular attributes of objects. Incorporating these bands results in larger data sets, more complex data storage, and greater difficulties with preprocessing (such as smoothing and noise reduction) and post-processing (such as image segmentation and pattern recognition) [53, 54]. The large volume of data, along with the variety of formats, spatiotemporal resolutions, and uncertainties, poses several challenges for big data use. These elements make it more difficult to interpret data in real-time, extract useful information, and automate data analysis processes [55]. Satellite imagery, however, has several drawbacks. The majority of operational imagery has a spatial resolution of 15–60 m, making it challenging to locate small, irrigated regions that, when combined, may cover a considerable area of the globe. Because of similarities in their spectral signatures, distinguishing irrigated fields from non-irrigated plots is challenging in humid regions [56]. Furthermore, it is challenging to identify agricultural fields using remote sensing because irrigated landscapes are usually classified as regions challenging to map [57, 58].

FUTURE PROSPECTS OF HYPERSPECTRAL REMOTE SENSING IN FERTILIZER MANAGEMENT

Further research and development in remote sensing technologies can significantly cut farming costs and improve yields. Integration of artificial intelligence with advanced IoT systems will also play a significant role in plant growth prediction. It can also be used to mitigate losses by predicting calamities and detecting diseases. The development of various devices and sensors will also broaden the scope of remote monitoring, increasing precision and helping us work with additional factors. Improvements in communication and data systems will also enable us to handle large datasets and analyze large patches. Moreover, integration of these developments will eventually protect produce from unforeseen conditions, thus providing the upcoming generation with ample crops.

CONCLUSION

This chapter discusses various applications of hyperspectral RS in agriculture, with a primary focus on the applications, benefits, and drawbacks of RS for optimizing fertilizer use and nutrient mapping. In this chapter, various studies highlighted the use of remote sensing in agriculture, with more focus on fertilizer use optimization. This gives insights into the future of sustainable and smart agriculture, which aims to enhance food production while utilizing the limited resources at hand.

REFERENCES

[1] Campbell JB, Wynne RH. Introduction to remote sensing. Guilford press 2011.

[2] Navalgund R R, Jayaraman V, Roy P S. Remote sensing applications: An overview. current science 2007; 1747-66.

[3] Sishodia RP, Ray RL, Singh Sensing SK. Applications of remote sensing in precision agriculture: a review. Remote 2020; 12(19): 3136. [http://dx.doi.org/10.3390/rs12193136]

[4] Ali A, Kaul HP. Monitoring yield and quality of forages and grassland in the view of precision

agriculture applications—a review. Remote Sens (Basel) 2025; 17(2): 279. [http://dx.doi.org/10.3390/rs17020279]

[5] Ray AS. Remote sensing in agriculture. Int J Environ Agric Biotechnol 2016; 1(3): 362-7. [http://dx.doi.org/10.22161/ijeab/1.3.8]

[6] Wang L, Qu JJ. Satellite remote sensing applications for surface soil moisture monitoring: A review. Front Earth Sci China 2009; 3(2): 237-47. [http://dx.doi.org/10.1007/s11707-009-0023-7]

[7] Xu N, Daccache A, Ahmadi A, Houtz D, Perez-Barquero FP. Soil moisture estimation with microwave remote sensing: A systematic review and meta-analysis. Int J Digit Earth 2025; 18(1): 1-27. [http://dx.doi.org/10.1080/17538947.2025.2468413]

[8] Gao Y, Lian X, Ge L. Inversion model of surface bare soil temperature and water content based on UAV thermal infrared remote sensing. Infrared Phys Technol 2022; 125: 104289. [http://dx.doi.org/10.1016/j.infrared.2022.104289]

[9] Luo Y, Huang H, Roques A. Early monitoring of forest wood-boring pests with remote sensing. Annu Rev Entomol 2023; 68(1): 277-98. [http://dx.doi.org/10.1146/annurev-ento-120220-125410] [PMID: 36198398]

[10] Zheng Q, Huang W, Xia Q, *et al.* Remote sensing monitoring of rice diseases and pests from different data sources: A review. Agronomy (Basel) 2023; 13(7): 1851. [http://dx.doi.org/10.3390/agronomy13071851]

[11] Omia E, Bae H, Park E, *et al.* Remote sensing in field crop. Remote Sens (Basel) 2023; 15(2): 354. [http://dx.doi.org/10.3390/rs15020354]

[12] Salcedo FP, Cutillas PP, Cabañero JJA, Vivaldi AG. Use of remote sensing to evaluate the effects of environmental factors on soil salinity in a semi-arid area. Sci Total Environ 2022; 815: 152524. [http://dx.doi.org/10.1016/j.scitotenv.2021.152524] [PMID: 34954179]

[13] Shanmugapriya P, Rathika S, Ramesh T, Janaki P. Applications of remote sensing in agriculture-A Review. Int J Curr Microbiol Appl Sci 2019; 8(1): 2270-83. [http://dx.doi.org/10.20546/ijcmas.2019.801.238]

[14] Khanal S, Kc K, Fulton JP, Shearer S and Ozkan E. Remote sensing in agriculture—accomplishments, limitations, and opportunities. Remote Sensing 2020; 12(22): 3783. [http://dx.doi.org/10.3390/rs12223783]

[15] Karunathilake EMBM, Le AT, Heo S, Chung YS, Mansoor S. The path to smart farming: Innovations and opportunities in precision agriculture. Agriculture 2023; 13(8): 1593. [http://dx.doi.org/10.3390/agriculture13081593]

[16] Grisso R D, Alley M M, Thomason W E, Holshouser D L, Roberson G T. Precision farming tools: variable-rate application. 2011.

[17] Ilyas Q, Ahmad M, Mehmood A. Automated estimation of crop. Bioengineering (Basel) 2023; 10(2): 125. [http://dx.doi.org/10.3390/bioengineering10020125] [PMID: 36829619]

[18] Liu J, Xiang J, Jin Y, Liu R, Yan J, Wang L. Boost precision agriculture with unmanned aerial vehicle remote sensing and edge intelligence: A survey. Remote Sens (Basel) 2021; 13(21): 4387. [http://dx.doi.org/10.3390/rs13214387]

[19] Kavipriya J, Vadivu G. Exploring crop 2024 international conference on advances in computing, Communication and Applied Informatics (ACCAI). 1-5.

[20] Yao J, Wu J, Xiao C, Zhang Z, Li J. The classification method study of crops remote sensing with deep learning, machine learning, and Google Earth engine. Remote Sens (Basel) 2022; 14(12): 2758. [http://dx.doi.org/10.3390/rs14122758]

[21] Kussul N, Lavreniuk M, Skakun S, Shelestov A. Deep learning classification of land cover and crop. IEEE Geosci Remote Sens Lett 2017; 14(5): 778-82.
[http://dx.doi.org/10.1109/LGRS.2017.2681128]

[22] Singh G, Singh S, Sethi G, Sood V. Deep learning in the mapping of agricultural land use using Sentinel-2 satellite data. Geographies 2022; 2(4): 691-700.
[http://dx.doi.org/10.3390/geographies2040042]

[23] Wang L, Wang J, Liu Z, Zhu J, Qin F. Evaluation of a deep-learning model for multispectral remote sensing of land use and crop classification. Crop J 2022; 10(5): 1435-51.
[http://dx.doi.org/10.1016/j.cj.2022.01.009]

[24] López-Andreu FJ, Erena M, Dominguez-Gómez JA, López-Morales JA. Sentinel-2 images and machine learning as tool for monitoring of the common agricultural policy: Calasparra rice as a case study. Agronomy (Basel) 2021; 11(4): 621.
[http://dx.doi.org/10.3390/agronomy11040621]

[25] Lakra D, Pipil S, Srivastava PK, Singh SK, Gupta M, Prasad R. Soil moisture retrieval over agricultural region through machine learning and sentinel 1 observations. Frontiers in Remote Sensing 2025; 5: 1513620.
[http://dx.doi.org/10.3389/frsen.2024.1513620]

[26] Zhai W, Cheng Q, Duan F, Huang X, Chen Z. Remote sensing-based analysis of yield and water-fertilizer use efficiency in winter wheat management. Agric Water Manage 2025; 311: 109390.
[http://dx.doi.org/10.1016/j.agwat.2025.109390]

[27] Li S, Jin Z, Bai J, Xiang S, Xu C, Yu F. Research on fertilization decision method for rice tillering stage based on the coupling of UAV hyperspectral remote sensing and WOFOST. Front Plant Sci 2024; 15: 1405239.
[http://dx.doi.org/10.3389/fpls.2024.1405239] [PMID: 38911973]

[28] Zhang K, Cao Q, Song X, *et al.* Remote sensing approaches for crop nutrition diagnosis and recommendations for nitrogen fertilizers in rice at canopy level. Arch Agron Soil Sci 2023; 69(14): 2878-97.
[http://dx.doi.org/10.1080/03650340.2023.2180146]

[29] Yu F, Bai J, Jin Z, Zhang H, Guo Z, Chen C. Research on precise fertilization method of rice tillering stage based on UAV hyperspectral remote sensing prescription map. Agronomy (Basel) 2022; 12(11): 2893.
[http://dx.doi.org/10.3390/agronomy12112893]

[30] Srivastava K, Pandey PC, Sharma JK. An approach for route optimization in applications of precision agriculture using UAVs. Drones (Basel) 2020; 4(3): 58.
[http://dx.doi.org/10.3390/drones4030058]

[31] Kumarasiri UWLM, Ariyawansha T, Kulasekara BR. Use of drone imagery to predict leaf nitrogen content of sugarcane cultivated under organic fertilizer application Tropical Agricultural Research 2024; 35(1).
[http://dx.doi.org/10.4038/tar.v35i1.8700]

[32] Bonfil DJ, Michael Y, Shiff S, Lensky IM. Optimizing top dressing nitrogen fertilization using VENμS and Sentinel-2 L1 data. Remote Sens (Basel) 2021; 13(19): 3934.
[http://dx.doi.org/10.3390/rs13193934]

[33] Munir S, Seminar KB, Sudradjat , Sukoco H, Buono A. The use of random forest regression for estimating leaf nitrogen content of oil palm based on sentinel 1-A imagery. Information (Basel) 2022; 14(1): 10.
[http://dx.doi.org/10.3390/info14010010]

[34] Munnaf MA, Guerrero A, Calera M, Mouazen AM. Precision nitrogen fertilization for opium poppy using combined proximal and remote sensor data fusion. Remote Sens (Basel) 2023; 15(23): 5442.

[http://dx.doi.org/10.3390/rs15235442]

[35] Diaz-Gonzalez FA, Vuelvas J, Correa CA, Vallejo VE, Patino D. Machine learning and remote sensing techniques applied to estimate soil indicators – Review. Ecol Indic 2022; 135: 108517. [http://dx.doi.org/10.1016/j.ecolind.2021.108517]

[36] Vasu D, Singh SK, Ray SK, *et al.* Soil quality index (SQI) as a tool to evaluate crop productivity in semi-arid Deccan plateau, India. Geoderma 2016; 282: 70-9. [http://dx.doi.org/10.1016/j.geoderma.2016.07.010]

[37] Das AC, Noguchi R, Ahamed T. An assessment of drought stress in tea plantation areas in Bangladesh using optical and thermal remote sensing: A climate change Perspective In Remote Sensing. Singapore: Springer Nature Singapore 2024; pp. 23-47.

[38] Zhang X, Liu D, Ma J, Wang X, Li Z, Zheng D. Visible near-infrared hyperspectral soil organic matter prediction based on combinatorial modeling. Agronomy (Basel) 2024; 14(4): 789. [http://dx.doi.org/10.3390/agronomy14040789]

[39] Khalil SK, Khalaf AB, Bader BR. Studying the relationship between some spectral evidence and the nutritional elements of citrus orchards in baqubah IOP Conference Series: Earth and Environmental Science . IOP Publishing 2024; 1371: p. (10)102025.

[40] Wang J, Yang J, Li Z, *et al.* Research on soil erosion based on remote sensing technology: a review. Agriculture 2024; 15(1): 18. [http://dx.doi.org/10.3390/agriculture15010018]

[41] Xu Y, Smirnov M, Kohler MC, *et al.* A survey of wireless soil sensing technologies. IEEE Access 2024; 12: 12010-38. [http://dx.doi.org/10.1109/ACCESS.2024.3352006]

[42] Boiarskii B, Hasegawa H. Comparison of NDVI and NDRE indices to detect differences in vegetation and chlorophyll content. Journal of Mechanics of Continua and Mathematical Sciences 2019; 4: 20-9. [http://dx.doi.org/10.26782/jmcms.spl.4/2019.11.00003]

[43] Jang J D. Evaluation of thermal-water stress of forest in southern Québec from satellite images. 2004.

[44] Heisel F, Sowinska M, Miehé JA, Lang M, Lichtenthaler HK. Detection of nutrient deficiencies of maize by laser induced fluorescence imaging. J Plant Physiol 1996; 148(5): 622-31. [http://dx.doi.org/10.1016/S0176-1617(96)80083-6]

[45] Paul M, Debnath S, Debnath T, Rogiers S, Baby T, Rahaman DM. Hyperspectral imaging to detect age, defects and individual nutrient deficiency in grapevine leaves, arXiv preprint arXiv 2020; 05197.

[46] Duarte A, Borralho N, Cabral P, Caetano M. Recent advances in forest insect pests and diseases monitoring using UAV-based data: A systematic review. Forests 2022; 13(6): 911. [http://dx.doi.org/10.3390/f13060911]

[47] Ni-Meister W, Lee S, Strahler AH, *et al.* Assessing general relationships between aboveground biomass and vegetation structure parameters for improved carbon estimate from lidar remote sensing. J Geophys Res Biogeosci 2010; 115(G2).

[48] Power D J. What is a DSS. The On-line executive journal for data-intensive decision support 1997; 1(3): 223-32.

[49] Zhang K, Cao Q, Song X, *et al.* Remote sensing approaches for crop nutrition diagnosis and recommendations for nitrogen fertilizers in rice at canopy level. Archives of Agronomy and Soil Science 2023; 69(14): 2878-2897. [http://dx.doi.org/10.1080/03650340.2023.2180146]

[50] Munns R, Passioura JB, Colmer TD and Byrt CS. Osmotic adjustment and energy limitations in crop yield under water stress. Plant, Cell & Environment 2025; 43(5): 1089-1106. [http://dx.doi.org/10.1111/pce.13729]

[51] Khalifeh AF, Alqammaz A, Khasawneh AM, Abualigah L, Darabkh KA, Zinonos Z. An

environmental remote sensing and prediction model for an IoT smart irrigation system based on an enhanced wind-driven optimization algorithm. Comput Electr Eng 2025; 122: 109889. [http://dx.doi.org/10.1016/j.compeleceng.2024.109889]

[52] Mustafa G, Hayat N, Alotaibi BA. How and why to prevent over fertilization to get sustainable crop. Academic Press 2023; pp. 339-54. [http://dx.doi.org/10.1016/B978-0-443-18675-2.00019-5]

[53] Khanal S, Kc K, Fulton JP, Shearer S, Ozkan E. Remote sensing in agriculture—accomplishments, limitations, and opportunities. Remote Sens (Basel) 2020; 12(22): 3783. [http://dx.doi.org/10.3390/rs12223783]

[54] Jia B, Wang W, Ni X, *et al.* Essential processing methods of hyperspectral images of agricultural and food products. Chemom Intell Lab Syst 2020; 198: 103936. [http://dx.doi.org/10.1016/j.chemolab.2020.103936]

[55] Yang C, Yu M, Hu F, Jiang Y, Li Y. Utilizing Cloud Computing to address big geospatial data challenges. Comput Environ Urban Syst 2017; 61: 120-8. [http://dx.doi.org/10.1016/j.compenvurbsys.2016.10.010]

[56] Ozdogan M, Yang Y, Allez G, Cervantes C. Remote sensing of irrigated agriculture: Opportunities and challenges. Remote Sens (Basel) 2010; 2(9): 2274-304. [http://dx.doi.org/10.3390/rs2092274]

[57] Loveland TR, Reed BC, Brown JF, *et al.* Development of a global land cover characteristics database and IGBP DISCover from 1 km AVHRR data. Int J Remote Sens 2000; 21(6-7): 1303-30. [http://dx.doi.org/10.1080/014311600210191]

[58] Friedl MA, McIver DK, Hodges JCF, *et al.* Global land cover mapping from MODIS: algorithms and early results. Remote Sens Environ 2002; 83(1-2): 287-302. [http://dx.doi.org/10.1016/S0034-4257(02)00078-0]

CHAPTER 9

Study on Harnessing Remote Sensing for Advanced Wildlife Monitoring and Conservation

Anamika Larhgotra[1,*] and **Navpreet Kaur Walia**[1]

[1] *Department of CSE, Chandigarh University, Mohali, India*

Abstract: Remote sensing is growing rapidly as a valuable and, at times, critical technology in monitoring the environment. This allows large-scale data acquisitions for ecological applications. The chapter describes the impact of integrating remote sensing into wildlife monitoring and conservation, particularly Hyperspectral Remote Sensing (HRS), on sustainable agriculture. Monitoring of wildlife changes with the ongoing advancements like satellite imagery, drone sensor-based techniques, and AI technologies. This helps to map habitats, estimate populations, and monitor biodiversity. On the other hand, HRS has a crucial role to play in agriculture through more detailed spectral data, enhancing productivity through crop health assessment and soil and water-resource management.

The chapter discusses some of the recent methodologies used in wildlife conservation, such as species tracking with GPS collars, vegetation mapping with multispectral imagery, and machine learning ecosystem classification. For sustainable agriculture in hyperspectral data, precision farming, disease detection, and yield have potential applications. This chapter compares how these two areas relate through comparative analysis to show that ecological and agricultural monitoring could evolve together using remote sensing technologies. A case study demonstrates the application of integrated remote sensing in an agro-ecological landscape in terms of how habitat conservation can be made to coincide with agricultural sustainability. Additionally, a thorough literature review synthesizes key research works, for presentation in tabular comparison, demonstrating methodologies and applications. Also, there is a flow chart that represents the different components and processes involved in wildlife monitoring and conservation through remote sensing technologies.

Keywords: Artificial Intelligence, Agriculture, Ecology, Hyperspectral remote sensing, Machine learning, Remote sensing, Sustainability, Wildlife monitoring.

* **Corresponding author Anamika Larhgotra:** Department of CSE, Chandigarh University, Mohali, India; E-mail: annularhgotra@gmail.com

Sartajvir Singh, Neelam Dahiya, Maged Mohammed, Abdullah Alzharihi & Vishal Dutt (Eds.)

INTRODUCTION

Hyperspectral Remote Sensing (HRS) is a sophisticated technology that gathers data in hundreds of close spectral bands and enables detailed analysis of surface materials. These features allow farmers to make effective decisions and implement sustainability and precision agriculture. HRS facilitates monitoring crop health, early disease and nutrient deficiency detection, and measurement of soil quality parameters like moisture, salinity, and organic content. These features allow farmers to make effective decisions, minimize input waste, and increase productivity in a responsible, environmentally friendly way. The current developments in remote sensing technologies have expanded opportunities in wildlife monitoring and conservation efforts that will enable a whole series of applications, such as wildlife conservation and sustainable agriculture. These are used to unleash the benefits of biodiversity management through the unprecedented capabilities to acquire real-time information on the distribution of species, habitat conditions, and dynamics within ecosystems. Remote sensing technologies, for example, satellite imagery, aerial photography, and unmanned aerial vehicles, possess the extraordinary ability to monitor large and inaccessible regions [1]. Such an ability allows researchers and conservation managers to track and monitor the status of wildlife populations and their habitats across vast spatial and temporal scales. Most importantly, these technologies will inform and enable policymakers and decision-makers to provide the necessary information to define and implement appropriate strategies for sustainable development and effective biodiversity conservation. This chapter is primarily concerned with the technological and methodological foundations of remote sensing and also focuses on the likely transformative potential of the technology in responding to the global challenges posed by biodiversity loss and food security. They allow a variety of diverse applications, for example, wildlife conservation and sustainable agriculture, within these broad areas. This includes habitat monitoring, species tracking, and biodiversity assessment by wildlife conservation. Sustainable agriculture, on the other hand, generates profits from hyperspectral imaging for crop health, soil fertility, and water resource management [2].

The nexus of these two areas revolves around environmental sustainability as a common goal. Both of these require precise acquisition, processing, and analysis, with remote sensing technology playing a critical role in the chapter on AI and ML techniques for processing remote sensing data for predictive modelling, anomaly detection, and decision support. Through integration of remote sensing techniques, conservationists and agricultural planners can integrate ecological preservation with sustainable food production [2]. Computer-based simulation techniques, such as geographic information systems, active and passive RADAR, and lidar systems, are being used with critical importance for real-time monitoring of biodiversity.

METHODOLOGIES

There are no limits to the types of data that can be acquired, processed, and analysed for AI/ML applications. Satellite-based sources such as Landsat and Sentinel-2 can be used to capture habitat data, while drone-mounted thermal imaging can be used to locate animal movements as part of remote sensing technologies for wildlife monitoring. Real-time species tracking is enabled by IoT devices such as GPS collars. The application of AI-powered models with neural networks includes CNN for species detection and Random Forest for habitat classification in data processing. NDVI and other spectral types assess vegetation health, and habitat-suitability assessments depend on them. GIS-based tools combine spatial data for habitat mapping and land-use monitoring. For instance, in India, Kaziranga National Park uses drones equipped with AI to detect illegal poaching, demonstrating how remote sensing technology is advancing conservation efforts.

Among these techniques is the mapping of the essential areas.

Remote sensing enables extensive use of techniques for acquiring information about the world's surface without physically touching the Earth's surface. Some of the key methodologies under wildlife monitoring are:

- **Satellite Imagery**: These satellites measure a number of different wavelengths of electromagnetic radiation through optical, infrared, and radar sensors [3]. They cover large areas and can thus detect habitat, vegetation patterns, and land-use changes that affect wildlife distribution and behaviour.
- **Aerial Imagery**: Aircraft and drones have comparatively higher resolution imagery and flexible data-acquisition modalities to provide detailed surveys of particular areas and record dynamic events, such as wildlife migrations or human-wildlife conflicts [4].
- **Acoustic Monitoring**: Passive acoustic sensors listen to animal vocalizations to provide information on species abundance and distribution, and, to some extent, behaviour.
- **Thermal Imaging**: With thermal sensors, heat signatures can be observed, enabling the identification and tracking of animals and the monitoring of their physiological processes under changing environmental conditions, especially for nocturnal species [5].

Key components of remote sensing are depicted in Fig. (**1**).

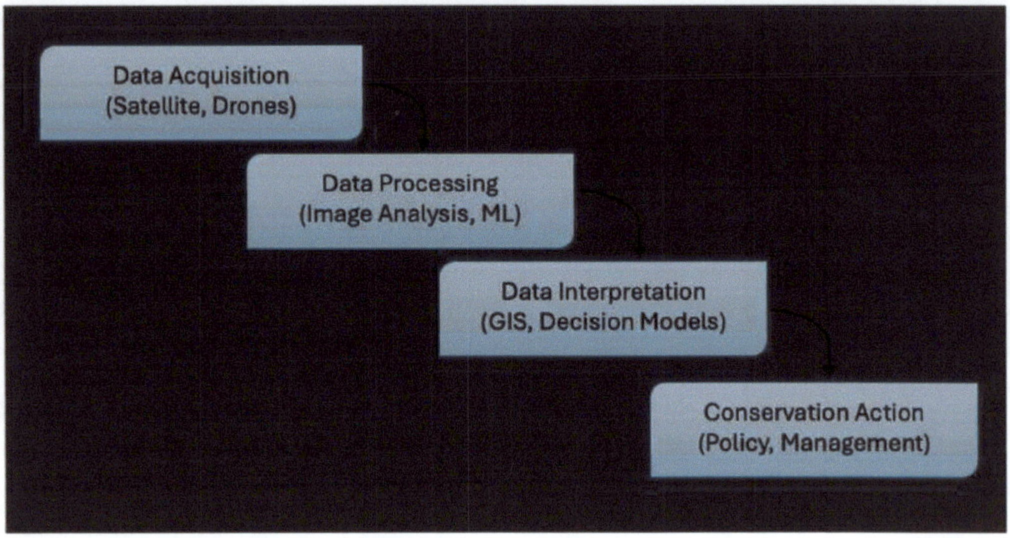

Fig. (1). Components of wildlife monitoring using remote sensing.

Remote sensing depends mainly on 4 prominent components, as shown in Fig. (**1**). This begins with capturing real-time data from devices such as cameras, drones, and sensors. From there, it is transmitted for preprocessing and building a knowledge base, on which the algorithms are eventually applied. The relevant data can be derived from models and prototypes, which lead to concrete conservation actions.

LITERATURE REVIEW

The use of remote sensing is a significant way to transform wildlife monitoring and conservation through large-scale environmental evaluation using satellites, drones, and aerial imagery. Many studies have already discussed solution-based approaches in biodiversity tracking, habitat mapping, and environmental change detection. Turner *et al.* (2015) integrated various multispectral and hyperspectral sensors into GIS for habitat classification, enabling conservationists to better monitor areas of high biodiversity. As Pettorelli *et al.* (2017) noted, thermal and optical sensors combined with machine learning models, such as Convolutional Neural Networks (CNNs), can detect species presence and estimate population densities with an accuracy that will leave you breathless.

Recent advances in remote sensing and AI have enhanced wildlife monitoring capabilities. One outstanding example is the study by Norouzzadeh *et al.* (2018) [5], which features automated species classification powered by deep learning algorithms applied to millions of camera-trap images, resulting in reduced manual work and greater accuracy. Wall *et al.* (2021) described real-time tracking of migrating species using GPS-enabled collars and IoT sensors to time interventions during human-wildlife conflict situations. Additionally, Asner *et al.* (2019) [6] conducted LiDAR-based studies on 3D habitat modeling to facilitate the assessment of forest canopy structures for the conservation of arboreal species.

However, challenges remain, including methodological constraints, weather-related issues, restricted access to data, and the cost of sensor deployment, which affect the efficiency of these approaches. The next frontier for research involves multi-sensor platforms equipped with AI-powered decision support systems, aiming to address these limitations and provide a more holistic and sustainable approach to wildlife conservation through remote-sensing technologies.

Substantial deep learning architectures, such as CNNs, have been used to process data from satellites and drones for remote sensing to automatically identify animal species [6]. Improved monitoring has been achieved, leading to less manual observation in far-flung regions. Additionally, spectral unmixing techniques differentiated crop features from mixed pixels. These studies resulted in higher predictions of crop yield and provided accurate indications of the timing of irrigation, fertilization, and early disease detection. Many existing research studies and allied findings for wildlife monitoring are presented in Table **1**.

Table 1. Analysis of various research papers.

Research Topic	Year of Publication	Emphasis	Methodology Used	Key Findings	Scope
"Combining Remote Sensing and GIS"	2019	Habitat-Crop Interaction	GIS + AI models	Balanced land-use models	AI-powered real-time data systems
"Hyperspectral Imaging in Agriculture"	2020	Precision Agriculture	Spectral Unmixing, CNNs	Higher crop yield predictions	Enhanced AI-driven forecasting
"Remote Sensing for Wildlife Conservation"	2021	Wildlife Monitoring	ML for species detection	Improved monitoring accuracy	Large-scale deployment needed
"Climate-Driven Remote Sensing Eco-Agricultural Systems"	2022	Eco-Agricultural Systems	Time-series analysis	Climate-resilient practices	Climate change adaptation models

(Table 1) cont.....

"Multispectral Image Processing for Land Cover Classification"	2018	Land Use Monitoring	ML-based Image Processing	Accurate land cover mapping	Advanced AI integration
"AI-Driven Satellite Imaging for Forest Fire Detection"	2023	Disaster Monitoring	AI + Satellite Imagery	Early wildfire detection	Global wildfire management
"Remote Sensing for Biodiversity Hotspot Identification"	2021	Biodiversity Assessment	Deep Learning and GIS	Improved ecosystem monitoring	Biodiversity conservation policies
"Smart Agriculture with IoT and Hyperspectral Sensors"	2020	Precision Farming	IoT + Spectral Analysis	Enhanced precision farming	Automated farm management
"Automated Land Use Detection with AI-Powered Drones"	2022	Environmental Monitoring	Drone + AI models	Efficient land use analysis	Scalable environmental management
"Real-Time Wildlife Tracking Using IoT-Enabled Devices"	2019	Wildlife Tracking	GPS + IoT Devices	Real-time animal tracking	Improved anti-poaching systems
"Data-Driven Sustainable Agriculture Using AI and Remote Sensing"	2023	Sustainable Agriculture	AI-Based Crop Prediction	High crop yield accuracy	Scalable AI-driven agriculture

The research in "Hyperspectral Imaging for Crop Disease Detection" (Zhang *et al.*, 2020) demonstrates the efficiency of hyperspectral imaging in detecting early-stage fungal infections of wheat using machine learning classifiers with more than 90% accuracy. The article "Soil Property and Hyperspectral Remote Sensing in Precision Agriculture" (Li & Wang, 2021) investigates the use of hyperspectral cameras mounted on UAVs for crop health and nitrogen monitoring, enhancing site-specific fertilizer application.

A detailed analysis of related research has been conducted from different perspectives and is presented in Table **1**. This table provides information on the core ideas, methodologies, and findings of some crucial research papers in the same domain.

ADVANCES WITH AI/ML TECHNIQUES

AI and machine learning are increasingly essential and facilitate simpler, more efficient solutions to various problems. They are being implemented for real-time monitoring and at different tiers for detecting and conserving wildlife and supporting agriculture. The following are some examples:

Data Acquisition Using IoT Sensors

- Example: Acoustic sensors placed in forests capture animal calls and illegal gunfire.
- Research Proof: Wiggins *et al.* (2020) used IoT-enabled acoustic sensors to monitor bird migration patterns in North America [5].

Habitat Mapping Using AI/ML

- Example: Satellite imagery analyzed with CNNs for forest cover change detection.
- Research Proof: Rodríguez-Galiano *et al.* (2019) used deep learning models for large-scale habitat mapping in Amazon rainforests [7].

Species Identification by means of ML Models

- Example: Camera trap images are analyzed through models based on ResNet for species category classification.
- Research Proof: Norouzzadeh *et al.* employed deep CNNs to automatically classify animal species from millions of camera-trap images [7].

Poaching and Threat Detection Using IoT

- Example: IoT-enabled collars are used for tracking elephant migrations, where the authorities receive real-time alerts on entering danger zones.
- Research Proof: Wall *et al.* demonstrated a real-time elephant tracking methodology developed in Africa using IoT-based GPS collars.

Fig. (**2**) below depicts the flowchart for monitoring wildlife in Real Time.

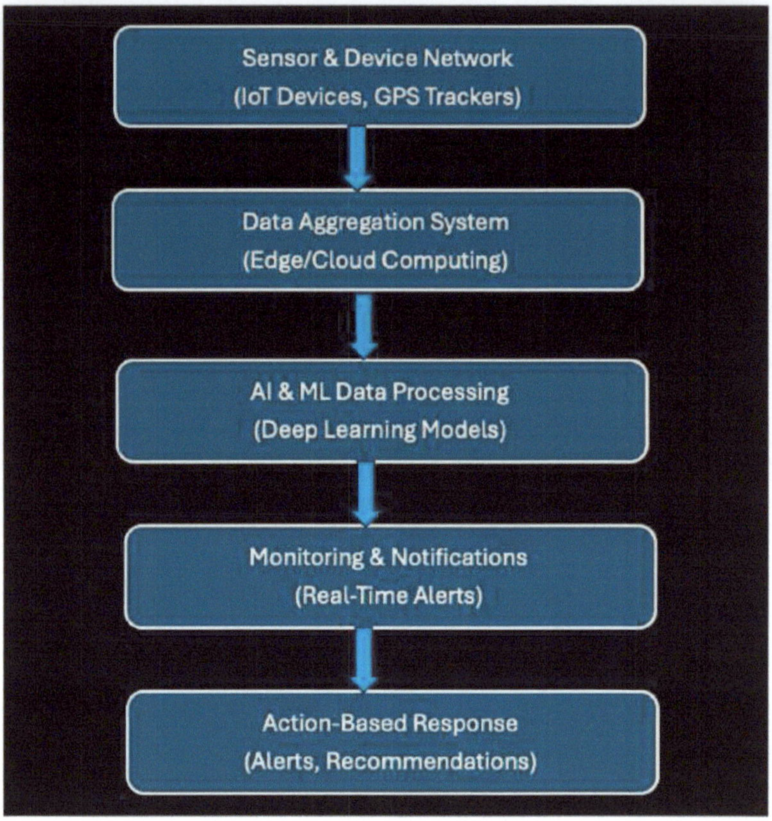

Fig. (2). Steps of real-time monitoring of wildlife scenarios.

The monitoring and safeguarding of wildlife needs dynamic approaches. These approaches should be flexible enough to be adopted in real time to avoid malfunctions. Furthermore, efficient monitoring goes well with devices equipped to capture streaming or dynamic inputs. After that, appropriate alignment with the suitable model and aggregation smoothens the monitoring process. Alerts are issued to notify of sudden rehabilitation or counterattacks in the event of disturbances to wildlife safety. Proper execution and arrangements create positive scenarios that align actions to strengthen the system.

For end-to-end monitoring of the ecosystem of wildlife and agriculture, the steps are shown below:

The end-to-end monitoring process, as shown in Fig. (**3**), is crucial for connecting the steps of wildlife safeguarding. It should be adopted as it provides a clear path to prevent sudden hindrances in planning and allows timely action on received real-time alerts. This monitoring tracks every event and changing situation in the wildlife ecosystem.

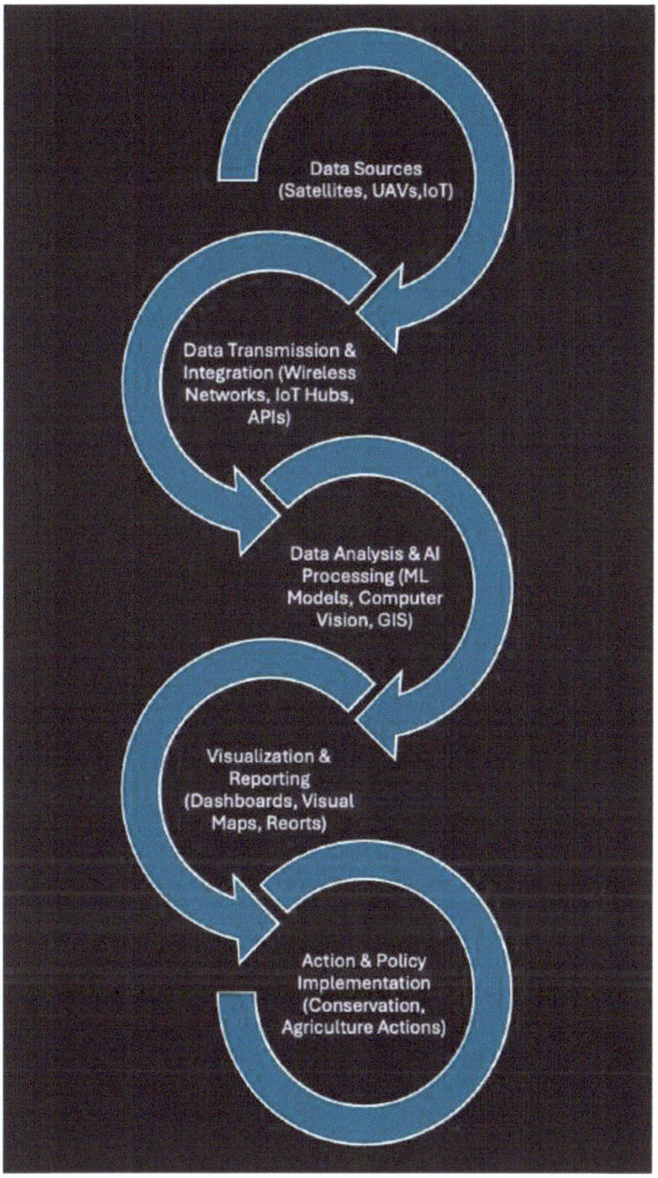

Fig. (3). End-to-end monitoring with AIML.

The end-to-end monitoring and integration of AIML capabilities have widened the scope of monitoring and safeguarding the ecosystem of animals in their respective niches.

MERITS AND DEMERITS

A readout of all arguments for and against wildlife monitoring and sustainable agriculture under the prevailing situation is presented below. These points have the potential to provide insights into trends and gaps in research.

Merits

Wildlife Monitoring

- Large Scale Monitoring: Enables observation of vast and remote areas.
- Non-Invasive: Minimizes human-wildlife conflicts.
- Immediate Data: Facilitates instant decision-making concerning conservation.

Sustainable Agriculture

- Efficient Utilization of Resources: Water and fertilizers, as well as pesticides, are better managed.
- Highly Accurate: Allows early detection of crop diseases and soil deficiencies.
- Environment: Conducive to the promotion of eco-friendly farming practices.

Demerits

Wildlife Monitoring

- High cost: Drones and satellite imagery equipment are expensive.
- Complexity of Data Processing: It requires skills in ML and GIS.
- Weather Dependence: Cloud cover reduces data quality.

Sustainable Agriculture

- **Initial Investment:**There are high technology setup and maintenance costs.
- **Limited Accessibility**: Technology may be prohibitive for some of the smallholders.
- **Data Privacy Issues:** Sensitive data could be misused.

Table **2** presents the advantages and disadvantages of using hyperspectral remote sensing in agriculture. This will give an idea of the use of the technique in sustainable farming.

Table 2. Comparison between the advantages and limitations of hyperspectral remote sensing in sustainable farming.

Advantages	Limitations
Enables **early detection** of crop stress, diseases, and nutrient deficiencies	**High cost** of sensors and processing tools
Provides **non-destructive and high-resolution data**	Requires **skilled personnel** for data processing and interpretation
Supports **site-specific management** and precision farming	**Large data volume** makes storage and processing computationally intensive
Helps in **soil quality assessment** (moisture, salinity, organic content)	**Atmospheric conditions** (*e.g.*, cloud cover) affect satellite data accuracy
Improves **yield prediction** and resource optimization	**Limited accessibility** for small-scale farmers, especially in developing regions
Allows integration with **AI/ML models** for automation	**Calibration and preprocessing** are time-consuming and require domain knowledge

COMPARISON AND CONNECTION TO SUSTAINABLE AGRICULTURE

Hyperspectral remote sensing can capture different electromagnetic wavelengths, producing very high-resolution, detailed spectral signatures of the Earth's surface [7]. Although it has advantages, HRS has some limitations. The technology is still quite costly, and hence less affordable for smallholder farmers. Moreover, hyperspectral data processing demands advanced software and skilled experts. Satellite-based HRS systems could also be impacted by cloud cover and atmospheric disturbances, reducing their reliability under some conditions. The above data has a direct relationship with wildlife conservation when integrated with sustainable agriculture for ecosystem management. Remote sensing, AI/ML, and IoT are essential to both wildlife conservation and sustainable agriculture in India and the globe. The IRS and CARTOSAT are among the remote sensing technologies in India that support monitoring biodiversity-rich ecosystems, such as the Western Ghats and the Sundarbans [8]. Sensors such as AVIRIS, PRISMA, EnMap, and others are used to support hyperspectral monitoring, and these advancements have provided a versatile spectrum for visualizing scenes in the wildlife ecosystem. Hyperspectral imaging supports sustainable farming by monitoring crop health and soil fertility, like those in Punjab and Maharashtra [9].

Globally, satellites such as Sentinel-2 and Landsat have enabled precision agriculture in the U.S., while drones have enhanced anti-poaching patrols in national parks across Africa [10]. The technologies applied in both areas include Geographic Information Systems (GIS) for spatial analyses, AI-based species recognition for wildlife, and crop classification in agriculture. For example, drones equipped with thermal cameras in Kaziranga National Park can detect poachers, and IoT sensors attached to agricultural soils in Andhra Pradesh measure soil moisture to enable water-efficient farming. AI/ML models, such as CNNs, classify wildlife from remote sensing data and analyze crop diseases [11].

Although the objectives differ, wildlife monitoring focuses on habitat conservation, whereas agriculture emphasizes food security and resource optimization. Integrated frameworks could balance conservation with agricultural expansion in sustainable systems through climate-resilient and data-driven decision-making, both in the Indian and global contexts [12].

Common Usage Scenarios and Intersections

- **Land Use and Cover Monitoring:** Continuous land cover monitoring is used for both wildlife conservation and agriculture to detect, as well as assess, habitat suitability for species or crops.
- **Monitoring Health and Stress in Vegetation:** HRS supports the assessment of vegetation health, which is linked to habitat quality in wildlife conservation and crop productivity in agriculture [13].
- **Climatic Impact Assessment-**It assesses spatial and temporal results of environmental stressors such as drought, flood, and fire regarding natural habitat and agricultural lands.
- **Water Resource Management**: It assesses water availability, which is critical for wildlife survival and also important for irrigation planning.
- **Mapping Biodiversity and Crop Diversity:**It involves the identification of plant species for conservation and as crop varieties for sustainable farming.
- **Innovative Connections:** Eco-Agro system monitoring involves combined wildlife-agriculture monitoring to ensure effective land management and reduce conflicts between expansion agriculture and habitat preservation.
- **Integrated Landscape Management Models:** The eventual creation of models that merge habitat conservation with agricultural productivity will guarantee both environmental and economic sustainability.
- **Early Warning Systems**: Use of predictive models *via* HRS for pest outbreaks, habitat degradation, and agricultural yield forecasting, benefiting both spheres.

Integrated ecological management becomes more attainable with the association of remote sensing in wildlife monitoring with hyperspectral applications in sustainable agriculture [14]. Such arrangements will ensure biodiversity conservation and, at the same time, provide resources used sustainably, thereby fostering a resilient environmental balance. Sustainability is a core need to strengthen the monitoring process of the wildlife ecosystem. It offers an opportunity to lead or to create a healthy, bright future. If sustainability is adopted, then harshness in nature can be reduced. Sustainable agriculture can be used to safeguard and reduce attacks on wild animals, as it fulfils the greedy needs of humans, which in turn align with supporting the wildlife environment and minimising the human desire to destroy wild ecosystems [15]. Some points on wildlife monitoring and sustainable agriculture are depicted in Table **3** below.

Differentiated criteria for wildlife monitoring and sustainable agriculture are shown in the table below:

Table 3. Comparison between wildlife monitoring and sustainable agriculture.

Criteria	Wildlife Monitoring and Conservation	Sustainable Agriculture
Data Acquisition	Satellite imagery, drones	Hyperspectral sensors
Applications	Habitat mapping, species tracking	Crop health, soil analysis
Techniques	ML models for classification	Spectral unmixing, regression
Challenges	Data availability, processing time	Cost, spatial resolution
Future Potential	Automated ecosystem monitoring	Precision farming systems

Integration of remote sensing, AIML, and IoT is also on the rise and is being embraced to strengthen efforts in wildlife conservation and to adopt sustainable agriculture for the better health of the Ecosystem [16]. These three technologies have given rise to many new opportunities, and a basic illustration of their proceedings is shown below.

The integration of remote sensing, AIML, and IoT, as depicted in Fig. (**4**), provides a basis for utilizing these services to develop a conservation approach for wildlife. This collaboration is directly focused on habitat planning, tracking, threat detection, and conservation of the animals' niche.

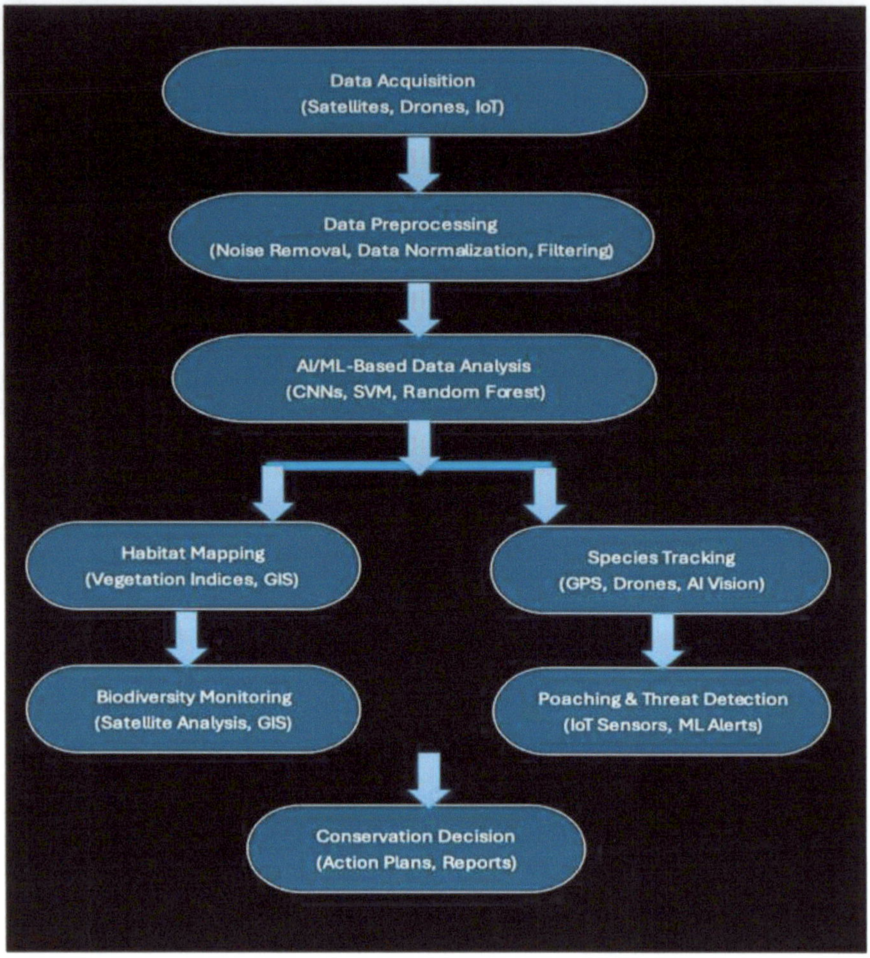

Fig. (4). Integrated proceedings of remote sensing, AIML, and IoT for wildlife monitoring.

APPLICATIONS

Case Study 1: Integrated Remote Sensing in Wildlife Conservation and Sustainable Agriculture

This case study demonstrates how remote sensing technology serves wildlife conservation and sustainable agricultural management in the Amazon Basin. The multispectral and hyperspectral data captured by Sentinel 2 were used to deliver land cover classification while simultaneously mapping habitat and identifying different crop types. Artificial intelligence image processing has been used to detect deforestation, monitor migratory species, and predict crop yields [17]. This is an example of an integrated approach in showing the contribution of remote sensing to a balanced ecosystem while boosting agricultural productivity.

Case Study 2: AI-facilitated Cameras for Early Bushfire Detection in Australia

This case is in Victoria, Australia, where AI cameras are deployed in remote outback areas for bushfire detection. These cameras operate round-the-clock, with detection capabilities of up to 20 kilometers, and report to authorities as soon as fires are detected. For implementation, seven cameras are installed in the western area of the state, capturing real-time images analyzed by AI for smoke or fire. The number of unplanned fires detected so far has increased, at times saving up to six minutes compared to human observation. Early detection has improved response times, enabling more prompt containment and reducing potential damage. This success has led to plans for scaling the initiative.

Case Study 3: AI in US Agroecosystems Regenerative Agriculture

AI and digital technologies are revolutionizing regenerative agriculture in the US by improving soil health and CO_2 sequestration. Companies like Agri-carbon and Yard Stick use robotics to automate soil analysis, including soil core extraction and spectral probes. Digital soil maps contribute to predicting soil organic content using machine learning and remote-sensing data, in addition to monitoring soil to assess the impacts of different agricultural practices. AI is making regenerative agriculture more accessible and cost-effective: it provides accurate estimates for carbon markets and supports reductions in atmospheric CO_2 through budget-friendly interventions.

Case Study 4: AI-Cattle Monitoring in Queensland, Australia

The AI monitoring system for cattle has been developed through a collaboration between the Queensland Department of Agriculture and Fisheries and InFarm. The system aids in identifying areas for increased production while maintaining biosecurity considerations.

A prototypical automated camera system records and detects cattle without manual input, focusing on identifying cows and calves due to the low fertility rate. The system generated approximately 750,000 images and 86,000 videos, which were used to develop AI algorithms for continuous remote surveillance. This technology promises productivity gains by detecting issues such as injuries or disease symptoms at the earliest possible stage, consistent with the visions of the AgTech Roadmap in adoption, adaptation, and advancement.

DEVICES AND TOOLS

The devices and tools mentioned in Tables **4-8** are significant in the conservation process and are mainly centred on harnessing technologies to provide services to wildlife. The applications of AI/ML and IoT for remote sensing have given wings to the conservation domain. Many pieces of equipment are installed for different applications, helping unravel the impediments posed by wildlife protection and monitoring. Habitat monitoring, crop health assessment, and disaster management are conducted through satellites such as Landsat and drones fitted with thermal and optical sensors. Real-time tracking and environmental data are made possible by IoT devices, including GPS collars, environmental sensors, and acoustic detectors. AI tools, such as TensorFlow and QGIS, process this information to enable predictive analysis, decision-making, and visualization. Integration of these devices ensures seamless data collection and processing with actionable insights [18]. For instance, forest cover changes are detectable through drones, while soil sensors enable precision farming by monitoring water and nutrient levels. Interconnected systems optimize the productivity of ecological conservation and agriculture. For example, drones combined with AI are used for forest fire detection. Additionally, IoT sensors are deployed to monitor water intake on farms, and AI/ML tools assist in wildlife species classification [19]. Several classes of devices and tools are as follows:

- **Remote Sensing Devices**

Table 4. Features of remote sensing devices.

Device/Tool	Description	Application	Example
Satellites (Landsat Sentinel-2)	Earth-observing satellites that capture multispectral and hyperspectral images.	Land cover mapping, habitat monitoring, crop health analysis.	Landsat-8, Sentinel-2
UAVs/Drones	Unmanned aerial vehicles with various sensors like RGB, thermal, and LiDAR.	Real-time monitoring of wildlife and agricultural fields.	DJI Matrice 300 RTK
Spectrometers	Devices that measure spectral signatures of vegetation and soil.	Crop and soil health monitoring.	ASD FieldSpec 4
LiDAR Sensors	Laser-based sensors that create 3D maps of terrain and forests.	Habitat structure mapping, forest inventory.	Velodyne LiDAR
Thermal Cameras	Capture heat signatures of animals and plants.	Wildlife detection, poaching prevention.	FLIR Vue Pro R

• AI/ML Tools

Table 5. Features of AI/ML tools.

Tools	Description	Application	Example
Google Earth Engine	Cloud-based geospatial analysis platform.	Satellite image processing, habitat monitoring.	Google Earth Engine
TensorFlow	Open-source ML framework.	Image recognition, crop health analysis.	TensorFlow for ML
QGIS	Open-source GIS tool.	Mapping and spatial data analysis.	QGIS
ArcGIS	Open-source GIS tool.	Data visualization, spatial modelling.	Esri ArcGIS
YOLO (You Only Look Once)	Real-time object detection ML model.	Animal tracking and identification.	YOLOv4

• IOT Devices

Table 6. Features of IoT devices.

Device/Tool	Description	Application	Example
GPS Trackers	GPS-enabled collars or tags for tracking wildlife.	Migration tracking, animal behaviour monitoring.	Smart Paws GPS Collars
Environmental Sensors	Sensors measuring temperature, humidity, and air quality.	Micro-climate monitoring, habitat assessment.	LoRa Environmental Sensors
Acoustic Sensors	Record and analyse environmental sounds.	Poaching detection, animal call identification.	AudioMoth
Soil Moisture Sensors	Measure water content in soil.	Precision irrigation, crop monitoring.	Vegetronix VH400
Weather Stations	Collect climate data like temperature and wind speed.	Climate change monitoring, yield prediction.	Davis Vantage Pro2

• Data Processingand Visualisation Tools

Table 7. Features of visualisation tools.

Tool	Description	Application	Example
AWS Ground Station	Cloud service for satellite data retrieval.	Data analysis for conservation projects.	Amazon AWS Ground Station
R-Studio	Statistical computing and analysis tool.	Environmental data processing.	RStudio

(Table 7) cont.....

MATLAB	Computational tool for data analysis.	Remote sensing data modelling, ML.	MATLAB for AI/ML
Tableau	Data visualization and business intelligence tool.	Data-driven decision making.	Tableau Dashboard
Google Colab	Cloud-based ML and AI development environment.	AI model training and deployment.	Google Colabgi

In effect, the inclusion of IoT, AI/ML, and remote-sensed data has revitalized wildlife monitoring and protection. It bridges the gap between real-time and large-scale environmental data collection and analysis (and does so more comprehensively). Thus, remote-sensing satellites, such as Sentinel-2 and even drones, will be able to provide high-resolution imagery, which will be important for habitat mapping and deforestation detection (Turner *et al.*, 2015). AI/ML models such as CNNs and Random Forests help classify species and detect poaching activities from drone footage and camera trap data (Norouzzadeh *et al.*, 2018). The tools mentioned in Table **6** provide information on technologies that can be harnessed to benefit wildlife and to create models and analyses to track animal activities.

IoT technology, such as GPS collars and acoustic sensors, can be used to track animal movements and detect environmental sounds, which can inform biodiversity assessments [19]. Predictive ML algorithms analyze this data to forecast future migration routes, critical habitat loss, and climate effects. Real-time poaching detection, achieved by combining drones with AI-based object detection, has been employed in Africa's national parks [20].

Hyperspectral remote sensing in agriculture employs a range of sophisticated tools and equipment to gather, process, and analyze spectral data. The key hardware includes hyperspectral cameras, spectroradiometers, drones (UAVs), and satellite sensors, which capture high-resolution images over hundreds of spectral bands. These instruments allow non-destructive monitoring of crops and soil conditions, as well as early detection of diseases and nutrient deficiencies. Platforms such as ENVI, ERDAS Imagine, and QGIS, in combination with machine learning algorithms, enable hyperspectral data processing and analysis. Applications include precision fertilization, weed and pest detection, yield estimation, and soil variability mapping, making these technologies essential for data-driven and sustainable agriculture. To provide more information about hyperspectral tools and their associated applications, Table **8** is provided below:

Table 8. Hyperspectral tools and associated applications in sustainable agriculture.

Tool / Platform Name	Agricultural Item	Application / Use Case
Headwall Nano-Hyperspec	Crop Leaves (*e.g.*, wheat, rice)	Early detection of nutrient deficiency and disease stress
Specim IQ (Handheld Camera)	Fruits and Vegetables (*e.g.*, tomatoes, apples)	Quality inspection, ripeness evaluation, and sorting based on spectral signatures
AVIRIS (NASA)	Large-scale Farmlands	Crop type classification, soil moisture mapping, and yield estimation
HyPlant (ESA Project)	Forest Crops / Tree Plantations	Monitoring photosynthetic activity and plant health
UAV-mounted Hyperspectral Sensors	Field Crops (*e.g.*, maize, soybean)	Precision farming: monitoring growth stages, detecting weeds and pests
Spectroradiometer (*e.g.*, ASD FieldSpec)	Soil samples, Plant Canopies	Measuring reflectance for soil nutrient mapping and crop stress analysis
HySpex Cameras	Grains and Pulses	Post-harvest quality analysis and contamination detection
PRISMA (Italian Satellite Mission)	Regional Agricultural Zones	Land use classification, water stress detection, and monitoring of agricultural expansion

By scaling down the efforts put in by field workers and enhancing the accuracy of ecological monitoring, data-driven wildlife conservation is prescribed.

RESEARCH ANALYSIS

The fusion of remote sensing with AI/ML and IoT for wildlife monitoring toward sustainable agriculture has a significant scope for research. In wildlife monitoring, advanced research on habitat modeling can be pursued using 3D LiDAR technology and AI-powered biodiversity indexing [20]. Another possible study could include the combination of real-time IoT-based sensor systems with ML models for predictive poaching detection and forecasting of animal behavior. Research in precision agriculture would also be very helpful by developing AI algorithms that can aid in the prediction of crop disease using hyperspectral imaging. One real-world use of HRS is in wheat cultivation, where hyperspectral imaging is used to identify nitrogen deficiency far earlier than visual symptoms appear. By detecting this condition early, farmers can deliver fertilizers more precisely and effectively, saving money and minimizing environmental damage. Interventions targeted in this manner advance sustainable agriculture by optimizing resource use and minimizing chemical runoff. Hyperspectral sensing allows for non-destructive, high-precision crop examination. It can detect stressors early, facilitate site-specific management, and enhance decision-making.

The technology has direct benefits for increased yields, efficient resource use, and environmentally friendly agriculture. Integration of climate-resilient models through spaceborne datasets and AI-driven weather forecasting could be another crucial area. Wider scalability can be achieved through data fusion techniques incorporating satellite, drone, and field-level data. Cross-domain research could involve creating unified eco-agriculture frameworks that balance conservation with food security [21]. Table **9** lists different parameters by which the hyperspectral technique can be viewed. It provides analyses of the techniques used, the targeted area, shelf life, and key findings to assess a crop and the area in which it can be sown.

Table 9. Parameter-based comparison of hyperspectral remote sensing technique.

Technique Used	Usage / Target Area	Key Finding	Shelf Life / Validity
Vegetation Index Analysis (NDVI, *etc.*)	Crop health monitoring	Detects chlorophyll content and vegetation vigor	Seasonal / Crop cycle-specific
Spectral Signature Analysis	Disease and nutrient stress detection	Identifies spectral shifts indicating plant stress	Valid per crop type and growth stage
Soil Spectral Mapping	Soil property assessment (*e.g.*, moisture, salinity)	Determines spatial variability in soil characteristics	Valid for 1–2 years (depends on land use changes)
Time-Series Hyperspectral Monitoring	Crop yield prediction, growth tracking	Tracks growth stages and biomass development	Valid throughout the crop growth period
Machine Learning Classification Models	Crop type mapping, weed detection	Accurately differentiates crop types and invasive species	Model updates required every season
Anomaly Detection using PCA/ICA	Pest outbreak prediction, abnormal changes	Highlights deviations from typical crop behaviour	Short-term (real-time or within season)

However, the challenge remains to reduce deployment costs, enable real-time data processing, and trigger policy-driven implementations, making this area very fruitful for interdisciplinary research and opportunity creation. Possible research domains in this field are:

Wildlife Monitoring

- Scarner AI Models: Formulate deeper learning for future prospects of species behavior prediction.
- Threat Monitoring in Real Time: IoT sensors linked to real-time AI alert systems.

- Biodiversity Index Map: Global biodiversity indexing through remote sensing fusion.

Sustainable Agriculture

- Management of Waterwise Irrigation-AI water-saving optimization using real-time spectral data.
- Soil Health Monitoring: Live HRS real-time soil fertility monitoring systems.
- Models for Climate Change Adaptation: Prediction of long-term yield under different climate scenarios.

Integrated Research Scope

- Eco-Economic Agricultural Consortium: Establish very similar models in conservation and agricultural productivity, unmapped.
- Use of AI in Landscape Management: Hyperspectral action analytics-based predictive models integrating multispectral and hyperspectral data for eco-agricultural land management.
- Techniques for Data Fusion: Research on combined use of LiDAR, multispectral, and hyperspectral data for integrated ecosystem monitoring.

Patents provide an indication of the extent of research in a particular field. Moreover, some of the patent ideas related to wildlife monitoring and conservation are stated in Table **10** below:

Table 10. Analyses of patents related to wildlife conservation.

Project Title	Description / Mechanism	Core Methodology	Year	Status	Impact / Benefits
Artificial Intelligence and IoT Driven Technologies for Environmental Monitoring	Integrates AI, sensors, and IoT devices to monitor environmental pollution, utilizing machine learning methods to predict and track pollution changes.	A system that leverages AI and IoT for real-time environmental pollution monitoring and prediction.	2024	Research ongoing; potential patent applications in development.	Improves environmental monitoring accuracy, aiding in pollution control and policy-making.

(Table 10) cont.....

Spectral Intelligence: AI-Driven Hyperspectral Imaging for Sustainable Agriculture	Applies AI to analyses hyperspectral imaging data for optimizing resource utilization and minimizing environmental impacts in agriculture.	A method that uses AI to process hyperspectral data, enhancing decision-making in sustainable agriculture practices.	2023	Research published; technology adoption in early stages.	Promotes sustainable agriculture by providing detailed insights into crop health and resource needs.
Ensuring Agricultural Sustainability through Remote Sensing in the Era of AI	Combines remote sensing technologies with AI to monitor and ensure agricultural sustainability, focusing on crop and environmental factors.	A framework that integrates AI and remote sensing for comprehensive agricultural monitoring to support sustainability.	2021	Research published; implementation in pilot projects.	Supports sustainable farming practices through advanced monitoring and data analysis.
From Field to the Cloud: AI in Regenerative Agriculture	Utilizes AI and digital technologies to enhance regenerative agriculture practices, focusing on soil health and carbon sequestration.	An approach that applies AI to improve soil health monitoring and promote regenerative agriculture techniques.	2024	Research ongoing; early adoption by agricultural technology companies.	Advances regenerative agriculture by providing tools for better soil management and carbon sequestration tracking.
Environmental Sensing: Tracking Forest Fires and Threatened Species	Develops environmental sensing technology for monitoring forests, detecting wildfires, and tracking threatened species using advanced sensors.	Innovations in environmental sensors designed to provide real-time data on forest conditions and wildlife presence.	2024	Research and development in progress; prototypes being tested.	Enhances forest management and conservation efforts through improved monitoring capabilities.

Information on patents in the field of wildlife conservation provides analyses of the needs and researchers' efforts to develop technologies for this purpose.

CONCLUSION

Remote sensing, associated with AI/ML techniques, has changed wild animal monitoring and conservation. Real-time and comprehensive data access allows researchers and conservationists to make well-informed decisions and carry out conservation measures against endangered species and biodiversity for future generations. Future improvements in remote-sensing and AI systems are expected to maximize our potential in understanding and conserving animal life in a rapidly changing world. From habitat mapping to poaching detection, these technologies ensure precise data-driven decisions. The integration of remote sensing, AI/ML, and IoT in wildlife monitoring and sustainable agriculture offers immense potential for addressing the challenges facing environmental and agricultural systems. Future improvements would aim at near-real-time systems, automated data analysis, and climate-resilient models. Such advancements could promote precision farming at scale in India's agricultural sector, using hyperspectral imaging and IoT-based soil sensors to ensure sustainable food production. Similarly, national parks like Kaziranga could deploy more AI-powered drones and GPS-enabled collars for improved species tracking and anti-poaching efforts. This would lead to engagement with global trends toward edge AI, which processes data on-site, thereby reducing latency in remote areas. Subsequently, it would enable AI-driven predictive modelling for forest cover changes, crop yield, and overall sustainability.

To address these challenges, future work needs to aim at creating affordable and user-friendly HRS devices, especially handheld or drone-based sensors that can be used for on-site measurements. Merging hyperspectral information with AI and ML algorithms can enhance simplicity in interpretation and make decision-making more automated. Additionally, open-access datasets and tools would enable broader use and stimulate both field-based and academic innovation. From a deployment perspective, small-scale pilot tests on specific crops or regions should first be implemented to gain experience step by step. Data pre-processing, including calibration and noise reduction, is necessary to improve accuracy. Integrating hyperspectral data with other data types, such as weather or soil sensor data, also results in greater depth of analysis. Ultimately, coordination with agronomists and local experts ensures that interpretations are context-oriented and useful in practice.

In summary, hyperspectral remote sensing is full of potential to make agriculture a more efficient and sustainable industry. With the right investment in accessibility, education, and integration, the technology has the potential to enable farmers and researchers to effectively counter productivity as well as environmental issues.

Future work may possibly incorporate multi-sensor platform combinations using LiDAR and multispectral satellites to enable cross-domain monitoring. The convergence of all these would be based on eco-agriculture frameworks, aligning habitat conservation with agricultural productivity. Policymakers have prioritized the need to focus on data-sharing platforms, reduce implementation costs, and strengthen the legal framework to address such problems. As these efforts take root, remote sensing, AI/ML, and IoT will remain core technologies for enabling intelligent, efficient, and future-ready conservation and agricultural practices that support ecological balance and global food security. Future research efforts should focus on integrating multi-sensor platforms with predictive models to enhance ecosystem sustainability, while considering agricultural productivity and global biodiversity conservation.

REFERENCES

[1] Wu X. Deep learning for wildlife monitoring and conservation: A review. IEEE Access 2020; 8: 161653-72.
[http://dx.doi.org/10.1109/ACCESS.2020.3020807]

[2] Cristóbal J, Poyatos R, Ninyerola M, Llorens P, Pons X. Combining remote sensing and GIS climate modelling to estimate daily forest evapotranspiration in a Mediterranean mountain area. Hydrol Earth Syst Sci 2011; 15(5): 1563-75.
[http://dx.doi.org/10.5194/hess-15-1563-2011]

[3] Huang C-L. Deep learning-based object detection for wildlife conservation: A review. IEEE Access 2020; 8: 127677-94.
[http://dx.doi.org/10.1109/ACCESS.2020.3009041]

[4] Du Y. Deep learning for wildlife monitoring using remote sensing: A review. Remote Sens 2020; 12(15): 2375.
[http://dx.doi.org/10.3390/rs12152375]

[5] Marques CS. Wildlife monitoring using unmanned aerial vehicles (UAVs): A review. IEEE Access 2019; 7: 118866-84.
[http://dx.doi.org/10.1109/ACCESS.2019.2937033]

[6] Luo J. Deep learning for wildlife habitat mapping and monitoring: A review. IEEE Geosci Remote Sens Mag 2019; 7(4): 92-105.
[http://dx.doi.org/10.1109/MGRS.2019.2941228]

[7] Zhao K. Deep learning for wildlife monitoring: A review. IEEE Trans Geosci Remote Sens 2019; 57(11): 8174-97.
[http://dx.doi.org/10.1109/TGRS.2019.2919996]

[8] Zheng G. Deep learning for wildlife monitoring: A survey. IEEE Access 2018; 6: 4161-73.
[http://dx.doi.org/10.1109/ACCESS.2018.2796738]

[9] Zhou W. Deep learning for wildlife conservation: A review. IEEE Access 2018; 6: 3232-45.
[http://dx.doi.org/10.1109/ACCESS.2018.2808325]

[10] Pappas CC. Remote sensing IEEE Geosci Remote Sens Mag 2017; 5(1): 8-22.
[http://dx.doi.org/10.1109/MGRS.2017.2682058]

[11] Li H. Deep learning in remote sensing: A review. IEEE Geosci Remote Sens Mag 2017; 5(4): 8-22.
[http://dx.doi.org/10.1109/MGRS.2019.2921780]

[12] Ferreira LG. Unmanned aerial vehicles (UAVs) for wildlife monitoring: A review. IEEE Access 2016; 4: 7181-94.
[http://dx.doi.org/10.1109/ACCESS.2016.2602951]

[13] Wittemyer G. Poaching and the international ivory trade. Proc Natl Acad Sci USA 2010; 107(19): 8136-41.
[http://dx.doi.org/10.1073/pnas.0910939107]

[14] Hansen MC, Potapov PV, Moore R, *et al.* High-resolution global maps of 21st-century forest cover change. Science 2013; 342(6160): 850-3.
[http://dx.doi.org/10.1126/science.1244693] [PMID: 24233722]

[15] Joshi C. A review of remote sensing applications for wildlife monitoring and conservation. Remote Sens 2018; 10(4): 554.
[http://dx.doi.org/10.3390/rs10040554]

[16] Turner W. Remote sensingRemote sensing for conservation biology. Springer 2003; pp. 3-22.

[17] Benelli A, Cevoli C, Fabbri A. In-field hyperspectral imaging: An overview on the ground-based applications in agriculture. J Agric Eng 2020; 51(3): 129-39.
[http://dx.doi.org/10.4081/jae.2020.1030]

[18] Zhu X. Integrating genomics and remote sensing technologies for wildlife monitoring. Anim Mol Breed 2024; 14

[19] Kommalapati J, Dasari S B, Pidaparthi H. Drone-based elephant detection and counting with YOLOv5. 2024 4th Int Conf Pervasive Comput Soc Netw (ICPCSN). 527-32.
[http://dx.doi.org/10.1109/ICPCSN.2024.1234567]

[20] Dasari K, Ali MA, Shankara NB, Reddy KD, Bhavsingh M, Samunnisa K. A novel IoT-driven model for real-time urban wildlife health and safety monitoring in smart cities. 2024 8th Int Conf I-SMAC (IoT Soc Mob Anal Cloud) (I-SMAC). 122-9.
[http://dx.doi.org/10.1109/I-SMAC61858.2024.10714601]

[21] Vyshnavi MRV, Menon NV, Tharneesh P. Wildlife management system—Integrating location tracking, healthcare management, and QR-based incident reporting. 2024 15th Int Conf Comput Commun Netw Technol (ICCCNT). 1-6.

CHAPTER 10

Advancement in Remote Sensing and GIS for Sustainable Groundwater Monitoring

Neha Bhati[1,*], **Narayan Vyas**[2] and **Ashutosh Pagrotra**[3]

[1] *Department of Research and Development, Flexxited, Bangalore, India*

[2] *Department of Computer Science and Engineering, Vivekananda Global University, Jaipur, India*

[3] *Department of Biomechatronics, National Taiwan University, Taipei, Taiwan*

Abstract: This chapter discusses advanced approaches in remote sensing and Geographic Information Systems (GIS) technology for sustainable groundwater monitoring. The extraction and management of groundwater are fundamental to human survival, but aquifer depletion has emerged as a critical issue. Recent advancements in satellite platforms, such as Gravity Recovery and Climate Experiment (GRACE), Landsat, and hyperspectral remote sensing technologies, enable high-resolution, continuous monitoring of groundwater levels, recharge zones, and land use dynamics. Together with GIS, they can contribute to the spatial assessment of critical recharge zones, groundwater depletion, and agriculture-based water use. Artificial Intelligence (AI) and Machine Learning (ML), when embedded into the groundwater monitoring framework, allow automating the data analysis workflow and help in making better predictions that further assist in facilitating real-time decision-making. As case studies show, these tools have greatly enhanced the sustainability of groundwater across regions. Lastly, the chapter discusses the innovations in hyperspectral imaging, AI-driven analytics, and remote sensing, which are going to be the future of groundwater resource management.

Keywords: Geographic Information Systems (GIS), Groundwater Monitoring, Gravity Recovery and Climate Experiment (GRACE), Machine Learning (ML), Remote Sensing, Sustainability.

INTRODUCTION

Overview of Groundwater Importance and Global Water Crisis

Groundwater is a natural resource used for drinking water, irrigation, and industrial use. It comprises around one-third of global freshwater and is a key

* **Corresponding author Neha Bhati:** Department of Research and Development, Flexxited, Bangalore, India; E-mail: nehabhati184@gmail.com

Sartajvir Singh, Neelam Dahiya, Maged Mohammed, Abdullah Alzharihi & Vishal Dutt (Eds.)

drought mitigation buffer [1]. Many rural and some urban populations rely on groundwater as a significant source of water supply [2]. Yet, for the past few decades, their underground reserves of freshwater have been drawn down at an unprecedented rate through unsustainable extraction and overexploitation of groundwater. The ongoing water crisis is being aggravated due to several factors, including the rapid rise in world population, escalating climate variability, and extreme weather events like extended droughts and flash floods. Several large areas in South Asia, the Middle East, and most of North America are experiencing a state of severe water inadequacy, with many reports showing a rapid decline in groundwater levels and a corresponding decrease in storage capacity [3]. These trends threaten the water security of millions around the world.

Need for Remote Sensing and GIS in Groundwater Monitoring

Traditional groundwater monitoring techniques are extensively used but are expensive, labour-intensive, and limited in the spatial context [4]. Due to these limitations, modern technologies have been adopted and developed, including remote sensing and Geographic Information Systems (GIS) for more efficient and accurate groundwater monitoring. These methods offer low-cost, high-resolution information on the water table and recharge area. Remote sensing facilitates large-scale groundwater monitoring by measuring gravity anomalies, soil moisture, and land cover changes [5]. These images are used to ascertain trends over time, which can tell us when aquifers are becoming less sustainable and whether they are still healthy. For example, Satellites like GRACE detect variations in Earth's gravitational field, which, through modeling, provide insights into global water storage changes, including groundwater.

In contrast, GIS is an integrative spatial analysis tool that combines multiple datasets such as topography, geology, and hydrology. GIS facilitates groundwater identification, recharge zone mapping, future prediction of water over time, and helps with informed decision-making to ensure sustainable groundwater overlaid with varied data layers [6]. The integration of remote sensing and GIS has transformed groundwater monitoring, allowing water managers to implement proactive water management strategies that reduce depletion risks, enhance water resource planning, and secure sustainable management in the long term [7]. These technologies are helping to overcome the various bottlenecks in the scarcity and depletion of water. Satellite technology, as adapted in capturing and analysing land surface data for groundwater assessment, is shown in Fig. (**1**).

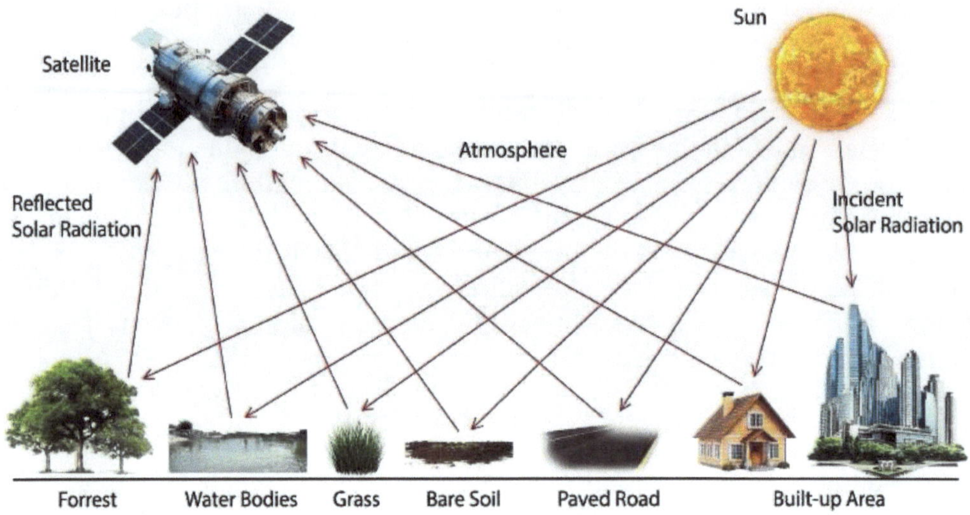

Fig. (1). Brief overview of the working of a satellite.

Objectives of the Chapter

In this chapter, the authors investigate the developments of remote sensing and GIS technologies that contribute to sustainable groundwater monitoring. The chapter will (a) emphasize that groundwater is a critical resource and has challenges in managing it worldwide, (b) understand the growth of remote sensing technologies and detect groundwater levels and quality, (c) explore how remote sensing and GIS systems are integrated to understand groundwater systems holistically, and (d) identify gaps in current groundwater monitoring capabilities and explore future trends, challenges, and technological advancements.

UNDERSTANDING GROUND WATER SYSTEMS

Basics of Ground Water Hydrology

Groundwater, stored in aquifers, is mapped using remote sensing to detect gravity anomalies and geophysical surveys to assess subsurface structures. Groundwater is the water that percolates into aquifers, which are rock formations in the Earth's geologic structure where water accumulates and is stored, providing a reliable source of fresh water for drinking or irrigation projects in villages [8]. Groundwater is integral to the Earth's available water reservoirs for ecosystems, agriculture, and human use. The groundwater cycle is interrelated with the hydrologic cycle, which includes precipitation, infiltration, percolation, and recharge [9]. Rainwater enters the ground and passes through soil layers to recharge aquifers. The time it takes for an aquifer to recharge depends on soil porosity, land cover, and overall climatic conditions [10].

There are various types of aquifers:

- Unconfined Aquifers: Recharge can occur from the land surface, and water can move in or out of such an aquifer. These are refueled by rainwater or surface water and are at risk of contamination [11].
- Confined Aquifers: An aquifer trapped between two impermeable rock layers, so the water is under pressure. Unconfined aquifers, often shallower, are more susceptible to surface contamination and typically recharge faster than confined aquifers, depending on local conditions [12].

From rivers to lakes and oceans, groundwater slowly flows through this network of aquifers toward natural discharge points, where it can be used as a source of fresh water for extended periods.

Key Challenges in Groundwater Management

Although groundwater is considered a sustainable resource, its availability is increasingly threatened due to over-harvesting and contamination. Another serious issue is the over-extraction of groundwater in rural and urban areas [13]. In many instances, this is being extracted at a rate greater than it can be naturally replenished, causing aquifers to be slowly drained. Prolonged groundwater pumping leads to declining water levels, increasing extraction costs, and challenges. For worst-case scenarios, aquifers may face permanent depletion [14]. Another major problem is environmental contamination caused by human activity. Additionally, due to climate change, rainfall patterns have been disturbed, leading to an increase in droughts, which hurt the aquifers' natural recharge [15]. The increasing dependence on groundwater, due to the deterioration of surface water sources, highlights the vital need for sustainable management of groundwater [16]. The characteristics of groundwater make it inherently difficult to monitor; the resource does not exist in visible geometries as do lakes or rivers. This, in turn, results in inefficient water policies and inappropriate use due to a lack of real-time, precise data. Particularly in coastal zones, excessive groundwater extraction can lead to saltwater from the ocean entering freshwater aquifers (a process known as saltwater intrusion), contaminating the water and making it unsuitable for agriculture or domestic use [17]. Finally, groundwater governance is also weak in many areas. Unclear water rights and weak regulations often lead to the misconception that groundwater is abundant and freely available.

The Crucial Role of Sustainable Groundwater Monitoring

Sustainable groundwater monitoring is crucial to sustainably managing this vital resource. Monitoring helps to manage our water resources better. Sustainable groundwater management is essential due to the following points. Resource conservation plays a vital role in sustainable groundwater management. By monitoring the aquifer, areas that use too much water can be controlled through water use restrictions and managed depletion by water managers [18]. Preventing contamination is another crucial benefit, as groundwater monitoring can detect contamination issues early on. Of course, the earlier one detects these types of pollutants infiltrating groundwater supplies, the safer it is for those who rely on that water supply, whether for agriculture, industry, or drinking [19]. Climate change adaptation also relies heavily on such monitoring. Regularly monitoring groundwater helps assess how climate change affects groundwater resources, allowing changes in management and preparation for drier conditions or changing weather patterns [20]. Additionally, policy and planning are significantly strengthened through accurate groundwater data. Governments, water management authorities, and policymakers require accurate and up-to-date groundwater data to plan for sustainable development, regulate usage, and formulate policies. Monitoring systems serve data-driven decision-making [21].

EVOLUTION OF REMOTE SENSING FOR GROUNDWATER MONITORING

Traditional Groundwater Monitoring Techniques

Traditionally, groundwater monitoring was considered a time-consuming process, as it relied on physical procedures such as drilling wells and setting up piezometer devices used to measure water depth for level measurements [22]. Although these manual methods were accurate, they came with several limitations. First, they were highly labor-intensive; a considerable number of personnel and a significant amount of time were required to establish and operate monitoring stations [23]. Second, the data collected was often sparsely distributed, as each monitoring point served as an individual data source. This setup failed to capture the broader dynamics of the entire aquifer system effectively [24]. Lastly, the cost of drilling wells and installing monitoring equipment was relatively high, especially in remote or hard-to-reach areas, making it financially challenging to scale such monitoring efforts. These challenges have prompted the use of remote sensing for broader spatial and temporal data coverage. Hyperspectral and microwave remote sensing have further enhanced groundwater studies. Hyperspectral remote sensing captures detailed spectral data to map surface features, such as soil moisture and vegetation, that indicate potential groundwater recharge zones [25]. Microwave remote sensing, especially Synthetic Aperture Radar (SAR), helps detect soil moisture levels and land subsidence caused by groundwater extraction [26]. These technologies provide all-weather, high-resolution monitoring, making groundwater assessment more effective. By integrating these advanced remote sensing techniques with GIS, groundwater monitoring has become more precise and efficient for sustainable management.

Introduction to Remote Sensing: Key Technologies and Advancements

Remote sensing involves collecting information about the surroundings using sensors on satellites, airplanes, or drones [27]. It plays a crucial role in indirectly monitoring groundwater, measuring parameters such as soil moisture, land use, and land cover, as well as groundwater recharge. The massive amounts of data that these sensors generate require sophisticated analysis, and here, AI and ML make all the difference [28]. Optical sensors, such as RGB, acquire visible and near-infrared radiation, which measure vegetation health, land cover, and surface water bodies, which are indispensable in groundwater recharge estimation [29]. Microwave sensors, in contrast, can penetrate cloud cover and provide information about soil moisture and surface water regardless of weather, including snow and ice [30]. In addition, radar sensors will be used to view the surface subsidence due to over-extraction of groundwater. The practice of employing AI and ML in remote sensing for groundwater monitoring has been dramatically accelerated. AI enables automated processing of large-scale satellite imagery, identifying trends in groundwater depletion, recharge, and land use changes with minimal human intervention [31]. Using ML algorithms on retro and live data provides a better predictive modelling of groundwater levels, and can assist in locating areas at risk, well ahead of depletion. Remote sensing data can be classified into groundwater recharge zones using various deep learning techniques, including Convolutional Neural Networks (CNNs) for multispectral and hyperspectral imagery data [32]. Moreover, the AI-based abnormality detection will help to detect unusual fluctuations in groundwater and take steps well in advance in water-stressed regions. This combination of advances in remote sensing, connecting AI and ML analytics, has led to completely automated, on-demand, and much more accurate mentalities of groundwater resources through these technologies.

Satellite-Based Groundwater Monitoring: GRACE, Landsat, and Other Key Platforms

Table **1** presents key remote sensing satellites for groundwater monitoring, detailing their technology and specific applications in detecting groundwater changes, land use patterns, and soil moisture levels.

Table 1. Key remote sensing satellites for groundwater monitoring.

Satellite	Technology Used	Purpose
GRACE [33]	Gravity Field Measurement	Detect groundwater depletion
Landsat [34]	Optical/Infrared Imagery	Monitor land use and recharge zones
SMAP [35]	Microwave Radiometer	Measure soil moisture levels
Sentinel-1 [36]	Synthetic Aperture Radar	Track surface deformation and subsidence

Satellite missions have been a significant contributor to groundwater monitoring, providing critical data to enhance monitoring capabilities. For example, the GRACE satellites monitor changes in the gravity field of Earth caused by the movement of water masses [37]. GRACE detects large-scale groundwater changes by measuring gravity anomalies caused by subsurface water mass variations. GRACE has long enabled scientists to assess regional groundwater changes, even in locations where local field measurements are sparse, through the Groundwater Mass Balance approach. The Landsat series of satellites has produced a wealth of high-resolution optical and infrared imagery that is extremely useful for deriving information about land use, vegetation, and groundwater recharge areas [38]. Landsat imagery also facilitates the assessment of groundwater resource sustainability in agricultural and urban environments by monitoring land cover change. The Soil Moisture Active Passive (SMAP) mission provides surface and root-zone moisture information, which directly impacts our potential to understand groundwater recharge and water resources [35]. On the other hand, European Space Agency Sentinel missions provide high-resolution Synthetic Aperture Radar (SAR) imagery to monitor land surface motion, see for example, surface water matter and deep ground settlement as a result of underground water over-extraction [39]. Meanwhile, hyperspectral sensors, which offer a continuous spectrum of wavelengths, are opening up new applications of remote sensing for groundwater studies by providing more accurate information on geological formations, soil moisture, and vegetation health [40]. Adding these sensors enhances the levels of mapping associated with groundwater recharge due to the identification of land cover, soil permeability, and water retention characteristics. Further, thermal infrared hyperspectral imagery may inform subsurface moisture changes, thus contributing to our understanding of groundwater storage dynamics. Their combined use of hyperspectral and SAR data, duly integrated and analysed with AI, achieves an unprecedented power of groundwater resources assessment, enabling sounder and more effective water management solutions [41].

REMOTE SENSING TECHNOLOGY ADVANCEMENTS

Remote Sensing Techniques for Groundwater Monitoring (Optical, Radar, and Microwave)

Remote sensing enhances traditional groundwater monitoring by collecting data on soil moisture and recharge zones. Optical remote sensing is one of the primary methods, utilizing visible and infrared sensors to characterize the spatial distribution of land cover changes, vegetation condition, and surface water bodies [42]. These optical sensors can also be used to analyze the effects of any change in land use, such as deforestation or urbanization, on groundwater evolution. Another critical method is ground subsidence monitoring by radar remote sensing. Specifically, ground surface deformation from over-extraction of groundwater has been successfully detected using Synthetic Aperture Radar (SAR) sensors. The application of this is reasonably practical, especially in regions where land settlement occurs as a result of over-extraction of groundwater. Furthermore, microwave remote sensing has a distinct advantage over optical sensors, whereby it can penetrate cloud cover and operate in all-weather conditions [43]. Among soil moisture sensors, microwave-based sensors are critical as soil moisture is a direct determinant of groundwater availability. This is important as data obtained from these sensors can also identify temporal changes in surface water, which can provide additional information about groundwater recharge variability through time.

Integration of AI and Machine Learning (ML) in Remote Sensing for Groundwater Analysis

Breakthroughs in AI and ML are transforming the way remote sensing information is interpreted, providing new and simplified applications for groundwater monitoring and management [44]. AI can reduce both the effort required and the time taken to process large amounts of satellite imagery and other remote sensing data, enabling the training of models on past patterns to identify shifts in groundwater levels quickly [45]. This will also reduce the need for manual intervention and help speed up the analysis proccss. In addition to that, the ML algorithms improve the prediction accuracy *via* assimilation of remote sensing inputs with climate data and land use patterns for predicting groundwater levels, recharge rates, and potential depletion risks. Such predictive abilities enable improved decision-making. AI-based models enable the development of groundwater management strategies by providing comprehensive scenario analyses. Combining the potential of AI with remote sensing and big data enables increasingly precise, data-driven decision-making that bolsters global action for sustainable groundwater management [46].

ROLE OF GIS IN GROUNDWATER MAPPING

Groundwater resource visualisation, analysis, and management are predominantly based on geoinformation systems, and these systems, when combined with remote sensing, make groundwater monitoring more effective and comprehensive [47]. GIS excels in spatially representing groundwater data, enabling large-scale analysis of aquifer characteristics and trends. GIS provides dynamic and near-real-time details on groundwater levels and ground recharge zones, land use/land cover patterns, including remote sensing data, which is often utilized in sustainable groundwater management [48]. The spatial specificity of GIS enables the delineation of important groundwater areas and time-series analysis of variations in groundwater levels through multi-temporal satellite data. GIS, in combination with remote sensing, can also detect trends in groundwater depletion, delineate recharge areas, and assess potential groundwater stress based on environmental parameters, including soil type and land cover, and climatic factors [49].

Integration of remote sensing data has dramatically advanced the application of GIS technology for groundwater sustainability. This means that detailed maps can be developed that define aquifer extents, well & high recharge zones, and contamination sites using remotely sensed data [50]. With GIS, land use patterns, rainfall distribution, and even vegetation indices calculated from satellite images could be integrated to provide a better assessment of groundwater availability [51]. Particularly, satellite data can be used in combination with GIS-based spatial interpolation techniques, which perform excellently for the monitoring of groundwater fluctuations over time. Moreover, remote sensing datasets, such as GRACE, Landsat, and Sentinel, could be integrated with GIS tools to develop predictive models for forecasting groundwater depletion and risk evaluation for sustainable management. It combines hydrological modeling with real-time remote sensing observations and assists policymakers and water resource managers with data-driven decision-making affected by multiple uncertainties. In conclusion, the integration of perspectives through GIS and remote sensing under the same umbrella of a research theme helped streamline successful, timely, and large-scale/synoptic evaluations of aquifer sustainability. Now, through high-resolution satellite imagery and GIS-based models, decision-makers can target water conservation strategies that will help with the long-term sustainability of these groundwater resources [52].

INTEGRATION OF IMAGERY AND GIS FOR GROUNDWATER DETECTION

Remote Sensing And GIS Technologies Synergy

The integration of remote sensing and GIS technologies has significantly enhanced groundwater monitoring capabilities. It uses remote sensing, a satellite-based technique that allows for the repeated acquisition of broad-scale information needed for land use, soil moisture, and topographic conditions over large areas [53]. This technique is associated with GIS technology, which enables detailed analysis and visualization of the collected data. In combination, they provide capabilities that none could provide on their own. A great benefit is automated data integration, which allows for remote sensing inputs (satellite imagery, soil moisture estimations) to be natively imported into GIS for spatial analysis and mapping. Furthermore, GIS-based mapping tools improve decision-making by providing stakeholders with intuitive visualizations of groundwater activity that assist in the formulation of groundwater policy and more effective resource allocation [54]. GIS integrates remote sensing data, such as rainfall, land cover, and temperature, with hydrological models to simulate groundwater flow and recharge. Such models provide a window not only into more contemporary groundwater behaviour, but also into future groundwater states and areas with potential depletion risk [55].

Remote Sensing and GIS-Integrated Groundwater Model Development

The integration of RS and GIS technologies has resulted in complex groundwater models that provide great insight into aquifer processes and assist in the management of sustainable water resources. These models use spatial data derived from remote sensing, such as rainfall distribution and land use maps, and couple them with hydrological models to simulate groundwater flow [56]. By studying how recharge rates are affected by factors such as precipitation, land use, and soil type, they provide water managers with valuable insights to inform future planning. Moreover, these models can provide time-series forecasts of groundwater table changes when they are integrated with GIS analysis of satellite imagery.

Predictive Modelling and Forecasting for Groundwater Sustainability

Remote sensing and GIS data integration support geodata mining and predictive modeling for groundwater sustainability. These models are based on historical records of groundwater levels, rainfall, and usage for different purposes in the area where there is satellite data, collected from the remote sensing equipment, in real time. They can forecast groundwater level changes based on climate and extraction patterns, and estimate safe yield ratios for the majority of aquifers, meaning they can assess the sustainability of current usage under differing management strategies and apply across historical or recent timeframes of recharge variability. In addition, these models will also allow for the current regions that are most at risk for shortages to be identified, allowing conservation to be done strategically. Recent advances have enhanced the precision of these predictive models by incorporating ML algorithms along with remote sensing and GIS data [57]. Consequently, such models have become indispensable tools for assessing groundwater sustainability and for the better examination and development of improved resource planning and management at the regional and global scales.

REMOTE SENSING AND GIS APPLICATIONS IN SUSTAINABLE GROUNDWATER MANAGEMENT

Groundwater is one of the most vital natural resources for sustainable management, and remote sensing and GIS play a significant role as catchment-based water resources monitoring and planning tools [58]. Notable applications include identifying groundwater recharge zones by utilizing remote sensing data to pinpoint areas where precipitation or surface water infiltrates the soil and reaches groundwater aquifers. These tools also aid in understanding soil types, vegetation, and rainfall distribution, enabling the identification, definition, and protection of recharge areas to maximize groundwater potential. GIS plays a crucial role in this process. In recent years, satellites such as GRACE, which track tiny variations in the Earth's gravity field, have been used to monitor groundwater depletion [59]. Combined with GIS, these data allow water authorities to identify at-risk areas and manage groundwater extraction accordingly. Agriculture is the primary consumer of groundwater, and remote sensing and GIS enable ongoing assessment of irrigation impacts on groundwater reserves [60]. This includes technologies that sense soil moisture and monitor water use by crops, resulting in more efficient farming practices and sustainable food production systems. GIS mapping for water conservation and groundwater stewardship supports planning of water conservation projects, such as rainwater harvesting and afforestation, and addresses issues detectable at the space level [61].

CONCLUSION

This chapter provides a comprehensive review of sustainable groundwater monitoring through remote sensing and GIS technology. Technologies like GRACE (Gravity Recovery and Climate Experiment) and Landsat, as well as spatial analysis through GIS, help monitor groundwater levels, identify recharge zones, and manage water table depletion to avoid a major water crisis on a global scale. However, issues related to data quality, cost limitations, and legal considerations hinder the full potential of these tools. In contrast, the combination of AI, IoT, and Big Data transforms groundwater monitoring by enabling real-time data analysis, predictive modeling, and automated decision-making. By utilizing massive datasets from satellites, sensors, and hydrological models, AI-powered algorithms can detect anomalies and predict trends in groundwater depletion with high accuracy. Smart sensors equipped with IoT track groundwater levels, extraction rates, and water quality to facilitate proactive resource management. Predicting groundwater trends relies on integrated knowledge from diverse information sources, such as climate data, land use changes, and hydrological patterns, which are incorporated into data-driven modeling approaches known as Big Data analytics, enhancing predictive capabilities and refining groundwater conservation strategies.

REFERENCES

[1] Prapanchan VN, Subramani T, Karunanidhi D, Gopinathan P. Groundwater quality assessment for drinking and irrigation purposes and its human health risks in the Sevathur mine region, south India. Desalination Water Treat 2024; 320: 100883. [http://dx.doi.org/10.1016/j.dwt.2024.100883]

[2] Yar P. Urban development and its impact on the depletion of groundwater aquifers in Mardan City, Pakistan. Groundw Sustain Dev 2020; 11: 100426. [http://dx.doi.org/10.1016/j.gsd.2020.100426]

[3] Amparo-Salcedo M, Pérez-Gimeno A, Navarro-Pedreño J. Water security under climate change: challenges and solutions across 43 countries. Water 2025; 17(5): 633. [http://dx.doi.org/10.3390/w17050633]

[4] Yadav A, Raj A, Yadav B. Enhancing local-scale groundwater quality predictions using advanced machine learning approaches. J Environ Manage 2024; 370: 122903. [http://dx.doi.org/10.1016/j.jenvman.2024.122903] [PMID: 39413632]

[5] Ibrahim A, Wayayok A, Shafri HZM, Toridi NM. Remote sensing technologies for unlocking new groundwater insights: a comprehensive review. J Hydrol X 2024; 23: 100175. [http://dx.doi.org/10.1016/j.hydroa.2024.100175]

[6] Burayu DG, Karuppannan S, Shuniye G. Geospatial mapping of groundwater potential zones using multi-criteria decision analysis and GIS fuzzy logic in Dabus Sub-Basin, western Ethiopia. Quaternary Science Advances 2025; 18: 100275. [http://dx.doi.org/10.1016/j.qsa.2025.100275]

[7] Monir MM, Sarker SC, Islam ARMT. A critical review on groundwater level depletion monitoring based on GIS and data-driven models: Global perspectives and future challenges. HydroResearch 2024; 7: 285-300. [http://dx.doi.org/10.1016/j.hydres.2024.05.001]

[8] Adiat KAN, Kolawole AO, Adeyemo IA, Akinlalu AA, Afolabi DO. Assessment of groundwater resources from geophysical and remote sensing data in a basement complex environment using fuzzy-topsis algorithm. Results in Earth Sciences 2024; 2: 100034. [http://dx.doi.org/10.1016/j.rines.2024.100034]

[9] Mensah JK, Ofosu EA, Yidana SM, Akpoti K, Kabo-bah AT. Integrated modeling of hydrological processes and groundwater recharge based on land use land cover, and climate changes: A systematic review. Environ Adv 2022; 8: 100224.

[http://dx.doi.org/10.1016/j.envadv.2022.100224]

[10] Gebreslassie H, Berhane G, Gebreyohannes T, Hagos M, Hussien A, Walraevens K. Water harvesting and groundwater recharge: a comprehensive review and synthesis of current practices. Water 2025; 17(7): 976.
[http://dx.doi.org/10.3390/w17070976]

[11] Hocking M, Kelly BFJ. Groundwater recharge and time lag measurement through Vertosols using impulse response functions. J Hydrol (Amst) 2016; 535: 22-35.
[http://dx.doi.org/10.1016/j.jhydrol.2016.01.042]

[12] Meles MB, Bradford S, Casillas-Trasvina A, *et al.* Uncovering the gaps in managed aquifer recharge for sustainable groundwater management: A focus on hillslopes and mountains. J Hydrol (Amst) 2024; 639: 131615.
[http://dx.doi.org/10.1016/j.jhydrol.2024.131615]

[13] Alao JO, Bello AY, Lawal HA, Abdullahi D. Assessment of groundwater challenge and the sustainable management strategies. Results in Earth Sciences 2024; 2: 100049.
[http://dx.doi.org/10.1016/j.rines.2024.100049]

[14] Jódar J, Urrutia J, Herrera C, Custodio E, Martos-Rosillo S, Lambán LJ. The catastrophic effects of groundwater intensive exploitation and Megadrought on aquifers in Central Chile: Global change impact projections in water resources based on groundwater balance modeling. Sci Total Environ 2024; 914: 169651.
[http://dx.doi.org/10.1016/j.scitotenv.2023.169651] [PMID: 38159766]

[15] Abanyie SK, Apea OB, Abagale SA, Amuah EEY, Sunkari ED. Sources and factors influencing groundwater quality and associated health implications: A review. Emerg Contam 2023; 9(2): 100207.
[http://dx.doi.org/10.1016/j.emcon.2023.100207]

[16] Cook PG, Shanafield M, Andersen MS, *et al.* Sustainable management of groundwater extraction: An Australian perspective on current challenges. J Hydrol Reg Stud 2022; 44: 101262.
[http://dx.doi.org/10.1016/j.ejrh.2022.101262]

[17] Prusty P, Farooq SH. Seawater intrusion in the coastal aquifers of India - A review. HydroResearch 2020; 3: 61-74.
[http://dx.doi.org/10.1016/j.hydres.2020.06.001]

[18] Chen J, Wu H, Qian H, Li X. Challenges and prospects of sustainable groundwater management in an agricultural plain along the Silk Road Economic Belt, north-west China. Int J Water Resour Dev 2018; 34(3): 354-68.
[http://dx.doi.org/10.1080/07900627.2016.1238348]

[19] Ejiohuo O, Onyeaka H, Akinsemolu A, *et al.* Ensuring water purity: Mitigating environmental risks and safeguarding human health. Water Biology and Security 2025; 4(2): 100341.
[http://dx.doi.org/10.1016/j.watbs.2024.100341]

[20] Davamani V, John JE, Poornachandhra C, *et al.* A critical review of climate change impacts on groundwater resources: a focus on the current status, future possibilities, and role of simulation models. Atmosphere (Basel) 2024; 15(1): 122.
[http://dx.doi.org/10.3390/atmos15010122]

[21] Gregory A, Kelly E, Landa S, *et al.* Challenges and opportunities for enhancing groundwater data access and usability in low- and middle-income countries: insights and recommendations from WaSH researchers and practitioners. J Water Sanit Hyg Dev 2024; 14(10): 929-37.
[http://dx.doi.org/10.2166/washdev.2024.066]

[22] Masood A, Tariq MAUR, Hashmi MZUR, *et al.* An overview of groundwater monitoring through point-to satellite-based techniques. Water 2022; 14(4): 565.
[http://dx.doi.org/10.3390/w14040565]

[23] Essamlali I, Nhaila H, El Khaili M. Advances in machine learning and IoT for water quality

monitoring: A comprehensive review. Heliyon 2024; 10(6): e27920. [http://dx.doi.org/10.1016/j.heliyon.2024.e27920] [PMID: 38533055]

[24] Lyons KJ, Ikonen J, Hokajärvi AM, *et al.* Monitoring groundwater quality with real-time data, stable water isotopes, and microbial community analysis: A comparison with conventional methods. Sci Total Environ 2023; 864: 161199. [http://dx.doi.org/10.1016/j.scitotenv.2022.161199] [PMID: 36581300]

[25] Lubczynski MW, Leblanc M, Batelaan O. Remote sensing and hydrogeophysics give a new impetus to integrated hydrological models: A review. J Hydrol (Amst) 2024; 633: 130901. [http://dx.doi.org/10.1016/j.jhydrol.2024.130901]

[26] Hrysiewicz A, Holohan EP, Donohue S, Cushnan H. SAR and InSAR data linked to soil moisture changes on a temperate raised peatland subjected to a wildfire. Remote Sens Environ 2023; 291: 113516. [http://dx.doi.org/10.1016/j.rse.2023.113516]

[27] Jafarbiglu H, Pourreza A. A comprehensive review of remote sensing platforms, sensors, and applications in nut crops. Comput Electron Agric 2022; 197: 106844. [http://dx.doi.org/10.1016/j.compag.2022.106844]

[28] Soori M, Arezoo B, Dastres R. Artificial intelligence, machine learning and deep learning in advanced robotics, a review. Cognitive Robotics 2023; 3: 54-70. [http://dx.doi.org/10.1016/j.cogr.2023.04.001]

[29] Kumar S, Arya S, Jain K. A SWIR-based vegetation index for change detection in land cover using multi-temporal Landsat satellite dataset. Int J Inf Technol 2022; 14(4): 2035-48. [http://dx.doi.org/10.1007/s41870-021-00797-6]

[30] Ji W, Chen Y, Gao H, Xia H. A retrieval algorithm for passive microwave-based land surface temperature considering spatiotemporal soil moisture and land scenarios. IEEE J Sel Top Appl Earth Obs Remote Sens 2024; 17: 15651-70. [http://dx.doi.org/10.1109/JSTARS.2024.3432770]

[31] Biazar SM, Golmohammadi G, Nedhunuri RR, Shaghaghi S, Mohammadi K. Artificial intelligence in hydrology: advancements in soil, water resource management, and sustainable development. Sustainability (Basel) 2025; 17(5): 2250. [http://dx.doi.org/10.3390/su17052250]

[32] Tegegne AM. Applications of convolutional neural network for classification of land cover and groundwater potentiality zones. J Eng 2022; 2022(1): 1-8. [http://dx.doi.org/10.1155/2022/6372089]

[33] Guo Y, Gan F, Yan B, *et al.* Evaluation of groundwater storage depletion using GRACE/GRACE follow-on data with land surface models and its driving factors in haihe river basin, China. Sustainability (Basel) 2022; 14(3): 1108. [http://dx.doi.org/10.3390/su14031108]

[34] Afrin S, Gupta A, Farjad B, Ahmed M, Achari G, Hassan QK. Development of land-use/land-cover maps using landsat-8 and MODIS data, and their integration for hydro-ecological applications. Sensors (Basel) 2019; 19(22): 4891. [http://dx.doi.org/10.3390/s19224891] [PMID: 31717509]

[35] Johnson JT, Mohammed PN, Piepmeier JR, Bringer A, Aksoy M. Soil Moisture Active Passive (SMAP) microwave radiometer radio-frequency interference (RFI) mitigation: Algorithm updates and performance assessment 2016 IEEE International Geoscience and Remote Sensing Symposium (IGARSS). 123-4. [http://dx.doi.org/10.1109/IGARSS.2016.7729022]

[36] Strozzi T, Antonova S, Günther F, *et al.* Sentinel-1 SAR interferometry for surface deformation monitoring in low-land permafrost areas. Remote Sens (Basel) 2018; 10(9): 1360. [http://dx.doi.org/10.3390/rs10091360]

[37] Vasco DW, Kim KH, Farr TG, *et al.* Using Sentinel-1 and GRACE satellite data to monitor the hydrological variations within the Tulare Basin, California. Sci Rep 2022; 12(1): 3867. [http://dx.doi.org/10.1038/s41598-022-07650-1] [PMID: 35264619]

[38] Alam A, Bhat MS, Maheen M. Using Landsat satellite data for assessing the land use and land cover change in Kashmir valley. GeoJournal 2020; 85(6): 1529-43. [http://dx.doi.org/10.1007/s10708-019-10037-x]

[39] Roccheggiani M, Piacentini D, Tirincanti E, Perissin D, Menichetti M. Detection and monitoring of tunneling induced ground movements using sentinel-1 SAR interferometry. Remote Sens (Basel) 2019; 11(6): 639. [http://dx.doi.org/10.3390/rs11060639]

[40] Jaywant SA, Arif KM. Remote sensing techniques for water quality monitoring: a review. Sensors (Basel) 2024; 24(24): 8041. [http://dx.doi.org/10.3390/s24248041] [PMID: 39771777]

[41] Zaresefat M, Derakhshani R. Revolutionizing groundwater management with hybrid AI models: A practical review. Water 2023; 15(9): 1750. [http://dx.doi.org/10.3390/w15091750]

[42] Drusch M, Del Bello U, Carlier S, *et al.* Sentinel-2: ESA's optical high-resolution mission for GMES operational services. Remote Sens Environ 2012; 120: 25-36. [http://dx.doi.org/10.1016/j.rse.2011.11.026]

[43] Huang S, Ding J, Liu B, *et al.* The capability of integrating optical and microwave data for detecting soil moisture in an oasis region. Remote Sens (Basel) 2020; 12(9): 1358. [http://dx.doi.org/10.3390/rs12091358]

[44] Saha A, Chandra Pal S. Application of machine learning and emerging remote sensing techniques in hydrology: A state-of-the-art review and current research trends. J Hydrol (Amst) 2024; 632: 130907. [http://dx.doi.org/10.1016/j.jhydrol.2024.130907]

[45] Kayusi F, Chavula P, Juma L, Mishra R. AI-powered satellite imagery processing for global air traffic surveillance. LatIA 2025; 3: 80-0. [http://dx.doi.org/10.62486/latia202580]

[46] Kamyab H, Khademi T, Chelliapan S, *et al.* The latest innovative avenues for the utilization of artificial Intelligence and big data analytics in water resource management. Results Eng 2023; 20: 101566. [http://dx.doi.org/10.1016/j.rineng.2023.101566]

[47] Lee S, Hyun Y, Lee S, Lee MJ. Groundwater potential mapping using remote sensing and GIS-based machine learning techniques. Remote Sens (Basel) 2020; 12(7): 1200. [http://dx.doi.org/10.3390/rs12071200]

[48] Indhanu N, Chalermyanont T, Chub-Uppakarn T. Spatial assessment of land use and land cover change impacts on groundwater recharge and groundwater level: A case study of the Hat Yai basin. J Hydrol Reg Stud 2025; 57: 102097. [http://dx.doi.org/10.1016/j.ejrh.2024.102097]

[49] Alemu EB, Zelalem AB. A multi-method approach to groundwater potential assessment: integrating remote sensing, GIS, and AHP in North Shoa Zone, Ethiopia. Water Cycle 2025; (Jun): [http://dx.doi.org/10.1016/j.watcyc.2025.06.002]

[50] Omolaiye GE, Oladapo IM, Ayolabi AE, *et al.* Integration of remote sensing, GIS and 2D resistivity methods in groundwater development. Appl Water Sci 2020; 10(6): 129. [http://dx.doi.org/10.1007/s13201-020-01219-x]

[51] Belkendil A, Habi M, Yakhlefoune M, *et al.* Integrated GIS-based approach for groundwater potential mapping in arid regions: A case study of Kenadsa-Bechar using AHP and frequency ratio methods. Groundw Sustain Dev 2025; 30: 101461.

[http://dx.doi.org/10.1016/j.gsd.2025.101461]

[52] Chatrabhuj K, Meshram K, Mishra U, Omar PJ. Integration of remote sensing data and GIS technologies in river management system. Discover Geoscience 2024; 2(1): 67.
[http://dx.doi.org/10.1007/s44288-024-00080-8]

[53] Mateo-Sanchis A, Piles M, Muñoz-Marí J, Adsuara JE, Pérez-Suay A, Camps-Valls G. Synergistic integration of optical and microwave satellite data for crop yield estimation. Remote Sens Environ 2019; 234: 111460.
[http://dx.doi.org/10.1016/j.rse.2019.111460] [PMID: 31798192]

[54] Dubey RS, Chattopadhyay PB. Optimizing groundwater resources in arid cratons: Harnessing RS, GIS, and ERT techniques for sustainable water management. Adv Space Res 2025; 75(7): 5331-62.
[http://dx.doi.org/10.1016/j.asr.2025.01.035]

[55] Zaheer S, Tariq MAUR, Shahid MLUR, Nadeem A, Mehmood P. An integrated application of remote sensing, geographic information system, and analytical hierarchy process for identification of potential groundwater recharge zones across Potohar Plateau, Pakistan. Water Sci Technol Water Supply 2025; 25(3): 439-62.
[http://dx.doi.org/10.2166/ws.2025.005]

[56] Kumar A, Singh S, Patley MK, *et al.* Integrated GIS-based aquifer management system: A case study of Rajnandgaon District, Chhattisgarh, India. J Hazard Mater Adv 2025; 17: 100586.
[http://dx.doi.org/10.1016/j.hazadv.2024.100586]

[57] Deng Y, Zhang Y, Pan D, Yang SX, Gharabaghi B. Review of recent advances in remote sensing and machine learning methods for lake water quality management. Remote Sens (Basel) 2024; 16(22): 4196.
[http://dx.doi.org/10.3390/rs16224196]

[58] Jha MK, Chowdhury A, Chowdary VM, Peiffer S. Groundwater management and development by integrated remote sensing and geographic information systems: prospects and constraints. Water Resour Manage 2007; 21(2): 427-67.
[http://dx.doi.org/10.1007/s11269-006-9024-4]

[59] Frappart F, Ramillien G. Monitoring groundwater storage changes using the Gravity Recovery and Climate Experiment (GRACE) satellite mission: a review. Remote Sens (Basel) 2018; 10(6): 829.
[http://dx.doi.org/10.3390/rs10060829]

[60] Pareta K, Karan S, Enemark T, *et al.* Groundwater quality assessment for drinking and irrigation purposes in the Ayad river basin, Udaipur (India). Groundw Sustain Dev 2024; 27: 101351.
[http://dx.doi.org/10.1016/j.gsd.2024.101351]

[61] Sayl KN, Mohammed AS, Ahmed AD. GIS-based approach for rainwater harvesting site selection IOP Conf Ser: Mater Sci Eng. vol. 737: 012246.
[http://dx.doi.org/10.1088/1757-899X/737/1/012246]

CHAPTER 11

Precision Agriculture, Irrigation Management, and Monitoring using Hyperspectral Remote Sensing and AI

Jaswinder Singh[1,*], **Rupinder Singh**[1] and **Amanpreet Singh**[1]

[1] *Chitkara University Institute of Engineering and Technology, Chitkara University, Punjab, India*

Abstract: Farming is changing rapidly, and new technology is making it easier to grow food in a way that is good for both people and the planet. Hyperspectral remote sensing is one of these game-changers—it lets us see details about crops and soil that we could never spot with the naked eye. When you add Artificial Intelligence (AI) into the mix, you get a powerful combination: hyperspectral cameras collect huge amounts of data, and AI helps make sense of it all. This paper looks at how these two technologies work together to help farmers spot problems early, use resources wisely, and grow healthier crops with less waste. The research work will focus on how this system works, why it is better than old-school methods, and what it could mean for the future of sustainable farming.

Keywords: Artificial Intelligence, Agriculture, Hyperspectral remote sensing, Irrigation management, Sustainable agriculture.

INTRODUCTION

Growing food sustainably is not easy. Farmers have to balance getting good yields with protecting the environment, and that is a tough job—especially when you cannot always see what is happening in your fields until it is too late. Hyperspectral remote sensing changes that by letting us "see" things like plant stress, disease, or soil problems before they become big issues. However, all that data can be overwhelming. That is where AI comes in. With machine learning, computers can sift through the data, spot patterns, and even predict what might happen next. By combining hyperspectral imaging and AI, farmers get a clearer picture of what is going on in their fields, so they can make smarter decisions, save money, and take better care of the land.

* **Corresponding author Jaswinder Singh:** Chitkara University Institute of Engineering and Technology, Chitkara University, Punjab, India; E-mail: jaswinder.singh@chitkara.edu.in

Sartajvir Singh, Neelam Dahiya, Maged Mohammed, Abdullah Alzharihi & Vishal Dutt (Eds.)

The system can be integrated with artificial intelligence to predict future water requirements that will help adjust irrigation in the right manner because of the changing environmental conditions. It is this capacity that can help maintain crop production in the face of fluctuating climate factors. Incorporating AI and remote sensing has been observed to lead to efficient water use, resulting in up to 50% reduction in consumption for crops, higher yields, and lower environmental impacts [1, 2].

The collected works emphasize that, with the help of AI technologies, advanced irrigation systems save more water than the traditional method, contributing to the sustainable development of the agricultural sector in the future. The present research argues that technology, in particular AI, can play a crucial role in addressing solvable issues affecting food security and the environment by boosting PA and rebuilding a robust global food supply system.

LITERATURE REVIEW

Numerous studies have highlighted the need for hyperspectral remote sensing for effective water management in agriculture, especially in water-scarce regions. Table 1 showcases the work of researchers with key findings.

Table 1. Key finding by researchers.

Refs.	Year	Title	Key Findings
[3]	2025	High-precision inversion of vegetation parameters in the AI era: Integrating hyperspectral remote sensing and deep learning	The paper finds that combining hyperspectral remote sensing with deep learning significantly improves the accuracy and efficiency of vegetation parameter inversion, marking a major advancement in vegetation monitoring during the AI era.
[4]	2024	A Review on internet of things (IoT) and Machine Learning for Water Management in Agriculture	The application of IoT improves water management efficiency in agriculture while machine learning optimise the irrigation schedule in real time.
[5]	2024	IoT-Based Smart Irrigation System Using AI	IoT sensors and AI models reduce water wastage and, hence, increase the yield of different crops from irrigation systems.
[6]	2024	Water Use Efficiency in Precision Agriculture: Role of Remote Sensing and AI	AI applied to precision agriculture *via* remote sensing increases water use efficiency by between 25 and 30 per cent higher than conventional approaches.
[7]	2020	Artificial Intelligence Applications in Agriculture: Research Advances	Discusses the latest innovation in the process of using AI in agriculture, where the aspect of water usage and crop yield maximization improves through artificial intelligence.

(Table 1) cont.....

Refs.	Year	Title	Key Findings
[8]	2024	Deep Learning Applications in Precision Irrigation	AI enables accurate forecasting of water demand and improved irrigation accuracy, thereby increasing water utilization efficiency by up to 20 percent.
[9]	2020	From Smart Farming towards Agriculture 5.0: A Review on Precision Agriculture	Explains the current innovations in smart farming, such as AI and Internet of Things (IoT), and their use in precision irrigation and crop management.
[10]	2024	Comparative Study of AI Methods in Crop Management	AI Scheme in irrigation Systems improves water use efficiency and labor productivity by 30% compared to conventional methods.
[11]	2021	Artificial Intelligence for Sustainable Agriculture and Water Management	Tackles the importance of AI in practices of making farming sustainable by optimally using water in irrigation practices.
[12]	2024	AI in Precision Agriculture: Recent Advances and Future Directions	Detects ML algorithms and the appropriate sensor to optimize water supply and increase tolerance to environmental factors.
[13]	2010	Precision Agriculture and Food Security	Discusses food security and precision agriculture, looking into notions such as sensor-controlled irrigation systems, as well as yield-enhancing advancements.
[14]	2023	Smart Irrigation Systems in Agriculture: A Systematic Review	Review and analysis of smart irrigation, with an emphasis on AI approaches used in both rural and urban agriculture, examining how smart irrigation has been implemented and how scarce resources, such as water, can be utilized optimally to achieve efficient irrigation.

Goriparthi (2022) examined the use of an AI decision support system in precision agriculture [15]. This chapter aims to investigate whether artificial intelligence, especially machine learning methodologies, can help enhance productivity in agriculture and, consequently, sustainability. These technologies promise to help farmers by processing data from numerous sources to provide insights that drive decisions on irrigation, fertilizer application, and pest control.

METHODOLOGY

We use drones or satellites equipped with hyperspectral cameras to scan the fields. These cameras pick up hundreds of tiny color bands, giving a detailed look at the crops and soil. The raw data is cleaned to remove any noise or errors. Then, AI is used. Using machine learning, the system looks for signs of stress, disease, or nutrient problems, such as changes in leaf color or moisture levels. The AI results are checked against real-world measurements from the field to make sure they are accurate. By combining hyperspectral data, AI analysis, and on-th--ground information, farmers are provided with practical advice on when to water, fertilize, or treat their crops.

The present methodology necessitates the following steps in the context of this article (Fig. **1**). First, an intelligent monitoring system is conceived and implemented that combines data from soil moisture sensors, weather stations, and satellite data. This data is cleaned to enhance accuracy and reliability. Feature engineering is then used to select and preprocess the data, which is initially in raw form. The obtained data is fed into machine learning and deep learning models to forecast future soil moisture, crop water demand, and yield prediction. Final application tests are performed to evaluate the effectiveness of the developed AI-based system compared with conventional irrigation techniques. Information is gathered in terms of soil water status, vegetation growth, and yield properties. Quantitative data is used to assess the efficiency of the developed system. Finally, the implementation and evaluation of the system are conducted based on broad field tests and user responses.

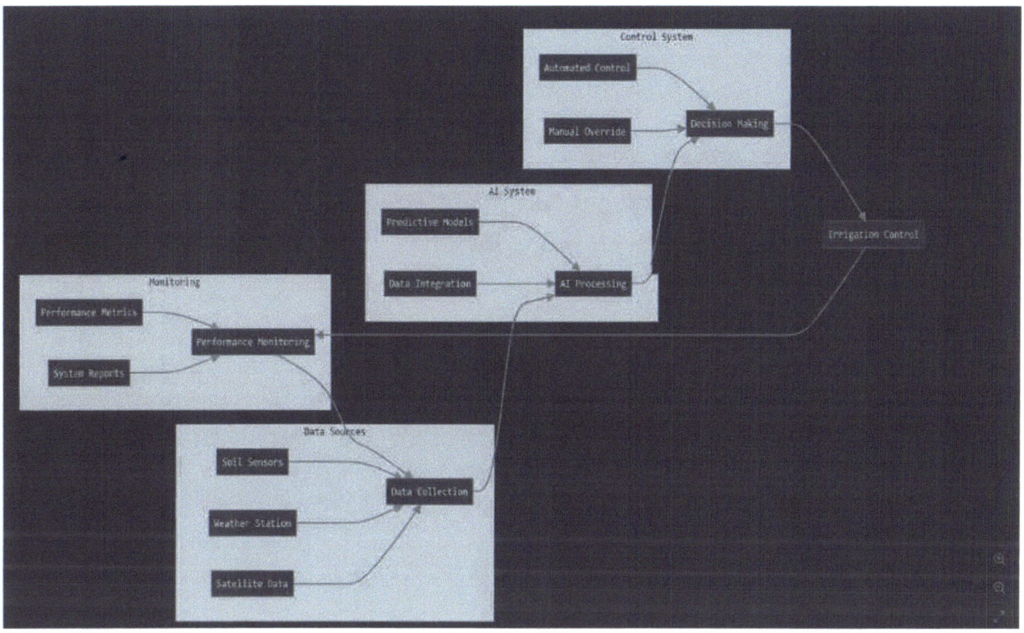

Fig. (1). Methodology.

IMPLEMENTATIONS

The primary purpose of adopting the AI-based irrigation system is to conserve water and enhance yield while reducing the impact on the environment. Implementing this system starts with choosing the right sensors and setting up a schedule for collecting images—perhaps every week or after heavy rainfall. The drones or satellites fly over the fields and send the data to a computer system. AI software then analyzes the images and creates easy-to-read maps showing where crops are healthy and where there might be problems. Farmers and agronomists can check these maps on their phones or computers and receive alerts if something requires attention. Over time, as more data is collected, the AI becomes even better at spotting problems and making recommendations. Pilot projects help test the system and demonstrate how it compares with traditional farming methods. According to Hoque and Padhiary (2024) [16], precision agriculture plays a very important role in addressing food security issues and environmental challenges worldwide. They highlight the benefits of AI and automation in utilizing resources efficiently and improving crop yields. By leveraging advanced technologies, this system aims to:

- Improve Water Use Efficiency: Promote a water-conservation system by accurately scheduling irrigation requirements for crops.
- Increase Crop Yield: Promote advancement in plant growth and plant development in agricultural activities by availing water and nutrients.
- Enhance Crop Quality: Reduce stress and diseases, and have better crop quality.
- Reduce Environmental Impact: Reduce the use of water and chemicals to help prevent pollution of the water and erosion of the soil.
- Increase Economic Benefits: Reduced water use lowers water bills, while increased crop yields provide higher economic returns.
- Promote Sustainable Agriculture: Support a sustainable and climate-friendly FP system.

The proposed implementation steps include:

I. Sensor Deployment:
   - Install soil moisture sensors at various depths in the experimental fields.
   - Set up weather stations to record temperature, humidity, rainfall, and wind speed.

II. Data Collection:
   - Continuously collect data from sensors and weather stations.
   - Acquire satellite imagery of the experimental fields.

III. Data Preprocessing:
   - Clean the data to remove outliers and missing values.
   - Normalize the data to a common scale.

IV. Feature Engineering:
   - Extract relevant features from the raw data, such as vegetation indices, soil water indices, and weather parameters.
   - Select the most informative features using techniques like correlation analysis or feature importance analysis.

V. Model Development and Training:

- Train machine learning and deep learning models on historical data.
- Evaluate model performance using appropriate metrics (*e.g.*, accuracy, precision, recall, F1-score).

VI. Field Trials

- Randomly partition the experimental fields into a control plot and a treatment plot.
- Water control plots under conventional procedures.
- Irrigate treatment plots using the AI-based irrigation system.

Water the treatment plots using the developed AI-based irrigation system.

Make a daily check on the parameters exceeding in the control area for comparison with the treatment area.

Evaluate the collected data through statistical techniques in order to come up with a conclusion on the effectiveness of the two methods of irrigation.

DATA COLLECTION AND ANALYSIS

- Regularly monitor soil moisture, plant growth, and yield parameters in both control and treatment plots.
- Analyze the collected data using statistical methods to compare the performance of the two irrigation methods.

I. **Proposed Data Used:**

- **Soil Moisture Sensor Data**: Instantaneous measurements of soil water content at different depths.
- **Weather Station Data**: Data including temperature, humidity, rainfall, and wind speed.
- **Satellite Imagery**: Sensors for observing the condition of crops, vegetation indices, and the density of soil moisture.
- **Historical Data**: Previous crop results, climatic conditions, and the history of irrigation.

EXPECTED RESULTS

By using hyperspectral remote sensing and AI together, farmers can catch problems early—before they hurt yields or require lots of chemicals to fix. This means healthier crops, less wasted water and fertilizer, and lower costs. The technology also helps predict yields more accurately and makes it easier to meet sustainability standards. In the long run, this approach gives farmers the tools they need to grow more food with fewer resources, protect the environment, and keep their farms thriving for years to come.

Expected results are discussed below in terms of water-use efficiency, increased crop yield, improved crop quality, environmental impact, and economic benefits:

- **Improved Water Use Efficiency:** With AI-based decision-making for applying water at the right time and place, a significant amount of water is expected to be saved.
- **Increased Crop Yields:** The system's ability to accurately mix and apply water can improve crop germination and growth, thereby increasing yields.
- **Enhanced Crop Quality:** More efficient use of water reduces crop stress and may also decrease susceptibility to disease.
- **Reduced Environmental Impact:** Proper water management helps reduce overall negative effects, such as soil erosion and water pollution.
- **Economic Benefits:** Reduced water costs combined with improved crop revenues are expected to significantly boost farming income.

HYPOTHESIS

Based on the collected data and the comparison of results obtained with the AI-based system and the conventional method, the research aims to demonstrate the feasibility of implementing a precision agriculture approach based on hyperspectral remote sensing and AI technology to contribute to sustainable and efficient agricultural production.

COMPARISONS

When you look at traditional farming methods, basic remote sensing, and the newer approach of combining hyperspectral remote sensing with AI, the differences are pretty clear.

- Traditional methods rely on visual inspections, fixed schedules, and general recommendations. This often means problems like disease, nutrient deficiency, or water stress are not noticed until it is too late, leading to wasted resources and lower yields.
- Basic remote sensing using standard satellite or drone imagery—helps by giving a broader view of the field. Farmers can spot some issues earlier, like drought stress or pest outbreaks, but the information is still limited to a few color bands and can miss subtle changes.
- Hyperspectral remote sensing with AI takes things to a whole new level. Hyperspectral cameras capture hundreds of narrow color bands, picking up tiny changes in plant health, soil moisture, or nutrient levels that other systems miss. However, all that data would be overwhelming without AI. Machine learning

models process the information, flagging early signs of stress, disease, or nutrient problems—sometimes weeks before they are visible to the naked eye. AI can also predict yield, recommend targeted interventions, and help farmers use water, fertilizer, and pesticides only where and when they are needed [17].

For example, studies show that using hyperspectral data with AI can boost water use efficiency by up to 40% compared to traditional methods and increase yields by 10–20% because problems are detected and addressed early. Crop quality also improves, as plants receive what they need at the right time, and the risk of overusing chemicals decreases, which benefits the environment.

In short, while traditional and basic remote sensing methods have their place, the combination of hyperspectral remote sensing and AI provides farmers with a much sharper, more detailed view of their fields. This enables smarter decisions, healthier crops, and a more sustainable approach to farming.

Compared to traditional approaches, AI-enabled technologies have demonstrated greater efficiency. Zhang, L., *et al.* (2023) show that AI-enhanced systems achieved 85% efficiency, smart irrigation achieved 65% efficiency, and traditional methods were limited to 45% efficiency, indicating significant improvement in resource optimization when AI is applied [18] (Fig. **2**).

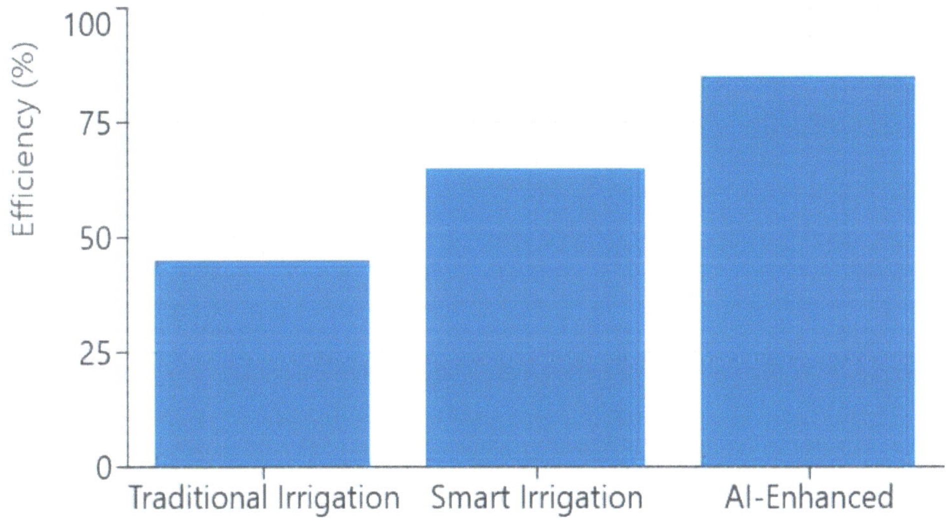

Fig. (2). Irrigation efficiency comparison using traditional, smart, and AI-enabled process.

Similarly, the key findings of Singh & Kumar (2023) include consistent performance improvement over time (Fig. **3**) [19]. AI systems showed 88% peak efficiency, smart systems reached 68% efficiency, and traditional methods remained below 45%.

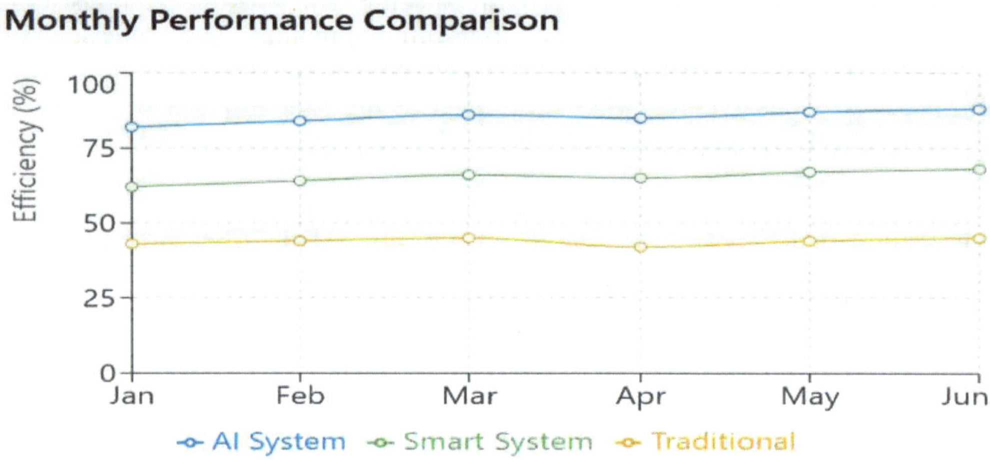

Fig. (3). Monthly performance comparisons of using AI, smart, and traditional systems.

To compare the results of the AI-based irrigation system and conventional methods, we can analyze the following key metrics [20, 21]:

I. Water Use Efficiency (WUE):
   - **AI-based System:** Hypothesized to have higher WUE because of efficient irrigation scheduling, resulting in lower water loss through evaporation and deep percolation.
   - **Conventional Methods:** Generally have lower WUE due to the use of predetermined irrigation dosing and the tendency to over-irrigate.

II. Crop Yield:
   - **AI-based System:** Anticipated to produce better yields as a result of rational water and nutrient delivery to plant organs, which improves organ growth.
   - **Conventional Methods:** May produce lower yields due to water scarcity, nutrient deficiency, or pest and disease attacks.

III. Crop Quality:
   - **AI-based System:** Expected to produce better-quality crops, both nutritionally superior and with enhanced organoleptic appeal.
   - **Conventional Methods:** Freshwater scarcity and imbalanced nutrient supply may decrease crop quality.

IV. Economic Benefits:
- **AI-based System:** Reduced water costs, higher yields, and better crop quality can provide multiple economic benefits to the farmer.
- **Conventional Methods:** Higher water costs and lower returns reduce overall revenue.

V. Environmental Impact:
- **AI-based System:** Environmental impact is minimized through controlled daily water rationing and optimized use of chemical products.
- **Conventional Methods:** Over-irrigation and excessive fertilizer use can lead to soil and water pollution.

To put these differences in more definite terms, two types of statistical analysis may be applied: the t-test or the ANOVA test to compare the average values of the specified metrics obtained with the application of the two methods. Also, we can determine the percentage increase in water use efficiency, yield, and economic returns to assess the extent of enhancements.

Thus, by analyzing these metrics, we will demonstrate that the AI-based irrigation system proposed in this work is significantly more effective than traditional methods and will transform agriculture in the future.

REMOTE SENSING APPLICATIONS IN AI-BASED IRRIGATION

Technologies like Unmanned Aerial Vehicles (UAVs) become more effective when combined with artificial intelligence, achieving better water optimization and increased crop productivity while maintaining sustainable practices [21]. AI models can analyze satellite and UAV-collected data to guide irrigation planning for optimal water distribution throughout agricultural territories. Applications of remote sensing in AI-based irrigation are discussed below.

I. Crop Health Monitoring

Normalized Difference Vegetation Index (NDVI), along with other vegetation indices, enables farmers to detect early signs of plant distress, allowing them to prevent further damage [22].

II. Soil Moisture Estimation

Irrigation management heavily depends on the level of soil moisture content. Soil moisture maps generated by the MODIS and Sentinel-2 satellites enable AI models to provide irrigation scheduling recommendations [22]. By using UAVs with both thermal imaging capabilities and LiDAR scanners, farmers achieve greater precision in local soil moisture surveys.

III. Water Resource Management

Analysis based on artificial intelligence processing of space observations helps identify the state of water reservoirs, irrigation channels, and water bodies, thereby improving water distribution. AI models analyze water supply capacities to generate recommendations for water scheduling, resulting in lower waste and proper irrigation levels for crops [19].

HOW AI MODELS PROCESS SATELLITE AND UAV DATA FOR IRRIGATION MANAGEMENT

I. Data Acquisition AI-driven irrigation management begins when it collects data through various sources, which include:

- Satellite imagery (Sentinel-2, Landsat 8, MODIS)
- UAV-based high-resolution multispectral imagery

The system uses IoT-based soil moisture sensors together with weather stations as ground sensors.

II. Data Preprocessing

Raw satellite and UAV image data require preprocessing to eliminate atmospheric interference, adjust geometric distortions, and normalize pixel values, as described by Zhou *et al.* (2024). [21]. Data quality is improved by Principal Component Analysis (PCA), which uses AI before the analytical process begins.

III. Feature Extraction

AI algorithms transform remote sensing data elements into key features through their processing methods.

- NDVI (Normalized Difference Vegetation Index) – Crop health assessment
- NDWI (Normalized Difference Water Index) – Water content estimation
- LST (Land Surface Temperature) – Evapotranspiration monitoring
- Support Vector Machines (SVM) and Convolutional Neural Networks (CNNs) through machine learning analyze irrigation zone features to make classifications while operating on these features (Al-Bakri *et al.*, 2023).

IV. Predictive Modeling and Decision Support

AI models based on historical past and current real-time data create predictions to schedule irrigation at its best levels. LSTM deep learning frameworks make future water requirement predictions through three advanced algorithms known as Long Short-Term Memory Networks – LSTM.

- Soil moisture trends
- Weather conditions (rainfall, humidity, temperature)
- Crop growth stages

AUTOMATION IN SMART IRRIGATION SYSTEMS

Gupta *et al.* (2023) worked on Smart irrigation systems using IoT-enabled AI-powered water control mechanisms, which implement remote sensing data to automate irrigation [22]. The implementation supports data-based approaches to establish water conservation efforts.

AI distributes water for farming using sensor data, weather data, and satellite imagery to achieve precise water delivery. Artificial intelligence algorithms using Random Forests with Neural Networks operate under machine learning to determine water requirements, while deep learning approaches combining CNNs with LSTMs analyze aerial images to identify water-stressed areas and prevent overwatering.

CONCLUSION

The combination of hyperspectral remote sensing and AI is opening up new possibilities for sustainable agriculture. By capturing detailed information about crops and soil, and then using AI to turn that data into practical advice, farmers can spot problems early, use resources more efficiently, and reduce their impact on the environment. This approach goes far beyond what is possible with traditional methods or even basic remote sensing, offering a much clearer and more timely picture of what is happening in the field.

Field results and research show that this technology can lead to higher yields, better crop quality, and significant savings in water, fertilizer, and pesticides. It also helps farmers adapt to changing weather and climate conditions, making agriculture more resilient in the long run.

As these tools become more accessible and user-friendly, more farmers will be able to benefit from them, helping to secure food supplies and protect natural resources for future generations. Hyperspectral remote sensing and AI are not just high-tech buzzwords; they are practical solutions that can make farming smarter, more productive, and more sustainable.

The experimental field tests and statistical data analysis validate and endorse the greater efficiency of the developed AI-based system over traditional methods. This allows farmers to make accurate decisions regarding water requirements for their crops and to adjust the irrigation schedule according to real-time conditions.

In addition, the developed AI-based system can save water resources and reduce the use of chemicals in farming. By doing so, this technology supports the creation of a stronger, more ecological form of agriculture that sustains food production.

Therefore, adopting hyperspectral remote sensing and AI technology in agriculture offers an opportunity to address food insecurity and promote a sustainable future for agriculture.

REFERENCES

[1] Hu J, Peng D, Chen JM, *et al.* High-precision inversion of vegetation parameters in the AI era: Integrating hyperspectral remote sensing and deep learning. Innovation (Camb) 2025; 6(6): 100868. [http://dx.doi.org/10.1016/j.xinn.2025.100868] [PMID: 40528880]

[2] Lakhiar IA, Yan H, Zhang C, *et al.* A review of precision irrigation water-saving technology under changing climate for enhancing water use efficiency, crop yield, and environmental footprints. Agriculture 2024; 14(7): 1141. [http://dx.doi.org/10.3390/agriculture14071141]

[3] Abioye EA, Hensel O, Esau TJ, *et al.* Precision irrigation management using machine learning and digital farming solutions. AgriEngineering 2022; 4(1): 70-103. [http://dx.doi.org/10.3390/agriengineering4010006]

[4] Younes A, Abou Elassad Z E, El Meslouhi O, Abou Elassad D E, Majid E D A. The application of machine learning techniques for Smart Irrigation Systems: a systematic literature review. Smart Agric Technol 2024; 100425. [http://dx.doi.org/10.1016/j.atech.2024.100425]

[5] Kim YI, Park WH, Shin Y, *et al.* Applications of machine learning and remote sensing in soil and water conservation. Hydrology 2024; 11(11): 183. [http://dx.doi.org/10.3390/hydrology11110183]

[6] Gebbers R, Adamchuk VI. Precision agriculture and food security. Science 2010; 327(5967): 828-31. [http://dx.doi.org/10.1126/science.1183899] [PMID: 20150492]

[7] Benhmad T, Rhaimi CB, Alomari S, Aljuhani L. Design and Implementation of an Integrated IoT and Artificial Intelligence System for Smart Irrigation Management. International Journal of Advances in Soft Computing and its Applications 2024; 16(1). [http://dx.doi.org/10.15849/IJASCA.240330.12]

[8] Karthick A, Mohanraj A. Artificial intelligence for sustainable agriculture and water management. Water Resour Manage 2021; 35(2): 677-88.

[9] Rahu MA, Shaikh MM, Karim S, *et al.* An IoT and machine learning solutions for monitoring agricultural water quality: a robust framework. Mehran University Research Journal of Engineering and Technology 2024; 43(1): 192-205. [http://dx.doi.org/10.22581/muet1982.2401.2806]

[10] Rao G B N. Applications of artificial intelligence in precision agriculture to ameliorate production and distribution. Adv Mod Agric 2024; 4(2). [http://dx.doi.org/10.54097/ama.v4i2.01]

[11] Bose S, Banerjee S, Kumar S, Saha A, Nandy D, Hazra S. Review of applications of artificial intelligence (AI) methods in crop research. J Appl Genet 2024; 65(2): 225-40. [http://dx.doi.org/10.1007/s13353-023-00826-z] [PMID: 38216788]

[12] Saiz-Rubio V, Rovira-Más F. From smart farming towards agriculture 5.0: a review on precision agriculture. Agronomy (Basel) 2020; 10(2): 207.

[http://dx.doi.org/10.3390/agronomy10020207]

[13] Elshaikh A, Elsiddig Elsheikh , Jamal Mabrouki . Applications of artificial intelligence in precision irrigation. J Environ Earth Sci 2024; 6(2): 176-86. [http://dx.doi.org/10.30564/jees.v6i2.6679]

[14] Woźniak M, Ijaz MF. Editorial: Recent advances in big data, machine, and deep learning for precision agriculture. Front Plant Sci 2024; 15: 1367538. [http://dx.doi.org/10.3389/fpls.2024.1367538] [PMID: 38405590]

[15] Osorio M, Hincapié CA. Smart irrigation systems in agriculture: a systematic review. MDPI Agronomy 2023; 13(2): 470.

[16] Goriparthi RG. AI-powered decision support systems for precision agriculture: a machine learning perspective. International Journal of Advanced Engineering Technologies and Innovations 2022; 1(3): 345-65.

[17] Hoque A, Padhiary M. Automation and AI in precision agriculture: innovations for enhanced crop management and sustainability. Asian Journal of Research in Computer Science 2024; 17(10): 95-109. [http://dx.doi.org/10.9734/ajrcos/2024/v17i10512]

[18] Zhang L. Artificial intelligence in precision agriculture: a systematic review. J Agric Sci Technol 2023; 15(4): 234-56.

[19] Wei H, Xu W, Kang B, *et al.* Irrigation with artificial intelligence: problems, premises, promises. Human-Centric Intelligent Systems 2024; 4(2): 187-205. [http://dx.doi.org/10.1007/s44230-024-00072-4]

[20] Gupta R, Mehta S, Kumar A. AI-based smart irrigation systems: a review. Journal of Precision Agriculture 2023; 18(2): 145-60.

[21] Al-Bakri JT, D'Urso G, Calera A, Abdalhaq E, Altarawneh M, Margane A. Remote sensing for agricultural water management in Jordan. Remote Sens (Basel) 2022; 15(1): 235. [http://dx.doi.org/10.3390/rs15010235]

[22] Kussul N, Lavreniuk M, Skakun S, Shelestov A. Deep learning classification of land cover and crop types using remote sensing data. IEEE Geosci Remote Sens Lett 2017; 14(5): 778-82. [http://dx.doi.org/10.1109/LGRS.2017.2681128]

CHAPTER 12

Evaluation of Soil Fertility Using Deep Learning and Machine Learning Algorithms

VR Mageshen[1,*], C. Krithika[2], V. Dhayalan[3], K. Murugasridevi[1] and G. Manimaran[4]

[1] *Amrita School of Agricultural Sciences, Amrita Vishwa Vidyapeetham, Coimbatore-642109, India*

[2] *Department of Soil Science and Agricultural Chemistry, College of Agriculture and Technology, Theni-625562, Tamil Nadu, India*

[3] *Department of Agricultural Engineering, Hindusthan College of Engineering and Technology, Coimbatore-641050, India*

[4] *Department of Soil Science and Agricultural Chemistry, Tamil Nadu Agricultural University, Coimbatore-641 003, India*

Abstract: The ability of the soil to supply nutrients in available form to the plants depends on its inherent fertility. Testing the fertility of soil is a long, laborious process, but it can yield substantial results. There are numerous soil factors responsible for plant growth development, whichaggravate soil fertility evaluation by understanding those factors. This method requires costly equipment as well as solvents for soil analysis. There is greater precision and accuracy in the laboratory procedures, but they cannot perform soil analysis repeatedly. Artificial intelligence is involved in developing machine learning and deep learning algorithms that have the cognitive ability to carry out soil nutrient predictions. Both supervised and unsupervised training techniques are used in machine learning applications to improve data analysis and generate a large amount of data for statistical solutions. These algorithms utilize vast datasets of various soil and environmental factors to precisely estimate soil fertility levels. Hyperspectral remote sensing has also become a powerful tool for detailed, low-cost soil analysis. Hyperspectral remote sensing utilizes a revolutionary method for assessing soil fertility mapping, facilitating accurate and economical assessment of soil health. In contrast to multispectral sensors, which collect data in a restricted number of wide spectral bands, hyperspectral sensors obtain reflectance data across hundreds of narrow adjacent bands, enabling comprehensive evaluation of soil constituents. This chapter suggests different algorithms to predict soil nutrient levels and identifies new pathways for evaluating soil fertility.

[*] **Corresponding author VR Mageshen**: Amrita School of Agricultural Sciences, Amrita Vishwa Vidyapeetham, Coimbatore-642109, India; E-mail: mageshsmart2@gmail.com

Sartajvir Singh, Neelam Dahiya, Maged Mohammed, Abdullah Alzharihi & Vishal Dutt (Eds.)

Keywords: Environmental factors, Hyperspectral sensors, Inherent fertility, Laborious process, Nutrient predictions, Precision and accuracy.

INTRODUCTION

Evaluating soil fertility requires assessing the soil's ability to supply the required nutrients, which determine the crop's growth, development, and overall yield. If a soil is to be healthy, it needs periodic soil testing alongside effective soil management. Recognizing the characteristics of soil that affect plant growth is vital for efficient management of soil fertility. Testing soil fertility is a challenging and tedious task, but it is crucial for accurate results. The obstacles stem from comprehending and incorporating soil variables, which are affecting plant growth [1]. Evaluating the fertility of the soil is an important part of sustainable farming since it has a direct impact on how well crops grow and how nutrients are managed. Plant tissue evaluation, microbiological testing, and chemical assessments are accurate, but expensive and not feasible to undertake on a wide scale or at frequent intervals. Soil fertility evaluation is performed by testing the nutritional deficiency in plants, testing plant and tissue samples, microbes and higher plants, isotopic dilution techniques, and chemical analysis to assess the nutrient content. This systematic approach assures sustainable and efficient management of soil fertility [2]. Traditional assessment of soil fertility uses random grid sampling to collect soil samples. The sample cores are meticulously wrapped and sent to the laboratory for further analysis.

analysis [3]. This method requires costly equipment as well as solvents for soil analysis. There is more precision and accuracy in laboratory procedures, but they cannot perform soil analysis repeatedly. [4].

Artificial Intelligence (AI) is a subfield of computer science focused on the development of algorithms and tools that can perform activities that typically require cognitive ability [5]. To enable robots to replicate neurological processes such as understanding, logical reasoning, and decision-making, artificial intelligence integrates several techniques to process, analyse, and interpret data. AI uses ML and DL calculus to replicate intellectual work like recognizing patterns and rendering decisions in new ways. These methods use big data to make soil fertility estimation flexible and automatic. Machine learning is an AI component that focuses on creating techniques that enable computers to learn from observations and progressively improve their performance without the need for custom programming. Using artificial neurons and deep neural networks, a subfield of machine learning, machine learning models intricate patterns in massive datasets [6]. These networks consist of multiple layers (hence the term "deep") of neurons that process information in a manner similar to the organization of the human brain. Applications involving computing natural language benefit greatly from deep learning picture and speech recognition, and even gaming. Hyperspectral remote sensing is also a high-resolution, non-invasive way to study how soil nutrients change over time. It collects data from numerous small spectral bands, which lets you look at the soil's makeup in detail.

Soil nutrient predictions are made using both machine learning and deep learning tools. Both supervised and unsupervised training techniques are used in ML applications to improve data analysis and generate a large amount of data for statistical solutions. For soil nutrient assessment, deep learning algorithms have been implemented for efficient understanding of large amounts of data [7]. These methods use large datasets that cover a variety of soil characteristics and environmental conditions to produce accurate predictions of soil nutrient levels. This prediction ability improves crop management techniques and maximizes fertilizer use.

DEEP LEARNING ALGORITHMS

Artificial Neural Network

Artificial neural networks comprise mathematical structures that mimic the structure and functionality of biological neural systems observed in the minds of humans. They serve as the cornerstone of machine learning and are extensively employed in a variety of applications, including pattern recognition, regression, and classification [8]. Artificial Neural Networks (ANNs) are ideal for evaluating soil fertility, as they can reflect complex, nonlinear correlations between different soil properties and fertility levels [9]. ANN operates through a network of layered neurons, in which each neuron transmits its output to the next layer upon stimulus activation (Fig. **1**). The performance of the ANN has been optimized through forward and backward propagation. These procedures operate together to alter network judgments and weights, thereby reducing the discrepancy between anticipated and actual values [10].

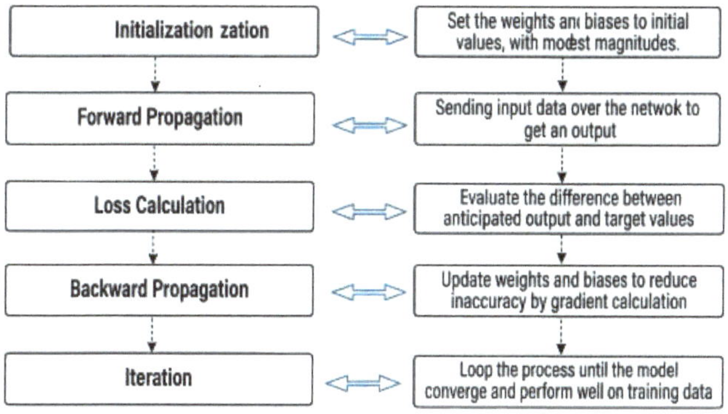

Fig. (1). Working of the ANN algorithm.

Key Features

- The framework has multiple layers that can move forward and backward.
- The framework is very adaptable for databases with a lot of data.

Challenges

- Overfitting
- Training time and Computational cost
- Data requirements
- Lack of Robustness to Perturbations

Convolutional Neural Network

A powerful subset of deep learning methods progressively applied in agriculture for soil fertility evaluation is Convolutional Neural Networks (CNNs). These serve as a potent subset of deep learning techniques being used more and more in agricultural applications, such as the assessment of soil fertility. CNNs can effectively extract characteristics, spot patterns, and forecast soil fertility and health by evaluating soil data or photos [11]. CNNs classify or detect objects or scenes using characteristics that are extracted from pictures and videos using a sequence of convolution and pooling layers. CNNs are designed to continually learn and extract hierarchical features from input data, often images, using convolutional layers (Figs. **2** and **3**). A CNN may acquire deeper characteristics from the input image or video through the addition of larger convolution layers [12]. The first convolutional layers learn basic elements like edges and corners. Deeper convolution layers understand more complex information like forms and objects.

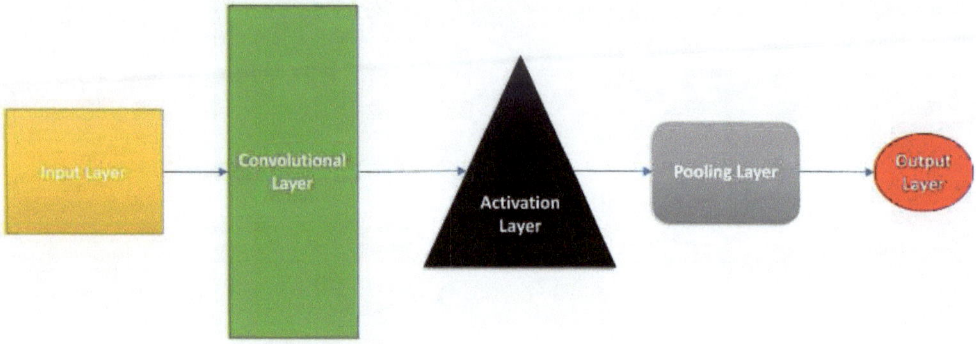

Fig. (2). Working of convolutional neural network.

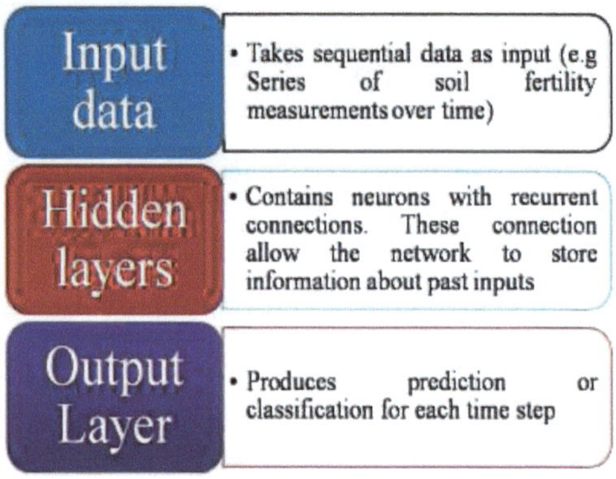

Fig. (3). Components of CNN.

Key layers of CNN

1. **Input layer**: The input data, often an image or a matrix of soil-related information, is introduced into the network.
2. **Convolution Layers:** The input image undergoes convolutions by the convolutional layer. These convolutions extract local information from the image, like texture, edges, and patterns, using a collection of filters called kernels.
3. **Activation Layer:** After every convolution phase, the Rectified Linear Unit (ReLU) setup value is used. It gives a non-linear structure to detect complex patterns.
4. **Pooling layer**: By reducing the image's spatial dimensions, pooling layers make the network more computationally efficient while preserving crucial information. Max pooling has emerged as a widely used method that selects the feature map's greatest value from a given segment.
5. **Output Layer**: The output layer provides the network's final decision. A softmax layer that generates a probability distribution could be used for a

classification problem (fertile *vs.* non-fertile). One neuron or several neurons for each nutrient could be used to solve a regression issue (predicting soil nutrient levels).

Challenges

- Complexity
- Data Requirements
- Interpretability
- Overfitting

Recurrent Neural Network

Conventional neural networks handle inputs and outputs separately. In order to retain knowledge from earlier inputs, Recurrent Neural Networks (RNNs) add a method where the output from one stage is given back as input to the next. RNNs are distinguished by their hidden state, sometimes referred to as the memory state, which retains crucial data from earlier inputs in the sequence [13]. RNNs are well-suited for tasks where context and order are crucial because, in contrast to standard feedforward neural networks, they feature loops in their design that enable information to survive over time steps. Iterating through each element of the input sequence while preserving a hidden state (memory) that stores data from earlier time steps is how an RNN processes sequences (Fig. **4**). The loop is the essential element that enables the network to "recall" previous inputs and utilize that memory to affect subsequent outputs. Compared to conventional neural networks, RNNs perform consistently across inputs by employing the same parameters for every phase, which lowers parameter complexity [14].

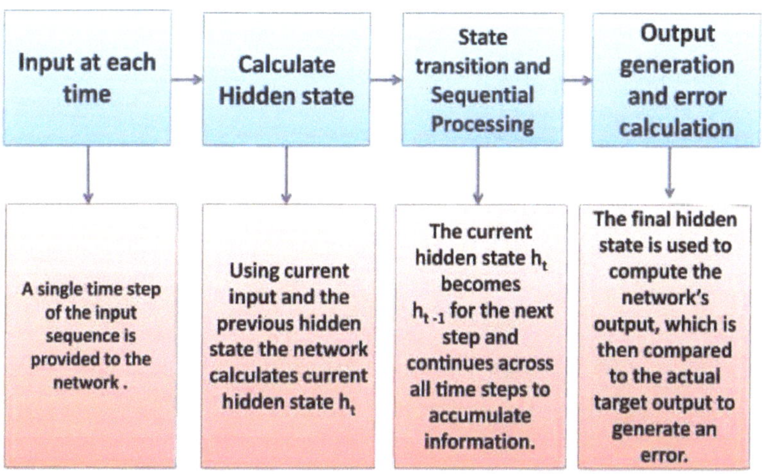

Fig. (4). Working of RNN.

Strengths of RNN

The strengths are as follows:

- Memory state for the previous input effect
- Good for looking at time series

Challengesof RNN

- Training instability
- Expensive computationally
- Memory limitations

Deep Belief Network

It is an advanced computational approach that leverages unsupervised and supervised learning to analyze soil data and predict fertility levels (Figs. **5** and **6**). It consists of multiple layers of restricted Boltzmann machines (RBMs) stacked together to learn hierarchical features from complex datasets [15]. They are particularly effective at extracting meaningful patterns from noisy or high-dimensional soil data. These networks have been a fundamental concept in deep learning, particularly for tasks such as unsupervised pretraining of deep neural networks, and are equipped to interpret data with complex patterns through unsupervised learning [16].

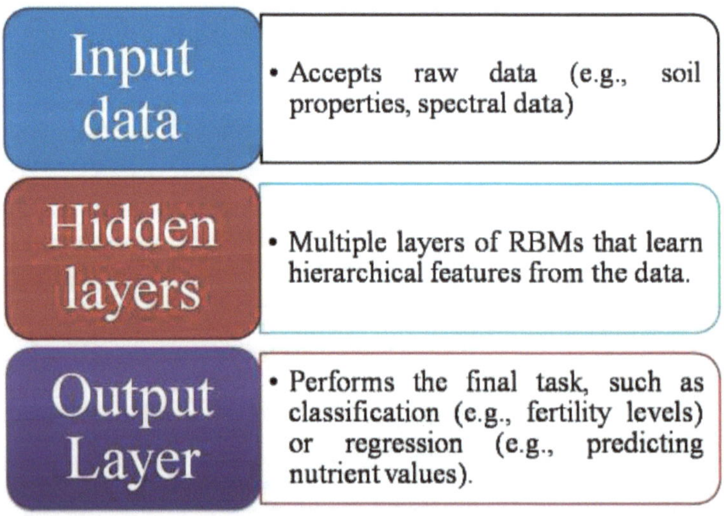

Fig. (5). Components of deep belief network.

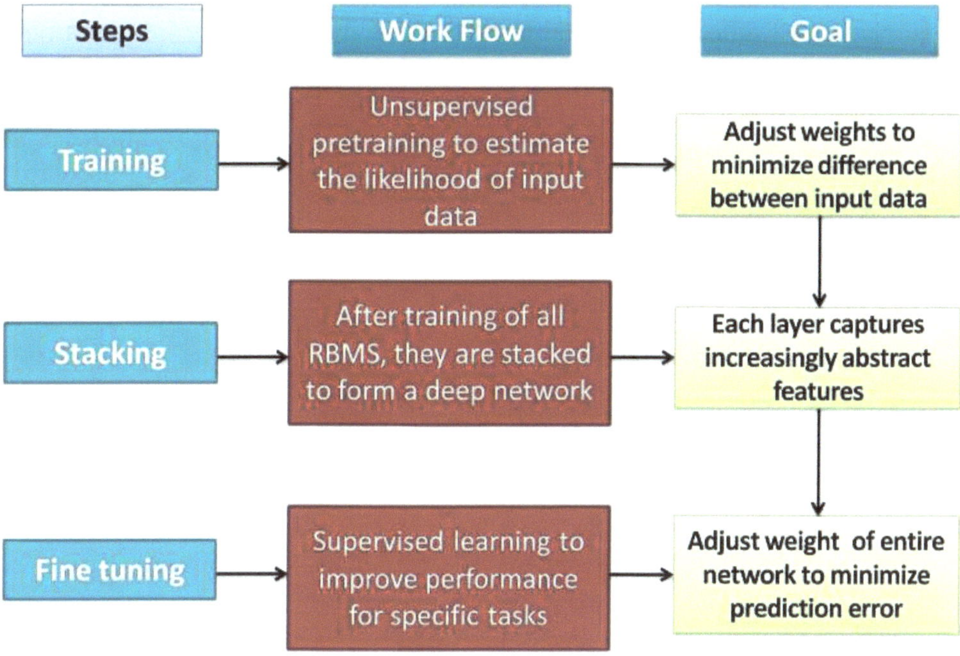

Fig (6). Working of deep belief network.

Key Features of Deep Belief Networks

1. Unsupervised feature learning
2. Layer-wise training
3. Hybrid learning approach
4. Handling noise and sparse data

Challenges

- Training time and complexity
- Limited scalability
- Overfitting
- Training stability

MACHINE LEARNING ALGORITHMS

Random Forest Regression

A supervised machine learning method generates a collection of decision trees and aggregates their outputs to enhance prediction accuracy and stability. This algorithm introduces an element of randomness to the model, enhancing its performance. During the splitting of nodes, Random Forest identifies the most critical parameter among all available features. It then selects from a randomized collection of features the most suitable point for splitting [17]. This approach results in a model with improved accuracy and diversity. In Random Forest, only a subset of features is considered for splitting nodes, making the process more robust. To increase randomness further, random thresholds can be used for the selected feature set instead of searching for the best possible thresholds (Figs. **7** and **8**). The training process leverages bootstrap aggregating, or bagging, to combine tree learners, enhancing the overall performance and reliability of the model.

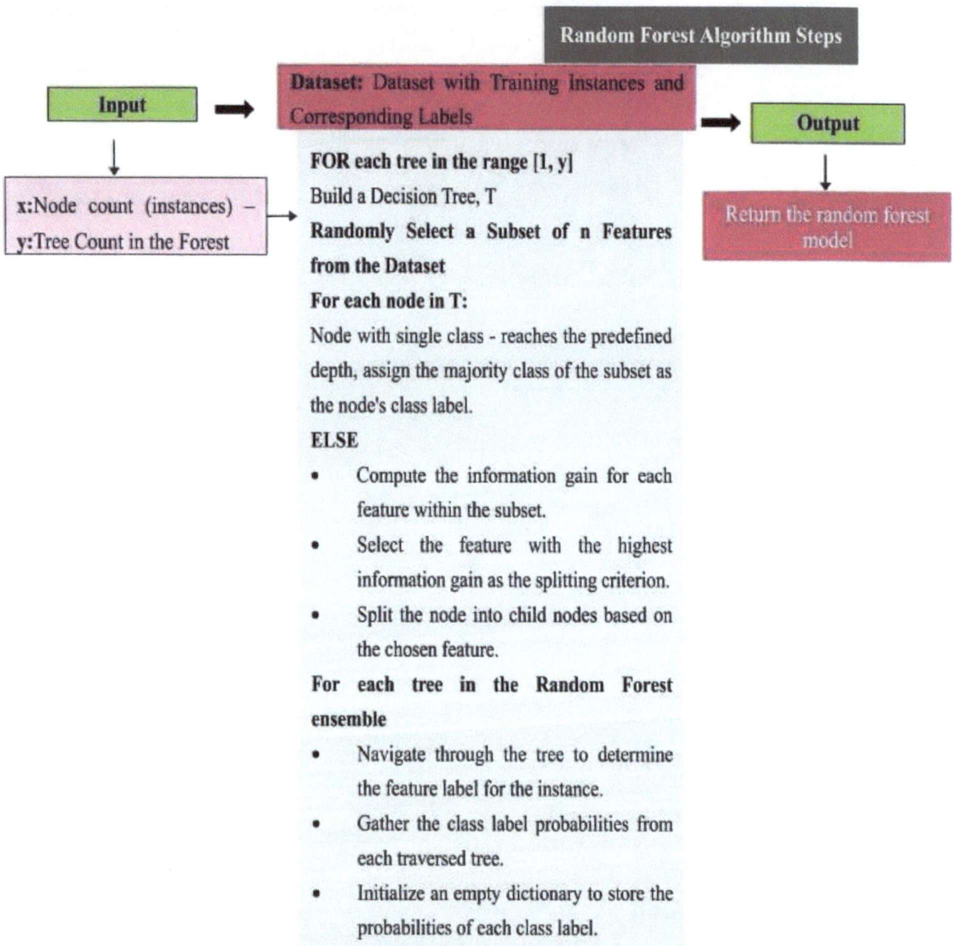

Fig. (7). Steps in the random forest algorithm.

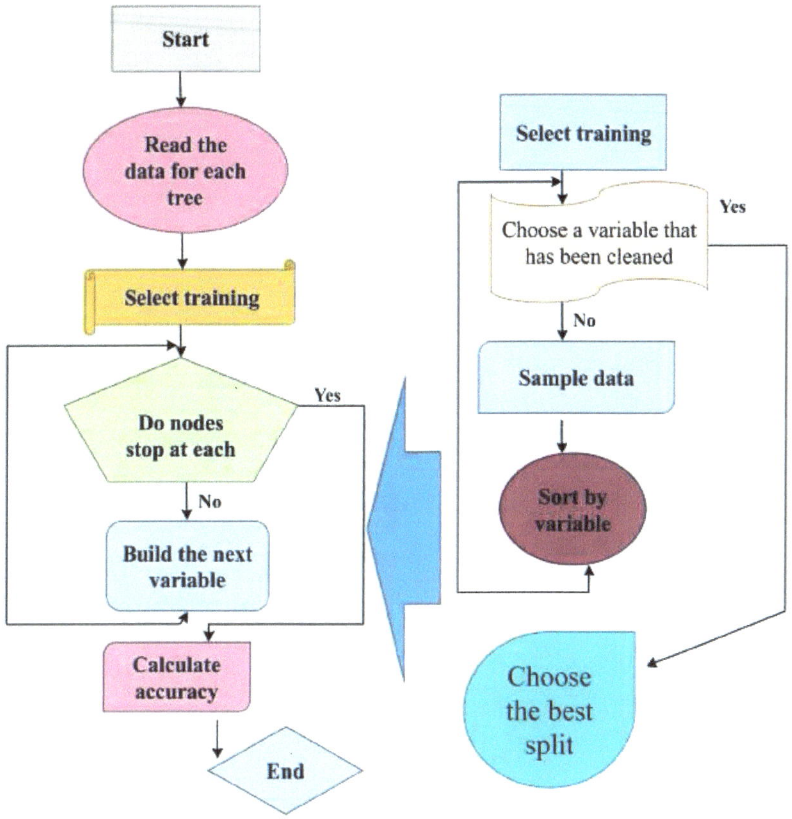

Fig. (8). Stages in the random forest algorithm.

Classification is the process of anticipating future occurrences based on present facts. Once a classification algorithm is developed, it is applied to the training dataset utilizing a range of classification techniques. Random Forest is a collective strategy that blends diverse decision trees to improve forecast accuracy. In a Random Forest, random samples are drawn from the dataset, and a decision tree is built for each model. This method is performed several times, with a new random sample selected for each iteration [18]. As a result, a diverse set of trees is constructed, each generating its own predictions. To combine these predictions into a final output, methods like averaging or majority voting are employed, ensuring a more robust and reliable result.

Key Features of Random Forest Aggression

- Does a good job of dealing with multicollinearity
- Strong and less likely to get overfit
- Can do both classification and regression jobs

Challenges in Random Forest Aggression

- Model Interpretability
- Overfitting
- High computational cost
- Imbalance data
- Loss of spatial or temporal correlation

Linear Regression

To determine a linear relationship and evaluate the spatial distribution of a dependent factor, linear regression is used, with a set of indigenous spectral data, terrain attributes, and climatic factors serving as independent variables [19]. Soil characteristics are identified as variables of dependency in this study.

Linear regressionmodels are commonly represented in the following form:

$$y = a + \sum bi\, xi \; +/\!- \mathcal{E}i$$

In this model, “y” = the dependent factor (soil parameter),

“xi” = predictors, “n” is the approximate number of predictors,

“a” = intercept, “bi” are the partial regression variables

“ε” = standard error.

Regional distribution of the feature of interest is then predicted using a regression model and the independent variables.

R’s **“lm”** package was employed to perform Multiple Linear Regression (MLR) analysis. The prediction matrix was developed by stacking experimental samples across spectral and spatial components and removing irrelevant data. The resulting matrix served as the prediction set, and each soil feature was separately modeled as the response (dependent) variable. The residual mean error and adjusted R^2 were computed for each model, and variables significant at the 1% level were identified.

Multicollinearity, which happens when variables have a high degree of correlation, is a frequent problem in regression models. To mitigate this issue and reduce multicollinearity, a stepwise regression analysis was initially performed. This approach selects a subset of uncorrelated predictors essential for modelling each soil parameter. Stepwise regression identifies the most significant predictors based on their statistical relevance, employing techniques such as forward selection, backward elimination, or a combination of both [20].

Despite the sole exception of carbon, which was picked in 53% of cases, each soil component had a typical selection rate of less than 50% of the original determinants. Although Random Forest Regression (RFR) is not as influenced by the multiple linearity problem, a similar set of variables was utilized for the RFR analysis to guarantee uniformity in the assessment with RFR.

Key Features in Linear Regression

- Easy to understand and use
- Works well with small datasets
- Measures the effect of predictors
- Assumes linearity

Challenges in Linear Regression

- Receptive to multiple linearity
- Needs to reduce the number of dimensions (for example, stepwise regression)
- Not as good for complicated nonlinear soil behaviour

Naive Bayes Algorithm

This method analyses fertilizer use statistics, computing odds for each category to identify the most likely one (Figs. **9** and **10**). The split validation approach, which separates the input information into distinct sets of training and testing to gauge the model's efficacy, was used to assess the correctness of the algorithm [21].

A Naive Bayes classifier is a straightforward probabilistic classification method in machine learning, belonging to a larger family of classifiers. It is based on Bayes' theorem, assuming feature independence [22]. Class labels are estimated based on the probability of a given instance. Naive Bayes requires only a small amount of training data to accurately predict class labels, making it highly efficient. This algorithm is particularly effective for datasets with multiclass predictors.

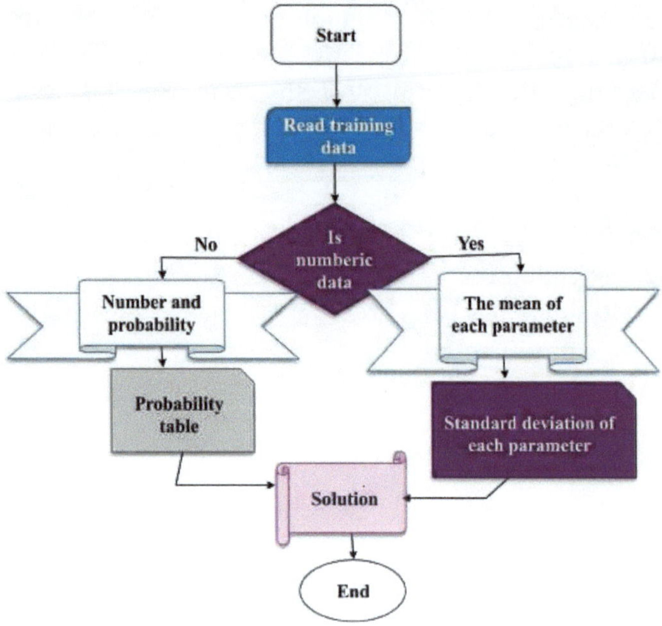

Fig. (9). Analysis stages of the naive bayes algorithm.

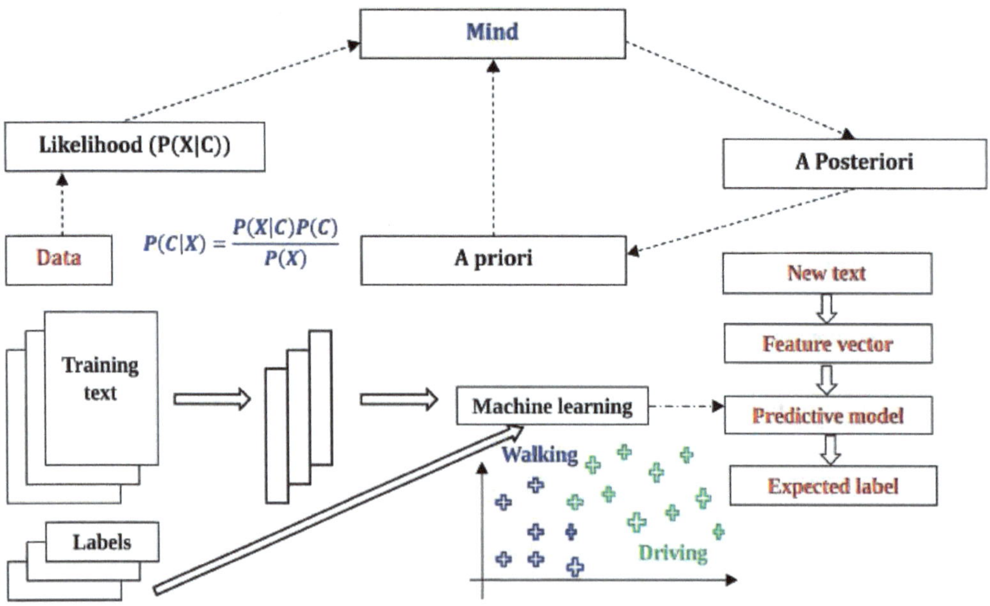

Fig. (10). Process and procedure of the naive bayes algorithm for classifying data.

Strength of Naive Bayes Algorithm

- Rapid and simple to understand
- Works effectively with datasets that have more than one class

Challenges of the Naive BayesAlgorithm

- Assumption of a distinct feature
- Zero likelihood problem
- Imbalanced class responsiveness
- Unfavourable estimation of probabilities

Multinomial Logistic Regression (MLR)

A generalised linear model is used to analyse response variables with several categories [23]. It aids in estimating the probable abundance of each soil type appearing in the investigated region. The MLR employs a non-linear log conversion to determine the likelihood of happening for any combination of dependent variable categories (in this example, soil class "y") using explanatory variables. Unlike linear regression models, MLR exhibits a sigmoidal curve, which distinguishes it from linear regression. MLR has been evaluated for soil mapping in various contexts, including soil data acquisition methods, landscape forms, and soil categorization. Because of discrepancies in data processing, there was a comparison between MLR and other algorithms in mapping soil, with accuracy differences observed depending on factors such as sampling schemes, covariate resolution and scale, landscape patterns, and the specific level and use of soil classification.

Field surveys and lab studies are costly aspects of soil mapping, and data retrieved from older soil polygon maps are usually used instead. This technique was assessed by many scientists, who have since made it popular; nonetheless, they all relied on traditional scale maps (1:50000) [24 - 26]. Likewise, another scientist evaluated MLR by comparing the usage of historical data to ground data from soil pits. The findings showed that MLR performance was improved when using an MLR-bagging approach, as opposed to a single MLR model [27].

Six seasonal variables, four soil attributes, and their interactions were evaluated using logistic regression to determine the influence of eight visual soil health indices. The algorithms, which incorporated soil and climatic factors, accounted for a considerable percentage of the differences in visual indicators. Separate algorithms were developed for each visual indication, taking into account both acidic-to-neutral and alkaline soils [28].

Strength of Multinomial Logistic Regression

- Can withstand several classes
- Interpretable model
- Mathematical framework
- Adaptable predictors

Challenges of Multinomial Logistic Regression

- Multicollinearity
- Requires plenty of data
- Overfitting
- Inability to operate with little data

HYPERSPECTRA REMOTE SENSING IN SOIL FERTILITY MAPPING

Hyperspectral remote sensing has established itself as a potent tool for nutrient mapping, providing precise spectral data that facilitate reliable assessment of soil attributes [29]. In contrast to multispectral sensors, which collect information in a restricted, wide spectral bands, hyperspectral sensors obtain reflectance data across hundreds of narrow, adjacent bands, enabling comprehensive evaluation of organic matter, macronutrients, micronutrients, and soil moisture (Table **1**). Hyperspectral remote sensing delivers a revolutionary method for assessing soil fertility mapping, facilitating accurate and economical assessment of soil health [30]. Revolutions in sensor software and information extraction methods will further integrate into precision agriculture and healthy land use, enhancing production and preserving the environment.

Table 1. Hyperspectral Sensors used in soil fertility mapping.

S. No	Hyperspectral Sensors	Properties
1	AVIRIS (Airborne Visible/Infrared Imaging Spectrometer)	Used for soil nutrient mapping, carbon assessment, and contamination studies.
2	Hyperion (onboard EO-1 satellite)	Monitors farmland deterioration and nutrient levels.
3	PRISMA (PRecursoreIperSpettraledellaMissioneApplicativa)	Precision agriculture, soil health assessment, and environmental monitoring.
4	EnMAP (Environmental mapping and Analysis program)	Identifies soil characteristics as well as fertility variations over vast areas.
5	HySpex	High Spectral and Spatial resolution for soil and crop monitoring

CONCLUSION

By allowing computers to automatically evaluate enormous volumes of data, spot trends, and draw conclusions without explicit programming, machine learning is revolutionizing a number of industries. The industrial sector, banking, and autonomous systems will expand as the discipline develops, offering more effective solutions to pressing issues. Machine learning systems can replicate some features of human learning and decision-making by producing predictions and decisions that become progressively more accurate through training on large datasets and ongoing improvement based on new information.

REFERENCES

[1] Alaoui A, Barão L, Ferreira CSS, Hessel R. An overview of sustainability assessment frameworks in agriculture. Land (Basel) 2022; 11(4): 537. [http://dx.doi.org/10.3390/land11040537]

[2] Lawrence PG, Roper W, Morris TF, Guillard K. Guiding soil sampling strategies using classical and spatial statistics: A review. Agron J 2020; 112(1): 493-510. [http://dx.doi.org/10.1002/agj2.20048]

[3] Guo M. Soil health assessment and management: Recent development in science and practices. Soil Syst 2021; 5(4): 61. [http://dx.doi.org/10.3390/soilsystems5040061]

[4] Çakmakçı R, Salık MA, Çakmakçı S. Assessment and principles of environmentally sustainable food and agriculture systems. Agriculture 2023; 13(5): 1073. [http://dx.doi.org/10.3390/agriculture13051073]

[5] Khaleel M, Jebrel A, Shwehdy DM. Artificial intelligence in computer science: international journal of electrical engineering and sustainability 2024; 1-21.

[6] Taherdoost H. Deep learning and neural networks: decision-making implications. Symmetry (Basel) 2023; 15(9): 1723. [http://dx.doi.org/10.3390/sym15091723]

[7] Folorunso O, Ojo O, Busari M, *et al.* Exploring machine learning models for soil nutrient properties prediction: A systematic review. Big Data and Cognitive Computing 2023; 7(2): 113. [http://dx.doi.org/10.3390/bdcc7020113]

[8] Rakshit Khajuria and S.S. Sunanda. A survey of existing leaf disease techniques using artificial neural network. International Journal of Computer Trends and Technology (IJCTT) 2018; 59(1): 2231-803. [http://dx.doi.org/10.14445/22312803/IJCTT-V59P109]

[9] Sujatha M, Jaidhar CD. Machine learning-based approaches to enhance the soil fertility. Expert Syst Appl 2023; 122557. [http://dx.doi.org/10.1016/j.eswa.2023.122557]

[10] Gülcü Ş. Training of the feed forward artificial neural networks using dragonfly algorithm. Appl Soft Comput 2022; 124: 109023. [http://dx.doi.org/10.1016/j.asoc.2022.109023]

[11] Attri I, Awasthi LK, Sharma TP, Rathee P. A review of deep learning techniques used in agriculture. Ecological Informatics 2023; p. 102217. [http://dx.doi.org/10.1016/j.ecoinf.2023.102217]

[12] Liu Y, Pu H, Sun DW. Efficient extraction of deep image features using convolutional neural network (CNN) for applications in detecting and analysing complex food matrices. Trends Food Sci Technol

2021; 113: 193-204.
[http://dx.doi.org/10.1016/j.tifs.2021.04.042]

[13] Mienye ID, Swart TG, Obaido G. Recurrent neural networks: A comprehensive review of architectures, variants, and applications. Information (Basel) 2024; 15(9): 517.
[http://dx.doi.org/10.3390/info15090517]

[14] Sangiorgio M, Dercole F. Robustness of LSTM neural networks for multi-step forecasting of chaotic time series. Chaos Solitons Fractals 2020; 139: 110045.
[http://dx.doi.org/10.1016/j.chaos.2020.110045]

[15] Jain S, Sethia D, Tiwari KC. A critical systematic review on spectral-based soil nutrient prediction using machine learning. Environ Monit Assess 2024; 196(8): 699.
[http://dx.doi.org/10.1007/s10661-024-12817-6] [PMID: 38963427]

[16] Nivaashini M, Priyanka G, Aarthi S. Deep Neural Machine Translation (DNMT). Hybrid deep learning architecture-based english-to-indian language translation. automatic speech recognition and translation for low resource languages 2024; pp. 331-73.
[http://dx.doi.org/10.1002/9781394214624.ch16]

[17] Sun Z, Wang G, Li P, Wang H, Zhang M, Liang X. An improved random forest based on the classification accuracy and correlation measurement of decision trees. Expert Syst Appl 2024; 237: 121549.
[http://dx.doi.org/10.1016/j.eswa.2023.121549]

[18] Lan T, Hu H, Jiang C, Yang G, Zhao Z. A comparative study of decision tree, random forest, and convolutional neural network for spread-F identification. Adv Space Res 2020; 65(8): 2052-61.
[http://dx.doi.org/10.1016/j.asr.2020.01.036]

[19] Taripanah F, Ranjbar A. Quantitative analysis of spatial distribution of land surface temperature (LST) in relation Ecohydrological, terrain and socio- economic factors based on Landsat data in mountainous area. Adv Space Res 2021; 68(9): 3622-40.
[http://dx.doi.org/10.1016/j.asr.2021.07.008]

[20] Ullmann T, Heinze G, Hafermann L, Schilhart-Wallisch C, Dunkler D. for TG2 of the STRATOS initiative. Evaluating variable selection methods for multivariable regression models: A simulation study protocol. PLoS One 2024; 19(8): e0308543.
[http://dx.doi.org/10.1371/journal.pone.0308543] [PMID: 39121055]

[21] Prathivi R, Sharifzadeh S, Sharifzadeh S. Performance evaluation of naive bayes algorithm for classification of fertilizer types. Telematika 2022; 15(1): 57-69.
[http://dx.doi.org/10.35671/telematika.v15i1.1410]

[22] Rrmoku K, Selimi B, Ahmedi L. Application of trust in recommender systems—utilizing naive Bayes classifier. Computation (Basel) 2022; 10(1): 6.
[http://dx.doi.org/10.3390/computation10010006]

[23] Hosmer DW, Lemeshow S. Applied logistic regression. New York: John Wiley & Sons 1989.

[24] Giasson E, Figueiredo SR, Tornquist CG, Clarke RT. Digital soil mapping using logistic regression on terrain parameters for several ecological regions in Southern Brazil. Springer 2008; pp. 225-32.
[http://dx.doi.org/10.1007/978-1-4020-8592-5_19]

[25] Kempen B, Brus DJ, Heuvelink GBM, Stoorvogel JJ. Updating the 1:50,000 Dutch soil map using legacy soil data: A multinomial logistic regression approach. Geoderma 2009; 151(3-4): 311-26.
[http://dx.doi.org/10.1016/j.geoderma.2009.04.023]

[26] ten Caten A, Dalmolin RSD, Pedron FA, Mendonça-Santos ML. Regressões Logísticas Múltiplas: fatores que influenciam sua aplicação na predição de classes de solos. Rev Bras Ciênc Solo 2011; 35(1): 53-62.
[http://dx.doi.org/10.1590/S0100-06832011000100005]

[27] Heung B, Ho HC, Zhang J, Knudby A, Bulmer CE, Schmidt MG. An overview and comparison of

machine-learning techniques for classification purposes in digital soil mapping. Geoderma 2016; 265: 62-77.
[http://dx.doi.org/10.1016/j.geoderma.2015.11.014]

[28] Teixeira F. The effects of climate and soil properties on the magnitude of the visual soil quality indicators: a logistic regression approach. AIMS Geosci 2023; 9(3): 492-512.
[http://dx.doi.org/10.3934/geosci.2023027]

[29] Benipal DS, Pasricha NS, Singh R. Potassium release to proton saturated resin and its diffusion characteristics in some alluvial soils. Geoderma 2006; 132(3-4): 464-470.
[http://dx.doi.org/10.1016/j.geoderma.2005.06.007]

[30] Abdulraheem MI, Zhang W, Li S, Moshayedi AJ, Farooque AA, Hu J. Advancement of remote sensing for soil measurements and applications: A comprehensive review. Sustainability (Basel) 2023; 15(21): 15444.
[http://dx.doi.org/10.3390/su152115444]

CHAPTER 13

Advanced Remote Sensing Techniques for Monitoring Agricultural Changes

Jay Arindam Maity[1], **Sangeetha Annam**[1,*] and **Akinchan Maity**[1]

[1] *Chitkara University Institute of Engineering and Technology, Chitkara University, Punjab, India*

Abstract: Agricultural activity is of great importance for a sustainable future and economic growth. With limited resources and manpower, it is important to use them efficiently for optimum results. Smart agricultural systems incorporating remote sensing tools can help optimize and simplify agricultural systems. Ensuring food security, maximizing resource use, and tackling climate variability all depend on monitoring agricultural developments. Because they offer quick, precise, and scalable insights regarding crop development, soil health, and environmental effects, advanced methods of remote sensing have completely changed this process. Precision farming and sustainable land management are supported by these methods, which integrate high-resolution information with machine learning, artificial intelligence, and geospatial technologies. This chapter discusses the potential applications and methodology for applying remote sensing for improved yields of crops. A literature review of different implementations and solutions proposed by other researchers in the field of agriculture using remote sensing is also discussed.

Keywords: Precision agriculture, Remote sensing, Smart agricultural systems.

INTRODUCTION

The growing world population means a growing need for resources and food supply. This increased requirement, if not satisfied, is a great threat to the quality of life and a sustainable future. To circumvent this issue, given the limited availability of resources, more efficient and sustainable solutions need to be brought to life. A clear requirement for a growing population is food; this means an increased requirement for higher-quality and efficient crop production. To ensure better crop production on a large scale, the extent of crops also needs to be monitored efficiently. For this, remote sensing can be implemented to get insights about different parameters relating to crop growth on a wide range.

* **Corresponding author Sangeetha Annam**: Chitkara University Institute of Engineering and Technology, Chitkara University, Punjab, India; E-mail: a.sangeeta@chitkara.edu.in

Sartajvir Singh, Neelam Dahiya, Maged Mohammed, Abdullah Alzharihi & Vishal Dutt (Eds.)

Remote Sensing Evolution

With the advent of imaging and satellite technologies paired with Artificial Intelligence (AI), the capabilities of remote sensing have improved significantly. Remote sensing is the process of using recording equipment that is not in close proximity to the features being observed (usually from a certain distance), in order to gather and measure data on certain characteristics of materials, objects, or occurrences. RS employs two different types of sensors, namely active sensors and passive sensors. Natural radiations that are reflected or released from the earth are detected by passive sensors. On the other hand, active sensors (like LIDAR and RADAR) are those that emit electromagnetic radiation of their own. RS is extensively used in the fields of agriculture, geostatistics, disaster management, climate monitoring, biodiversity monitoring, *etc.* Remote sensing in the hyperspectral range records hundreds of continuous, narrow spectral bands, permits thorough examination of soil composition, crop health, and nutrient status, identifies crop disease, stress, and nutritional deficits early, and supports mapping soil health and applying fertilizer precisely. Employing RS-based solutions for various real-life problems tends to be more efficient compared to traditional approaches.

Methods and Techniques of Remote Sensing

As discussed above, RS is used to extract meaningful information about a physical entity or region without coming in physical contact with it. The same can be implemented with different methodologies, each with its own advantages and limitations. In this section, the different methodologies and the technologies they employ are presented.

Satellite-Based Remote Sensing

Satellite-based RS technologies typically depend on electromagnetic radiation for collecting information, which may use Synthetic Aperture Radar (SAR) or Multispectral Imaging (MI). An imaging radar installed on a moving platform is called a SAR [1]. The meaning behind "Synthetic Aperture" in SAR springs from the nature of the radar, which "simulates" a larger aperture by using the motion of a satellite platform. In SAR, Electromagnetic (EM) waves of varying wavelengths and intensities are successively broadcast, just as in a traditional radar. An energy pulse is released, reacts with physical structures, and is then backtracked to the SAR for imaging. Applications for SAR are numerous and include mapping wetlands [2], following oil spill routes [3], and researching icebergs [4]. MI in Satellite-based RS is implemented by detecting radiation across different bands or wavelengths reflected or emitted by the planet. The data from the sensors is then used to create images that resemble photographs captured by a camera high in space. Multispectral (MS) imaging is the most popular technique for gathering data about vegetation. These MS photos are typically obtained from satellites or airplanes, although they are typically costly. Furthermore, cloud cover frequently affects satellite data, which presents a problem for image interpretation. Unmanned Aerial Vehicle (UAV)-based MS image acquisition is a flexible and useful method. Depending on the geographic area, medium-sized and big farms choose to use this strategy to varying degrees. The adoption rate for crop farms in the USA is 67%, which is significantly higher than the average of 25% for the EU [5].

Aerial Remote Sensing

Aerial Remote Sensing employs airborne platforms that are not necessarily satellite-based and are usually close to the observed area. For this, platforms like UAVs or aeroplanes are embedded with RS tools to gather data [6]. Compared to satellite-based solutions, Aerial RS tends to be cheaper and more accessible, given the high cost of implementation of satellites and other tools used for satellite-based RS [7]. Due to the limited number of satellites and their reliance on the weather, using satellite imagery is very expensive and not feasible for small farms [8]. These factors make satellite imagery impractical. Commercial flights were the most practical means of acquiring aerial photos until recently, but they are still very expensive and scarce because there are so few businesses that specialize in this activity. Numerous businesses devoted to the production of small UAVs have been bolstered by the development of compact integrated inertial sensors and the decline in the price of high-precision GPS receivers, making UAVs an efficient and practical solution for many farmers.

A cutting-edge imaging technique called hyperspectral remote sensing (HRS) gathers and analyzes data from all over the electromagnetic spectrum. Hyperspectral sensors measure reflectance in hundreds of small, contiguous bands, usually between 400 and 2500 nanometers (visible to shortwave infrared), in contrast to standard imaging systems that only record a few spectral bands (such as red, green, blue, or near-infrared). Hyperspectral sensors pick up on how an object transmits, reflects, or absorbs light. Each element has a distinct spectral signature, including water, plants, dirt, *etc.* HRS can precisely identify and measure particular materials or circumstances by examining these spectral characteristics.

Use of Hyperspectral Remote Sensing in Agriculture

In the field of agriculture, various parameters affect overall crop production and therefore need to be optimized for better yields and sustainability. However, manually measuring these parameters through traditional methods can be time-consuming and require significant manpower. Utilizing RS technologies for this task is more efficient and requires less manpower. With the help of remote sensing, various crop-related parameters can be accessed, enabling decisions to improve crop yields and reduce resource waste. This process of using RS to access crop information and, based on that, implement appropriate agricultural activities/solutions is called Precision Agriculture (PA). For PA, Decision Support Systems (DSS) are often implemented for making optimum decisions. With great accuracy and precision, HRS enables both farmers and scientists to promote sustainable farming methods, optimize resource use, and monitor crop health.

Fig. (**1**) shows an overview of the implementation of remote sensing in agriculture.

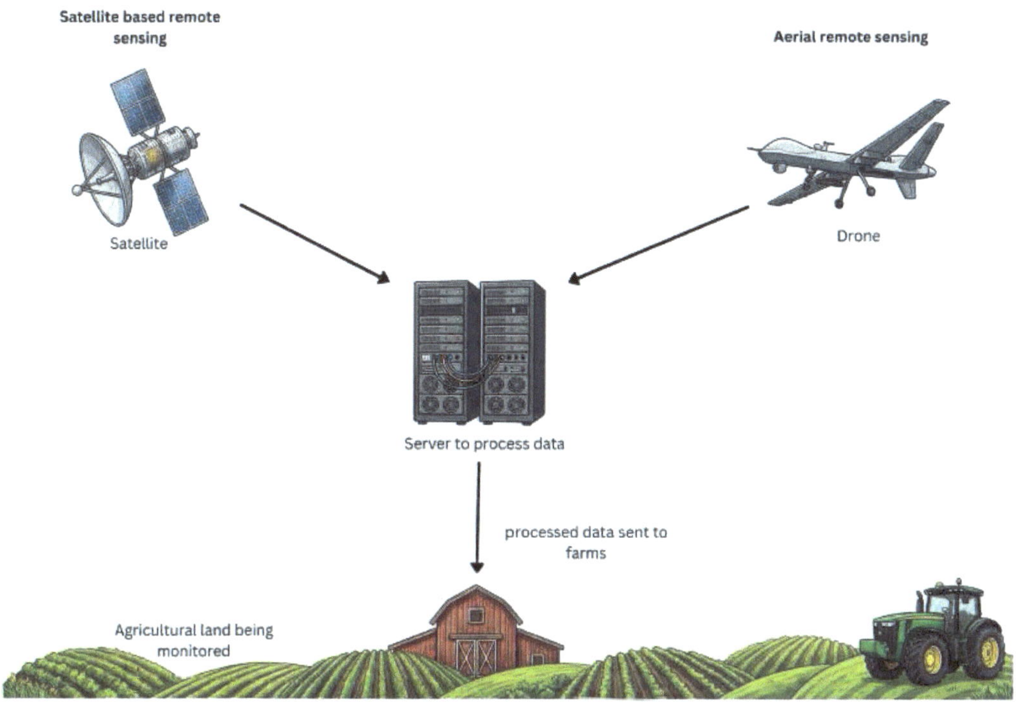

Fig. (1). Aerial and satellite-based remote sensing in agriculture.

To better understand the role of RS in PA and the different methodologies related to it, a review of the literature on the works of different researchers is presented.

METHODOLOGIES USED IN HYPERSPECTRAL RS

HRS is often used in PA for its ability to provide data across a large region of land at once (relative to traditional techniques, where data may be collected manually for each crop). There exists a number of RS techniques targeting a wide range of agricultural parameters. The process of gathering, processing, and evaluating high-resolution spectrum data from hundreds of adjacent spectral bands is known as hyperspectral remote sensing, or HRS. At different phases of the hyperspectral procedure, different approaches and techniques are employed to extract relevant information from this complicated dataset. In this section, the methodologies used by researchers, along with their outcomes, are discussed.

The authors in a previous study [9] aimed to demonstrate how a learning community method, proposed by the Upper Midwest Aerospace Consortium (UMAC), combines application development, data supply, and training to give remote sensing technology-based management tools to precision farmers. Their training involved demonstrating imaging and mapping technologies by educating farmers about these applications and technologies through "hands-on" training seminars. The study also aimed to collaborate with farmers for collaborative learning and experimentation, the results of which were used for the research of improved PA technologies. The authors applied RS technologies for tasks of monitoring crop (wheat) with Normalized Difference Vegetation Index, monitoring field conditions and stress detection, mapping regions for variable rate application of nitrogen and assessing its results, detecting any infestation or disease, and assessing any damage. In another study [10], the authors discussed the growing trend of optimizing fertilization techniques using data from RS systems to achieve higher yields, sustained use, and an environmentally friendly approach to fertilizer. The study highlighted the drawbacks of conventional fertilization approaches and discussed the advantages and common methodologies of modern precision agriculture solutions for optimizing fertilizer use. The common methodology discussed included mapping nutrient-deficient regions for fertilizer application; the mapping data is usually derived from RS technologies. In a study [11], the authors explained the concept of Microwave RS and its applications in drought monitoring. The study explored the current state of Microwave RS, discussing its advantages and challenges. Using various satellite- and model-based data sets on rainfall, SM, vegetation, and their combinations, a case study over Senegal illustrated the potential of microwave remote sensing for drought monitoring. The authors [12] used UAVs to study potato fields with an objective to assess and improve the performance of current radiometric correction methods in different lighting scenarios, with a focus on radiometric accuracy and homogeneity, for more accurate RS data. The authors [13] discussed the applications and drawbacks of different RS techniques for crop classification, primarily focusing on Deep Learning methods, such as CNNs for image classification and their advantages over Machine Learning approaches. In another study [14], the authors discussed applications of RS using UAVs and Artificial Intelligence in disease detection of different crops. Optical imaging instruments attached to UAVs are used to obtain crop image data, which is then processed by ML, DL, or statistical methods for crop disease assessment.

There are many more similar studies that employ HRS technologies to enhance crop yield. Some more related studies are shown in Table **1**.

Table 1. Studies using HRS in agriculture.

Ref No.	Year	Objective	Sensing Type	Region of Study
[15]	2024	Study agricultural water productivity	Geospatial	Lebanon
[16]	2024	Evaluate soil moisture content	UAV	Jinzhong, China
[17]	2024	Corn Yield Estimation	UAV	Liaoning Province, China
[18]	2025	Access Weed Infestation Level	UAV, Geospatial	Zhytomyr Oblast, Ukraine
[19]	2025	Drought Assessment	Geospatial	Tamil Nadu, India
[20]	2025	Agricultural Burn Area Detection	Geospatial	Punjab, India
[19]	2025	Crop Identification and Acreage Estimation	Geospatial	Anand, Gujarat, India

All the applications discussed in this section focus on obtaining information about one or more agricultural factors of the crops. A qualitative introduction about each of these factors is provided in the following section to better understand what affects crop growth.

AGRICULTURAL FACTORS TO MONITOR WITH HYPERSPECTRAL RS

As stated above, agriculture involves a wide range of factors that ultimately affect the yield of crops. High-resolution spectrum data over hundreds of bands is captured using Hyperspectral Remote Sensing (HRS), which makes it possible to monitor a variety of agricultural parameters. This makes it possible to identify, measure, and record the traits of plants and soil that are crucial for sustainable agriculture and precision farming. For PA, there is a need to understand and mitigate any problem that may be related to any of the above factors. Therefore, it is important to properly study and understand these factors. The main agricultural factors that are measured with RS techniques for crop monitoring are soil health, plant health, water quality, and weather. A brief explanation of what these factors are is provided in this section.

Soil Health

Soil quality and its nutrient content are the most significant factors that affect a plant's health and the crop's yield. It is important to ensure that the soil being used for agriculture is healthy and does not lose its fertility over time, for better use of land resources. The factors that are actively used in the evaluation of SQI are discussed in this section. Fig. (**2**) highlights the factors that affect soil health.

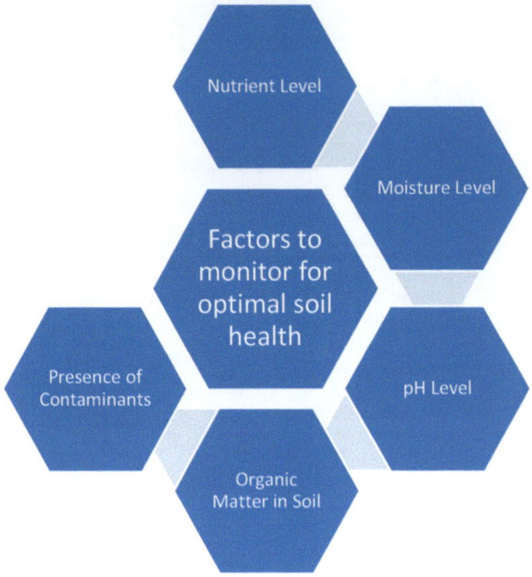

Fig. (2). Factors to monitor for optimal soil health.

Nutrient Level

The nutrient level of the soil is one of the most important factors for plant growth. The presence of macronutrients (Nitrogen, Phosphorus, Potassium) and micronutrients (Iron, Zinc, and Manganese) is essential for plant growth [21]. Lack of these nutrients can lead to stunted plant growth or disease. If these nutrients are in excess, this may lead to poisoning of plants, ultimately damaging the crop and yield. To prevent any kind of damage, remote monitoring of nutrient levels is very essential.

Soil Type and Soil Texture

To grow a specific crop, while expecting maximum yields, it is important to determine the best soil type required for the crop. One of the most significant analyses for soil type detection is texture analysis [22]. This also helps in the estimation of soil properties like water retention, nutrient levels, and porosity.

Moisture Index

The moisture index of soil is also a key factor for the growth of plants; one of the main reasons for this is the plant's need for water to absorb nutrients from the soil and photosynthesis [23]. Lack of proper moisture levels makes the plant wilt and have slower growth rates. On the other hand, excess moisture makes the plants rot or prone to fungal diseases. All this makes it very essential to monitor the moisture content of the soil.

pH Level

pH of soil affects the availability of nutrients in soil; the ideal pH range for soil is about 6.0 to 7.5. Acidic soil can cause a deficiency of nutrients, such as phosphorus, calcium, and magnesium, while also increasing aluminium toxicity [24]. If the soil is alkaline, it can limit the intake of iron, manganese, and phosphorus. To prevent any kind of nutrient deficiency and have the ideal nutrient intake, it is important to monitor and account for the pH levels of the soil.

Soil Organic Matter

Organic matter in soil is another very important factor for maintaining ideal soil health. A soil with good organic matter has better water and nutrient retention capabilities and more nutrient cycling due to enhanced microbial activities [25]. All these capabilities of organic matter in soil lead to better plant health, resulting in ideal produce. Thus, soil organic matter is another factor that cannot be ignored and therefore must be monitored through remote sensing.

Presence of Contaminants

The presence of any kind of contaminant could be lethal for plant growth in many ways. The presence of heavy metals (lead, arsenic, and cadmium) in soil can be toxic for plants [26]. Pesticides and herbicides also act as contaminants; they may poison the plant's produce and also disrupt the microbial life in soil [27]. Monitoring of contaminants through remote sensing can better help understand the steps that can be taken to prevent any kind of negative damage to plants.

These factors, although useful for the identification of soil health, can be difficult to compare or provide a proper scale for measuring soil health. For this, a Soil Quality Index (SQI) is needed, which provides a framework for analysing soil health. This soil quality index may be used to map fertile soil areas [28].

Plant Growth and Health

The main objective of using hyperspectral RS in agriculture is to ensure that crops grow optimally; plant growth rate and plant health cannot be ignored. Some of the factors responsible for plant growth and health are shown in Fig. (**3**) and discussed below.

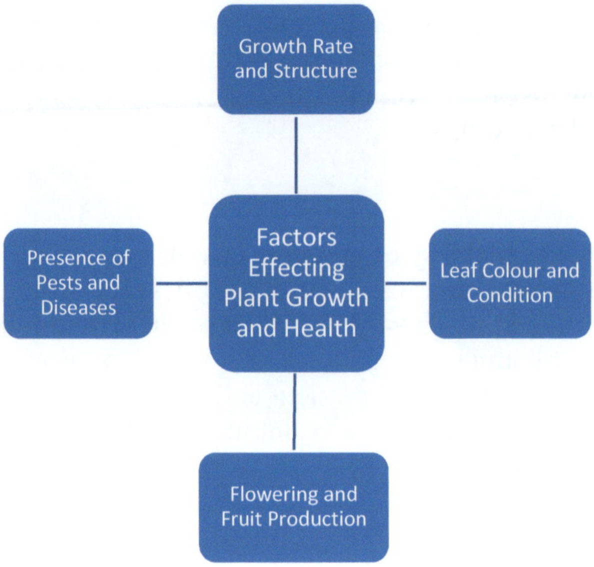

Fig. (3). Factors affecting plant growth and health.

Any of the listed factors can result in a significant decline in plant growth and health.

Growth Rate and Structure

One of the signs of optimal plant health is its growth rate and structure. Signs of ideal growth rate include new plant parts (leaves, stems, roots), a strong and upright structure with no weak stems. The presence of well-spaced branches is also another sign of healthy growth. Monitoring of these factors through remote sensing helps in the detection of anomalies before they can happen.

Leaf Colour and Condition

Leaf colour and condition also help in the determination of plant growth and health. For most plants, vibrant green leaves are considered healthy, and other shades might indicate some underlying problem. Yellow leaves indicate poor nitrogen levels, overwatering, and poor drainage. Brown leaves indicate a lack of water, salt buildup, or wind damage. Purple leaves indicate phosphorus deficiency. Spots/holes in leaves and curly leaves indicate the presence of pests and diseases.

Flowering and Fruit Production

Flowering and fruit production are also ways to evaluate plant growth. A healthy plant has regular blooming and fruiting, where flowers are bright, and fruits are well-formed. The presence of no flowers or fruits is an indication of a lack of nutrition, inadequate light, or stress. These factors can also indicate other issues, such as overfertilization and pollination problems. Monitoring flowering and fruit production through remote sensing can also be beneficial.

Pest and Disease Signs

Signs of pests and disease are also factors to look for when monitoring plant growth and health. Ideally, a plant should have no visible insect damage or disease spots. Strong and resilient stems are also an indication of the absence of pests and diseases. Presence of pests and diseases is indicated by chewed leaves, sticky residue on leaves, white powdery or black mould, and wilting despite good care. Monitoring of these factors through remote monitoring can help understand these symptoms in early stages and prevent excessive damage to plants.

Weather and Environmental Indices

Weather and environmental indices also play a key role in plant growth, especially in the case of agriculture. There are various factors that are discussed further, which will add to the importance of considering environmental indices in plant growth. Fig. (**4**) illustrates the weather and environmental indices that affect agricultural growth.

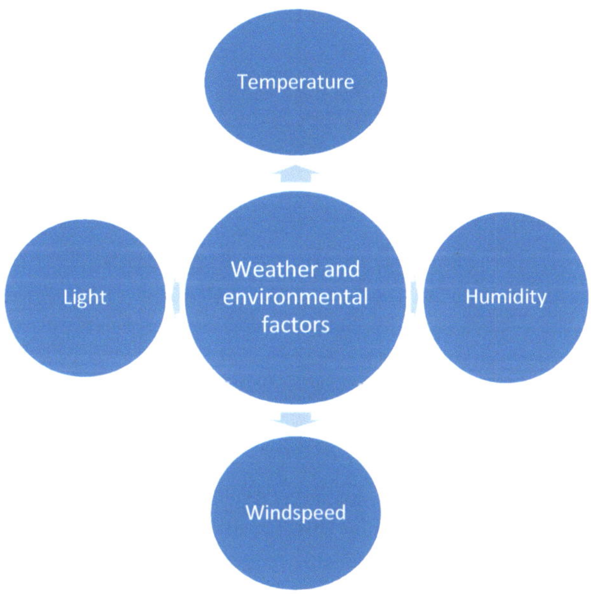

Fig. (4). Weather and Environmental indices for agricultural analysis.

All these factors, when monitored through remote sensing, ensure that a wide range of data is covered in the most precise and efficient manner.

Effects of Temperature

Environmental and root temperatures also play a significant role in plant health analysis [29, 30]. Some plants may require higher temperatures for ideal growth, and some may require lower temperatures. Hence, the effects of temperature cannot be ignored while monitoring for crop growth. For some plants, lower temperatures may decrease the enzyme activity photosynthesis, and growth.

Effects of Humidity

The humidity (air moisture level) of the region also affects crop growth significantly. Maintaining the humidity levels in the plant (high humidity) can promote plant growth by keeping the stomata open, which enables photosynthesis to continue and reduces dehydration [31]. Further, low humidity conditions have been observed to assist in plant water loss and to reduce Carbon Dioxide (CO_2) diffusion. From the above, it is obvious that the humidity levels play a big role in plant growth, as they directly influence the process of photosynthesis in plants.

Effects of Light

Since plants are sedentary and photoautotrophic, the constantly shifting light environment has a significant impact on them during their whole life cycle. Through the process of photosynthesis, higher plants convert solar energy into chemical energy. The main pigment involved in photosynthesis, chlorophyll A, absorbs light at a wavelength of 430–662 nm. Chlorophyll plays a crucial part in the energy transfer to the reaction centre. Chlorophyll B helps organisms transform light spectrum energy into chemical energy by absorbing blue light with wavelengths between 453 and 642 nm [32]. Throughout their life cycle, they also employ light as an informational signal to regulate a wide range of physiological responses [33].

Effects of Wind

It is well known that plants develop differently in windy conditions than in less windy conditions: roses grow shorter, and trees bend leeward. Furthermore, wind frequently causes irrevocable harm to plants, such as windthrow, branch breakage, and leaf tearing [34]. Different wind conditions have also been studied to affect the extent of photosynthesis [35]. From this discussion, the effects of wind on plant growth can be well understood.

With a brief overview of these different parameters, there is still a need to discuss ways of how these parameters may be measured and processed. The same will be discussed in the following section, with reference to various solutions proposed by researchers.

TECHNIQUES FOR PROCESSING AND MONITORING THE DATA THROUGH HYPERSPECTRAL REMOTE SENSING

In this section, the applications and methodologies of RS used for accessing valuable data on the agricultural factors discussed above are reviewed. With hundreds of spectrum bands per pixel, Hyperspectral Remote Sensing (HRS) creates massive, high-dimensional datasets. Throughout the workflow, from raw data gathering to final analysis and interpretation, a number of sophisticated data processing techniques are employed to extract usable information for agricultural monitoring and other applications. Various techniques include pre-processing, dimensionality reduction, classification using machine learning and deep learning algorithms, vegetation and soil indices, *etc.* Numerous studies employ RS in agriculture. Some of them are discussed here. In a study [36], the authors applied IoT and RS-based solutions for analysing soil health and weather conditions and used them for precision agriculture. The authors in another study [37] utilized remote sensing data from the Landsat Enhanced Thematic Mapper (ETM) for soil texture estimation. The remote sensing data obtained from LANDSAT was evaluated using three different methods: multiple stepwise regression (MSR) based on the correlation between remote sensing data and the amounts of sand, silt, and clay in the surface soil; kriging the amount of sand, silt, and clay in the surface soil; and cokriging with data from remote sensing. The authors [38] employed UAV drones for plant health monitoring by analysing different plant health factors. Using a variety of sensors and cameras, the drone technology automatically takes pictures of diseased plants. Following feature extraction, image data was processed using deep learning or conventional machine learning algorithms. Using histogram equalization techniques, features were taken out of plant photos. This helped assess plant health and detect diseases using UAV drones and optical images. Table **2** showcases studies that aimed to monitor soil factors using RS. Common abbreviations used in the table include Infrared (IR), Near Infrared (NIR), Short Wave Infrared (SWIR), Visible (VIS), Thermal Infrared (TIR), Microwave (MW), and Visible Near Infrared (VNIR).

Table 2. Soil factors and the types of imaging used to analyse them.

Ref No.	Soil Factor Monitored	Type of Imaging
[39, 40]	Nutrient Level	IR
[41, 42]	Texture	NIR, VIS

(Table 2) cont.....

Ref No.	Soil Factor Monitored	Type of Imaging
[43 - 45]	Moisture	MW, TIR
[46, 47]	pH	NIR, VIS
[48, 49]	Organic Matter	VIS, NIR, SWIR
[50 - 52]	Contaminant	VNIR, SWIR, TIR

This data, obtained from RS alone is not practical unless used to optimize crop production. This is discussed in the subsequent section, which covers the workflow and integration of RS data with Decision Support Systems.

Workflow and Integration with Decision Support Systems

The data obtained from various sources, including hyperspectral RS, integrated with decision support systems, enables advanced implementation of agricultural solutions in precision agriculture. For example, creating a map of the region from the obtained data and analyzing it to identify areas where fertilizer or water may be required. Finally, this allows automation of supplementary fertilization or irrigation through Variable Application Systems [53]. The exact process is discussed in detail in this section.

Models that employ information and communication technology for intricate accounting and result evaluation are known as Decision Support Systems (DSSs). Numerous methods, such as process-based, empirical, and/or Artificial Intelligence (AI) techniques, can be used to develop these models. In agriculture, empirical models are statistical models based on observations between variables; process-based models are typically mathematical representations of biogeochemical and physical systems; and machine learning models generate predictions based on patterns identified in the data set. The special suitability of ML/AI models for Precision Agriculture (PA) stems from the fact that they learn as new input data is supplied, which sets them apart from process-based and empirical models [54].

Current Limitations

There are several hindrances to the use of remote sensing in current times. These factors reduce the efficiency of remote sensing significantly. One of these factors is existing technology. Existing technologies, such as satellites and some sensors, are too expensive for agricultural remote sensing and may also be prone to errors and technical malfunctions. All these factors make the existing technology difficult to work with for remote sensing. Another factor that limits the use of remote sensing techniques is weather conditions. Unfavourable weather conditions like storms, heavy rain, high temperatures, *etc.*, can create a negative impact on agricultural fields, destroying the crops and thus rendering the entire process of remote sensing useless. Animals can also cause significant damage to agricultural fields, which cannot currently be addressed in a timely manner with remote sensing. Fig. (**5**) provides a pictorial representation of the limitations of remote sensing technologies.

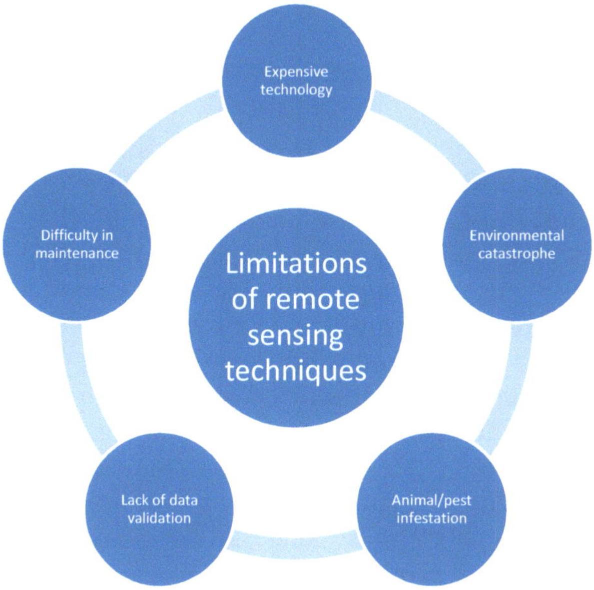

Fig. (5). Limitations of remote sensing techniques.

Methods of hyperspectral remote sensing are also slowed down by latency in data processing and transmission, which can be a significant hindrance to real-time field monitoring. Validation of data is another problem faced by remote sensing; this is mainly because monitoring large fields is a difficult task for an individual, and confirmation of data insights may take more time if using other means. Maintenance of devices and technology used in RS is also difficult. All these factors make the process of remote sensing unreliable at the current time. Further, similar limitations of RS technologies are discussed in other studies [55 - 58].

FUTURE SCOPE

With some advancements, hyperspectral RS could be the next essential tool for modern agricultural practices. One such advancement is the integration of artificial intelligence for advanced decision support systems. The integration of artificial intelligence will account for more conceivable factors and guide better decisions for optimal yields. Improvements in technology and sensors will also increase the accuracy and reliability of remote sensing systems, and their increased efficiency can also be used for large-scale monitoring practices, reducing the overall costs and making it an ideal choice for evaluating fields. Increased awareness of technological growth will also help farmers better adapt and use these technologies to their advantage, resulting in more efficient production and workflows. Increased funding from NGOs and governmental organisations will also help in the research and development of remote monitoring systems.

CONCLUSION

With the advent of technology and the growing needs of humanity, it is important to effectively use our knowledge and resources available to ensure a sustainable future. For this, the significance of sustainable agriculture was discussed in this chapter. With limited agricultural land, the need for improving agricultural yields is recognized. Employing smart agricultural solutions involving remote sensing has shown great potential in improving and making the process of agriculture much more efficient. Processing and keeping an eye on preprocessing, dimensionality reduction, classification, and machine learning approaches are all necessary for hyperspectral data. HRS is a key component of precision agriculture and environmental monitoring because of these techniques, which enable accurate evaluation of crop health, soil quality, and agricultural change detection. Any limitations that still exist need to be analysed for potential solutions, ensuring sustainable development and economic growth.

REFERENCES

[1] Franceschetti G, Lanari R. Synthetic aperture radar processing. CRC press 2018. [http://dx.doi.org/10.1201/9780203737484]

[2] Brisco B. Mapping and monitoring surface water and wetlands with synthetic aperture radar Remote Sensing of Wetlands: Applications and Advances. 2015; pp. 119-36.

[3] Zhang Y, Li Y, Lin H. Oil-spill pollution remote sensing by synthetic aperture radar Advanced geoscience remote sensing, 2. 2014; pp. 27-50. [http://dx.doi.org/10.5772/57477]

[4] Akbari V, Brekke C. Iceberg detection in open and ice-infested waters using C-band polarimetric synthetic aperture radar. IEEE Trans Geosci Remote Sens 2018; 56(1): 407-21. [http://dx.doi.org/10.1109/TGRS.2017.2748394]

[5] Bai A, Kovách I, Czibere I, Megyesi B, Balogh P. Examining the adoption of drones and categorisation of precision elements among Hungarian precision farmers using a trans-theoretical model. Drones (Basel) 2022; 6(8): 200. [http://dx.doi.org/10.3390/drones6080200]

[6] Yao H, Qin R, Chen X. Unmanned aerial vehicle for remote sensing applications—A review. Remote Sens (Basel) 2019; 11(12): 1443. [http://dx.doi.org/10.3390/rs11121443]

[7] Jang G, Kim J, Yu JK, *et al.* Cost-effective unmanned aerial vehicle (UAV) platform for field plant breeding application. Remote Sens (Basel) 2020; 12(6): 998. [http://dx.doi.org/10.3390/rs12060998]

[8] Cucho-Padin G, Loayza H, Palacios S, Balcazar M, Carbajal M, Quiroz R. Development of low-cost remote sensing tools and methods for supporting smallholder agriculture. Applied Geomatics 2020; 12(3): 247-63.
[http://dx.doi.org/10.1007/s12518-019-00292-5]

[9] Seelan SK, Laguette S, Casady GM, Seielstad GA. Remote sensing applications for precision agriculture: A learning community approach. Remote Sens Environ 2003; 88(1-2): 157-69.
[http://dx.doi.org/10.1016/j.rse.2003.04.007]

[10] Radočaj D, Jurišić M, Gašparović M. The role of remote sensing data and methods in a modern approach to fertilization in precision agriculture. Remote Sens (Basel) 2022; 14(3): 778.
[http://dx.doi.org/10.3390/rs14030778]

[11] Vreugdenhil M, Greimeister-Pfeil I, Preimesberger W, *et al.* Microwave remote sensing for agricultural drought monitoring: Recent developments and challenges. Frontiers in Water 2022; 4: 1045451.
[http://dx.doi.org/10.3389/frwa.2022.1045451]

[12] Wang Y, Kootstra G, Yang Z, Khan HA. UAV multispectral remote sensing for agriculture: A comparative study of radiometric correction methods under varying illumination conditions. Biosyst Eng 2024; 248: 240-54.
[http://dx.doi.org/10.1016/j.biosystemseng.2024.11.005]

[13] Bouguettaya A, Zarzour H, Kechida A, Taberkit AM. Deep learning techniques to classify agricultural crops through UAV imagery: a review. Neural Comput Appl 2022; 34(12): 9511-36.
[http://dx.doi.org/10.1007/s00521-022-07104-9] [PMID: 35281624]

[14] Shahi TB, Xu CY, Neupane A, Guo W. Recent advances in crop disease detection using UAV and deep learning techniques. Remote Sens (Basel) 2023; 15(9): 2450.
[http://dx.doi.org/10.3390/rs15092450]

[15] Safi C, Pareeth S, Yalew S, van der Zaag P, Mul M. Estimating agricultural water productivity using remote sensing derived data. Model Earth Syst Environ 2024; 10(1): 1203-13.
[http://dx.doi.org/10.1007/s40808-023-01841-z]

[16] Qu T, Li Y, Zhao Q, *et al.* Drone-based multispectral remote sensing inversion for typical crop soil moisture under dry farming conditions. Agriculture 2024; 14(3): 484.
[http://dx.doi.org/10.3390/agriculture14030484]

[17] Qu G, Shuai Y, Shao C, Peng X, Huang J. County scale corn yield estimation based on multi-source data in liaoning province. Agronomy (Basel) 2023; 13(5): 1428.
[http://dx.doi.org/10.3390/agronomy13051428]

[18] Skydan V, Pazych V M, Petruk T V. Utilizing remote sensing data to ascertain weed infestation levels in maize fields. 2025.

[19] Murugesan E, Shanmugamoorthy S, Veerasamy S, Sivakumar V. Drought assessment in Coimbatore South region, Tamil Nadu, India, using remote sensing and meteorological data. J Earth Syst Sci 2025; 134(1): 40.
[http://dx.doi.org/10.1007/s12040-024-02487-w]

[20] Chauhan KK, Lunagaria MM. Remote sensing. International Journal of Environment and Climate Change 2025; 15(1): 1-11.
[http://dx.doi.org/10.9734/ijecc/2025/v15i14668]

[21] Yahaya SM, Mahmud AA, Abdullahi M, Haruna A. Recent advances in the chemistry of nitrogen, phosphorus and potassium as fertilizers in soil: A review. Pedosphere 2023; 33(3): 385-406.
[http://dx.doi.org/10.1016/j.pedsph.2022.07.012]

[22] Hristov B. The importance of soil texture in soil classification systems. J Balk Ecol 2013; 16(2): 137-9.

[23] Hunt ED, Hubbard KG, Wilhite DA, Arkebauer TJ, Dutcher AL. The development and evaluation of a soil moisture index. Int J Climatol 2009; 29(5): 747-59. [http://dx.doi.org/10.1002/joc.1749]

[24] Treder W. Variation in soil pH, calcium and magnesium status influenced by drip irrigation and fertigation. J Fruit Ornam Plant Res 2005; 13(1/4): 59.

[25] Beyer L, Blume HP, Elsner DC, Willnow A. Soil organic matter composition and microbial activity in urban soils. Sci Total Environ 1995; 168(3): 267-78. [http://dx.doi.org/10.1016/0048-9697(95)04704-5]

[26] Ashraf M A, Maah M J, Yusoff I. Soil contamination, risk assessment and remediation Environmental risk assessment of soil contamination, 1. 2014; pp. 3-56.

[27] Gunstone T, Cornelisse T, Klein K, Dubey A, Donley N. Pesticides and soil invertebrates: A hazard assessment. Front Environ Sci 2021; 9: 643847. [http://dx.doi.org/10.3389/fenvs.2021.643847]

[28] Paz-Kagan T, Zaady E, Salbach C, *et al.* Mapping the spectral soil quality index (SSQI) using airborne imaging spectroscopy. Remote Sens (Basel) 2015; 7(11): 15748-81. [http://dx.doi.org/10.3390/rs71115748]

[29] Körner C. Significance of temperature in plant life Plant growth and climate change 2006; 48-69. [http://dx.doi.org/10.1002/9780470988695.ch3]

[30] Kaspar TC, Bland WL. Soil temperature and root growth. Soil Sci 1992; 154(4): 290-9. [http://dx.doi.org/10.1097/00010694-199210000-00005]

[31] Chia SY, Lim MW. A critical review on the influence of humidity for plant growth forecasting. IOP Conf Series Mater Sci Eng 2022; 1257(1): 012001. [http://dx.doi.org/10.1088/1757-899X/1257/1/012001]

[32] Mohamed SJ, Rihan HZ, Aljafer N, Fuller MP. The impact of light spectrum and intensity on the growth, physiology, and antioxidant activity of lettuce (Lactuca sativa L.). Plants 2021; 10(10): 2162. [http://dx.doi.org/10.3390/plants10102162] [PMID: 34685971]

[33] Kami C, Lorrain S, Hornitschek P, Fankhauser C. Light-regulated plant growth and development. Curr Top Dev Biol 2010; 91: 29-66. [http://dx.doi.org/10.1016/S0070-2153(10)91002-8] [PMID: 20705178]

[34] de Langre E. Effects of wind. Annu Rev Fluid Mech 2008; 40(1): 141-68. [http://dx.doi.org/10.1146/annurev.fluid.40.111406.102135]

[35] Sinoquet H, Le Roux X, Adam B, Ameglio T, Daudet FA. RATP: a model for simulating the spatial distribution of radiation absorption, transpiration and photosynthesis within canopies: application to an isolated tree crown. Plant Cell Environ 2001; 24(4): 395-406. [http://dx.doi.org/10.1046/j.1365-3040.2001.00694.x]

[36] Singh DK, Sobti R, Jain A, Malik PK, Le DN. LoRa based intelligent soil and weather condition monitoring with internet of things for precision agriculture in smart cities. IET Commun 2022; 16(5): 604-18. [http://dx.doi.org/10.1049/cmu2.12352]

[37] Liao K, Xu S, Wu J, Zhu Q. Spatial estimation of surface soil texture using remote sensing data. Soil Sci Plant Nutr 2013; 59(4): 488-500. [http://dx.doi.org/10.1080/00380768.2013.802643]

[38] Neupane K, Baysal-Gurel F. Automatic identification and monitoring of plant diseases using unmanned aerial vehicles: A review. Remote Sens (Basel) 2021; 13(19): 3841. [http://dx.doi.org/10.3390/rs13193841]

[39] Dhiman G, Bhattacharya J, Roy S. Soil textures and nutrients estimation using remote sensing data in north india - Punjab region. Procedia Comput Sci 2023; 218: 2041-8.

[http://dx.doi.org/10.1016/j.procs.2023.01.180]

[40] Zhang W, Zhu L, Zhuang Q, Chen D, Sun T. Mapping cropland soil nutrients contents based on multispectral remote sensing and machine learning. Agriculture 2023; 13(8): 1592. [http://dx.doi.org/10.3390/agriculture13081592]

[41] Silva E B, ten Caten A, Dalmolin R S D, Dotto A C, Silva W C, Giasson E. Estimating soil texture from a limited region of the visible/near-infrared spectrum. Digital soil morphometrics 2016; 73-87.

[42] Conforti M, Froio R, Matteucci G, Buttafuoco G. Visible and near infrared spectroscopy for predicting texture in forest soil: an application in southern Italy. iForest-Biogeosciences and Forestry 2015; 8(3): 339.

[43] Prigent C, Aires F, Rossow WB, Robock A. Sensitivity of satellite microwave and infrared observations to soil moisture at a global scale: Relationship of satellite observations to *in situ* soil moisture measurements. J Geophys Res 2005; 110(D7): 2004JD005087. [http://dx.doi.org/10.1029/2004JD005087]

[44] Hain CR, Crow WT, Mecikalski JR, Anderson MC, Holmes T. An intercomparison of available soil moisture estimates from thermal infrared and passive microwave remote sensing and land surface modeling. J Geophys Res 2011; 116(D15): D15107. [http://dx.doi.org/10.1029/2011JD015633]

[45] Akash M, Mohan Kumar P, Bhaskar P, Deepthi PR, Sukhdev A. Review of estimation of soil moisture using active microwave remote sensing technique. Remote Sens Appl Soc Environ 2024; 33: 101118. [http://dx.doi.org/10.1016/j.rsase.2023.101118]

[46] Marín-González O, Kuang B, Quraishi MZ, Munóz-García MÁ, Mouazen AM. On-line measurement of soil properties without direct spectral response in near infrared spectral range. Soil Tillage Res 2013; 132: 21-9. [http://dx.doi.org/10.1016/j.still.2013.04.004]

[47] Rodríguez-Pérez JR, Marcelo V, Pereira-Obaya D, García-Fernández M, Sanz-Ablanedo E. Estimating soil properties and nutrients by visible and infrared diffuse reflectance spectroscopy to characterize vineyards. Agronomy (Basel) 2021; 11(10): 1895. [http://dx.doi.org/10.3390/agronomy11101895]

[48] Rosero-Vlasova OA, Vlassova L, Pérez-Cabello F, Montorio R, Nadal-Romero E. Soil organic matter and texture estimation from visible–near infrared–shortwave infrared spectra in areas of land cover changes using correlated component regression. Land Degrad Dev 2019; 30(5): 544-60. [http://dx.doi.org/10.1002/ldr.3250]

[49] Oliveira KM, Gonçalves JVF, Furlanetto RH, *et al.* Predicting particle size and soil organic carbon of soil profiles using VIS-NIR-SWIR hyperspectral imaging and machine learning models. Remote Sens (Basel) 2024; 16(16): 2869. [http://dx.doi.org/10.3390/rs16162869]

[50] Mezned N, Alayet F, Dkhala B, Abdeljaouad S. Field hyperspectral data and OLI8 multispectral imagery for heavy metal content prediction and mapping around an abandoned Pb–Zn mining site in northern Tunisia. Heliyon 2022; 8(6): e09712. [http://dx.doi.org/10.1016/j.heliyon.2022.e09712] [PMID: 35756131]

[51] Singh S. Mapping soil trace metal distribution using remote sensing and multivariate analysis. Environ Monit Assess 2024; 196(6): 516. [http://dx.doi.org/10.1007/s10661-024-12682-3] [PMID: 38710964]

[52] Cristina dos Reis Medeiros S, Del Papa Moreira Scafutto R, Roberto de Souza Filho C. Temporal analysis of emissivity variation of mineral substrates impregnated with hydrocarbons: Significance for oil exploration and environmental pollution monitoring. Fuel 2024; 375: 132590. [http://dx.doi.org/10.1016/j.fuel.2024.132590]

[53] Mehedi IM, Hanif MS, Bilal M, Vellingiri MT, Palaniswamy T. Remote sensing and decision support

system applications in precision agriculture: Challenges and possibilities. IEEE Access 2024; 12: 44786-98.
[http://dx.doi.org/10.1109/ACCESS.2024.3380830]

[54] Brugler S, Gardezi M, Dadkhah A, Rizzo DM, Zia A, Clay SA. Improving decision support systems with machine learning: Identifying barriers to adoption. Agron J 2024; 116(3): 1229-36.
[http://dx.doi.org/10.1002/agj2.21432]

[55] Khanal S, Kc K, Fulton JP, Shearer S, Ozkan E. Remote sensing in agriculture—accomplishments, limitations, and opportunities. Remote Sens (Basel) 2020; 12(22): 3783.
[http://dx.doi.org/10.3390/rs12223783]

[56] Ozdogan M, Yang Y, Allez G, Cervantes C. Remote sensing of irrigated agriculture: Opportunities and challenges. Remote Sens (Basel) 2010; 2(9): 2274-304.
[http://dx.doi.org/10.3390/rs2092274]

[57] Ge Y, Thomasson JA, Sui R. Remote sensing of soil properties in precision agriculture: A review. Front Earth Sci 2011; 5: 229-38.
[http://dx.doi.org/10.1007/s11707-011-0175-0]

[58] Cottrell B, Kalacska M, Arroyo-Mora JP, *et al.* Limitations. Remote Sens (Basel) 2024; 16(13): 2463.
[http://dx.doi.org/10.3390/rs16132463]

CHAPTER 14

Remote Sensing for Precision Agriculture: Optimizing Fertilizer Use through Nutrient Mapping

Jaspreet Singh[1], **Rupinder Singh**[2,*], **Amanpreet Singh**[2] and **Jaswinder Singh**[2]

[1] *Department of Computer Science & Engineering, Chandigarh University, Mohali-140413, Punjab, India*

[2] *Chitkara University Institute of Engineering and Technology, Chitkara University, Punjab, India*

Abstract: Efficient use of fertilizers is of utmost importance in sustainable agriculture, as it leads to higher crop yields and limits environmental pollution. Fertilizer application in the traditional way usually overapplies or underspends, causing nutrient imbalances, soil degradation, and environmental pollution. A new application of remote sensing technology in precision agriculture is that of accurate and timely measurement of the levels of soil nutrient availability and crop health. Remote sensing combines satellite imagery, drone-based sensors, and spectral analysis to obtain the most accurate mapping, enabling site-specific fertilizer application. By focusing on this data-driven approach, not only is fertilizer use optimized, but crop productivity is increased, costs are reduced, and environmental risks are mitigated. This chapter examines under what conditions remote sensing is used in nutrient mapping, how it is used, and the comparative merits. It also touches on the integration of remote sensing with artificial intelligence, machine learning, and IoT-enabled smart agriculture for better decision-making. Finally, the chapter discusses the challenges of using remote sensing for fertilizer optimization, as well as current trends in digital agriculture, including government initiatives, policies, and frameworks that support e-governance in agricultural practices.

Keywords: Cost reduction, Crop health, Food security, Precision agriculture, Remote sensing, Satellite imagery.

INTRODUCTION

In the last few decades, agriculture has undergone significant technological changes to achieve greater efficiency while ensuring sustainability. That is why there is a need for innovative ways to optimize agricultural practice to meet the needs of an increasing population and food demand. Fertilizer application is one

[*] **Corresponding author Rupinder Singh**: Chitkara University Institute of Engineering and Technology, Chitkara University, Punjab, India; E-mail: rupinder.1153@chitkara.edu.in

of the significant factors affecting agricultural output. However, the application of traditional fertilizer management techniques relies mainly on empirical practices, that is, they often use excessive or insufficient nutrient application. The contributing causes to this are such inefficiencies that lead to soil degradation, low crop yields, and environmental pollution. Precision agriculture can now be practiced despite the unavailability of real-time, accurate spatial data, with the help of remote sensing, which provides real-time, spatially accurate data for the optimal distribution of fertilizer, minimization of waste, and improved soil health.

The word remote sensing means the use of satellites, data, and drones to monitor various factors of agriculture. These technologies allow farmers to monitor nutrient deficiencies and predict crop health, among other things, and then apply fertilizers where needed. Geographic Information Systems (GIS) and Global Positioning Systems are further integrated to increase the accuracy of nutrient mapping and thus the efficacy of field (site-specific) fertilization [1]. The usefulness of GIS-based nutrient maps is especially in differentiating areas of variation in soil fertility within a given area and in making informed decisions about fertilizer application rates for these parcels. Fig. (**1**) depicts satellite-based nutrient monitoring, drone-based imaging, GIS mapping of soil, variable-rate fertilization, and field-based smart sensors.

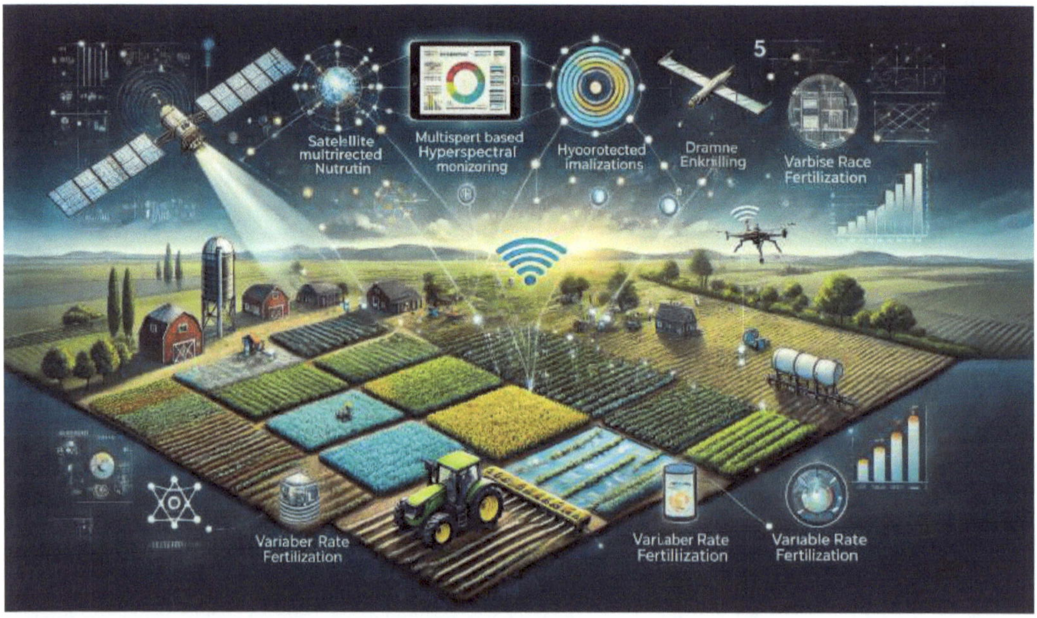

Fig. (1). Role of remote sensing in precision agriculture [4].

Benefits of Remote Sensing in Nutrient Management

Multispectral and Hyperspectral imagery provide a means for fine-scale soil and crop analysis using remote sensing techniques. Data are collected at a few broad spectral bands for multispectral imaging and at hundreds of narrow bands for hyperspectral imaging, which are sufficient to obtain a more precise measurement of nutrient levels [1]. Also adding to the crop stress and soil properties that affect nutrient availability are thermal imaging and LiDAR. The use of these technologies improves nutrient management in the following ways:

- **Early Detection of Nutrient Deficiencies**: Remote sensing aids in the early identification of areas of fields that can be fertilized proactively before symptomology becomes visible.
- **Efficient Resource Allocation:** It aids in reducing waste, lowering costs, and minimizing environmental impacts. Inefficient fertilizer application can also increase resource use by having farmers apply fertilizers only where they are actually needed.
- **Time and Labor Savings:** Remote sensing saves time and costs, allowing for the substitution of labor and the time-intensive sampling of soil by hand.
- **Data-Driven Decision Making**: Advanced analytics and AI-powered models increase prediction accuracy to develop the best fertilizer application strategy.

A major advantage of remote sensing in fertilizer optimization is the ability to implement Variable Rate Technology (VRT). Such an approach enables differential fertilizer application depending on real-time nutrient assessments and hence reduces costs and environmental impact. FAO (2020) reports that studies show that precision fertilization using remote sensing data can lead to yield increases of 20 to 30 percent and reductions in fertilizer waste of 20 to 25 percent. Dynamic soil health monitoring provides a balance between sustainable agriculture and maintaining productivity.

The analysis of how remote sensing can optimize fertilizer use for nutrient mapping is provided at length in this chapter. It examines different remote sensing techniques, their applicability, and the use of AI-driven decision-making techniques for precision agriculture. This chapter will, through case studies and comparative analyses, present the future prospects of digital agriculture and sustainable nutrient management to the best of our knowledge.

REMOTE SENSING TECHNIQUES FOR NUTRIENT MAPPING

Data from soil and crops are collected remotely using satellites and UAV (drone) sensors, and analyzed for different soil and crop parameters that constitute remote sensing. Fig. (**2**) illustrates the remote sensing data collection process, showcasing different methods, including satellites, drones, and ground-based sensors. The nutrient availability, deficiency, and poor soil health are viewed differently from various techniques of remote sensing. The most common methods of using remote sensing for mapping nutrients are explored here.

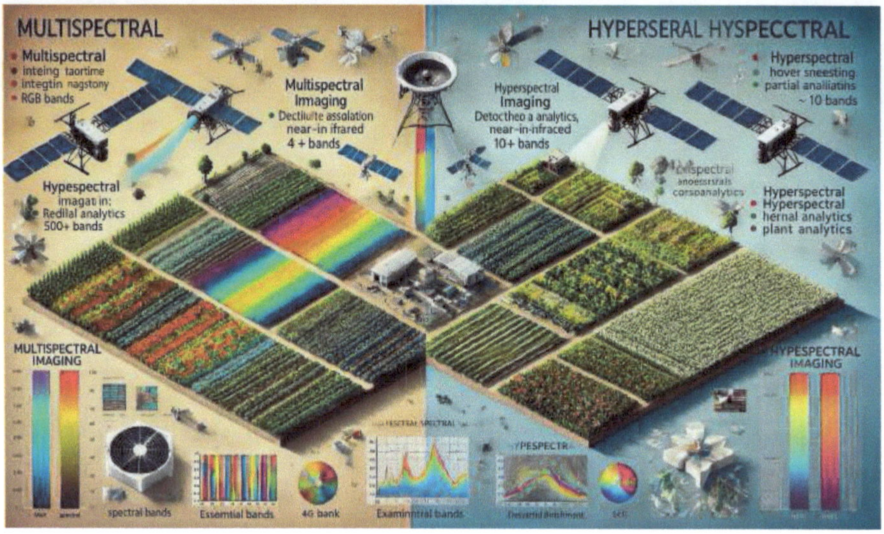

Fig. (2). Multispectral *vs* hyperspectral imaging [5].

Multispectral and Hyperspectral Imaging

Major remote sensing techniques for assessing nutrients can be seen in Fig. (**3**), including multispectral and hyperspectral imaging [2, 3]. For example, these various imaging techniques use data collected over a number of distinct wavelengths of the electromagnetic spectrum to detect very small changes in plant health and in soil properties. Table **1** represents the comparison of multispectral and hyperspectral imaging based on various features like bands, resolution, complexity, and application.

Table 1. Multispectral *vs* hyperspectral imaging [5].

Feature	Multispectral Imaging	Hyperspectral Imaging
Number of Bands	4–10	100+
Resolution	Moderate	High
Data Complexity	Lower	Higher
Application	General vegetation monitoring	Detailed nutrient analysis

- For general vegetation monitoring and feeding large-scale nutrient variations, Multispectral Imaging (MSI) acquires data across a few narrow spectral bands (about 4–10), and the utility of MSI lies in these two scenarios.
- On the other hand, hyperspectral imaging can capture hundreds of narrow spectral bands to provide more detailed analysis of nutrient deficiencies, chlorophyll content, and soil composition.

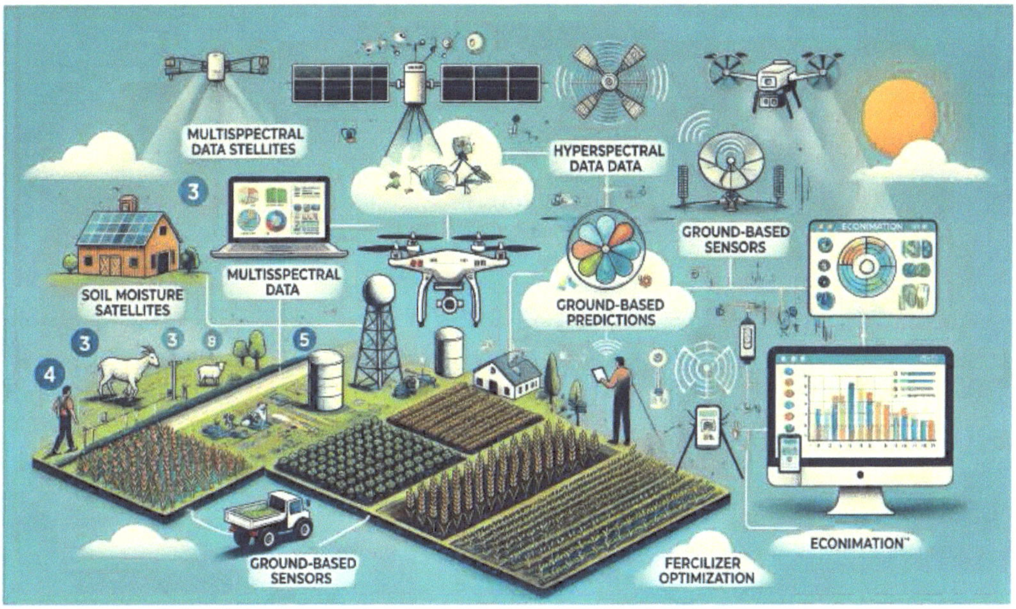

Fig. (3). Remote sensing data collection process [6].

Thermal Imaging

Thermal imaging is another critical technique used in remote sensing for nutrient mapping. It detects temperature variations in crops, which can indicate stress due to inadequate or excessive nutrient levels. Thermal cameras, mounted on UAVs or satellites, capture infrared radiation emitted by plants, helping to identify areas with poor nutrient uptake.

- **Advantages:** Provides real-time assessment of crop stress and helps in early detection of nutrient deficiencies.
- **Limitations:** Requires calibration with environmental temperature data to avoid misinterpretation.

LiDAR (Light Detection and Ranging)

LiDAR is a remote sensing technique that uses laser pulses to generate high-resolution maps of soil texture, elevation, and moisture levels. These factors play a crucial role in nutrient distribution within the soil [2]. LiDAR is particularly useful in:

- Identifying variations in soil structure that affect nutrient retention.
- Assessing terrain elevation to optimize irrigation and fertilizer application.
- Mapping field topography for precision agriculture applications.

(Diagram showcasing different remote sensing data collection methods, including satellites, drones, and ground-based sensors.)

Satellite-Based Remote Sensing

Satellite imagery plays a fundamental role in large-scale nutrient mapping. Satellites equipped with multispectral, hyperspectral, and thermal sensors provide continuous monitoring of soil and crop health [3]. Some commonly used satellites for agricultural remote sensing include:

- **Landsat Series**: Provides long-term data on vegetation health and soil conditions.
- **Sentinel-2:** Offers high-resolution multispectral imaging for nutrient and water stress assessment.
- **MODIS:** Useful for large-scale climate and vegetation monitoring.

UAV (Drone) Remote Sensing

Drones equipped with advanced sensors provide high-resolution imagery and real-time data collection for precision agriculture. UAVs are increasingly used for site-specific nutrient mapping because they:

- Offer flexibility in monitoring small to medium-sized farms.
- Provide rapid, on-demand data collection.
- Enable targeted application of fertilizers through integration with VRT (Variable Rate Technology).

Spectral Vegetation Indices for Nutrient Mapping

Spectral vegetation indices derived from remote sensing data play a crucial role in nutrient mapping, as illustrated in Table **2**. These indices include:

Table 2. Common spectral vegetation indices and their applications [7].

Vegetation Index	Purpose	Application in Nutrient Mapping
NDVI	Vegetation health assessment	Identifies nitrogen deficiency
SAVI	Adjusts for soil effects	Useful in sparse vegetation areas
NDRE	Chlorophyll & nitrogen detection	Effective for precision fertilization

- **Normalized Difference Vegetation Index (NDVI):** Measures chlorophyll content and overall plant health.
- **Soil-Adjusted Vegetation Index (SAVI):** Adjusts for soil reflectance variations.
- **Normalized Difference Red Edge Index (NDRE):** Sensitive to chlorophyll content and nitrogen levels in plants [4].

Ground-Based Remote Sensing

Ground-based remote sensing uses *in situ* sensors to measure soil and crop properties directly. These sensors can be integrated with IoT and machine learning models to provide:

- Real-time soil nutrient analysis.
- Precise calibration of satellite and UAV data.
- Automated decision-making for fertilizer application.

ROLE OF REMOTE SENSING IN FERTILIZER OPTIMIZATION

Remote sensing plays a crucial role in optimizing fertilizer application, ensuring that nutrients are supplied in the right amount, at the right time, and in the right place. This section explores how remote sensing contributes to fertilizer efficiency.

Site-Specific Nutrient Management (SSNM)

Remote sensing enables **Site-Specific Nutrient Management (SSNM)** by providing high-resolution spatial data on soil and crop nutrient status. Technologies, such as **multispectral imaging, hyperspectral imaging, and thermal sensors,** allow farmers to identify nutrient-deficient areas and apply fertilizers accordingly [5].

- **Benefits**: Reduces over-fertilization, minimizes nutrient runoff, and improves crop productivity.
- **Challenges**: Requires advanced data processing and integration with precision agriculture systems.

Variable Rate Technology (VRT) Integration

Variable Rate Technology (VRT) uses remote sensing data to adjust fertilizer application rates in response to real-time soil and crop conditions, as illustrated in Fig. (**4**) [8]. UAVs and satellite imagery provide precise maps that guide automated fertilizer spreaders [6].

- **Advantages:** Enhances resource efficiency and lowers input costs.
- **Implementation:** Requires GIS-based mapping and automated fertilizer application equipment.

Fig. (4). Remote sensing-based variable rate technology [8].

(Illustration depicting how remote sensing data is used to guide variable rate fertilizer application.)

Reduction of Environmental Impact

Excessive fertilizer use leads to **nutrient leaching, water pollution, and greenhouse gas emissions**. Remote sensing helps mitigate these environmental risks by:

- Monitoring nitrogen and phosphorus levels in soil and water bodies [7].
- Preventing overuse of fertilizers in sensitive ecosystems.
- Promoting eco-friendly, data-driven fertilization practices.

Real-Time Decision Support Systems

Remote sensing data, when integrated with **artificial intelligence (AI) and machine learning (ML)**, enhances real-time decision-making for fertilizer management [8]. Decision Support Systems (DSS) analyze historical and real-time data to generate precise fertilization recommendations.

- **Components of DSS:** AI-based nutrient modeling, IoT-based field sensors, and cloud computing.
- **Outcome:** Increases accuracy in nutrient application and enhances agricultural sustainability.

Remote sensing is revolutionizing fertilizer optimization by enabling precision agriculture techniques such as SSNM, VRT, and real-time decision support. By leveraging multispectral, hyperspectral, and AI-driven analytics, farmers can maximize yield while minimizing costs and environmental impacts. Table **3** lists the benefits of remote sensing in fertilizer optimization. Future advancements in remote sensing, combined with government initiatives, will further enhance sustainable fertilizer management in global agriculture.

Table 3. Benefits of remote sensing in fertilizer optimization [9].

Benefit	Description
Cost Reduction	Minimizes unnecessary fertilizer use
Environmental Safety	Reduces nutrient runoff and pollution
Yield Improvement	Enhances crop growth and nutrient absorption
Sustainability	Supports long-term soil health and fertility

Practical Implementation Tips

A systematic, feasible process for successfully utilizing remote sensing in precision agriculture should also be developed. Start out at a pilot area, where methods can be tried, before moving to whole farms. Monitor nutrient dynamics through the entire crop cycle with multi-temporal imagery, calibrate satellite or UAV data with field-based sample measurements, or calibrate, always. It is important to choose the right sensing platform, *i.e.*, a satellite covering a wide area or UAVs to map detailed information. Use several vegetation indices (NDVI, SAVI, *etc.*) coupled with free-of-charge utilities such as Google Earth Engine or QGIS to process and analyze pictures inexpensively. Prepare prescription maps that account for management variable-rate fertilizer efficiency and ensure a match between machinery. Engage and educate participants actively and teach farmers how to read maps and bring the information to the ground. Monitoring after the applications using follow-up imagery is useful in the evaluation of effects and individual improvements. By recording every use of fertilizers, yield, and imaging data in detail, one can continuously improve practices and make more effective decisions even in the next season. Table **4** demonstrates the implementation tips.

Table 4. Useful practices in applying remote sensing in nutrient mapping and fertilizer optimization.

S. No.	Implementation Tip	Description
1	Start with a Pilot Zone	Begin with a small, manageable field to test and refine remote sensing and nutrient mapping.
2	Use Multi-Temporal Imagery	Capture images at various crop stages to monitor nutrient changes over time.
3	Combine Remote Sensing with Ground Truthing	Validate imagery with soil/leaf sample data to enhance mapping accuracy.
4	Choose the Right Remote Sensing Platform	Use satellites for large farms; drones/UAVs for detailed analysis in smaller areas.
5	Apply Multiple Vegetation Indices	Use NDVI alongside others, such as SAVI and GNDVI, for better interpretation of nutrient status.
6	Leverage Open-Source Tools	Employ tools like Google Earth Engine, SNAP, and QGIS for image analysis at minimal cost.
7	Generate Prescription Maps for VRA	Convert nutrient maps into machine-readable formats for variable-rate fertilizer application.
8	Involve and Train Farmers	Conduct training sessions to help farmers understand and use the technology effectively.
9	Monitor Post-Fertilization Response	Use follow-up imagery to evaluate the impact of optimized fertilizer application.
10	Maintain Records for Continuous Improvement	Keep detailed logs on application rates, yields, and sensor data for ongoing model refinement.

CHALLENGES AND LIMITATIONS

While remote sensing has revolutionized fertilizer optimization, several challenges and limitations hinder its widespread adoption and effectiveness, as illustrated in Table 5. These challenges can be categorized into technological, financial, environmental, and operational constraints.

Table 5. Comparison of key challenges in remote sensing for fertilizer optimization [10].

Challenge Category	Challenges	Impact on Fertilizer Optimization	Possible Solutions
Technological	Data Processing Complexity	Requires advanced AI, GIS, and machine learning expertise	Develop user-friendly AI-based platforms
-	Nutrient Detection Accuracy	Environmental factors affect spectral reflectance	Improve multispectral and hyperspectral calibration
Financial	High Initial Costs	Expensive UAVs, satellites, and data processing tools	Government subsidies and cost-sharing programs
-	Accessibility for Small Farmers	Limited affordability in rural areas	Provide community-based sensor access
Environmental	Weather & Cloud Interference	Reduces the effectiveness of satellite imaging	Use UAV-based or ground-based sensors as alternatives
Operational	Integration with Traditional Methods	Farmers may resist adopting remote sensing technology	Offer training programs for farmers

Technological Challenges

Data Processing and Interpretation Complexity

Remote sensing generates vast amounts of multispectral, hyperspectral, and thermal imaging data, requiring sophisticated processing techniques. Converting raw sensor data into actionable fertilizer recommendations involves:

- **Advanced Image Processing Algorithms** – Requires expertise in GIS mapping, AI, and machine learning for accurate nutrient assessment [9].
- **High-Resolution Data Storage & Management** – Managing large-scale farm data demands cloud-based platforms with secure storage.
- **Calibration Issues** – Remote sensors must be frequently calibrated for **atmospheric correction and soil reflectance variation**, which adds complexity [10].

Accuracy Limitations in Nutrient Detection

- **Multispectral imaging** may not differentiate between different nutrient deficiencies effectively.
- **Hyperspectral Imaging** is more precise but is computationally expensive and requires high expertise.
- Variability in weather conditions, soil type, and crop species can reduce the accuracy of remote sensing models.

Financial and Infrastructure Challenges

High Initial Investment and Maintenance Costs

- **Satellite Imaging and UAV-based Sensors** require significant capital investment.
- **Precision Farming Technologies**, including Variable Rate Technology (VRT) and IoT-based decision systems, are expensive to deploy [11].
- **Data Processing Software and Cloud Integration** add operational expenses.

Limited Accessibility for Small-Scale Farmers

- **High-Cost Barriers** restrict the adoption of remote sensing by small and medium-sized farmers.
- **Lack of Technical Training** in remote sensing interpretation limits usability among rural farmers.

Environmental and Operational Constraints

Influence of Weather and Atmospheric Conditions

- **Cloud cover, fog, and extreme weather conditions** can reduce the effectiveness of satellite-based nutrient assessment [12].
- **Variability in sunlight intensity** affects multispectral and hyperspectral imaging results.
- **Rainfall and soil moisture variation** influence spectral reflectance, leading to inaccurate data readings.

Data Integration Challenges with Traditional Farming Practices

- Farmers accustomed to **conventional fertilizer application** may struggle to adapt to **AI-driven precision agriculture**.
- There is a**lack of compatibility** between different **sensor technologies, GIS software, and farm management systems**.
- **Inconsistent Internet Connectivity** in rural regions affects real-time remote

sensing data transmission [12].

FUTURE PROSPECTS AND TECHNOLOGICAL ADVANCEMENTS IN REMOTE SENSING FOR FERTILIZER OPTIMIZATION

As precision agriculture continues to evolve, remote sensing technologies are expected to become more accurate, cost-effective, and widely accessible. Several emerging trends and advancements aim to overcome existing limitations while enhancing the efficiency of fertilizer application (Table **6**).

Emerging Trends in Remote Sensing for Agriculture

Integration of Artificial Intelligence (AI) and Machine Learning (ML)

- **AI-driven Algorithms** improve remote sensing data analysis by detecting **nutrient deficiencies** with higher accuracy [13].
- **Deep Learning Models** analyze spectral signatures of crops and recommend precise fertilizer applications.
- AI-based **Predictive Analytics** help in forecasting soil nutrient requirements based on **historical climate and crop growth data**.

Adoption of Internet of Things (IoT) and Smart Sensors

- **IoT-based soil sensors** provide real-time monitoring of nutrient levels, **complementing remote sensing data** [14].
- **Wireless sensor networks (WSNs)** automate fertilizer management by integrating **ground-based and aerial remote sensing**.
- IoT enables seamless data transmission from UAVs and satellites to **cloud-based decision support systems (DSS)**.

Advances in Hyperspectral and Thermal Imaging

- Next-generation **hyperspectral cameras** with ultra-high spectral resolution will improve **nutrient identification accuracy**.
- **Thermal imaging enhancements** will provide better detection of plant stress related to **nutrient deficiency and water imbalance** [15].

Technological Advancements Driving Future Adoption

Integration of Blockchain for Data Security and Transparency

- Blockchain ensures secure sharing of remote sensing data among farmers, agronomists, and policymakers.
- Smart contracts allow for automated fertilizer supply chain management based on real-time soil analysis.

Autonomous Drones and Robotics in Fertilizer Application

- **AI-powered UAVs** will not only capture **remote sensing images** but also deploy **site-specific fertilizers** in real-time.
- **Autonomous robots** equipped with **LiDAR**, **multispectral cameras, and nutrient applicators** will revolutionize precision farming [17].

Development of Cost-Effective Satellite Imagery Solutions

- Emerging low-cost **CubeSats and microsatellites** will provide **frequent, high-resolution images** for small-scale farmers.
- Enhanced **satellite constellations,** such as **Sentinel-2 and Landsat Next** will offer improved **spectral bands** for nutrient monitoring [18].

Table 6. Comparison of traditional *vs* future remote sensing technologies [11].

Feature	Traditional Remote Sensing	Future Technological Advancements
Data Accuracy	Moderate (Multispectral imaging)	High (Hyperspectral & AI integration) [19]
Cost	Expensive for small farmers	Affordable *via* CubeSats & IoT sensors [15]
Real-time Monitoring	Limited	Advanced IoT-based real-time sensing [15]
Automation	Manual processing required	AI-driven automated analysis & application [20]
Decision Support	Static data interpretation	Dynamic AI & blockchain-powered recommendations [25]

Government Policies and Global Initiatives Supporting Remote Sensing Adoption

- **The European Space Agency (ESA)** and **NASA** are expanding **satellite-based agricultural monitoring programs** [21].
- **The Indian Space Research Organization (ISRO)** is developing **affordable precision farming solutions for smallholder farmers [22]**.
- Governments worldwide are offering **subsidies for precision agriculture equipment, including UAVs and IoT sensors**.

Challenges in Implementing Future Technologies

While these advancements are promising, some challenges remain:

- **High initial costs** for AI-based hyperspectral imaging systems.
- **Data privacy concerns** regarding blockchain and cloud-based farming solutions.

- **Need for farmer training** to adopt AI-driven fertilizer management systems.

The future of **remote sensing in fertilizer optimization** is driven by **AI, IoT, robotics, and blockchain technologies [23-25]**. As innovations continue, remote sensing will become an **integral part of sustainable agriculture**, ensuring optimal fertilizer use while reducing environmental impacts. With government support and technological advancements, **precision agriculture will soon be accessible to all farmers, regardless of scale**. The limitations and strategic research opportunities can be summarized as represented in Table 7.

Table 7. Limitations and future research directions [15, 22, 24].

S. No.	Limitations	Future Research Directions
1	**Cloud cover and atmospheric interference** affect optical imagery quality.	Explore **radar-based remote sensing** and **AI-driven image reconstruction** for cloudy conditions.
2	**Limited access to high-resolution imagery** due to high cost and regulations.	Develop **low-cost UAVs, community drone programs**, and **open-access imaging platforms**.
3	**Ground truthing is labor-intensive** and not scalable across large areas.	Use **AI/ML models** trained on historical data to minimize ground sample dependency.
4	Lack of **real-time nutrient monitoring and recommendations**.	Integrate **IoT sensors** and **edge computing** for live nutrient tracking and on-site processing.
5	High **technical complexity** restricts adoption by small-scale or traditional farmers.	Design **user-friendly mobile apps** with intuitive interfaces and local language support.
6	**Models lack generalizability** across crops, regions, and seasons.	Develop **adaptive, self-learning algorithms** tuned to local agronomic conditions.
7	Incompatibility of tools with **Variable Rate Application (VRA) machinery**.	Promote **standardized formats** and **machine-t- -machine integration** for prescription maps.
8	Lack of **long-term studies** assessing economic and environmental impact.	Conduct **multi-season, field-scale trials** to validate benefits and refine methodologies.

CONCLUSION

Remote sensing has emerged as a transformative tool in optimizing fertilizer use for sustainable agriculture. By enabling precise nutrient mapping, it minimizes fertilizer wastage, enhances crop productivity, and reduces environmental degradation. Technologies, such as multispectral and hyperspectral imaging, LiDAR, thermal sensing, and AI-driven analytics, have revolutionized the way farmers assess soil fertility and apply fertilizers with unparalleled accuracy. Despite the significant benefits, challenges, such as high implementation costs, data processing complexities, and the need for farmer education, remain. However, the integration of Artificial Intelligence (AI), Machine Learning (ML),

Internet of Things (IoT), and blockchain is gradually addressing these barriers, making remote sensing more accessible and efficient. Looking ahead, continuous advancements in remote sensing, government support, and increased adoption of precision agriculture technologies will play a crucial role in achieving food security and environmental sustainability. By embracing data-driven solutions, the agricultural sector can optimize fertilizer use, improve soil health, and contribute to a greener, more efficient future. Remote sensing is not just a technological advancement—it is a critical enabler of modern, precision-driven, and sustainable farming practices. Its role in fertilizer optimization will only expand as innovation continues, ensuring a balance between agricultural productivity and ecological responsibility.

REFERENCES

[1] Mulla DJ. Twenty five years of remote sensing in precision agriculture: Key advances and remaining knowledge gaps. Biosyst Eng 2013; 114(4): 358-71.
[http://dx.doi.org/10.1016/j.biosystemseng.2012.08.009]

[2] Zhang Z, Li Y, Wang X. Applications of multispectral and hyperspectral remote sensing in precision agriculture: A review. Remote Sens 2021; 13(15): 2927.

[3] Gao B, Daughtry DJ, Doraiswamy PC. Hyperspectral remote sensing for monitoring agricultural crops. IEEE Trans Geosci Remote Sens 2020; 58(3): 1985-2003.

[4] Jones H, Sirault X. Thermal imaging and its applications in agriculture. Plant Methods 2022; 18(1): 92.
[PMID: 35780674]

[5] Huang Y, Zhao S, Liu J. The role of LiDAR Agric Sci 2019; 10(5): 126-35.

[6] Basso B, Antle J, Beasley RA. Precision agriculture Precis Agric 2016; 18(6): 1062-78.

[7] Zhou L, Yang M, Tang H. Assessing nitrogen and phosphorus levels in soil using remote sensing techniques. Environ Monit Assess 2022; 194(8): 533.
[PMID: 35763174]

[8] Li Y, Chen X, Zhang G. Artificial intelligence and machine learning in remote sensing for precision agriculture. Comput Electron Agric 2021; 189: 106418.

[9] Prasad TS, Rao PV. Integration of IoT and remote sensing in smart farming: A future perspective. IEEE Internet Things J 2022; 9(3): 2031-42.

[10] Surendran U, Nagakumar KCV, Samuel MP. Remote sensing in precision agriculture. Digital agriculture: A solution for sustainable food and nutritional security. Cham: Springer International Publishing 2024; pp. 201-23.

[11] Toselli M, Baldi E, Ferro F, Rossi S, Cillis D. Smart farming tool for monitoring nutrients in soil and plants for precise fertilization. Horticulturae 2023; 9(9): 1011.

[12] Yadav N, Sidana N. Precision agriculture technologies: analysing the use of advanced technologies, such as drones, sensors, and GPS, in precision agriculture for optimizing resource management, crop monitoring, and yield prediction. J Adv Zool 2023; 44

[13] Dahiya N, Singh S, Gupta S, *et al.* Detection of multitemporal changes with artificial neural network-based change detection algorithm using hyperspectral dataset. Remote Sens 2023; 15(5): 1326.

[14] Kumar Y, Garg P, Moudgil MR, *et al.* Enhancing parasitic organism detection in microscopy images through deep learning and fine-tuned optimizer. Sci Rep 2024; 14(1): 5753.

[http://dx.doi.org/10.1038/s41598-024-56323-8] [PMID: 38459096]

[15] Bhamini K, Kumar A, Magrey AH, Kulsoom S. The role of GIS and GPS in precision fertilization: optimizing nutrient management for sustainable cropping. Int J Res Agron 2025; 8: 260-7.

[16] Aarif KOM, Alam A, Hotak Y. Smart sensor technologies shaping the future of precision agriculture: recent advances and future outlooks. J Sens 2025; 2025(1): 2460098.

[17] Sobhy DM, Anandhi A. Soil nutrient monitoring technologies for sustainable agriculture: a systematic review. Sustainability 2025; 17(18): 8477.

[18] Maalini D, Kumar V, SR AK, Baskar M, Gopal G, Buvaneshwaran B. Machine learning-based soil nutrient analysis for optimized plant cultivation and precision agriculture. 2025 3rd International Conference on Artificial Intelligence and Machine Learning Applications Theme: Healthcare and Internet of Things (AIMLA). IEEE 2025; pp. 1-7.

[19] Cai B, Shi F, Geremew BA, *et al.* Precision agriculture techniques for optimizing chemical fertilizer use and environmental sustainability: a systematic review. Front Agron 2025; 7: 1665444.

[20] Nie J, Wu K, Li Y, Li J, Hou B. Advances in hyperspectral remote sensing for precision fertilization decision-making: a comprehensive overview. Turk J Agric For 2024; 48(6): 1084-104.

[21] Mehedi IM, Hanif MS, Bilal M, Vellingiri MT, Palaniswamy T. Remote sensing and decision support system applications in precision agriculture: challenges and possibilities. IEEE Access 2024; 12: 44786-98.

[22] van Breda SG, Mathijs K, Sági-Kiss V, *et al.* Impact of high drinking water nitrate levels on the endogenous formation of apparent N-nitroso compounds in combination with meat intake in healthy volunteers. Environ Health 2019; 18(1): 87.
[http://dx.doi.org/10.1186/s12940-019-0525-z] [PMID: 31623611]

[23] Gobler CJ, Burson A, Koch F, Tang Y, Mulholland MR. The role of nitrogenous nutrients in the occurrence of harmful algal blooms caused by Cochlodinium polykrikoides in New York estuaries (USA). Harmful Algae 2012; 17: 64-74.
[http://dx.doi.org/10.1016/j.hal.2012.03.001]

[24] Moody GJ, Oke RB, Thomas JDR. A calcium-sensitive electrode based on a liquid ion exchanger in a poly(vinyl chloride) matrix. Analyst (Lond) 1970; 95(1136): 910-8.
[http://dx.doi.org/10.1039/an9709500910]

[25] Chinthamu C, M N, M V P, *et al.* AI-driven smart washing machine with automatic drying: modeling and optimizing energy and water consumption. Proc 3rd Int Conf Optim Tech Field Eng (ICOFE-2024).

CHAPTER 15

Smart Irrigation Systems: A Review of Current Trends and Future Prospects

Nishu Bali[1] and **Deepika Chaudhary**[1,*]

[1] *Chitkara University Institute of Engineering & Technology, Chitkara University, Punjab, India*

Abstract: Crop health monitoring is one of the most critical aspects of farming to ensure the desired output from the cultivated crop. Timely and accurate irrigations ensure healthy and maximum fruit from the crop. Recent advancements in technologies, such as the Internet of Things and machine learning, and their notable contribution in various areas of agriculture, have motivated the present study to explore their use in monitoring various aspects related to field irrigation. The present study provides an extensive review of various proposed models used in the field of smart irrigation.

Keywords: IoT, Machine learning, Smart irrigation, Sensors.

INTRODUCTION

Agriculture is one of the most important and widely followed occupations in India. The ever-growing population of the world necessitates researchers to adopt farm practices that can be beneficial to the farmers as well as to the environment. Adoption of sustainable agriculture practices ensures maximum production from the grown crop and also helps protect our natural resources from depletion. According to statistics, the total irrigated area of India amounts to 96 million hectares, which is only 50% of the total cultivated land. The agricultural sector is one of the largest users of water resources, accounting for approximately 80% of the country's total water resources. The irrigation needs of the country are heavily dependent on two sources: groundwater (60%) and canal irrigation (40%) [1]. The continuous decrease in groundwater levels due to over-extraction in various agriculture-based states of India is alarming. The major states of India, such as Punjab, Rajasthan, and Haryana, are already struggling to cope with severe groundwater level depletion. In some states, the rate of fall of the groundwater table level has gone from 1-3 meters/year. According to the National Water Policy, by 2030, India's 2 billion population might face continuous stress due to

* **Corresponding author Deepika Chaudhary:** Chitkara University Institute of Engineering & Technology, Chitkara University, Punjab, India; E-mail:deepika.chaudhary@chitkara.edu.in

Sartajvir Singh, Neelam Dahiya, Maged Mohammed, Abdullah Alzharihi & Vishal Dutt (Eds.)

severe water scarcity [2]. The present erratic climatic conditions have led to protracted droughts and hefty rainfalls, giving a huge setback to both rainfed and irrigated fields. Some prominent and important Indian states like Karnataka, Maharashtra, and Andhra Pradesh faced consecutive droughts for multiple years, giving a huge blow to crop production in these states [3]. Many natural Irrigation structures (around 60%), like irrigation canals, are also not working optimally due to aging and poor maintenance. There is around 40-50% loss of water due to evaporation and seepage during flood irrigation. Thus, the farmers' dependence on groundwater and canal irrigation to fulfill their irrigation requirements has led them to huge yield losses. Also, continuous water pollution due to industrial discharge and agricultural waste in the form of fertilizer runoff has made much of the available irrigation water unfit for crops. The need of the hour is to discover ways of regulating irrigation practices on fields to ensure good health for the crop. Recent advancements in technology have proposed many promising solutions for sustainable agriculture practices.

ROLE OF TECHNOLOGY FOR SMART IRRIGATION

Traditional irrigation practices have proven to be inefficient in fulfilling the water needs of the crops. The unpredictable climatic variations have further compelled researchers worldwide to discover ways of coping with the changing climate and water scarcity problems. Advancements in the area of technology, in the form of IoT and machine learning, have shown promising results in the area of smart irrigation. Smart irrigation refers to the use of practices that can infer the water needs of the crop at the right time and provide the required amount of water without any wastage. Today, many sensors are available that can sense the needs of the crop based on the environment, which can be used by the farmer and researcher for optimum results. A network of sensors embedded in an automation system can provide the runtime data, which can be used for predictions and analysis using various data analytics tools and machine learning and deep learning algorithms. Various tools and technologies used in smart irrigation can be categorized as follows:

Sensors

One of the most crucial parts of any smart irrigation system is sensors that can sense and provide data on the condition of a crop. A wide range of sensors is provided to facilitate efficient use of water resources. These are as follows:

Soil Moisture Sensor

This type of sensor provides the state of moisture in the soil, which details whether there is any requirement for irrigation or not. Various types of soil moisture sensors are available. Figs. **(1a**, **b**, and **c)** show various types of soil moisture sensors. Different soil moisture sensors can be categorized as mentioned below.

a. **Resistive** Sensor- This type of sensor works on the principle of electrical resistance. The resistance between electrodes is gauged in the soil, which shows an inverse proportion to the moisture present in the soil.
b. **Tensiometric** Sensor- This type of soil sensor measures the suction or pull required by the roots of the plant to extract water from the soil. This suction is mapped with the soil moisture levels.
c. **Capacitive** sensor-This sensor is based on the soil dielectric constant, which varies with changes in soil moisture level [4].

(a) (b) (c)

Fig. (1). Types of soil sensors (**a**) Tensiometric Sensor [4]. (**b**) Capacitive Sensor [5] (**c**) Resistive Sensor [6].

Rainfall Sensors

Rainfall sensors provide an accurate amount of rainfall in a region. The data can be used to halt irrigation at the time of rain and if sufficient water has already been provided to the crop [7]. Various types of rainfall sensors are available:

a) **Tipping Bucket Rain Gauge**- This type of sensor collects rainwater in a bucket up to a specific level, and when water drips, a particular reading is saved. Fig. (**2**) shows the structure of a tipping bucket rain sensor.

Fig. (2). Tipping bucket rain gauge [7].

b) **Optical Rain Sensors** - This type of sensor uses light to sense the presence of a raindrop. Based on raindrops, rainfall intensity is measured. Fig. (**3**) shows the structure of the optical rain sensor.

Fig. (3). Optical rain sensor [8].

Temperature Sensors

Temperature sensors record the ambient air temperature of the environment, based on which the irrigation level required for the crop is decided [9]. Thermistors are the most widely used temperature sensors. These sensors are very sensitive to changes in environmental temperature. Other types of temperature sensors are thermocouples, resistance temperature detectors, infrared sensors, semiconductor temperature sensors, digital temperature sensors, and soil temperature sensors. Fig. (**4**) shows various forms of temperature sensors.

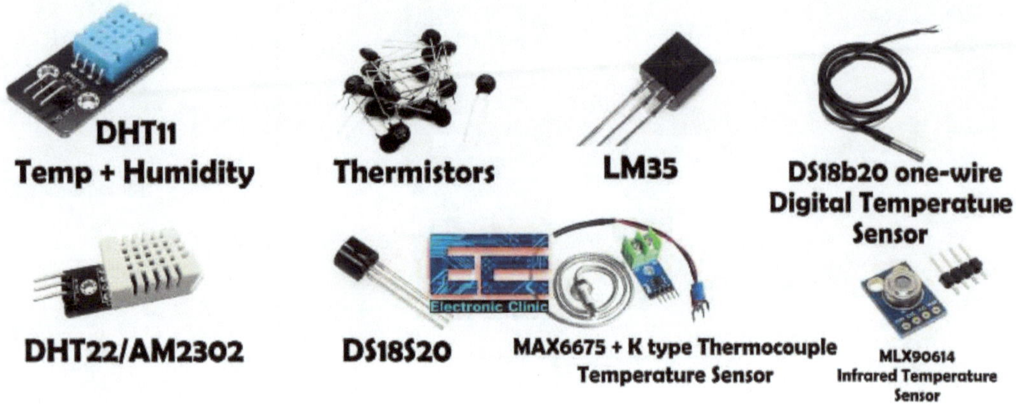

Fig. (4). Various kinds of temperature measuring sensors [10].

Solar Radiation Sensor

These sensors are used to gauge the intensity of solar radiation, leading to evaporation from crops and soil [11]. Fig. (**5**) shows the assembly of a solar radiation sensor. The evapotranspiration rate is further calculated based on the amount of evaporation. A pyranometer is a widely used solar radiation sensor.

Fig. (5). Solar radiation sensor [11].

Weather Stations

Weather stations are an integrated environment consisting of sensors to measure humidity, rainfall, temperature, solar radiation, and wind speed. These provide a comprehensive platform to provide an overview of climatic conditions. Based on this, the farmer can decide the irrigation schedules [12]. Fig. (**6**) displays the installation of a weather station.

Fig. (6). Installed weather station [12].

Flowmeters

Flow meters are used to check and control the amount of water in irrigation pipes. These flowmeters check for the presence of any cracks in the pipes and also regulate the amount of water flow in case the amount falls short of or exceeds the desired level [13]. Fig. (**7**) displays the basic structure of a flowmeter used to regulate the flow of water.

Fig. (7). Basic structure of a flowmeter [13].

Leaf Wetness Sensors

These sensors help in optimizing irrigation schedules based on the amount of water on the leaves of a plant to avoid any fungal infection to the plant due to dampness [14]. Decagon devices are one of the most commonly used leaf wetness sensors. Fig. (**8**) showcases the leaf wetness sensor assembly.

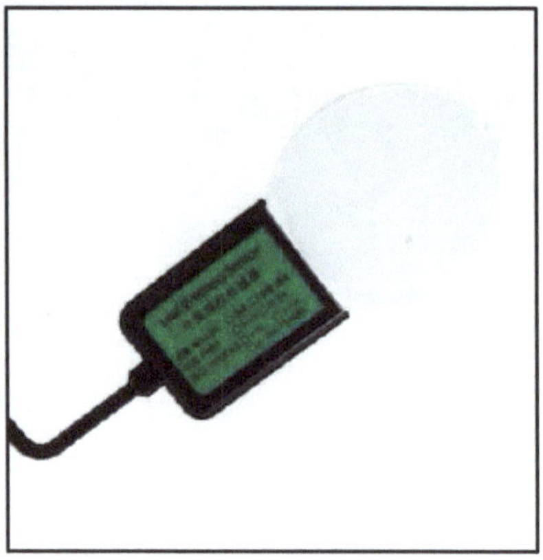

Fig. (8). Structure of a leaf wetness sensor [14].

UV Radiation Sensor

These sensors detect the plant stress level under exposure to UV radiation. LI-COR's LI-250A Light Meter is an important and commonly used UV radiation sensor [15]. Fig. (**9**) displays the structure of the UV radiation sensor.

Fig. (9). UV radiation sensor [15].

Automation and Control Systems

Based on the data received from various types of sensors, automation systems can be adjusted and designed to facilitate efficient irrigation and to avoid any wastage of water. The following are some of the automation systems.

Automated Irrigation Controllers- Irrigation controllers help the farmer in scheduling the irrigation frequency based on the data received from sensors and weather stations. These controllers can be programmed to schedule irrigation based on changing environmental conditions without any undue wastage of water.

Variable Rate Irrigation- Apart from the time of irrigation, the amount of irrigation is also a very important aspect to avoid any wastage of water resources. Variable rate irrigation controls the amount of water to be applied to different parts of the field based on the plant requirement, as per the sensor data.

Automated Drip Irrigation System- A drip irrigation system provides water to the roots of the plant. These systems can be automated by controlling their operation with controllers to avoid any wastage of water and to increase water use efficiency.

Internet of Things (IoT) and Cloud-based Platforms

IoT Incorporation- The Internet of Things integrates various sensor devices to create a network that communicates and sends real-time data on various devices like mobiles, computer systems, and tablets. This integration can provide real-time data to the farmer as and when required to perform effective irrigation practices on the field.

Cloud Platform- The data received from IoT devices can be stored and processed on clouds, facilitating decision-making and data analysis. Cloud platform offers various mobile applications and dashboards through which farmers can access and use the data for final decision-making. This also helps the farmer in remotely monitoring the fields as and when required.

Data Visualization- The data stored on the cloud can be fed to various data visualization tools to check the trends and patterns of water usage by plants, which can help in making further decisions.

Water Saving- Cloud-based platforms also offer advanced data analysis to suggest various water-saving strategies for the future. This can help the farmer in the judicious use of water resources.

Machine Learning and Artificial Intelligence

Machine Learning (ML) algorithms work on the principle of making the machine learn from previous data and use the learning to predict real-time data. This ability to predict dynamically changing data makes machine learning algorithms an important tool in the field of smart irrigation. Various areas in which machine learning can help in smart irrigation are as follows:

a. Machine learning algorithms can use historical weather and soil data to predict the future water needs of the plant, helping the farmer in making important irrigation decisions.
b. The prior knowledge of the water needs of the plant can help the farmer in planning precise irrigation amounts required by the plant without any wastage of water.
c. The field images captured by drones equipped with sensors can be fed to appropriate machine learning models to predict the areas of water stress in the field and help in the precise irrigation of the field.
d. Geospatial technologies, along with GPS, can help in finding the exact location of water stress in the field and can facilitate smart decisions regarding irrigation.

Automated Valves and Pumps

Various smart valves and pumps have been designed that help in remotely controlling the flow of water to various parts of the field. Based on the real-time data received from weather stations and various field sensors, the smart valves can be controlled remotely to close or open the valve as and when required. Also, Variable Frequency Drive pumps (VFD) help in adjusting the pressure of the water flow as per the requirements.

The integration of all tools and technologies to create a framework for smart irrigation is the need of the hour. Many studies have been done in the direction of creating and comparing traditional and smart irrigation practices. Section 3 discusses the methodology used for a systematic review of literature, followed by Section 4 presenting the various studies done in the area of smart irrigation.

METHODOLOGY

Many studies have been reported in the literature that discuss the use of tools and technologies to increase the efficiency of irrigation and avoid any wastage of water resources. To perform a systematic and detailed literature review on the topic, various keywords relevant to the domain were selected, such as smart irrigation, machine learning in smart irrigation, and IoT in irrigation, to search various conferences and journals indexed by scientific indexing services such as IEEE, Springer, Elsevier, and Taylor and Francis, to name a few. A total of 65 papers were identified, which were thoroughly scrutinized to find their relevance to the topic under study. Most of the studies were closely related to the topic. A total of 28 papers that were most related to the topic were finally selected and included in the study. Fig. (**10**) shows the methodology followed for a detailed literature review on the topic. The selected papers were further studied to find answers to some specific questions.

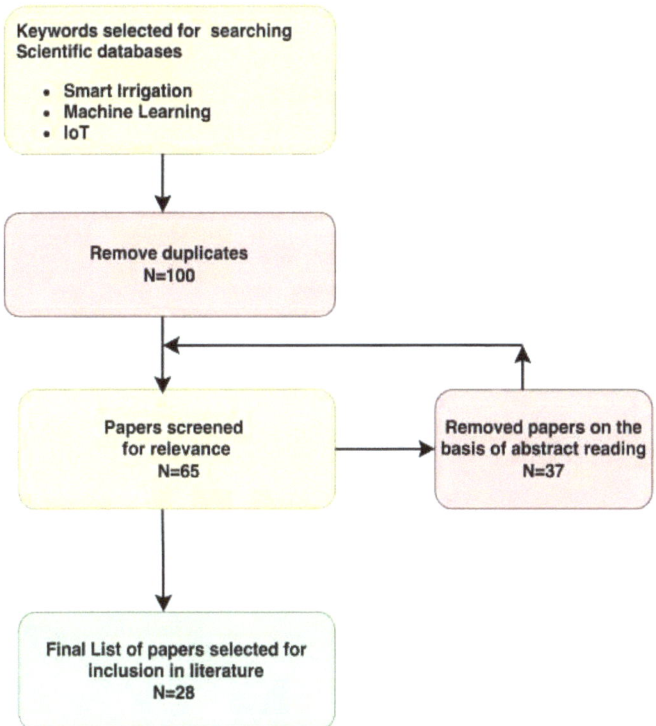

Fig. (10). Methodology used for systematic literature review.

1. What is the role of IoT and machine learning in improving the efficiency of field irrigation?
2. What were the drawbacks of traditional irrigation practices that have been overcome by smart irrigation?
3. How cost-effective is smart irrigation implementation in agriculture?
4. How can technologies be integrated to create a platform that can serve as a decision support system for farmers?

The following section discusses various studies done in the area of smart irrigation to find answers to the above-mentioned research questions.

EMERGING TECHNOLOGIES IN SMART IRRIGATION

Advancements in technology have contributed to various areas of agriculture, including crop disease prediction, yield prediction, weather forecasting, and identifying suitable crops for changing environments. Timely and precise irrigation is a critical aspect of farming that ensures healthy crop production. The availability of advanced sensors and their integration with IoT and cloud technologies has yielded significant results in smart irrigation. Moreover, the emergence of machine learning algorithms for predictive analytics on real-time data has further enhanced detailed irrigation practices. Several studies have explored the integrated use of these tools and techniques to improve water use efficiency in fields. Table **1** provides details of studies conducted by various researchers.

Table 1. Chronological review of literature on smart irrigation.

Year	Source	Technology Used	Summary
2024 [16]	*Journal of the Saudi Society of Agricultural Sciences*	Cloud computing, IoT, and embedded systems	The authors propose a comprehensive, efficient irrigation system using advanced sensors to send real-time data of the field to the ThingSpeak cloud and ThingView app. The system can help the farmer monitor his field remotely from any location, and the proposed system reported a 70% reduction in water usage for soil irrigation.
2024 [17]	*Results in Engineering, 22, 102283*	IoT, cloud computing, and big data	The authors propose a smart cloud-based irrigation system that can combine multiple small-scale farms and centralize their data. The system claims to optimize irrigation using big data and analysis. The proposed system is found to give promising results in water conservation.
2024 [18]	*Smart Agricultural Technology,* 100425	Machine learning Technique	The authors provide a comprehensive review of ML algorithms in the area of smart irrigation. Among the studied techniques, neural networks were found to give promising results, whereas SVM and ensemble models could not produce good results.

(Table 1) cont.....

Year	Source	Technology Used	Summary
[2023] [19]	*International Journal of Electrical and Electronics Engineering*, *10*(8), 224-234	IoT	In this study, the authors have designed an IoT-based system that optimizes water use by utilizing technology, integrating sensors, and automation. Using the Favoriot platform, the system monitors various parameters like soil moisture, humidity, and temperature. This system integrates the power of data analytics to forecast weather for enhanced efficiency and allows remote monitoring and control *via* cloud-based storage. This system promotes precise agriculture, reduces the wastage of water, and provides enhanced efficiency as well.
2023 [20]	*IEEE Access*.DOI 10.1109/ACCESS.2023.3251655	Wireless communication and IoT	The authors in this study highlight the importance of smart irrigation in sustainable agriculture and give a comprehensive overview of smart irrigation systems, as well as how these systems can be utilized for saving water using wireless communication, IoT, and automation technologies. Further to this, the study also compares the traditional and modern irrigation systems. The study also emphasized the integration of AI and machine learning for predictive analytics, which can make the decision-making process better.
2022 [21]	*Energy Reports*, *8*, 1025-1	Machine learning algorithms (KNN, logistic Regression, Neural Networks, SVM, and Naïve Bayes)	The authors proposed an irrigation prediction system using various machine-learning algorithms. Data was acquired from various sensors using the Node-RED platform and stored using MongoDB. Among various models studied, the K Nearest Neighbor model gave the best approximation (98.6%) with the lowest RMSE value of 0.12.
2022 [22]	*IFAC-PapersOnLine, 55(10), 3298-3303*	IoT	The authors propose an automatic irrigation system for mint crops using a soil moisture sensor in the root of the plant, a temperature sensor, and water flow sensors attached to the valve of a water pump. The assembly automatically switches on or off the water pumping motor based on soil moisture and temperature sensor values.

(Table 1) cont.....

Year	Source	Technology Used	Summary
2022 [23]	*Agronomy*, *12*(1), 212	LSTM model, IoT	Authors in the study propose a deep learning-based system that monitors the functioning of physical sensors installed on the field. The system proposes the concept of neural sensors that predict the values of sensors based on previous training data. The system was found to provide good and accurate results.
2022 [24]	*Applied and Environmental Soil* Science, *2022*(1), 7678570	Wireless network	The authors propose a wireless network-based smart irrigation system that predicts the threshold value to start irrigation based on the weather data and sensor data of soil samples. The system showed promising results with a classification accuracy of 89%
2021 [25]	*Complexity*, *2021*(1), 6691571	Ontology, IoT, and machine learning	The study proposes an irrigation system based on ontology and sensors for decision-making. The data from sensors and ontology are fed to the machine learning model (KNN) for final decision-making on irrigation.
2021 [26]	*Journal of Physics: Conference Series* (Vol. 1917, No. 1, p. 012028). IOP Publishing.	IoT	This paper presents a practical solution for precision-based agriculture wherein water supply is automated using a microcontroller-based approach. This system also utilizes the power of ATmega 328, and GSM modules, along with humidity and soil moisture sensors to control and monitor real-time environmental conditions. Another important characteristic, as proposed by the authors, is the closed-loop control mechanism. Using this mechanism, the water pumps are only activated when necessary.

(Table 1) cont.....

Year	Source	Technology Used	Summary
2021 [27]	*Agricultural Water Management, 245*, 106632	IoT, Machine learning	Authors in the study identified the importance of crop water uptake depth in determining the irrigation schedules. A regression equation was developed to measure dynamic water uptake depth based on soil moisture distribution for tomato crops. A guide based on irrigation to dynamic water uptake depth was proposed. The results showed that the water use efficiency of tomato plants improved when using the proposed system.
2019 [28]	*Computers and electronics in agriculture*, *162*, 979-990	Neural network and IoT	The authors propose a low-cost intelligent smart irrigation system that provides facilities like irrigation scheduling, an intelligent neural network-based decision system, and remote data monitoring. Results proved the proposed system to be an efficient and low-cost solution for farmer irrigation decision-making.
2019 [29]	*Procedia Computer Science*, *165*, 615-623	Fuzzy logic and IoT	The authors propose a smart irrigation system using sensors to capture real-time data and using fuzzy logic to operate the solenoid valves. Data was sent to the cloud, providing real-time data to the farmer. The Arduino was used to control the whole process and was supplied with solar power to operate.
2019 [30]	Agricultural Sciences, 10, 25-31	Arduino	The study proposes a smart irrigation system in which the water pumps operate as and when water is required based on data sent by sensors. The pumps are prioritized, and the damage to the pumps is avoided by switching off the pumps when there is no water available to pump. Results showed good performance of the proposed system.

(Table 1) cont.....

Year	Source	Technology Used	Summary
2019 [31]	*International conference on computing, communication, and intelligent systems (ICCCIS)* (pp. 327-330). IEEE	ARIMA and IoT	The study proposes a solution to the maintenance of greenbelts in smart cities. The proposed system provides a solution in the form of an innovative irrigation system that operates on the basis of soil moisture, temperature, and NPK sensor data. The ARIMA model predicts the operation of water pumps. The system also alerts the farmer if there is any quality issue with the plant in the field.
2019 [32]	*Computers & Electrical Engineering*, *73*, 180-193	Machine learning, IoT	The study proposes an automatic smart irrigation system based on the soil wetness status. The system captures the image of the farm to calculate the soil wetness level and sends data to the microcontroller. The microcontroller makes the decision and sends it to the farmer's mobile. The proposed model has reported a significant reduction in water use as compared to conventional drip and flood irrigation systems.
2019 [33]	*IEEE 9th International Conference on System Engineering and Technology (ICSET)* (pp. 96-101). IEEE	IoT	The authors in this paper have proposed an irrigation system that uses Arduino Mega 2560 as the main controller for the automation of the plant watering process based on real-time soil moisture levels. Along with the Mega 2560 controller, this system also uses DHT11 sensors and moisture sensors to monitor the humidity and soil conditions. The Blynk application is used for remote monitoring of the field. Whenever the soil moisture levels drop below a threshold, the water pump is activated. This system presents a novel solution for modern agriculture and gardening.
2019 [34]	*International conference on vision towards emerging trends in communication and networking (ViTECoN)* (pp. 1-11). IEEE	Machine learning, IoT	The authors in this study have leveraged the power of a machine learning algorithm for rainfall prediction. The smart irrigation system designed in this study not only integrates automatic irrigation but also employs Romyan's method to calculate water requirements through a web-based interface. The rainfall prediction works on parameters like temperature, humidity, soil moisture, and root length for making optimal watering schedules.

(Table 1) cont.....

Year	Source	Technology Used	Summary
2019 [35]	*International Ethical Hacking Conference 2018: eHaCON 2018, Kolkata, India* (pp. 395-403). Springer Singapore	IoT	The authors propose a smart irrigation prediction system based on soil moisture, temperature, and humidity, along with pollutants present in the air. The system uses machine learning to predict the water requirement of the plant based on the previous data and based on the environmental stats.
2018 [36]	*Journal of Cleaner Production, 175,* 670-682	Photovoltaic energy, IoT	The authors propose the use of renewable energy in the form of photovoltaic energy to operate irrigation pumps in the farms. A smart Photovoltaic irrigation manager (SPIM) system is proposed in which, instead of pressurized pumps, photovoltaic power is mapped with the energy required to pump irrigation water in farms. The proposed system, tested in southern Spain, showed satisfactory irrigation during the complete season with a reduction in CO2 emission by 1.2 tn.
2018 [37]	*Fifth HCT Information Technology* Trends (ITT) (pp. 175-179). IEEE	Fuzzy logic	Another study proposed a fuzzy logic and IoT-based smart irrigation system in which the wastage of water resources due to runoff was reduced and the time and duration of field irrigation were optimized. The system was found to provide a cost-effective solution to avoid wastage of water resources in irrigation.
2018 [38]	*Computers and Electronics in Agriculture, 155,* 41-49	Machine learning, IoT	The authors propose an efficient IoT-based irrigation system that uses machine learning to provide visualization and decision-making support to the user. The model uses both sensor data and weather prediction data to decide on the use of water for irrigation.
2018 [39]	*23rd International Scientific-Professional Conference on Information Technology* (IT) (pp. 1-4). IEEE	Wireless communication	Here, the authors propose a wireless sensor network-based solution that utilizes the power of Zigbee Communication for smart irrigation. Here, the XBee module is used to transmit the soil moisture level and air temperature data, which is collected through Arduino-based sensor nodes. Zigbee-based WSN ensures data transfers using minimal energy consumption.

(Table 1) cont.....

Year	Source	Technology Used	Summary
2017 [40]	In *3rd National* Conference on Intelligent Information and Computing Technologies (IICT '17) (pp. 1-5)	Arduino	The author proposes a field monitoring system that conveys the real-time statistics of the field using sensors and also prevents the entry of birds in the field using a PIR sensor. The details of the field will be conveyed to the farmer through a mobile message and a web application.
2016 [41]	In *2016, IEEE Bombay Section Symposium (IBSS)* (pp. 1-5). IEEE	IoT, wireless communication	This paper highlights how utilizing an embedded system for water usage for agriculture can be minimized. The designed system is powered by **Raspberry Pi** and **Arduino UNO**. It also integrates **sensors, relays, and solenoid valves** to automatically regulate water flow based on real-time soil conditions. The XBee module is used to transmit the data wirelessly, allowing remote monitoring and a web interface. Future enhancements like weather forecasting and solar power supply are also proposed by the authors, who will further enhance the utility of this system.
2015 [42]	In *2015, the 7th International Conference on Modelling, Identification and Control (ICMIC)* (pp. 1-6). IEEE	TCP/IP protocol, IoT	The authors propose a master-slave network of nodes connected through the XBee network. Fifteen farms were connected, each having a master node for final data communication. A TCP/IP network stack was used to communicate the real-time conditions of each farm to a PC. The proposed master-slave topology has proven to be a cost-effective alternative for efficient irrigation.
2014 [43]	*Advance in electronic and electric engineering*, *4*(4), 341-346	Solar power, IoT	Authors in this study use solar power to operate irrigation pumps along with water flow control using a moisture sensor. The proposed system is beneficial to farmers as it will help in electricity conservation while saving water.

CONCLUSION

Water is one of the most important natural resources on Earth. Being a perishable resource, its judicious use is important to sustain life on the planet. The present study focuses on the tools and techniques used for the safe use of this resource in agriculture, specifically in the irrigation of fields. Advancements in technology have led to the invention of new and efficient tools to reduce water wastage without compromising crop production. The fields of artificial intelligence, such as machine learning, deep learning, and IoT, have proven to be game changers in the area of smart irrigation. After a thorough study of the literature, the following conclusions are drawn:

a. Despite being an important field of AI, machine learning and deep learning have not been fully explored in smart irrigation. These fields, being efficient in making predictions on soil and weather conditions, can help cope with probable risks in irrigation.
b. The literature shows extensive use of sensors in the fields for fetching real-time data, but not much work has been done on the malfunction detection of sensors, which can lead to incorrect or malicious data. Neural sensors, as reported in one study [23], can be a beneficial solution to monitor the functioning and reliability of sensors deployed on farms.
c. Only one study has given attention to the water uptake depth of plants [27]. More work is required on this important concept to accurately predict the actual water requirements of plants.
d. The use of technologies in agriculture has increased the efficiency of farm practices and led to both quantitative and qualitative improvements in crop production. However, the extensive use of advanced sensors can increase overall expenses for small-scale farmers. Additionally, farmers need to be trained and educated to effectively utilize advanced techniques for the betterment of their crops.

FUTURE SCOPE

The literature studies in the field of smart irrigation have emphasized the importance of using advancements in information technology, such as IoT and artificial intelligence, for smart irrigation. The hybridization of machine and deep learning algorithms with IoT can generate predictive models for smarter irrigation solutions in the form of precise scheduling and accurate irrigation amounts. Recent advances in remote sensing, specifically in Hyperspectral Imaging (HSI), can be very beneficial for smart irrigation, as HSI can detect and capture a wide range of spectral bands, enabling efficient detection of water stress levels, diseases, and nutrient deficiencies before actual symptoms emerge. Future studies can explore the integration of HSI with current decision support systems to increase the efficiency of smart irrigation systems.

REFERENCES

[1] Singh S, Naz F. Changing cropping patterns on water-energy-food nexus and gaps in agricultural extension services in western Uttar Pradesh, India. Journal of Agricultural Extension 2025; 29(4): 1-0.

[2] Chakkaravarthy DN, Balakrishnan T. Water scarcity-challenging the future. Int J Agric Environ Biotechnol 2019; 12(3): 187-93.
[http://dx.doi.org/10.30954/0974-1712.08.2019.2]

[3] Datta P, Behera B, Rahut DB. Climate change and Indian agriculture: A systematic review of farmers' perception, adaptation, and transformation. Environ Chall (Amst) 2022; 8: 100543.
[http://dx.doi.org/10.1016/j.envc.2022.100543]

[4] Zhang X. Application of soil moisture sensors in precision agriculture: A review. Sensors (Basel) 2019; 19(15): 3194.

[5] Hrisko J. Capacitive soil moisture sensor theory, calibration, and testing. 2020; (2): 1-12.

[6] Selvaperumal A, Muthuchamy I. Irrigation Int J Agric Sci Res (Chennai) 2017; 7(1): 143-8.

[7] Mekonnen MM. Assessment of rainfall variability and its implications on irrigation management in semi-arid regions. Environ Sci Technol 2020; 54(9): 5282-9.

[8] Niubol Available from: https://www.niubol.com/Product-knowledge/What-is-an-Optical-Rain-Sensor.html

[9] Alkhatib A. The role of temperature sensors in improving water management in agriculture. Sensors (Basel) 2020; 20(8): 2314.
[PMID: 32325654]

[10] Temperature Sensor types & their use with Arduino, ESP8266, and ESP32. 2025. Available from: https://www.electroniclinic.com/temperature-sensor-types-their-use-with-arduino-esp8266-and-esp32/

[11] Elshahed M. Solar radiation-based smart irrigation system for precision agriculture. Comput Electron Agric 2020; 175: 105552.

[12] Soleimani M. The role of weather stations in optimizing irrigation schedules using real-time data. Agric Water Manage 2019; 216: 184-96.

[13] Gao X. Integration of flow meters and soil moisture sensors for efficient water management in smart irrigation systems. Water Resour Manage 2020; 34(5): 1475-87.

[14] Prashar P. Leaf. Environ Monit Assess 2017; 189(11): 575.
[PMID: 29052079]

[15] Mansour F. UV radiation sensors for irrigation management in semi-arid regions. Agric Syst 2021; 189: 103040.

[16] Morchid A, Muhammad Alblushi IG, Khalid HM, El Alami R, Sitaramanan SR, Muyeen SM. High-technology agriculture system to enhance food security: A concept of smart irrigation system using Internet of Things and cloud computing. J Saudi Soc Agric Sci 2024.
[http://dx.doi.org/10.1016/j.jssas.2024.02.001]

[17] Et-taibi B, Abid MR, Boufounas EM, *et al.* Enhancing water management in smart agriculture: A cloud and IoT-Based smart irrigation system. Results Eng 2024; 22: 102283.
[http://dx.doi.org/10.1016/j.rineng.2024.102283]

[18] Younes A, Abou Elassad Z E, El Meslouhi O, Abou Elassad D E, Majid E D A. The application of machine learning techniques for smart irrigation systems: A systematic literature review. Smart Agric Technol 2024; 100425.

[19] Abdikadir NM, Hassan AA, Abdullahi HO, Rashid RA. Smart irrigation system. International Journal of Electrical and Electronics Engineering 2023; 10(8): 224-34.
[http://dx.doi.org/10.14445/23488379/IJEEE-V10I8P122]

[20] Gamal Y, Soltan A, Said L A, Madian A H, Radwan A G. Smart irrigation systems: Overview. IEEE Access 2023.
[http://dx.doi.org/10.1109/ACCESS.2023.3251655]

[21] Tace Y, Tabaa M, Elfilali S, Leghris C, Bensag H, Renault E. Smart irrigation system based on IoT and machine learning. Energy Rep 2022; 8: 1025-36.
[http://dx.doi.org/10.1016/j.egyr.2022.07.088]

[22] Mezouari AE, Fazziki AE, Sadgal M. Smart irrigation system. IFAC-PapersOnLine 2022; 55(10): 3298-303.
[http://dx.doi.org/10.1016/j.ifacol.2022.10.125]

[23] Sami M, Khan SQ, Khurram M, *et al.* A deep learning-based sensor modeling for smart irrigation system. Agronomy (Basel) 2022; 12(1): 212.
[http://dx.doi.org/10.3390/agronomy12010212]

[24] Ndunagu JN, Ukhurebor KE, Akaaza M, Onyancha RB. Development of a wireless sensor network and IoT-based smart irrigation. Science 2022; 2022(1): 7678570.

[25] Munir MS, Bajwa IS, Ashraf A, Anwar W, Rashid R. Intelligent and smart irrigation system using edge computing and IoT. Complexity 2021; 2021(1): 6691571.
[http://dx.doi.org/10.1155/2021/6691571]

[26] Vimal SP, Sathish Kumar N, Kasiselvanathan M, Gurumoorthy KB. Smart irrigation system in agriculture. J Phys Conf Ser 2021; 1917(1): 012028. [IOP Publishing].
[http://dx.doi.org/10.1088/1742-6596/1917/1/012028]

[27] Liao R, Zhang S, Zhang X, Wang M, Wu H, Zhangzhong L. Development of smart irrigation systems based on real-time soil moisture data in a greenhouse: Proof of concept. Agric Water Manage 2021; 245: 106632.
[http://dx.doi.org/10.1016/j.agwat.2020.106632]

[28] Nawandar NK, Satpute VR. IoT based low cost and intelligent module for smart irrigation system. Comput Electron Agric 2019; 162: 979-90.
[http://dx.doi.org/10.1016/j.compag.2019.05.027]

[29] Sudharshan N, Karthik AVSK, Kiran JSS, Geetha S. Renewable energy-based smart irrigation system. Procedia Comput Sci 2019; 165: 615-23.
[http://dx.doi.org/10.1016/j.procs.2020.01.055]

[30] Ogidan OK, Onile AE, Adegboro OG. Smart irrigation system: a water management procedure. Agric Sci 2019; 10(1): 25-31.
[http://dx.doi.org/10.4236/as.2019.101003]

[31] Mitra A, Saini G. Automated smart irrigation system (ASIS). 2019 Int Conf Comput Commun Intell Syst (ICCCIS). 327-30.

[32] Barkunan SR, Bhanumathi V, Sethuram J. Smart sensor for automatic drip irrigation system for paddy cultivation. Comput Electr Eng 2019; 73: 180-93.
[http://dx.doi.org/10.1016/j.compeleceng.2018.11.013]

[33] Leh N A M, Kamaldin M S A M, Muhammad Z, Kamarzaman N A. Smart irrigation system using the Internet of things. 2019 IEEE 9th Int Conf Syst Eng Technol (ICSET). 96-101.
[http://dx.doi.org/10.1109/ICSEngT.2019.8906497]

[34] Kondaveti R, Reddy A, Palabtla S. Smart irrigation system using machine learning and IoT In 2019 international conference on vision towards emerging trends in communication and networking (ViTECoN). IEEE 2019; pp. 1-11.

[35] Dasgupta A, Daruka A, Pandey A, Bose A, Mukherjee S, Saha S. Smart irrigation: IOT-based irrigation monitoring system. Proceedings of International Ethical Hacking Conference 2018: eHaCON 2018, Kolkata, India. 395-403.

[http://dx.doi.org/10.1007/978-981-13-1544-2_32]

[36] Mérida García A, Fernández García I, Camacho Poyato E, Montesinos Barrios P, Rodríguez Díaz JA. Coupling irrigation scheduling with solar energy production in a smart irrigation management system. J Clean Prod 2018; 175: 670-82. [http://dx.doi.org/10.1016/j.jclepro.2017.12.093]

[37] Alomar B, Alazzam A. A smart irrigation system using IoT and fuzzy logic controller. 2018 Fifth HCT Inf Technol Trends (ITT). 175-9. [http://dx.doi.org/10.1109/CTIT.2018.8649531]

[38] Goap A, Sharma D, Shukla AK, Rama Krishna C. An IoT based smart irrigation management system using Machine learning and open source technologies. Comput Electron Agric 2018; 155: 41-9. [http://dx.doi.org/10.1016/j.compag.2018.09.040]

[39] Savić T, Radonjić M. WSN architecture for the smart irrigation system. 2018 23rd Int Sci-Prof Conf Inf Technol (IT). 1-4. [http://dx.doi.org/10.1109/SPIT.2018.8350859]

[40] Nandhini R, Poovizhi S, Jose P, Ranjitha R, Anila S. Arduino-based smart irrigation system using IoT. Conference on Intelligent Information and Computing Technologies (IICT '17). 1-5.

[41] Namala K K, AV K K P, Math A, Kumari A, Kulkarni S. Smart irrigation with an embedded system. 2016 IEEE Bombay Sect Symp (IBSS). 1-5.

[42] Zaier R, Zekri S, Jayasuriya H, Teirab A, Hamza N, Al-Busaidi H. Design and implementation of smart irrigation system for groundwater use at farm scale. 2015 7th Int Conf Model Identif Control (ICMIC). 1-6. [http://dx.doi.org/10.1109/ICMIC.2015.7409402]

[43] Harishankar S K U V S, Kumar R S, Sudharsan K P, Vignesh U, Viveknath T. Solar-powered smart irrigation system. Adv Electron Electr Eng 2014; 4(4): 341-6.

SUBJECT INDEX

A

Accuracy assessment 29, 32, 143
Accuracy assessment parameters 30
Accuracy limitations in nutrient detection 272
Acidic soil 249
Advanced image processing algorithms 271
Advanced remote sensing 243, 245, 247, 251, 253, 255
AI-based advisory mechanisms 85
AI-based crop prediction 174
AI-based irrigation system 106, 213, 215, 218, 219
AI-based models 118, 120, 201
AI-based nutrient modeling 269
AI-driven analysis 96
AI-powered analytics 2
AI-powered biodiversity indexing 187
AI-powered drones 174, 191
Airborne hyperspectral liDAR 56
Alternate wetting and drying (AWD) 119
ANN algorithm 227
ANOVA test 219
Application in nutrient mapping 267
Arduino-based sensor nodes 293
Artificial intelligence 2, 4, 36, 38, 150, 151, 210, 211, 212, 224, 225, 242, 243, 254, 255
ATmega 290
Autoencoders 109
Automated land use detection 174
Autonomous drones and robotics in fertilizer application 274
AVIRIS 179, 187, 238

B

Backscattered light method 60
Backward propagation 226
Band selection methods 109
Band transmittance 58
Basics of ground water hydrology 196
Batch normalization 94
Bayes' theorem 235
Bemisia tabaci 65
Bio-based approaches 7
Biochemical composition 67
Biodiversity assessment 170
Biodiversity index map 189
Biological neural systems 226
Biomass estimation 108, 156
Biophysical techniques 55
Blockchain technologies 98, 275
Boltzmann machines 230
Boosting grain 119

C

Calibration issues 271
Canopy temperature 41
Capacitive sensor 280
Carbon sequestration 190
Carotenoid reflectance index 59
CART classifier 145
Catchment-based water resources monitoring 204
Cation exchange capacity 158
Chemical indicators 158
Chlorophyll fluorescence 56
Chlorosis 51, 82, 95, 96
Class boundaries 144
Classification spectral unmixing 181
Climate change resilience 117
Climate variability 105, 118, 122, 242
Cloud-based geospatial analysis platform 185
Cloud computing 39, 42, 81, 150, 269, 288
CNN for species detection 171
CO2 sequestration 183
Convolutional layer (CL) 94, 227, 228
Crop productivity forecasting 101
Crop stress analysis 187
Cybersecurity 5

Sartajvir Singh, Neelam Dahiya, Maged Mohammed, Abdullah Alzharihi & Vishal Dutt (Eds.)

D

Data fusion techniques 188
Dataset split 94
Deep belief networks 230, 231
Deep learning models 85, 116, 147, 156, 175, 213, 215, 273
Deep Q-networks (DQNs) 117
DESIS 68
Dielectric constant 280
Dimensionality reduction 253, 256
Disease resistance 82
Drought assessment 247
Dynamic soil health monitoring 263

E

Early bushfire detection 183
Early identification of nutritional stress 154
Early warning systems 180
Eco-agro system monitoring 180
Edge computing 39, 155, 275
Electromagnetic radiation 51, 53, 171, 243
ELM (Extreme Learning Machine) 156, 157, 160
End-to-end monitoring 176, 177, 178
ENKF (Ensemble Kalman Filter) 156
Epicyclic gear train mechanisms 18
EVI (Enhanced Vegetation Index) 8, 11, 18, 96, 159

F

Feature extraction sublayer 94
Fertilizer optimization 150, 151, 153, 154, 156, 157, 159, 160, 161, 162, 163, 270, 271, 275, 276
Field heterogeneity 104
Fluorescence sensors 56, 159
Food security 118, 138, 170, 180, 188, 211, 212, 261, 276
Fuzzy logic 66, 291, 293

G

GaiaSky-mini 160
GBT (Gradient Boosting Trees) 136, 138, 141, 142, 143, 144, 146, 147, 148
GIS applications 62, 63, 204
Global biodiversity indexing 189
GNDVI (Green Normalised Difference Vegetation Index) 59, 270
GRACE (Gravity Recovery and Climate Experiment) 194, 195, 199, 200, 202, 204
Gradient boosting 107, 111, 114, 115, 118
Groundwater mass balance approach 200
Growing degree days (GDD) 118

H

Habitat classification 171, 172
Headwall Nano-Hyperspec 68, 187
High-performance computing (HPC) 2
Histogram equalization techniques 253
Host insect detected 59, 60
Hyperion EO-1 24, 27, 30, 32
Hyperspectral imaging (HSI) 23, 24, 38, 56, 67, 72, 95, 96, 104, 105, 109, 159, 174, 187, 264
HySpex 238

I

IEEE Access.DOI 289
Image segmentation 163
Infrastructure challenges 272
Integrated landscape management models 180
Internet of Things (IoT) 3, 80, 81, 87, 101, 102, 112, 114, 174, 211, 212, 273, 276, 285, 289, 290, 291, 292, 293, 294
Ips typographus outbreak 61

K

Kappa coefficient 29, 30, 31, 32, 143
Kjeldahl method 160
KNN 289, 290

L

Laboratory procedures 224, 225
Land surface temperature 220
Land Use and Land Cover (LULC) 31, 32, 112
Landsat-8 71, 97, 155, 184
Laser fluorosensor 54
Leaf Area Index (LAI) 102
Linear regression 107, 234, 235, 237
LSTMs (Long Short-Term Memory) 97, 112, 114, 147, 220, 221

M

Machine Learning (ML) 24, 38, 60, 101, 107, 113, 114, 155, 194, 224, 225, 226, 254, 256, 278, 279, 286, 289, 292, 293, 295
Macronutrients 158, 238, 248
Mapping pest incidence 66
Max pooling 94, 228
MDC (Minimum Distance Classifier) 23, 25, 26, 27, 29, 30, 31, 32
Micronutrients 83, 158, 238, 248
MLC (Maximum Likelihood Classifier) 23, 25, 26, 27, 28, 29, 30, 31, 32
MLR (Multiple Linear Regression) 157, 234, 237
MODIS 70, 97, 220, 266
Multispectral Imaging (MSI) 23, 38, 151, 159, 263, 264, 265, 266, 267, 272, 274

N

Naive Bayes 235
NDMI (Normalized Difference Moisture Index) 159
NDRE (Normalized Difference Red-Edge) 157, 267
NDVI (Normalized Difference Vegetation Index) 11, 17, 18, 44, 59, 85, 94, 95, 96, 99, 105, 159, 219, 220, 267
NDWI 38, 41, 42, 43, 46, 159, 220
Normalized Pigment Chlorophyll Index (NPCI) 59

O

Object detection 23, 155
Operational constraints 271, 272
Overfitting 140, 141, 144, 145, 227, 229, 231, 234, 238

P

PCA (Principal Component Analysis) 105, 109, 220
Pest outbreak prediction 60, 65, 69, 188
Photochemical Reflectance Index (PRI) 38, 59, 69, 95, 96
Photosynthesis 249, 252
Physiological changes 50, 67, 72
PIR sensor 294
Plunger rod 9, 10
Preemptive management of physiological disorders 83
Prescription maps 67, 69, 270, 275
PRISMA 68, 179, 187, 238
Proutista moesta 65

R

Random Forest (RF) 23, 24, 29, 30, 31, 32, 107, 112, 114, 118, 140, 141, 142, 144, 145, 146, 147, 155, 157, 232
Random Forest Regression (RFR) 231, 235
Real-time environmental pollution monitoring 189
Rectified Linear Unit (ReLU) 94, 228

Red-edge chlorophyll index 95
Reference samples 30, 31
ResNet for species category classification 175
Restricted Boltzmann Machines (RBMs) 230
RNN processes sequences 229

S

SAEs (Stacked Autoencoders) 109, 110
SAR data 108, 116, 200
SAVI (Soil Adjusted Vegetation Index) 38, 42, 60, 62, 159, 267, 270
Site-Specific Nutrient Management (SSNM) 119, 120, 267, 269
SMOTE (Synthetic minority oversampling) 45, 46, 47, 48, 166
Soil-Adjusted Vegetation Index 60, 267
Soil moisture Active Passive (SMAP) 200
SPA 156, 160
Spatial analysis techniques 66
Spectral vegetation indices for nutrient mapping 266
SQI (Soil Quality Index) 158, 248, 249
Structural Independent Pigment Index (SIPI) 60
Support Vector Machines (SVM) 42, 95, 113, 114, 136, 138, 141, 142, 144, 145, 146, 147, 148, 220
Synthetic Aperture Radar (SAR) 55, 151, 159, 199, 201, 243

T

Tableau dashboard 186
Tensiometric sensor 280
TensorFlow 42, 94, 114, 184, 185
Thermal Infrared (TIR) 159, 253, 254
Tipping bucket rain gauge 281
Training points 147

U

U-Net 155
UAS (Uncrewed Aerial Systems) 61
Upper Midwest Aerospace Consortium (UMAC) 246

V

Variable-Rate Application (VRA) 104, 154, 270, 275
ViTECoN 292
VNIR (Visible and Near-Infrared) 26, 68, 105, 139, 157, 199, 253, 254

W

Water Body in SVM 148
Water Requirement Satisfaction Index (WRSI) 118
Waterwise Irrigation-AI water-saving optimization 189
WOA-ELM 157, 160

X

Xanthophyll cycle 58
XGBoost-based soil quality prediction model 94

Y

YOLOv4 185

www.ingramcontent.com/pod-product-compliance
Lightning Source LLC
LaVergne TN
LVHW070946210926
848482LV00002B/113
* 9 7 9 8 8 9 8 8 1 3 9 8 7 *